~~Once~~ a Cheater...

~~ONCE~~ A CHEATER

People Tell You Who They Are Up Front

(a true story)

~~Once~~ a Cheater...

~~Once~~ a Cheater...

~~ONCE~~ A Cheater

People Tell You Who They Are Up Front

(a true story)

By Laurie Majka

~~Once~~ a Cheater...

Copyright © 2020 Laurie Majka

All rights reserved. No part of this book may be reproduced in any form or by any electronic or mechanical means, including information storage and retrieval systems, without permission in writing from the publisher, except by reviewers, who may quote brief passages in a review.

ISBN 978-1-7349672-3-4

Library of Congress Control Number

Editing by Marilyn Abrahamian

Cover design and images by Ryan Majka

Proof reading by Chuck Teater

S
Storm Publishing

Cave Creek, Arizona

Printed in the United States of America

First Edition August 22, 2020

Full Release March 24, 2021

For Permissions: Storm.Laurie@gmail.com

Visit https://www.LaurieMajka.com

~~Once~~ a Cheater...

To all of my Soul Mates,

Past, Present and Future...

Thank you for the lessons.

~~Once~~ a Cheater...

~~Once~~ a Cheater...

Table of Contents

Introduction iii
Chapter 1 Games People Play 1
Chapter 2 You Make My Dreams (Come True) 3
Chapter 3 The Long Run 7
Chapter 4 Magic Power 15
Chapter 5 Strange Magic 21
Chapter 6 If Looks Could Kill 25
Chapter 7 I Know You're Out There Somewhere 35
Chapter 8 Ready for Love 39
Chapter 9 Love Walks In 45
Chapter 10 Beginnings 49
Chapter 11 Is This Love 53
Chapter 12 I Want Your Sex 57
Chapter 13 Moondance 61
Chapter 14 Movin' Out 69
Chapter 15 Jane 73
Chapter 16 I Walk the Line 79
Chapter 17 Caught Up in You 83
Chapter 18 Believe in Me 87
Chapter 19 I'm Jealous 93
Chapter 20 So in to You 99
Chapter 21 Foolish Heart 105
Chapter 22 This Kiss 109
Chapter 23 Rock the Boat 117
Chapter 24 Spirits in the Material World 121
Chapter 25 You Can Do Magic 129
Chapter 26 What a Fool Believes 135
Chapter 27 Gold Dust Woman 137
Chapter 28 Get Outta My Dreams, Get into My Car 143
Chapter 29 Magic 147
Chapter 30 Waiting for a Star to Fall 153
Chapter 31 Silent Lucidity 155
Chapter 32 Hold the Line 163
Chapter 33 What You Won't Do for Love 167
Chapter 34 The Flame 171

~~Once~~ a Cheater…

Chapter 35 Insecure 175

Chapter 36 Little Lies 181

Chapter 37 I Won't Give Up 189

Chapter 38 I Don't Want to Be Your Friend 197

Chapter 39 She's Gone 203

Chapter 40 Love's a Hard Game to Play 211

Chapter 41 Can We Still Be Friends 215

Chapter 42 Promises, Promises 221

Chapter 43 Stop Draggin' My Heart Around 225

Chapter 44 Man on Your Mind 231

Chapter 45 Taken In 237

Chapter 46 Lost in Love 249

Chapter 47 Keep on Walking 257

Chapter 48 Misled 263

Chapter 49 Alibi... 267

Chapter 50 How Long (Has This Been Going On)... 271

Chapter 51 Don't Shed a Tear 281

Chapter 52 Someday..285

Chapter 53 The Captain of Hear Heart 289

Epilogue 291

Part 2 Lessons Learned..295

Your Soul's Vibration..297

Understanding Soul Mates.. 301

Twin Flames Explained, Kind-of...305

Soul Contracts 309

Free Will 315

People Tell You Who They Are Up Front 319

Learning to Trust Your Intuition 323

Forgiveness 327

Your Super Power 331

Real Love 335

Pick Them, Don't Pick Them 337

Psychedelic Healing Spiritual Journeys...339

Psychic Medium & Angel Connectors 341

Signs I Received While Writing This Book 345

Acknowledgements...351

About the Author 353

~~Once~~ a Cheater...

Introduction

You could call me a hypocrite for using this title; after all I did cheat on my husband. I even documented it in my first book: *Signs Surround You, Love Never Dies*. You can read all the details there. I guess that makes me knowledgeable about the subject – but not an expert, by any means. I only cheated one time. My previous history had been more of whistle blowing on cheaters, so the cheatee could pull the balance of power back towards themselves. I made a promise to myself that I would stand in my truth and never be unfaithful in a relationship again. I have vowed to exit a relationship before I ever starting something new with someone else. I believe intentions are what count the most. I understand the pitfalls of opening your energy and your heart to someone new when your heart is not really free to enter into that contract. I know how you can get sucked into a new relationship unexpectedly, like what happened to me with my affair. Everyone makes mistakes, and we can choose to correct past wrongs, move on and make better choices. That is how we learn, grow and evolve as Souls.

This title refers to the chronic cheater, the one who has a history, who knows the pitfalls and puts themselves in the trap anyway, or the person who deliberately sets out to deceive and has a game plan they follow. This title refers to the person who has lived a double life – and may even want to change their behavior but succumbs to the temptations anyway. Maybe they get a rush of excitement by having multiple people stroking their ego at the same time. Perhaps they enjoy feeling they are getting away with something. It could be that it makes them feel they're smarter than their partner, or maybe it gives them some sense of power. Maybe something is missing inside of them and they are looking to someone else to help fill that void. There are a million reasons why someone continues to cheat over and over again, but ultimately they just don't possess a strength of character or don't live by the same set of ethics most of society subscribes to. Or maybe they're in an unhappy, unfulfilling relationship they haven't had the courage to leave. There is also the argument of evolution and monogamy and whether humans were built to be in one monogamous relationship – or not. That is not for me to say.

I have written this book in two parts. The first part is my journey into this dark twisted foray. The second part analyzes the lessons learned and offers guidance – from my perspective – to help you see what I didn't see, couldn't see at the time, or maybe didn't *want* to see.

~~Once~~ a Cheater...

    I write a lot about the spiritual aspects of life. I will get into the deeper spiritual aspects of Soul contracts and life lessons in the second part of this book. I don't really believe in karma, as I feel it is the human ego wanting to judge what cannot be fully understood.

    I use a very specific writing style with a lot of ellipses, dashes and unconventional capitalizations. It is a style I developed over many years of writing my blog: Soul Heart Art, my inspirational art page designed to empower you to listen to the whispers of your Soul.

    Music is such an important part of my life, and it enhances a story. I often *think in* music, which means when things happen to me a song sometimes begins playing in my head to match the live action. As I was considering the content of each chapter in this book, a song would come to me. Each chapter is named for a song that expresses the mood of what was happening during those events, pulling the reader into the emotions I experienced. I have provided a Spotify link for you to connect with the songs representing each chapter. Spotify is a streaming audio platform that allows you access to millions of songs. There is a free version.

    I designed this book to be accompanied by the music, kind of like a soundtrack to the book. You may choose to listen to the song first, then read the chapter, or absorb the chapter and then reflect on it while listening to the song. Or, my favorite way, to softly play the song as a background enhancement *while* reading the chapter; I myself turn the repeat song feature on so the song plays in a loop. You can use this link at Spotify to access: *Once A Cheater NEW book by Laurie Majka*

https://open.spotify.com/playlist/3GdsSkrhZ7b7Ooom2YMeAc?si=kxOxrxFOREK9OilC4uNilg

    I believe we are all here on this Earth for soul growth. This is a journey we choose to take. To be here we must forget the *true* power of our Soul. The greatest lesson we are here to learn is LOVE. Love for others and love for ourselves; sometimes that lesson includes forgiveness. No lessons are ever lost, and if you learn something that helps you by reading my book, then I have gained more than I could ever lose...xo Laurie

~~Once~~ A Cheater...

Chapter 1

Games People Play

~Song by *Alan Parsons Project*

https://open.spotify.com/track/2gQsUHVFY4tpXc3AFU2mcS?si=Cw9oAJWzSlSPCAVYDxd9BQ

Mark Abrahamian had been my greatest spiritual teacher on this Earth. Now he was dead, destined to be my guide, guardian angel and teacher from across the veil. He had been gone only three short months when I connected with him through Moriah, an extraordinary medium. He was sharing words of wisdom and advice from his new enlightened perspective through her. She began:

"Sometimes when there are people on Earth who have the victim complex, they always have this deep feeling of guilt, and they make excuses and apologize all the time and say they're sorry. He [Mark] feels that people just get used to the victim language and don't want to make reparations. They apologize for their failure in advance, and they tell you who they are. So, he wants you to know if you went to a lawyer and you asked him to defend you in a lawsuit and the lawyer said, 'I'll sure try' – how would you feel? He just wants you to be aware; **as people tell you who they are, you're supposed to believe them in advance.** He worries that sometimes – although you are very savvy – you are not very good at listening to people when they tell you who they are. You aren't very good at believing them."

It had been over seven years since Mark delivered that message to me, and this was about to become one of my greatest spiritual lessons. It was going to hit me over the head in a way I could not have conceived of nor imagined. The *real* question was, would I survive the blow....

~~Once~~ A Cheater...

~~Once~~ A Cheater…

Chapter 2

You Make My Dreams (Come True)

~song by *Daryl Hall & John Oates*

https://open.spotify.com/track/4o6BgsqLIBViaGVbx5rbRk?si=TsfW5bpoSZamk673CzcAEw

On the afternoon of my 50th birthday party, sitting on the cream-colored leather couch in the living room of my house in Cave Creek, Arizona, my boyfriend Wylie had just arrived to help me set up for the party. He had himself passed this milestone three years before. He's a handsome man with a strong jawline, piercing blue eyes surrounded by laugh lines that had been etched over time by his boyish spirit. His full head of hair is short and flecked with gray more than anything else. He wore a short-sleeved button-down collared shirt with athletic shorts, which was about as dressed up as I had ever seen him. We had a lot to do before guests arrived, but first he wanted to give me my birthday present. He flashed me a smile with his perfect teeth that could have been straight out of a toothpaste commercial and unfolded a piece of paper. He began reading a poem he had written for the occasion.

Laur's 50th

It was a fine spring day

In the month of May

The 13th day if you insist

Was born a beauty in our midst

Laurie Ann was her given name

And from then the world was never the same

Into a beautiful woman she did grow

~~Once~~ A Cheater...

Loving and unique as we all know

A daughter, a friend and a committed mother
Radiant and intelligent like no other
Full of boundless energy and beaming with light
If adorned with wings, she would forever take flight

I didn't meet her until two years ago
In the bottom of Grand Canyon, I first witnessed her glow
And since that time our relationship has grown
Into the most amazing love I have ever known

Full of adventure, laughs and fun
Next we will embark on a most ambitious run
Back to the place whereby fate we did meet
Across the canyon and back on our two little feet

To all her friends she brings love and bliss
When she is not around, something is amiss
Nothing but the best we wish for her
And hope to have her around forever to be sure

As we celebrate Laur, our amazing friend
We will cherish and love her until the end
It's been 50 years since her fateful birth
Making better forever our planet Earth

~~Once~~ A Cheater...

My only response to that incredibly creative poem was tears – tears of joy and gratitude at having this wonderful man open his heart and shower his love on me. "...our relationship has grown into the most amazing love I have ever known"; that line certainly stood out *and* blew me away. It was, perhaps, the most he had ever expressed concerning our relationship and his love for me in the nearly two years we had been together.

Our relationship had taken off like a bullet train – completely unstoppable. We had certainly had our fair share of obstacles during our time together. When we first met he had only recently decided to end his 24-year marriage. I wasn't the catalyst, but I was certainly the accelerant that caused him to move out and to begin moving on. I wasn't part of his original plan. He had planned on getting divorced and having some time to process how things had gone off the rails in his marriage. Instead of taking that time, he spent the first six months of our relationship trying to keep me at arms-length – completely in denial of the serious relationship he had *not* planned on being in that had caught him completely unawares. It took almost two year for him to finally begin to let the relationship follow its natural course. We were now blissfully in love, the envy of anyone who saw us together – by just being near us; witnessing the feeling of our love and energy was palpable.

I kissed him passionately, wanting to linger in his words a few minutes longer before we had to get to work on the party preparations. He was a full seven inches taller than me, except I was wearing heels that closed a three-inch gap. My love language from the book *The Five Love Languages* was: "Words of Affirmation" and he was checking all the boxes. He wiped my tears away, laughing at my sensitivity. My heart was so full of joy. This was truly one of the happiest times I had ever experienced in my life. Nothing could ruin it! Wylie folded the paper he had read the poem from and stuck it back in his pocket. In a few short hours, my closest friends and family would be arriving to help me celebrate my birthday, two days before my actual birth date. Although the day was getting better by the minute, we needed to get back to work.

A few hours later, 100 of my friends and family were all gathered around the island in my kitchen and spilling over into the living room. My parents sat a few feet away beaming at me. My daughter Rachel stood on one side of me and Wiley on the other side with his arm tightly gripped around my waist. My constant companion *Storm* paced anxiously, barking near me – not sure what to make of all the commotion – just as the chorus of "Happy Birthday" rang out. When the song ended I made a wish and quickly blew out all 50 candles before that much fire power melted the cake.

While my friends were happily eating birthday cake and drinking, Wylie and I walked around visiting with everyone. There were about 25 people gathered in conversation halfway between where my office becomes one with my open-space living room. The group included my parents, my daughter, my aunt and several of my closest friends on the planet. Wylie removed the folded piece of paper from his shorts pocket, and began reading my very special birthday poem out loud to the entire group. Everyone was smiling and clapping as he finished the last line about me making forever better our planet Earth. I was so elated it felt like there were visible beams of happiness shooting out of my body! The true gift for me was not the poem; it was the *reading* of the poem in front of the most important people in my life. His gesture left me feeling euphoric and very special.

Around midnight the last of my friends, who had been moonlighting as the clean-up crew, left. We both collapsed into bed, exhausted but not too tired to make love. Our passion had been building all night. We fell asleep tangled up in each other's arms.

Chapter 3

The Long Run

~song by the *Eagles*

https://open.spotify.com/track/3MV4Upk8fO5sU2n3V03NWX?si=19hNHF1tTZa4uMkJPsORUQ

I woke up and reached across the bed to cuddle Wylie. He was wide awake lying next to me completely engrossed in what was on his phone screen. It was a common sight. I couldn't tell if he was playing one of his online games or if he was texting. He quickly glanced over at me, flashed a smile and said "Good morning," putting his phone aside long enough to give me a good-morning kiss.

Today was Mother's Day. Last year my birthday had fallen on Mother's Day. This year I would get to enjoy both holidays separately instead of simultaneously. Rachel, Wylie, and I had plans to meet my parents for a late breakfast to celebrate my mom and me. Then at two o'clock one of my best friends and everyday hiking partner, Stacy, and her husband Sal would be arriving in their new RV. My official birthday present would be a trip the four of us were taking to the Grand Canyon near Tusayan, Arizona. Tomorrow, on my actual birthday, Wylie and I were going to attempt a very challenging hike into the Grand Canyon. I was so excited I could hardly stand it.

This wouldn't be my first foray into the bottom of the Grand Canyon; it was to be my fifth trip there. But it was the most ambitious Grand Canyon hike I was to attempt to date. This was the famed Rim to Rim to Rim (R2R2R), a hike actually discouraged by the National Park Service because of the dangers it holds in distance and elevation gain and descent. It traversed a 41-mile route from the South Rim down into the bottom of the canyon all the way across and up to the top of the North Rim, then turning around and following the same trail back across and up the South Rim again – in one day! The elevation gain and descent was equivalent to climbing New York's Empire State building up and down seven times, equaling 21,561 feet.

Wylie had agreed to be my personal guide. I had coerced him into accompanying me and hiking it one last time for my 50th birthday. He agreed. It would be his birthday gift to me. He was a professional hiking guide and

~~Once~~ A Cheater...

mountaineer by trade. The Grand Canyon was his home away from home in that he guided there many times each season. He had accomplished this R2R2R hike twice before, and had officially checked it off his list *and* retired it. We had begun our training several months earlier. In addition to consistent hiking (which we both did regularly anyway) we had added trail running into the conditioning, since we planned to run eight miles each way on the more "flat" bottom of the canyon. All our training and preparation was about to be tested as we excitedly climbed into the RV to head to the Grand Canyon.

Knowing we would be getting up before midnight, Wylie and I catnapped on the drive. A couple hours into the trip we stopped at a restaurant along the route in Flagstaff, Arizona, to eat dinner. Wylie insisted on paying the entire bill for all four of us, declaring, "Stacy, you will never pay for a meal if I'm around!" Stacy was an extraordinary Real Estate Agent with a ton of connections, and she had many times over the past two years helped Wylie find new clients to sell our recently established Hiking Adventure trips to. The business was a professional guiding service offering high-end hiking trips, servicing various locations in the Southwest, all personally guided by Wylie or by me – since I did guide select trips on rare occasions for the business I had named and was instrumental in creating. Stacy had been a godsend to Wylie, often helping him fill up his trips in the eleventh hour.

After dinner we continued our drive and eventually set up camp in the Grand Canyon RV park. It was still relatively early and not yet dark when we decided to try to get to bed now. We planned to begin our R2R2R hike before midnight.

The alarm rang way too "early" at 11 p.m. We quickly dressed and gathered up our pre-prepped equipment and were on the trail by 11:40 p.m. We were working our way through five ecosystems including the boreal forest, the ponderosa pine forest, the pinyon-juniper woodland, desert scrub, and desert. It was only a few days before the full moon, but it was currently pitch-black dark. This was dark sky country and the moon would not be out for another two or so hours. We worked our way down the South Kaibab Trail, using headlamps, and began periodic trail running as we neared the bottom of the Grand Canyon. We made it to our first significant marker – Phantom Ranch – in record fashion at two hours, 20 minutes. Stacy had loaned us her inReach GARMIN emergency communication device. There was no cell service to be found in this remote part of the wilderness. We would need to rely on satellite connections. Stacy had pre-programmed messages into the device so we could quickly send them to her and Sal, keeping them abreast of our progress. I knew she would be shocked at the time we had made to this point. We ate a quick snack then began our eight-mile run.

Wylie and I had never trail-run together due to our heavy work/travel schedules, and our 35-minute distance from one another's homes. I hadn't run significantly since track in high school, so I really pushed myself during training, knowing Wylie was a natural-born runner. Luckily, I had over trained and the pace he set seemed more of a jog than a run to me. Wylie explained that we were making such good time we could conserve energy there. We began traversing over a series of metal and wooden bridges that crisscrossed back and forth over Bright Angel Creek. As we would reach the middle of each bridge, I would stop Wylie and we would take a moment to look up at the vast expanse of brilliant stars in the dark sky. There was not a soul – except us – to be found on these deserted trails. I really wanted to savor the journey while still crushing the time for completing the hike. After gazing at the stars for a minute – complete with a mini-make out session – Wylie would urge that we get going. This is the way we continued through what is known as "the box." It is a four-mile, narrow corridor of the trail that runs alongside Bright Angel Creek in the bottom of the canyon, surrounded by high rock walls on either side. This was the area we needed to avoid between 10 a.m. and 3 p.m. as it literally turns into an oven due to the intense direct sunlight retaining and radiating heat from the enormous rock walls. This trail offered little to no shade areas. It was a real pressure to get to the top of the North Rim and return to complete this part of the hike before 10 a.m.

The top of the North Rim sits at 8,803 feet in elevation and often has snow on the ground into the month of May. Therefore, the trailhead water isn't turned on until mid-May. We were hiking up to the North Rim only five days before opening weekend. We reached the top at the 6:41 hour mark, including stops. Wylie noted it was the fastest he had ever made it on that route. I beamed inside feeling proud of all the training time I had put in allowing me to keep pace with this incredibly in-shape man who had just 12 weeks earlier summited a 22,838-foot mountain.

We enjoyed our halfway point at the top and celebrated with a kiss, a selfie and an 11-minute, much deserved break. I don't know which perk I liked the best?! Feeling great with no fatigue or soreness, we began the 14-mile 6,000-foot descent. The R2R2R trail with the rock walls was also in my opinion the most beautiful part of the Grand Canyon, with its various shades of reds, oranges, terracotta, pale yellows and pinks. The sunlight was just beginning to hit the wall in the early morning hours, enhancing the colors from behind the shadows.

Alas, it was once again time to run the more "flat" semi-downward sloped part of the trail back toward Phantom Ranch. We had already reached the famed box area when I noticed my running pack was beginning to rub the skin off my shoulders. Not wanting to slow our pace, I endured the discomfort until I finally couldn't stand the pain any longer. I made Wylie stop to help me apply large, square band-aids to each shoulder, and Vaseline to help with the friction. It was a much needed break as my energy was dwindling because I was having trouble forcing myself to eat. Even my crushed potato chips that I had been so looking forward to eating were almost impossible to swallow, and I could only bring myself to eat a fraction of my salty snack. Nothing tasted good. Wylie happily finished them off for me.

~~Once~~ A Cheater...

My mind wandered off the pain in my shoulders to a story Wylie had told a group of hikers – at about this very spot – one year earlier when we were guiding a trip together in the Grand Canyon.

Years earlier Wylie was hiking his first R2R2R. He had separated from the group, keeping his own pace in the box corridor. It was completely dark in the early morning hours when Wylie's headlamp illuminated a group of three men off on the side of the trail. An older man was lying down and being tended to by two fellow hikers. Wylie is a Wilderness First Responder and has been trained to help in emergencies. He stopped, asking the men if they needed his help. They declined, waving him on and telling him their friend wasn't feeling well and just needed more rest time. Wylie urged them to feed the man some electrolytes which help regulate nerve and muscle function, hydrate the body, balance blood acidity and pressure, and help rebuild damaged tissue. He offered them some, but they assured him they had plenty and thanked him for the gesture. Wylie continued on the trail deep in thought about the sick man, hoping he would be alright. Several minutes later he felt a physical rush of air move through his body that caused his hair to instantly stand on end. It was the strangest sensation, something he had never experienced before and wasn't sure what it could be. He shook off the eerie feeling with a shiver and decided to run instead of walk for a while. Later that day he learned a man had died of heat exhaustion in the box corridor at the bottom of the canyon. Wylie instantly remembered the feeling he had had shortly after passing the men and realized he had felt the Spirit of the man pass through his own body shortly after the man's death as his Soul left its body. His hair once again stood up all over his body at the realization.

It was uncanny that we were in the same area where many people had died while hiking this gorgeous canyon. We continued our run toward Phantom Ranch, having cleared the most dangerous part of the hike. We reached Phantom Ranch at 10:45 a.m. and were welcomed by cool air conditioning as we entered the cantina. Wylie bought me an ice-cold lemonade which I transferred into my water bottle for later, and then he paid for a $1 refill that I promptly drank on the spot. We had made stellar time at 11 hours and five minutes. I sent Stacy an inReach message knowing she would be stunned by our pace.

It was imperative that Stacy monitor our progress – she would later have a very important job to do for us. From this point on we had two trail choices out of the canyon up to the top of the South Rim. We could either take the common, more crowded and longer route up Bright Angel trail or the shorter but steeper South Kaibab trail we had come down on. Wylie decided we were strong enough to make it up the extra 400 feet that would cut off about two miles. Now, 400 feet doesn't sound like it would be that much harder, but remember this would be an extra 400 feet added to the end of the 41 miles *after* already descending and climbing 21,120 feet! Not to mention, we would be climbing out in the hottest part of the afternoon in full sun with little to no shade. Plus there were a few bathrooms along the trail but NO water – none! Stacy's special job was to hike three miles and just under 2,000 feet down to Skeleton Point to bring us water. Wylie and I had hiked down to that point in 55 minutes with no break. Stacy was a pretty fast hiker, but she would also need enough notice to drive 20 minutes from the RV campground to the trailhead, then hike down carrying an extra 12 pounds of water weight.

We only allowed ourselves a quick five-minute break to soak our feet in the Bright Angel Creek before hitting the trail again to begin the last 6.5 mile, 4,870 feet, climb out of the canyon. The sun felt scorching in the 84 degree desert as we began our climb on the South Kaibab Trail, which is lined with hundreds of rock "steps" of varying height. My legs were in tremendous shape for this hike, but as we were climbing I could really feel the effort in my thighs for the first time today. It didn't help that I had acquired two medium-sized heart rocks I had found near the creek. Heart rocks are kind of my thing, and I had been collecting them and bringing them home from all over the world for many years. These two specimens seemed perfect for my collection. In the scope of things, the rocks themselves were not especially heavy, but Wylie admonished me for trying to carry them out, urging me to leave them behind. But my stubborn Taurus personality ignored his advice, thinking I could do it if I exerted a little extra effort, and I insisted on carrying them to the top of the canyon. After two grueling miles, I now understood how much the heart rocks were holding me back as I was finding it impossible to keep pace with Wylie. I reluctantly decided to prop them up along the side of the trail for others to admire. Wylie glanced back giving me an *I told you so* scoff.

I had been rationing my almost hot water for quite a while, and I knew I would be running out of water completely before we could finish our climb. Wylie was running low on water as well. I said a quick prayer asking God to *please* let Stacy be at her designated position. I kept glancing up toward where Skeleton Point would be somewhere out on the horizon, knowing it was still too early to see anyone. We were making progress up slowly and surely.

At some point, I could make out the figure of a person waaaay out in the distance. This person was waving both arms overhead signaling to someone below. Wylie exclaimed, "I think that's Stacy." Suddenly I recognized the color combination Stacy had been wearing, all those hours ago at the top of the trailhead. I felt a wave of relief rush over my body as I realized it *was* her; I spontaneously burst into tears at the comforting thought of her being there and supplying us with our much needed water. We made a few more unsanctioned stops in the shade, and as we got closer to Skeleton Point Stacy had bridged the gap and met us in the shade on the trail. She carried with her several hiking bladders each filled with ice-cold water. She helped me fill my bladder as my dexterity was no longer in top shape. Then she dumped the last of the water directly into my mouth letting it spill out both sides, soaking me in its refreshing coolness.

~~Once~~ A Cheater...

We all began climbing out together, with Stacy excitedly exclaiming how we were "killing it" by making such excellent time and how she and Sal had had to cut their exploring short to come help us at the trail. Most people moved out of our way, as "up" has the right of way on hiking trails, although not everyone is aware of this rule. Many people commented on our speed up the trail and asked us what part of the canyon we were hiking. Stacy did most of the talking for us, as we needed to preserve every breath; Wylie and I had realized several hours earlier that if we could keep this pace, we would be able to finish in under 15 hours.

We got a second wind and really began to hightail it out of the canyon, widening our gap with Stacy as she was still conversing with hikers along the route. What had taken us 55 minutes to hike down only took an additional 17 minutes to hike out, which seemed impressive considering the distance we had already covered.

At 14 hours and 51 minutes *with stops*, we had done it!!! I was absolutely exhilarated and barely sore. I truly would not have known from the condition of my body that we had just accomplished what Backpacker magazine lists as the second most difficult hike in America – *one way*, that is. ☺ We had accomplished something fewer than 1% of the five million annual visitors to the Grand Canyon ever do: we had ventured to the bottom of the Grand Canyon and up and back out again. *And* we had accomplished something even fewer people who hike into the Grand Canyon ever do; we completed a R2R2R in a single day, accomplishing it in 14 hours and 51 minutes with breaks – 13 hours and 30 minutes of actual hiking time. I don't know if I had ever felt more proud of any physical accomplishment I had ever made in my life. I felt more elated than tired as we sat there savoring our victory and waiting for Stacy to finish climbing out. When she reached the top of the trail, she hugged me and placed a sash around my body that read "50 and Fabulous."

We walked to the parking area where we had begun our journey many hours before in the darkness. Sal pulled the Jeep up to greet us, and Stacy took pictures to commemorate the occasion. We headed back to the RV for a much deserved dinner of pizza and beer – and chocolate bunnies left over from Easter for dessert, that I had saved for the occasion because I'm a chocolate fiend. Stacy also had birthday presents for me to open. I have to say it was the most memorable and amazing birthday I had ever experienced. What a way to celebrate 50 trips around the sun!

The next morning I could feel a little stiffness in my calves, when I descended the ladder from my bed located in the cab above the driver's seat, but nowhere else. Again, all of the dedicated training had really paid off! We ate a leisurely breakfast and everyone relaxed in the sun outside before packing up to head home.

~~Once~~ A Cheater…

On the drive home I turned my attention to my phone and social media, which I had taken a break from the day before. I had close to one hundred birthday wishes across all the social media platforms and I read them all and thanked everyone for the well wishes. I rarely post anything on Facebook – it had been about a year since I had posted something – but this was such a special accomplishment that I wanted to share it with everyone. Wylie also had a Facebook account, and we were connected to each other there. But I never linked us together romantically, out of respect for him not having told his kids about us. This was despite our being together nearly two years and his divorce just being finalized two months earlier. For that reason, I was careful to ask his permission before posting the celebratory picture of us at the top of the canyon with a description of our inspiring journey. I read it to him and he agreed it was fine. I felt like we were finally making progress and moving forward more as a couple, even though he still wasn't comfortable with the term "boyfriend" or "girlfriend" to describe us. Funny, he would use those words to describe other couples. He reasoned he hated labels that didn't really explain the depth and specialness of our relationship. It didn't matter; I was still flying high on cloud nine and felt satisfied and grateful for what we had, even if it still wasn't all I wanted it to be….

~~Once~~ A Cheater...

Chapter 4

Magic Power

~song by *Triumph*

https://open.spotify.com/track/0rzxZlSB2gjnSJinbtaz3v?si=YdEy_2xJSEyQKOcHkwepkw

Thomas John Flannigan was the name of a medium I had stumbled upon in a video series called *The Seatbelt Psychic* that had originally aired on the Lifetime channel. The premise was that Thomas posed as a rideshare driver, picking up unsuspecting customers in his car, then delivering messages from Spirit connecting them to their passed-away loved ones. It was fascinating to see the reactions from the rideshare clients when he would convey messages from loved ones on the Other Side. But the intriguing part for me, was his uncanny ability to channel names. Not just one or two names, but lots of names – in *every* reading. He would name people both alive and deceased, even connecting to great grandparents' names. The reason I highlight great grandparents names is because we live in a digitally connected world. If you wanted to boost ratings by naming names, producers could theoretically research the internet behind the scenes while Thomas was driving and "feed" him the information. I want you to think about your own specific social media feeds. If someone researched you, would they be able to dig up your great grandparents' names in mere seconds? Or come up with the name of a grandparent's deceased first wife, who wasn't even related to *you* in any way? The specific and detailed information he was giving his clients is what I call evidential information. And the abundance of those types of pertinent details, coupled with names, had me hooked in a matter of minutes. I am very familiar with mediums, but I had never witnessed one with skills like his. I binge watched the entire series and before I had even finished, I paid a visit to his website and booked a group-call session to have my own reading the next week. I also ordered his book *Never Argue With a Dead Person, True and Unbelievable Stories from the Other Side* so I could read it before my own reading. I was not disappointed.

    Mark, my own passed-away loved one, has never left me. Not that I get signs every day, but his songs continue to play beyond any kind of statistical norm. We had a whirlwind romantic relationship ten years ago. He was the lead guitarist for the band *Mickey Thomas' Starship* and he regularly sent me songs and song lyrics as signs that he was still around me. We were intimately connected through music in life, and now in death. He has been gone for seven

~~Once~~ A Cheater...

years now, yet his sign activity has greatly increased in recent months (or else I've gotten much better at picking up what he is putting down!) I joined the two-hour call with Thomas, excited for him to connect with Mark. In all of the medium readings I have had, no one has ever failed to connect to Mark. This was not a one-on-one reading like I usually have, but a group call. Thomas would be connecting, one at a time, with each of the six people on the video chat to give them an individual 15-minute reading. When it was my turn, Thomas allowed me two requests:

(1) *I would like you to connect with the man who passed away who was my greatest spiritual teacher and one of my greatest loves. I would like to understand his role in what I created spiritually since he left this world.*

(2) *Can you look at my current love as we are entering a new spiritual phase together, and speak to that.*

Thomas began by talking about my living arrangements, noting that it seemed like I lived in the Southwest and also in another location in the Midwest. He was certainly on the right track; I did live in the Southwest and was very frequently on an airplane to Kansas, in the Midwest for work. Thomas surprised me by mentioning my ex-boyfriend John by name, who was still living. John had absolutely no social media presence, and we had never been tied together in *any* way that could have been found through research online. We had only been together for ten months, but John had been significant in my life, teaching me some valuable spiritual lessons in love. Thomas noted we were no longer together as a couple.

Next, he connected with Mark – by name. A wave of relief washed over me. Now I could relax in the reading because Thomas had connected with the one and only person I needed to hear from. Mark wanted me to know he had a new project he had already begun working on with me. Thomas surmised, "I feel like he is a big thing. And he was spiritual on Earth..." Then the video call connection suddenly dropped. I instantly felt a full adrenalin rush of panic. Of course, my internet had chosen *this* moment to disconnect! I hurriedly ran through the house to connect my laptop – old school – directly to the ethernet, instead of going back through the wireless connection. I was reconnected within a minute, and Thomas didn't miss a beat:

"Mark's and your love was so strong and Mark has this really intense energy, it feels like when he comes through it blows up and that is why we disconnected. Gladys (my great grandmother) has a message for you."

I declined the offer to connect with her, because she had a tendency in the past to take over my readings, not allowing anyone else to speak. Thomas moved on asking, "Who is Jason?" I confirmed it was my ex-husband. He next asked, "Who died of a heart attack?" I confirmed that Mark had.

Thomas switched gears and brought up my second request inquiring about my current relationship, "Who is Kylie?"

[Me] *"Do you mean Wylie? He's my boyfriend."*

[Thomas] "*You are definitely Soul Mates, but you know you have more than one. Mark was a Soul Mate too. Hold on, let me get more connected to Wylie. Wylie, Wylie, Wylie. Oh, interesting. Is he an Aries?* [He was.] *I see you guys really continuing to build your dynamic together. I feel you are a spiritual teacher for him. I kind of feel like you put him on another path spiritually. Yes, you definitely did! Do you just want confirmation that Wylie is the right match for you?*"

[Me] "*I feel like he is my Twin Flame.*"

[Thomas] "*Totally, totally, totally! We can have many Soul connections and this has nothing to do with your Mark connection. This also is a major thing for you. Spirit is encouraging you to step out as a spiritual teacher. Use your artwork to stand as a body of work on its own, but step into this new spiritual work because people have a deep desire to connect with you – and to learn from you. I see you connecting with that aspect of things. You are a natural teacher. This is really about going into that kind of realm. Do you understand why I'm hearing the name _____* [He said the name of Wylie's youngest son.] *Then Thomas said who is _____? Is that his ex-wife?* [It was.] *Wylie has totally moved on. He's with you now. Spirit is showing me that energy was holding him back a little, but he has totally shifted that.*"

I was blown away. Thomas had brought up eight names in my short 15-minute reading. Usually a medium is not adept enough to give you even one name. He demonstrated this skill over and over again with the other people on the line, most impressively naming a woman's Japanese mother-in-law's unusual name. My reading was in no way generic, and could not have applied to anyone except me. I was intrigued by this "new spiritual work" Mark would be helping me with from the Other Side. But I was most excited about the messages pertaining to Wylie and our relationship.

Before we disconnected the call, Thomas told me he was going to be in Phoenix exactly one week from that day, and suggested I come to see him at the show. He would be conducting a large group reading where over 100 people would gather to receive messages from Spirit. Upon hearing about my incredible reading, my mom requested we go together. I purchased VIP tickets that would allow us to meet Thomas in person after the show.

Mom and I arrived at the venue early so we could get close seating, but were surprised our VIP tickets included seats in the first two rows. We sat in the second row slightly off center. Thomas started the show right on time, and before he could finish explaining how his connection to Spirit worked, Spirit began busting through with meaningful messages for people in the audience. About halfway through the show Thomas announced, "I have a message for someone here, whose father is still in the physical world but would never attend a show like this. His name is Chuck. Norma stands next to him, along with Gladys. *You have to know all three people so you would understand I am speaking to you.*"

I practically jumped out of my seat explaining Chuck was my skeptical dad. Norma was his deceased mother, and Gladys was my deceased great grandmother, whom he had brought up in my phone reading the previous week.

~~Once~~ A Cheater...

I pulled my mother into a standing position next to me, because the messages were just as much for her as they were for me. Thomas started giving us a message, then stopped mid-sentence and asked, "Who's Ivy? This message is for her too." I explained my mom Ivy was standing next to me. Thomas continued talking for a few more moments, then explained he had an urgent message for someone else and assured us he would return to talk to us again.

Several minutes later he was standing back in front of us and continued, "Ok, Chuck, Norma and Gladys..." But this time when I stood up along with my mom, Thomas said the messages were only for her, so I sat back down again. He began talking about a ring Gladys was going on and on about. Mom acknowledged having the ring.

[Thomas] *"I'm hearing a song – Spirit has been doing this more and more, and I'm not a singer so I'm not going to sing the song. But it's a song from the 80s.* He paused for a bit, listening, then said, *"Nothin's Gonna Stop Us Now."*

[Me, jumping up again] *"That's Mark!"*

[Thomas] *"How in the world is that song connected to Mark?"*

[Me] *"Mark was the lead guitarist for the band Starship. He probably played that song five hundred times in the 14 years he was with the band."*

[Thomas] *"Wow.* [Even Thomas seemed impressed.] *Well, Mark is stepping forward, and he's showing me that he's getting ready to do something very big in the world with you. He says you have been anxious about it, but he's telling me he doesn't want you to be anxious – he wants you to be excited! Who is Rachel?* ["My daughter," I confirmed.] *She is a very special Soul. She has been sent to heal the world. Who is Ryan?* ["My son," I said.] *He has been sent to protect the world. You have two very special children. Mark wants you to know he approves of Wylie."*

Thomas moved on to give messages to other people in the audience. My mom and I were both thrilled we had each been given special messages from Spirit. The icing on the cake was meeting Thomas in person and having him sign my book. I could not wait to tell Wylie about my reading!

The next day Wylie and I met to do a one-on-one CrossFit workout together and we got smoothies afterward. While we drank our smoothies, I told him about the mini reading I had received at the show. I described to him how Mark had communicated through Thomas that he would be helping me with this "new project" I was to bring into the world.

We left the smoothie shop to sit in my Jeep and finish our conversation. When I started the vehicle, the *Toto* song "Hold the Line" was playing. The radio screen, however, indicated *Bread* "Make it with You" was playing – except it wasn't. When the song "Hold the Line" ended, the screen updated to say *England Dan & John Ford Coley* "Nights Are Forever Without You" and that song began playing. I took pictures of both screens to document the unusual occurrence. Wylie was pretty amazed too, because he had heard a lot of the hype around my signs over the previous two years that we had been together – but had never experienced it for himself. I too was amazed. It had been several years since Mark had given me a sign of freezing my screen while playing another song in its place.

Chapter 5

Strange Magic

~song by the *Electric Light Orchestra*

https://open.spotify.com/track/7cY7GAhOWKPGDeFzKEAyj2?si=CTj-umFnSBqgSHRnA5TzYg

My two readings with Thomas were so impressive that I was ready to invest in something he offered called a "Psychic Remodel," where he would spend an entire day with you, at your house. He only did a couple of these a year, and I "knew" before I applied I would be one of them.

Thomas' assistant called me with the good news. Thomas would be at my home on July 13th – only a month away and two months after my birthday. I had a lot of work to do to prepare spiritually for his visit. I had begun a journal documenting all my spiritual journeys, and I wanted to add every reading I had had over the last seven years since Mark's death. I had had readings from psychic mediums, an energy healer, an angel connector, an astrologist and most recently an oracle. I always recorded my sessions. It was time to reach back into my archives, going back to 2012, to begin the task of documenting them and adding them to my journal. I wanted to see how the messages from Spirit had evolved over time, and having them all in one place would allow me to better assess them than I could do with my limited memories. Every night for a few weeks I would take a recording from oldest to newest and transcribe them. I was fascinated to discover a few consistent patterns related to what I had been told about my energy, my life's purpose and the work Spirit intended me to do. By the time I was to meet with Thomas, I truly believed I had been able to raise my vibration.

The day of the reading I made a quick run to the grocery store. As I pulled up to park the song "Guitar Man" by *Bread* began playing. Well, that was certainly a Mark song, in that he had been the lead guitarist of the band *Starship*! Once inside the store I quickly grabbed the few items I needed. I had not previously noticed music in the store, but all of the sudden I heard the beginning notes of the song "White Flag" by *Dido*. This was the title of a chapter in my book *Signs Surround You, Love Never Dies*. It was about Mark and had been written several years before but not yet published. I felt Mark was letting me know he was getting ready to communicate with me through Thomas. Lastly, a *Starship* song began playing on the short five-minute drive home. Three song signs in one trip. I knew Mark would not disappoint!

To clear out any negative energy, I prepared the house by lighting a bundle of sage then walking through every room letting the smoke infuse each area. I prayed out loud to God asking for "only love, light, and the highest and greatest good" to come into my home. Thomas texted me letting me know he was on his way. I was beyond excited to have six hours with him to connect with Spirit!

The day was filled with messages from many of my passed-away loved ones including my maternal and paternal grandparents, a few great grandparents, but mostly with Mark – it seemed since his passing he had become my primary guide. Thomas talked about what Mark had been creating with me from the Other Side since he left this Earth. I had been inspired to paint 40 paintings in 40 days shortly after Mark's death. They were all paintings of hearts flying, with inspirational messages. When I was getting close to finishing the last painting I realized I actually would complete the 40th painting on Mark's birthday. There was no way I could have planned that. Inspirational paintings continued to flood my mind after the first 40. After painting each one, I would write a *Soul Whisper* conveying a message of inspiration to accompany the painting. I had created 400 paintings in the seven years since he had been gone. When Thomas last connected to Mark, in my phone reading several weeks before, he had said "Mark is kind of a big thing." I couldn't wait to see what Thomas had to say today. "Some of the plans are changing." Thomas explained it this way: "When something happens in our lives, we get to choose how we respond. Let's pretend we are going to Vegas from Phoenix. We could take an airplane and that would be the fastest and most direct route. We could also drive from Phoenix; that would take a little longer than flying, but and we would still get there. Or we could even drive from Phoenix back to Chicago, then drive to Vegas. That would take the longest, but we would still eventually get to Vegas. Everything you went through with Mark's death presented choices for you to process and work through. Because of how you responded, other things have now shifted and changed. If you had responded differently things would've gone differently. You are now on the highest vibration of things. You had multiple paths to choose from – you chose the highest path, the quickest path, the fastest path. You are very, very, very psychic and very, very, very, intuitive. Spirit wants you to deepen and strengthen this part of yourself."

Then Thomas asked me, "Do you hear that?" I didn't hear anything at first, but then I heard faint music. Thomas took his phone out of his pocket and the music got louder. He turned his phone screen toward me showing his phone was playing a song, but added in wonderment that his phone didn't have any music downloaded on it. He said, "The song that's playing is "White Flag" by *Dido*. Now I was stunned! This was the *same song* that had been playing in the grocery store earlier. I told Thomas about the signs I had received before he arrived. He shook his head, laughed and added, "And even if I did have music on my phone, no offense, but I would not have *that* song!" We both laughed at his comment and the crazy confirmation Mark had sent.

Next, Thomas connected to my Spirit Team including Spirit Guides, Angels, and loved ones, like Mark, who were guiding me from the Other Side. Thomas talked a lot about my current life and also about my past, including information about my family, my ex-husband, my kids, and my relationship with Mark. Mark then brought up Wylie and my relationship. Thomas said, "Mark's energy kind of works with Wylie's energy." These were some of the important points he made...

Mark then explained that he had helped bring Wylie and me together after he was no longer in this world. Thomas went on to say, "There is now a part that went back for the love of Wylie." He meant Mark had a part in bringing Wylie and I together. "You are helping Wylie heal stuff from his childhood. When I connect to your relationship with him, you have a really strong connection. Thomas then said "Wylie has a very youthful energy and he can be boyish. I'm now being shown that Wylie and you are going forward in the world together. They show me that you know that too – but you get a little doubt that creeps in. But when you consciously think about it – you want to be with this guy. They are showing me that you are progressing, but there is still not that 100% foundation yet. It feels like you are on more stable ground, but you totally don't have all the anchors in. It's a little like you're fine, fine, fine – whoops – a little wobbly, then fine, fine, fine – whoops. Spirit wants you to know – PREDICTIVELY – like over the next few months, like by December, you should feel more like 150% on solid ground with Wylie. It's not really, for him, about other women. I don't see that it's about other women in his vibration – I don't see that he's putting out that energy." (I had not mentioned anything about other women.) "It's more of a – he has some things where Wylie feels like he hasn't kind of made it yet. Wylie feels like – I've got to do my own thing, have my own stuff." Then Thomas saw Wylie doing a lot of things with foreign countries: passports and plane trips across the world.

Thomas continued. "There is a lot of intention with Wylie that he doesn't want to mess this relationship up. He wants to keep this going! And you have this questioning – are we gonna go the whole distance? Spirit is showing me that when you tune in, you feel like – oh yeah, we are! But then there's a little doubt that creeps in from you. But I feel like the energy is going in that direction of getting to more. I see you shifting from boyfriend/girlfriend to partners – partnership! There's a lot of Soul Mate partnership energy. It feels like the dynamic of you're my boyfriend/I'm your girlfriend. And I see you are going to build this business together. It's going to intertwine your energies more. It's going to allow for a new type of intimacy and a new type of trust in something. As all that stuff starts to happen, it's really important that you guys are in a better place. But, I feel like Spirit is wanting you to know that some of this stuff is going to test your relationship a little bit. But I'm getting the feeling that this is going to be more of a positive test. It's going to be more of him showing you that he's capable of communicating in the right way – saying the right things. I feel like that stuff is going to be really important. So I feel like there will be some challenges with what to do with that. But I think it will be Okay! With Wylie I'm hearing Ayahuasca – is this new for him? They are showing me, because the medicine is in him now, it is still working in him. As the next few months unfold, the energy between you guys will also be unfolding in this way too – because the medicine is still working in him. Over the next few months, there will be some shifts with him. I don't want to say 'giving you more attention' – but I want to say 'being more allowing of the connection.' Were you really happy with Wylie at your 50th Birthday party? Spirit said Wylie really stepped it up! They want you to know that wasn't an act, that was real!"

The reading was everything I was hoping for and more. It was very healing, spiritually. I had gotten some answers about my relationship with Wylie. Thomas brought up so many pieces of information he could not have possibly known. I was especially intrigued about Spirit's acknowledgement of the spiritual medicine usage with Ayahuasca, and how that was "healing" Wylie. And although I felt good about my connection with Wylie, there was always a part of me that had been wary of his past. But maybe I needed to just trust that everything was unfolding as it should....

Chapter 6

If Looks Could Kill

~song by *Heart*

https://open.spotify.com/track/1mr9ZUNWfCUClBDhYbCErx?si=vC73d_4DRXuWam3aoNEjWA

Sitting at my home office desk, wrapping up the last of my Friday workday, I was ready for the weekend! Thomas' reading six days before had really inspired me to step up some inspirational projects I wanted to send into the world. I had some big plans for the next two days.

Wylie's guiding schedule had been really busy, and we only had a quick dinner that week to get together for the primary purpose of telling him all about my reading with Thomas. I wanted to share the insights from Spirit about him and about us. He was so tired that halfway through our dinner, while I was reading my notes, he actually began to fall asleep sitting up! He had never done that before. So we wrapped up our time together before I could really finish what I wanted to share with him. I was anxious to see him again when he returned from his Grand Canyon trip the next week – I wanted him to fully absorb the messages from Spirit.

Tonight, I had one hour before my friend Melinda would be arriving for dinner at my house. We had not seen each other since the couples Supai trip a few weeks before. My phone vibrated. It was a text from my good friend Shannon.

7-19-19 5:00 p.m.

[There was an image of my favorite picture of Wylie with the caption below:]

Wylie, 53 – Owner/Lead Adventure Guide at Vet Charity Adventures – United States Naval Officer

[Shannon] *Uh, I just logged back on to Bumble after months of being off...and this came up! I'm sure he doesn't realize it's still out there...you might want to help him hide that! Happy Friday, my friend!*

Bumble was a popular dating app geared toward women. The app would present pictures of potential suitors and you could swipe the picture to the right if you were interested in them, or swipe to the left if you didn't want to meet them. If the guy also swiped right on your picture, you were a "match." The

~~Once~~ A Cheater...

woman then had 24 hours to send a message to the man, and the man in turn had 24 hours to answer the woman's message. You would then be able to talk to each other to determine if you wanted to meet in real life. Shannon shared two more pictures from Wylie's Bumble profile.

[Laurie] *That pic at Antelope Canyon is since we've been together. I think the other one is really old. But the fact is, "Owner Lead Adventurer at Vet Charity Adventures" is brand new, like since January.*

[Shannon] 😨

[Laurie] *Shannon, I want you to know how grateful I am that you sent this. I want to believe there is an explanation, but because of the use of the Vet Charity Adventures – which he just named and started promoting this year – I don't see how there is anything but an intention to meet other people.*

By the time my friend Melinda arrived I was a MESS!! Although this would normally be something I would not tell anyone until there was more information, I told her the moment she arrived; I was not operating from a place of emotional intelligence. Feeling a full adrenaline rush, my thoughts were running wild as I was trying desperately to make sense of all this chaos. What I really needed was to see it for myself.

Installing Bumble on my phone, I then activated my old profile. After the breakup with my last boyfriend the year before, I had briefly tried Bumble. I paid for what they call *spotlight*, which matches you with every person who falls into your criteria. Moving at lightning speed, it still took me 20 minutes to swipe through every potential match on that app. Oddly, I couldn't find him! Then it dawned on me...wait...I was now 50 years old...Shannon is four years younger than me....OMG, I did not meet his criteria – I was too old! That fucker!!

Bumble actually verifies your personal information, and since I had already been in the system with my real age, I could not modify it. I needed a really big favor: I needed Melinda to set up a profile so we could search as "her" with a younger age – she was younger than me by two years. She reluctantly agreed, even though she was married and didn't really want to be on the site. First, she sent a text to her husband explaining in advance what we were going to do. Then we made her profile age 42 years young – I needed her to pose as younger than me but not too young. We found Wylie in minutes. Yep, it was him alright! I had him red-handed. The only problem was that he was at the bottom of the Grand Canyon at the moment and would not be home for me to confront him until Sunday. We didn't even have plans to see each other, because my daughter was coming home that day.

I launched into action – I delayed Rachel's arrival by one day and texted Wylie asking if we could see each other on Sunday night when he returned. He wouldn't get the message until Sunday late morning, but at least I had set the expectations into motion.

Melinda and I both cancelled our new Bumble accounts. It had cost me $75 between the two of us to "see for myself," but now at least I knew. This new information put quite a damper on the fun evening Melinda and I had planned together. I will be forever grateful she was on my calendar that night; Spirit knows in advance what is coming and what we ourselves can't see. I'm sure the Angels had sent the gentle, supportive, beautiful Soul of Melinda to be with me in my time of special need.

I now had 50 hours to sit on this before I would confront Wylie. That was going to feel more like 50 days! Instead of working on all the spiritual projects, as I had planned for the weekend, my plans were now diverted to preparing for my meeting with Wylie on Sunday. I re-read Thomas' notes from our reading, and now a few parts stood out to me differently:

There is still not that 100% foundation yet – I feel like Spirit is wanting you to know that some of this stuff is going to test your relationship a little bit. But I'm getting the feeling this test is going to be more positive. For him, it's not really about other women – I don't see in his vibration that it's about other women. I don't see that he's putting out that energy. It's more of a…Wylie has something where he feels like he hasn't kind of "made it" yet.

That comment about other women really got me. How in the world could it not be about other women when he was on a dating site to meet OTHER WOMEN??! I just didn't understand. My mind could not reconcile what he had said in my birthday poem, a few weeks before, with where we were at this moment. If I was honest with myself, he *had* acted very strangely on our recent couples hiking trip in June. I needed to have a plan to see him: I needed to know (1) what I wanted to ask, (2) what I needed to see, (3) what I would say, depending on his responses. Would he be defensive or honest? I didn't really know. I had been wary of a woman he fitness-trained and spent a lot of time with, and I was focused on that local threat. Maybe she was just a diversion to keep my attention off the real threat – **every other woman under 50 in the Phoenix area!!**

I spent the next day making lists and doing research. I had to download dumb Bumble again so I would be familiar with the app. I wanted to see if Wylie had chosen the "want to meet friends" mode (as he could have been looking for potential clients for our hiking business) or the "dating" mode. One thing was certain, 50 hours was more time than I wanted to wait in preparing for my meeting with him. I called a few of the closest people in my life to tell them what had happened – Dawn, Stacy, LeeAnn and Rachel. I was going to need all the moral support I could get. But at this point I didn't want too many people knowing, in case there really was some logical reason for all of this that I had not been able to figure out!

It was Sunday night and I was about to test my acting skills. I knocked on his door and was greeted with a big smile. I didn't have all the facts to convict Wylie, so before I exposed what I would never have wanted to know, I needed to do one thing first: I took his hand and dragged him into his office, opened my phone, and began playing the top three favorite songs from our Spotify *L.A. Woman* playlist. No matter what was going to happen in the next moment, I was utterly and completely *in love* with Wylie Heartley. We danced – the way we always danced, more of a stand-up make-out session than what could be called

~~Once~~ A Cheater...

dancing. In this moment, more than ever, I needed him to feel the full strength of our love as Twin Flames. I could feel he too was in love with me. You can fake what you say and how you say it, but you can't fake the feelings and emotions that are evoked in a make-out session. The whole truth was, I was so scared this might be the last time we were to ever again be in one another's arms....

As the third song was ending, I cradled his face in my hands, looked in his eyes and asked, "Wylie, do you have any idea how in love with you I am?" As I said those words, a steady stream of tears began to cascade out of my eyes and down onto my cheeks – partially from the emotions of loving him and partly because I knew what was coming next. There was a real possibility we may never be like this with one another again... He was used to me being emotional in moments like this because the depth of my love would often elicit this type of response from me. He smiled broadly and said he thought he might know what I was feeling and proclaimed his love as well. I gave him one final kiss, then stepped back from him and wiped the tears from my face.

I had a little folder with me where I had written all the notes I needed for this conversation. I wanted to start with what Thomas had revealed at my reading, especially since Wylie had been so tired last time we saw each other that he had not been able to fully absorb the messages. I read all of the condensed notes to him. Thomas had also shared information about Wylie's troubled relationship with his mother, and Spirit had a few things to say about his ex-wife and kids, as well. This time he listened, fully awake.

Next I told Wylie about a man I had met on my every-day hike, who was the CEO for a hospital, and who told me about his passion for helping vets. I was in the middle of one of my "commercials" about our Hiking Adventure business, when the CEO expressed wanting to connect with Wylie to discuss his Vet Charity. He wanted to share the information with some of the vets he knew. I explained to Wylie that the CEO had sent him two emails, and that he said Wylie had not yet responded to them. I wanted Wylie to tell me the story about **when** he established and created the Vet Charity name – I needed to compare the timeline with his Bumble profile. If I had somehow misunderstood and he had created it long ago, there was a possibility the Bumble account was *not* current, and this would explain things. As for the CEO's unanswered emails, Wylie had a history of missing important emails.

Wylie confirmed the Vet Charity name was born from the list of names we had spoken about at the beginning of the year. He then offered to find the emails from the CEO. We went to his computer and as he was scrolling, looking for the emails, I saw them...Bumble after Bumble after Bumble notifications. I was tempted in that moment to play dumb and ask him what they were, but I resisted because I had a better plan.

He found the email from the CEO and looked at it and said he would respond to it later. We sat back down on the floor again, and I asked him about his Grand Canyon trip. I then told him briefly about my weekend and casually said, "Oh, I want to tell you about what happened to Shannon. You know she has been off of all those dating sites for the last year, right?" He shrugged. "Well, she went back on them and she met this guy she is super interested in. Do you know what Bumble is?" I asked, innocently. He shook his head and said, as if guessing, "Some kind of dating app?"

I answered, "Yes, it's one of those where you swipe to the right if you like the guy and swipe to the left if you don't. You have got to see this guy she met..." and with that I opened my phone to Shannon's text picture of Wylie and shoved it up close so he could see it. I watched the color drain out of his face and continued: "Isn't he handsome? Do you think he would be interested in her? WHAT THE FUCK, WYLIE?!!"

He had been utterly and completely blindsided by my revelation, and I took full advantage as I needed to move quickly before he recovered. He admitted, "Yep, that's me." He knew there was nowhere to hide, so he fully owned it and at the same time immediately offered me an explanation. He claimed he just went on the app for fun, and that it was just a game – nothing more. He was using it for entertainment purposes and had already gotten bored with it and should have already deleted it.

I demanded, "Let me see your phone – I need to see for myself." The first thing I did was look at his Bumble app usage. I wanted to see how much time he had spent on the app over the last week. Thirty-eight minutes – ok, that was lower than I thought it was going to be, only five minutes a day. I opened the app and went right to the conversations he had been having with the women he matched with and began reading them, some of it out loud. I started at the top. The conversations contained a lot of lame questions, back and forth. There was no "Hey, baby," or "You're hot," or even anything that could be construed as interest. He would ask them a question, many times responding to their answers with a simple "Got ya." He was right; it looked more like entertainment. After reading the mundane conversations with about seven women, he began asking me for his phone back, telling me that was enough. I was tempted to go read his text messages too, but this wasn't about violating his privacy. It seemed clear that he had already broken our trust, and I did not know if this was going to be recoverable for me.

I only had one final question, "Did you meet any of these women?" I was expecting a "No" answer but was surprised when he said, "I met one for coffee." I just about lost my shit! In that moment I knew I was out of this relationship! I could not believe it!! Talking to them was bad enough – meeting one took this whole "game" to another level. I think he realized as soon as he saw my reaction *our* game was about to end. "So did you kiss her, have sex with her?" I asked. "No," he said, "It was all part of the game." He had heard that people on those apps use old pictures and misrepresent themselves. To see if it was true, he decided to meet the first woman he talked to, since they had had the longest conversation. He was totally disappointed. She didn't look like any of her pictures and – surprise – she was also over 50. She had lied about her age, reasoning that the cutoff for men she was interested in seemed to be 49. Funny – wasn't that Wylie's cutoff age too?

Then I realized my oversight – I had not read *this* woman's profile. Although, Wylie didn't know whose I had or hadn't read, and that may have been why he came clean and disclosed meeting her – not knowing if he was going to be caught in a lie when I asked.

I retorted, "So if she HAD looked like her picture – looked good – then you would have kissed her, slept with her, or seen her again?" He interrupted, saying he would never use an online site to meet someone for a *real* relationship because he would never find anyone like me on something like Bumble. I laughed at him! "*I* was on Bumble right before we started dating. If you had been there at the same time, we would have met – except I'm too old for you!" And I went OFF about this recently discovered age discrimination. I was thoroughly disgusted,

Wylie explained to me that he had been at a hotel with his 32-year-old co-guide the day before a Grand Canyon hike in June. There was nothing to do and they were bored, so they went through the co-guide's Bumble app to entertain themselves. The co-guide encouraged Wylie to download the app. He resisted at first, eventually succumbing to the "peer" pressure – of someone 21 years younger than himself. I reminded him, although this might have *felt* like a game to him, it was NOT a game to the women he was talking to – women who thought he was genuinely interested in them! I told him I might have been able to overlook the app usage, based on the conversations I had just read, but meeting someone in person took this to a whole new level. It was no longer a game to him, or to the woman he met – or to me. Because I was out!

I took the "If the relationship is over..." sheet out of my folder and began reading from it. I listed everything Wylie had in his possession that I wanted back – right now. Next I addressed the items of his I was storing at my house and told him he had 60 days to get them out – which I thought was pretty generous, and at the moment was considering throwing them out on the front lawn. I would be transferring the XM radio he had been using to Ryan. Lucky for me, he had just paid me $6,000 in outstanding permits for our Hiking Adventure business and no longer owed me any money from the business. He did owe me $8,000 for his half of our timeshare and was going to need to figure out how to pay me. Then, to remind him where we were two short months ago – I took a copy of my birthday poem out and began reading it out loud. At some point while reading it I broke down crying and just buried my head in my knees, sobbing for a few minutes. All the while, in my mind, I was trying to talk myself out of crying, telling myself to toughen up – there would be time for crying later! When I composed myself, I balled up the poem and threw it at him! It meant nothing to me now.

He expressed his deep apology and began talking about how this was all a symptom of his needing to take the break he never took after his divorce: He was so confused about not getting to take the break he needed "on his terms" – and it was now on my terms. He said he loved me and had simply thought that in time I would grow tired of him and the relationship would slow down, but that never happened – my feelings had just kept growing stronger. He never expected nor experienced anything like my love in his life! He also said that in his entire life he had never met anyone, in any sphere, that he thought was more amazing or whom he admired more than me. If I wasn't number one, then I was in the top

~~Once~~ A Cheater...

two, and that was why it had been so hard to find a way to take a break from our relationship.

I told him he had blown it with me! I had set the expectation from the beginning of our relationship, especially because of his past history: I had ZERO tolerance with ANY kind of cheating. And meeting some woman out on a date, even as mundane as coffee, was a violation of our relationship. I would *never* in the future be able to trust him again! He was a weak man masquerading in a strong man's body and I was seeing through his disguise for the first time.

I had said everything I wanted to say. There was nothing left to say. I stood up, gathered my purse, and my file folder of notes from Thomas and handed it to him. He now had in writing what I had told him about my session with Thomas. Then, without hugging him or saying another word, I walked out his front door. I heard him follow me out – I didn't look back. Instead, I got into my Jeep, started it, and left. I waited until I got to the highway before I let myself cry again. When I regained my composure, I began a series of phone calls. Everyone I had told was on standby, waiting to hear the outcome of our meeting.

When I arrived home, Rachel was there – thank God! I was so happy to see her. I had called before I was to meet Wiley to tell her what was going on and asked her to delay her trip home by one day. She knew I needed her and had headed to my house anyway. We talked for a really long time. Then I went to bed, knowing I was in for a fitful night of sleep. I awoke in the morning to Wylie's email.

From: Wylie Heartley

To: Laurie Majka

Date: 7-22-19 4:09 a.m.

Subject: Initial thoughts

Dearest Lauri,

Well I've been up since midnight. Not sure how I even fell asleep, but I was pretty exhausted from my trip, so I guess a little rest was in order.

I'm writing in a stream of consciousness fashion, so it might not make complete sense. I'll try to make it as clear as possible, but clarity is sometimes elusive. I'm also not going to pull any punches, so to speak. Some of what I write might be slightly misguided, but emotions can at times get the better of me. So I apologize for any hurtful things. They are not meant to be mean. I'm still feeling sorry, sad and confused.

So, strong work Laur! You got blindsided by my Bumble account and had to sit on it for 50 hours and get freaked out, and you were successful in returning the favor. I guess, I should at least be happy that you were the one to deliver the blow to me. You got the information secondhand, which is shitty for everyone. But hey, you totally returned the blindside, so well done!

~~Once~~ A Cheater...

As I said earlier, I'm sorry, sad and confused...

I'm sorry that you were blindsided.

I'm sorry that my actions hurt you.

I'm sorry that I betrayed your trust.

I'm sorry that you can never trust me again.

I'm sorry that you had to find out about the Bumble account in the way you did, especially since it was quite meaningless to me.

I'm sorry that I felt the urge to even set one of those things up in the first place, regardless of my intentions.

I'm sorry that I did not take it down when I realized how stupid it was and what a waste of time, especially given that I already had such an amazing person in my life.

I'm sorry to lose your bright smile, your warm embrace, your enthusiastic zeal for adventure, and your ability to bring out the best out in me.

I'm sad about the pain that I have caused you.

I'm sad when I replay the sight of your tears and anguish and realize that they were and are the result of my insensitivity and stupidity.

I'm sad to have lost your bright smile, your warm embrace, your enthusiastic zeal for adventure, and your ability to bring out the best out in me.

I'm sad that I didn't realize sooner that I needed to talk to you about how I was feeling and that I needed a break to sort shit out.

I'm sad that given what an amazing person you are, that I couldn't sort my shit out sooner.

I'm sad that I couldn't be as "all in" as you were.

I'm sad that I am still struggling with being in a totally committed relationship, even when in a relationship that is as amazing as ours.

I'm sad that I couldn't handle you.

I'm sad that I couldn't accept your love and reciprocate it as deeply as your feelings for me.

I'm confused because I didn't get to have the conversation that I needed to have with you on my terms, when I was ready.

I'm confused because I believe and believed in us so completely, that even though I was struggling, I thought the depth of your love and the breadth of our connection would be able to survive anything.

I'm confused that something so stupid and insignificant to me could cost so much — in fact, everything.

I'm confused that our relationship was "all or nothing" and that now we have only our memories.

I'm confused that I can't get over my "possession" obsession and couldn't just embrace being "your boyfriend."

I don't think this is a complete list but, as I've written this, I've also begun to have feelings of thankfulness.

I'm thankful for our adventures — trips, concerts, hikes, outings.

I'm thankful for our laughs, our talks and our sharing of ideas.

I'm thankful for being able to feel your love and passion and have someone who believed in me so much.

I'm thankful for our passion and romance.

I'm thankful for our time when we just hung out and playfully enjoyed our time together.

I'm thankful for your generosity and support.

I'm thankful for your creativity and thoughtfulness.

I'm thankful for your transparency and willingness to share your life with me.

I'm thankful that I got to meet your friends and share in the fun that you have with them.

I'm thankful for the support and love of your family.

I'm thankful for everything you taught me and shared with me spiritually and emotionally.

And out of thankfulness comes feelings of hope.

I hope that this is not the end of our relationship as I thought we had so much more to experience, build and share.

I hope that even if I am not "the one," that you find the love that you deserve.

To be continued.... Wylie~

~~Once~~ A Cheater...

~~Once~~ A Cheater...

Chapter 7

I Know You're Out There Somewhere

~song by *The Moody Blues*

https://open.spotify.com/track/0kINT1JI1ID4asUkfcJIVb?si=jg7KAITYRduWhHqN6SyIPA

To truly understand our relationship, I need to take you back to the beginning. Back before Bumble and birthday poems, before medium readings and make-out sessions, before R2R2R hikes – back to the Grand Canyon where it all started....

    Stacy and I had just finalized our plans to hike the Grand Canyon Rim2Rim (R2R). It was an ambitious endeavor – 25 miles in one day. North Rim to South Rim would be our route on opening day, the third weekend in May. It was not a trip for the faint of heart, nor to be prepared for lightly. We had hiked part of the route together one year earlier. That route took us down into the bottom of the canyon, where we dipped our feet in the freezing, emerald-green Colorado River, then turned around and climbed back out, We had hiked 17 miles in total. All the reservations for our new adventure had been made and we arranged for Sal and my then-boyfriend John to drop us off on one side, then drive around to meet us on the other.

    We had previously been pretty obsessed with getting reservations to actually stay overnight at the famous Phantom Ranch, the only hotel located at the bottom of the Grand Canyon. The National Park had a lottery for the reservations that would allow you to book 13 months in advance. You could call in to "win" them – concert style – and they would sell out in mere minutes. They were nearly impossible to get, as we discovered after making thousands of calls over several months, failing every time to win the "golden ticket."

    Stacy and I hiked and trained together nearly every morning. One day she excitedly told me about an intriguing phone call she had received from friends who were aware of her hiking passion. Four couples had planned a Grand Canyon trip, complete with cabin reservations at the famed Phantom Ranch. One couple had to bow out of the trip, and her friends wondered if Stacy and Sal might like to take their place. Sal had done his fair share of hiking in the Grand Canyon and had no interest in doing it again, but Stacy asked if I would be her "plus one." The only caveat was that the trip was to take place in the beginning of May – two

~~Once~~ A Cheater...

weeks before our already scheduled R2R excursion. I jumped at the chance to finally stay at Phantom Ranch, and we decided it would be an excellent rehearsal for our R2R trip. After these two trips took place, the only other Grand Canyon obsession we would have left would be to get reservations for Havasupai, a 20-mile round-trip hike into a different part of the Grand Canyon. It was was an Indian reservation owned by the Havasupai Indian tribe, whose name means blue-green waters. The sublime waters and many beautiful waterfalls beckoned to us and one day would be checked off our bucket list as well.

The trip to Phantom Ranch was structured so we would have an overnight first, at the top of the South Rim of the Grand Canyon. Early the next morning, we would descend 4,900 feet over seven miles with Stacy's couple friends who had invited us on the trip. We would carry only a medium-sized 20-pound backpack, stay overnight for two nights, then trek back out. The four of us left early in the morning for our descent into the canyon. Stacy and I had a lot more hiking experience than her friends, so toward the end we picked up the pace, leaving them behind, and arrived at Phantom Ranch before the rest of our group and before our cabin was ready. We ate our lunch next to Bright Angel Creek and then explored some trails around the ranch making good use of a few extra hours. In the late afternoon we entertained ourselves by watching a ranger show and visiting with the couples in our group. All meals were served at a building called The Canteen, in two sittings – an early one serving stew and a late one serving steak. We had the late sitting the first night, followed the next morning by the later breakfast. It was nice to be able to sleep in and eat a later breakfast.

We hiked some more the next morning and relaxed in the late afternoon, enjoying Phantom Ranch's famous lemonade. We showered afterwards and arrived for the early-sitting stew dinner in advance of The Canteen opening. I noticed a handsome hiker with a large group of people. He looked strong, and to be about my age. When the doors opened, each group was seated at their own table. The attractive man I had noticed outside was sitting directly in my line of vision at the opposite end of The Canteen, and he also noticed me; I couldn't be certain, but he seemed to catch my eye several times.

After dinner we planned to attend a late-night ranger talk. Stacy and I arrived early and saved seats for our couple friends. The ranger had also arrived early and was standing at the front waiting to begin. A few more early-comers arrived and the ranger began. "Since you're here early, does anyone have any questions about the Grand Canyon?" I raised my hand and asked what she could tell us about Havasupai. She replied that she had never been there, as it was in a different part of the Grand Canyon, but she had heard it was beautiful! A male voice a few rows over said, "I have information about Havasupai if you want to see me after." I turned to look and it was the handsome hiker. I smiled in response, thanked him and nodded that I would find him.

The ranger talk began with several stories about early pioneering adventures in the Grand Canyon. When it grew dark, she ended the talk with a bit of a ghost story. As soon as she finished, Stacy and I made a beeline for the handsome hiker, followed closely by our couple friends. Finding him, we all walked toward the sleeping quarters and stopped under the light of our cabin to talk. He introduced himself as Wylie and explained he was a professional hiking guide out of the Phoenix area. He was there guiding a trip with a group of hikers, and he also regularly guided Havasupai trips. He talked about the permit process and explained that, like the Phantom Ranch reservations, they had a lottery letting at the beginning of the year. If we had any interest in going this calendar year, the only way we could do it was through guiding companies who had already obtained reservations. He explained the trip itineraries but only had a vague idea of the trip cost. Two of the companies he guided trips for would still have availability for late summer to mid-fall, noting that we would probably want to avoid the very hot summer months. Stacy chimed in to say we were interested in booking a couples trip for herself and her husband and for me and my boyfriend. Wylie "traveled light" and did not have a card to give us but told us the names of the companies he guided for and suggested we could book a trip and ask for him.

When Stacy disclosed to Wylie that I had a boyfriend, I cringed. She *knew* I had been having significant issues with my relationship with John and wasn't sure he would remain my boyfriend for much longer. I had been dating him for eight months, and he was a really great guy whom I loved, but in all this time he had not been able to declare his love for me. Actually, he disclosed when I met him that at 51 years of age he had *never* been in love. Plus, he moved like the tortoise and I moved like the hare. We did have a great lifestyle connection and tons of fun together, and I don't think any other person had ever made me laugh as much as he did. But his inability to have deep conversations and to be more open, vulnerable and available had caused me great concern – so much so that it was known to Stacy and all my friends that I was giving our relationship three more months to turn around or I was pulling out. For that reason, I would have preferred that this man not know my dating status. I didn't see a ring on his finger, either.

The next morning we had the early 5:30 a.m. breakfast sitting in The Canteen. The handsome hiker was there with his group. I had forgotten his name. We said good morning, and I caught him watching me a couple times. There was no denying there was an obvious chemistry between us. I could physically feel it, and I think he could too.

Stacy and I went back to our cabin to change and pack up to hike out. We planned to be on the trail by 7 a.m. Her couple friends felt our pace was going to be too fast, so Stacy and I hiked out just the two of us. I asked her if she had remembered the handsome hiker's name. She thought it was Wylie and she remembered his last name too but wasn't sure of the spelling. About 30 minutes into the hike, we caught Wylie and his hiking group. As we were passing them, we asked Wylie to spell his full name and repeat the name of the companies he guided for, so we could request him as our guide if we booked a Havasupai trip.

A few minutes later we reached an outhouse. Stacy decided to use the bathroom one last time and change into shorts; she was growing hot already. I made a note in my phone about Havasupai and Wylie's name, so as not to forget it. Right about that time he caught and passed us. Stacy and I finished our break by taking a couple of pictures. We caught and passed Wylie and his group once more, right before we hit the difficult switchback climbing section called the Devil's Corkscrew. Stacy and I were quite a bit faster than Wylie's group, and I could see them down on the switchbacks as our gap grew larger and larger. Wylie looked like a really strong hiker, and I wondered how he felt hiking with people so much slower than him, and how annoying that must be.

Stacy and I made great time out of the Grand Canyon and treated ourselves to ice cream cones at the top. We then got into my car and headed back to Phoenix, having checked Phantom Ranch off our bucket list and feeling very prepared for our upcoming R2R trip. We would be back again in less than two short weeks.

Chapter 8

Ready for Love

~song by *Bad Company*

https://open.spotify.com/track/08JVaI77aIffNOwNjTOG4b?si=BkBC6rgtT8y4pqSNpOLdbQ

When I returned to Phoenix, I set out to find Wylie Heartly online. He had been on my mind and I was curious about him, and even more excited, after talking to him about the Havasupai itinerary, to book a trip. Plus, he had "heart" in his name. Everything in my life was centered around hearts; hearts for me were like apples for teachers. I found him on Facebook in about two minutes. I looked at his pictures and tried to determine his relationship status. There were a few pictures of him with a woman and two kids from five years before that were obviously family photos. I couldn't be sure if they were still together because there looked to be nothing current. But there was one recent birthday comment that made me suspect he might still have a wife. Well, it didn't really matter; I had a boyfriend, after all, and I was still truly interested in finding a way to go to Havasupai this year.

I also discovered a profile for him on the professional business site LinkedIn. Interesting – he was no *ordinary* hiking guide. According to his profile, he had graduated from the Naval Academy and had served as an officer in the Marines and fought in Desert Storm. He had owned a commercial real estate business, been a financial planner, and had had various other jobs before beginning a new career coaching CrossFit and guiding hikers professionally.

As we were not connected in any way, I sent him a private Facebook message that night on Messenger:

Hi Wylie, nice meeting you at Phantom Ranch! We made it out by 10 a.m. – what an awesome climb!! I would love to continue the convo about Havasupai Falls and other kewl hikes you have been on in the area. I'm up in Cave Creek...Laurie

He answered me instantly and we began a back-and-forth volley.

[Wylie] *You made great time out of the canyon!! Strong work!! It was a beautiful day, wasn't it?! I'd enjoy continuing our chat.*

~~Once~~ A Cheater… 40

May 9, 2017 8:35 p.m.

[Laurie] *It was such a beautiful day!! We left GC around noon and I was happy to see we dodged the bullet on the snow in Flagstaff this a.m.! What time did you climb out? You have got to be stronger than everyone you hike with. It must be hard to slow it down – but your group was moving pretty fast! I travel for work most weeks. I'm on a plane to KC right now. So far next week I don't travel but I may have to go to Ohio, so maybe we can continue the convo next week. I'm leaving next Thurs for GC again – R2R this time!*

[Wylie] *I got out with the last member of my group at 11:40. It can be challenging to go so slow, but I definitely get plenty of time to take in the beauty of the area – that's how I keep myself from going crazy when people move so slow!!! This week is pretty crazy for me as well. Full coaching schedule and leaving for Havasupai on Fri. back Sun. Next week might be a little more mellow, but back to Supai next Thurs. for a four day trip. You will have a great time on your R2R. Gonna be a big weekend for R2R folks!!! Is this your first time? If so, you will love it. The North Rim is so awesome and the drop into the canyon is spectacular from that side. Have a good trip to KC. And thank you for reaching out…I was hoping you would.*

  I had not imagined the connection – it was definitely there! I would need to be careful here. I had made a pact with myself long ago that I would never start a new relationship with anyone until I was truly free from an existing relationship. But I reasoned with myself that this was more like business. Sure, there was an attraction, but what I really needed from Wylie was help in deciding if I should go to Havasupai this year or wait until the following year to try to procure permits on my own. It seemed like going through a guide service was going to be expensive, and I was more of a do-it-yourself kind of gal anyway.

  We sent several messages back and forth the next day – each of us exposing a little bit of who we were, what we did, and where we grew up. But mostly we talked about hiking, and Wylie disclosed he had lived in Sedona, Arizona, for a few years. Sedona is a most spectacular place with hundreds of miles of hiking trails among the beautiful red rocks. Sedona was a big part of why I had moved to Arizona. I had plans to spend my birthday in a couple days hiking in Sedona with Stacy. I asked Wylie to make a few hiking recommendations, and mentioned that my kids would be coming home from college for my birthday and Mother's Day. He asked how many kids I had, their ages and where they were going to school. I asked him if he had any kids and he replied he had three, one daughter in college and two younger sons in high school. I asked him if they lived with him or their mom. He never answered. Just as I suspected. I texted Stacy: "Married!"

  Stacy and I had an amazing hiking experience on our R2R trip. We definitely were at an advantage, having trained in the Grand Canyon a couple weeks earlier. Our guys met us on the South Rim of the canyon and we were really feeling the 25-mile distance at dinner. When we got up to go to the bathroom, we hobbled there more than walked. We talked quite a bit on that trip about other hiking excursions we would like to take and agreed Havasupai was at the top of our list.

Sixteen days later, I received a message from Wylie apologizing for his "very delayed response." He was inquiring about our R2R trip. I waited a couple days to respond because I was traveling for work – and he *still* had not answered my question about who his kids lived with. I was puzzled why he had shared that he was "hoping" I would reach out if he was, indeed, in a relationship. I kept my responses all business and only about hiking, simply asking him how his Havasupai trip had been. It was a conversation that dead-ended very quickly.

In June, I took a ten-day trip with my boyfriend John to Yellowstone, where we spent most of our time with a large group of his friends, fishing. While we always had a great time together, a more intimate closeness and connection was missing in our relationship. We had planned to return home June 30 but extended our trip to July 3, which was by far the longest amount of time we had ever spent together. Before we left for the trip we had accepted an invitation to watch the fireworks on the Fourth of July with a group of my friends. John had met them twice before and liked them, but at the last minute he declined to go with me because we had been gone so long on the trip. He felt he just needed a break from people. While I could understand his sentiment, I am not the type of person who cancels plans. He had also been invited several other times to participate in various events with my group of friends and had many times declined. I was running out of excuses for him. My friends didn't understand why he wanted to spend less time with me, instead of more. It was a definite pattern resulting from dating a bachelor who had lived most of his life for himself, not having to make accommodations for anyone else. I was really disappointed that John wasn't going with me and asked if I could come talk to him about it.

While I was driving to his house, I had an overwhelming feeling it wasn't going to end well. The writing had been on the wall. John was a great listener and paid close attention to all I said. One of the issues I had with him was that he had not been able to embrace me as his girlfriend. When I met several of his friends over the course of our relationship, he always used the word "friend" to introduce me. I reminded him that he had even introduced me recently to his mail carrier as his "friend." Even though he would hug several of his guy friends and say he loved them, he had not been able to utter those words to me. He explained that he did love me but that he just moved very, very slowly. He said he hadn't really wanted a relationship when we met but had hoped for a solid friendship that would turn into more. I was puzzled, trying to understand why he had chosen to meet someone on a *dating site* in the first place if friendship was really the goal. I had a lot of friends already – I was looking for love. I had developed genuine feelings for this man and was pretty distraught. It was time for me to leave the relationship.

As I drove back to my house I could see firework displays all over the valley in every direction. They were all in celebration, but celebrating was the last thing I felt like doing.

I spent the next two weeks intermittently crying. I was really sad my relationship with John was over. He continued to reach out and text me over the next month, even a couple times calling me pet names and giving me small glimmers of hope that we might come back together as a couple. I wondered if

~~Once~~ A Cheater...

he might have realized in our time apart what he had given up with our relationship. I suggested we meet for dinner to discuss things, on what would have been the anniversary of our first date, August 22nd. He agreed to meet but then cancelled a week before, stating he was going to fly to another state to watch the solar eclipse. I noticed he had *not* suggested a future time to get together. He explained that he thought we were great friends and reminded me that *I* had ended the relationship, but that he valued my friendship and was happy I was in his life that way.

"Nope!" was my reply. "I can't do this. I can't text you and be your friend. You can't have me that way – it's too painful for me. I need to pull away and work through getting over this. I do know my own worth and I can't settle for someone who 'cares a lot' for me. I am so grateful for our time together – I learned a lot and I appreciate all the wonderful things you did for me and gave me. I want you to be happy and I hope you find that special relationship you are looking for with someone amazing." I was very picky with my friendships and there needed to be reciprocal energy to them. In response, he expressed that he was sorry I felt that way and it would be his loss. I shut the door completely on any type of future with John and put my focus back on work and my kids, who were far more deserving of my time and energy.

It was going to be hard to adjust to being alone again. My kids were both in college now, doing their own thing. I turned my attention back to a special project very close to my heart. When Mark had died several years before, I had been guided to begin painting inspirational art. Images of hearts flying would appear in my mind, and I would quickly sketch them on paper and paint them. I called them inspirational art because they would appear to me through some spiritual influence inspired from the Other Side. I would send each of them into the world through my Soul Heart Art Facebook page and website, which had a nice-sized following, With the eclipse coming up, I received a new vision to paint and spent several hours creating the painting. I named it "Rare Love," then wrote the following Soul Whispers to go with it:

> Rare Love is the merging of two Hearts into one – like a total solar eclipse, a rare event indeed. But a journey worth the wait and worth making the effort to seek out... Love will find a way...xo Laurie

As soon as I completed the painting, the thought of Wylie "popped" into my mind. Wow, I had not had a single thought of him in several weeks. I found it ironic that I thought of him right after writing about a "rare love" – and now my relationship situation had changed. It was time to figure out the mystery of our connection. I decided to send him a new message.

8-20-2017 10:01 p.m.

Hey Wylie! How are you? Can't believe my kids are back in school now – this summer flew! I'd really love to talk to you about Havasupai – let me know if you would be available to meet for lunch this week, Tues. or Wed. I meant to do this sooner but the work travel really got away from me.

8-21-2017 6:00 a.m.

Morning Laurie. Great to hear from you. I'm in Supai now but on my way out. Let's plan on Tues. for lunch. Send me a text or call me. Look forward to hearing from you.

Interesting – I now had a lunch "date" with Wylie on what would have been my one-year anniversary with John. Was it a foretelling of things to come? I decided to be open to love again….

Chapter 9

Love Walks In

~song by *Van Halen*

https://open.spotify.com/track/4vnj7Z2AYZxtVDmOWtZfO6?si=E4zf2d8iQAGrytrq-SrVwQ

I took extra care getting ready for my meeting with Wylie. He had already seen the plainest version of me when we first saw each other in the Grand Canyon. I was wearing a hat and only had mascara on for makeup. When I officially met him on the night of the ranger talk, I was not wearing a hat, I had taken a shower and washed my hair, but there were no hair dryers or curling irons, so I was the most down-to-earth version of myself. I wasn't sure why, but today I felt a need to make myself look especially pretty. I had curled my hair, put on full make-up, and was wearing jean shorts and an off the shoulder chocolate brown top with cute jewelry and heeled sandals. I took one final look at myself in the full-length mirror, and then joked with myself, wondering if Wylie would even recognize me.

    I had taken so much extra time getting ready, even going back twice for deodorant because I was so nervous that I was now going to be five minutes late to the restaurant. I texted Wylie, letting him know I was slightly behind schedule. He replied, "Relax."

    He was already seated at a table in the outside covered-patio area with his back to me. I recognized his broad shoulders immediately and said "Hello" as I walked in. He stood and turned to greet me with a hug, and I thought I detected a flash of appreciation in acknowledgement of how I appeared in his eyes. A big smile overtook his entire face.

    Wow. He was actually more handsome than I had remembered. His skin was slightly tanned and set off his light-blue eyes, also making his smile whiter. We visited a moment and casually looked at the menu. He suggested and ordered an appetizer. We talked about his recent trip to Havasupai, as that was the reason we were meeting, after all. His description of the exquisite waterfalls, and the trip design made me want to go there more than ever! I could practically feel the cool 70-degree water on this hot summer day. We talked about my job and work-travel and more about hiking adventures, and life in general. By the time we finished our appetizer, I had gotten up the courage to bring up the question he had *not* answered when we first started communicating. The bold me blurted it out, "So...when we first started talking, I asked if your kids lived with you or their mom, and you never answered me. Are you married, Wylie?" His answer was yes, he had been married for 24 years, but they had just decided on July 1st to get a divorce. It had been a long time coming. He planned to move out in September or October, and they were now in the process of working their way out of the marriage. I had not anticipated this answer and could not hide the happy surprise of it. I felt a giant grin form on my face before I could stop it – realizing he was actually free and at the same time realizing my reaction was *not* appropriate for this type of news. I immediately pulled both hands over my mouth, because the smile on my face was too big to be covered by only one hand! I quickly apologized and explained that I was actually sorry to hear he was to be going through a divorce, acknowledging how difficult it could be. But I was happy to know he was moving toward divorce, and I disclosed that I had *also* broken off the relationship with my boyfriend on July 4th. I found it interesting that we had both ended our relationships within three days of each other. Now it was his turn to let a large smile cross his face in reaction to *my* news. There was a very obvious chemistry, and I felt the electric connection between us.

    We continued our conversation, letting it go deeper into more personal areas of our lives, well after we had finished eating our lunch. In the two hours we spent talking, I learned we had a lot of similarities, including growing up in the Midwest. Our kids were close in age, and we had even been married the same number of years. Neither of us watched the news, followed politics or drank coffee. He was three years older than me, and I found him to be an excellent communicator – something that had been sorely lacking in my marriage. We both had a great love of – and spent quite a bit of time in – the outdoors. We even touched on a few more philosophical topics like judgement, and spirituality vs. religion. I really enjoyed this man's company – and he was pretty easy on the eyes, too. Although not my standard type, as I was usually more attracted to men with brown eyes and dark hair, whereas he had sandy-grey hair with blue eyes – no matter, I felt absolutely smitten.

    I had to get going back to work, and he needed to leave as well. I insisted on paying the bill because it had been my idea to meet to pick his brain about hiking, and he graciously accepted. We walked out together and were standing directly in front of the restaurant to say our goodbyes. As I reached out to hug him, he unexpectedly turned his face toward mine and passionately kissed me while thrusting his tongue in my mouth. I had not been expecting that and it felt like our kiss was off-sync. Plus, I felt instantly embarrassed being kissed in front of the restaurant's giant picture windows. He pulled back, grinning at me once more before we both turned to leave and find our vehicles.

    Well, any doubt I had of him not liking me had certainly been erased. Everything that had happened over the last almost two-and-a-half hours felt surreal and a bit "sparkly." I took a big breath to center myself before starting the drive home.

~~Once~~ A Cheater...

8-22-2017 1:48 p.m.

[Laurie] *Wow.*

[Wylie] *Ditto!!! Where did you come from?!*

[Laurie] *I know!! Crazy – but there are no accidents.*

[Wylie] *And I love your smile...lights up the world! So beautiful.*

[Laurie] *You gave me butterflies in my stomach.*

[Wylie] *I hope that's a good thing!? Btw...I really enjoyed kissing you.*

He called me and we talked for a little longer.

[Laurie] *Glad you called.*

[Wylie] *I really enjoyed talking to you, and I'm generally not this open and comfortable with someone so quickly, but with you it seems very natural. It's so refreshing that you have a depth to go with your beauty...rather rare in Scottsdale, AZ!*

[Laurie] *Hmmm. I'm full of surprises – you have only touched the tip of the iceberg, as I'm very deep.*

[Wylie] *Our paths have crossed and I'm excited to see where the journey takes us.*

[Laurie] *Me too.*

[Wylie] *I'm very glad you reconnected.*

[Laurie] *We have lots of time too – we will need to be patient, as you have a long journey ahead of you.*

[Wylie] *Agreed. And you excite me very much, so practicing patience will be challenging, but worthy. I think we are both at a bit of a crossroads so to speak in various aspects of our lives. So definitely an exciting time, and I feel thankful to have you to share it with, with no attachment to the outcome and totally up for enjoying the journey.*

[Laurie] *That just sounds so amazing!!!*

[Wylie] *Btw...for the record, I did not plan on kissing you today and generally don't when I first meet someone, but it felt right and I'm glad I did and I'm even happier that you didn't seem to mind.*

    What a strange comment – it was such a subtle wording, but I did not miss the "tell." Why would someone who had been married for 24 years mention not generally kissing someone when they first meet? That made no sense to me. There was definitely much I didn't know, and much to discover about this mystery man. I did not have a response to that message.

[Wylie] *Btw...you are the best surprise I've had in a long time. Very unexpected, but I'm thankfully happy that we finally connected again.*

[Laurie] *What a nice message to get, thank you. I'm happy we did too!*

Chapter 10

Beginnings

~song by *Chicago*

https://open.spotify.com/track/7xHJBSI1lwMpTJ3kcfvvsl?si=KIJYYfC8TISNBYjCR9gmIw

Wylie wasted no time scheduling a second date, but it was ten days before we could see each other again because of our work-travel. He decided to come my way and take me out for lunch. We decided on sushi, and I let him pick me up at my house. I had personally done a lot of work on my place and was excited to show him so he could see more of who I was.

  Our first kiss had bothered me a little, as it was a bit of a miss. He had not seemed to notice. I was excited to show off my kissing ability, because I thought it was going to be a place we would both excel. I did not have to wait long. When I answered the door he grabbed me, and this time we experienced our first *real* kiss together. I was not disappointed.

  The restaurant was only a few minutes from my house. Our talk at lunch was very similar to our first conversation, except that we spoke much less about hiking and more about who we were in the lives we had created before we met one another. He did tell me how he had recently guided a trip to Machu Picchu, Peru, and thought the beauty was unmatched. I was liking all I was learning about this man. Our conversation had an ease to it that seemed effortless, and it truly felt like I had known him forever. The energies between us seemed to dance and buzz, and play well together. Although I was enjoying our conversation immensely, I could not wait to kiss him again!

  On the drive back to my place he told me he never made the first "move" in a relationship – any move, if and when I was ready, would need to come from me. Hmmm, how strange for a guy. He said it was out of respect for taking the relationship at a pace that would feel comfortable for me. I agreed I needed to set the right expectations between us, because I knew he would be able to feel my excitement toward him, but I didn't want him to expect too much. I let him know I moved very slowly, and I could count my partners on one hand. He seemed very surprised by my revelation. I guess anyone would be surprised because of my age and potential life experiences. He didn't volunteer how many hands it would take to count his partners, but I knew he had been married for 24 years. Perhaps two hands would be more realistic, and maybe a couple of toes.

We wasted no time exploring each other's kissing abilities. He was pretty good, and we fit together perfectly. Kissing Wylie was going to be something I would want to do often and in great quantity. But it was only our second date, and I really needed to get to know him better first. I asked him about his marriage and why they were getting divorced. He told me the story of them meeting at the Naval Academy in college; how they had dated beyond that while each entered into service, him into the Marines and her into the Navy; and how they had dated long distance and dated others – her even once bringing another man to a family wedding, while he was in China. When he moved back to California from overseas, they resumed dating exclusively and eventually got married. Parts of the marriage were good – like his kids. But he had married her more out of comfort, as their relationship was easy. She understood him and they were fantastic friends, but he had not been attracted to her or in love with her for a very long time. While they were living in Sedona, he had wanted to get divorced and she had not. He really fought for it, finally coming to an agreement: in order to stay together, they would have an unconventional, open marriage. This arrangement allowed them to function.

He had not really been interested in sleeping around, because he enjoyed deeper, more meaningful relationships. He had entered into a couple of longer term relationships – one-and-a-half to two-and-a-half-years – that ended when he realized they were getting too serious and taking too much time away from his family. I was appalled at the information at first – shocked, really. I had only known one couple in an open relationship. It would never be my thing! He went into great detail about the circumstances and why it had happened. It seemed to be the product of a very dysfunctional childhood.

He described his mom as "batshit crazy" and on her sixth marriage. She had an undiagnosed personality disorder. She had challenged him in childhood with an "eggshell relationship" that had you either on her "good list" or "shit list" – only you never knew when you might step on an eggshell. Her love had been *very* conditional and could be doled out in smothering amounts, then just as easily reneged. Her love could not be trusted; it could be there one moment and just as easily gone the next. It made me sympathetic: this man had not experienced love he could trust.

In many ways, Wylie had inadvertently set up his life in such a way that he would experience a distrust in love again and again, in unhealthy relationships. I could not image it, because my own mom's love never wavered. I never had to wonder if it was there; it just always was. What a difficult way to grow up! I was worried, hearing his disclosure, because experiences in past relationships had taught me that a man at odds with his mother would certainly add challenges to a relationship. But he escaped her at 14 to a military high school, so he could follow his dream of getting into the Naval Academy. Perhaps he had overcome the challenge of a real relationship, and if not I was up to the challenge of showing him what it could be like.

Interestingly, Wylie's wife had been his safety net, yet that relationship hadn't worked for a variety of reasons. I asked if she had seen other men during their open marriage, though I suspected from his description of her that she had not. No, she had focused all of her time, energy and attention on the kids, even home schooling them – so much attention on them that she was called "Mom" even by Wylie. Hmmm, I was trying really hard to understand without judging, because you can judge all you want, but you can never truly understand why a situation is the way it is for a person unless you've stepped into their shoes and walked through their entire life.

Wylie had been unfaithful less than two years into the marriage. He hated the way it made him feel, and hated the sneaking, secrecy, lies and deceit. One day, he finally just came clean with her, admitting he wanted out of the marriage – not to be with anyone else, but wanted it for himself. The marriage wasn't working for him. She had NOT agreed to this, and together they picked a different path. Now here they were, ten years later, and she had asked him a very pivotal question: "Do you even want to be married to me anymore?" He had been asked this question by her before, but something made him stand in his truth on that day. Instead of his usual yes, he said, "No," he did not. It had been hard to say and she had not taken it well. They agreed it was time to divorce.

The reason he was telling me all this was because he felt he needed to be open and honest about his past: it was a product of having been in a marriage that wasn't right for him. He had wanted out for a long time, but at the same time didn't want to let his family down. I could totally relate: It had taken me over a year to get up the courage to even say the word "divorce" – and after being in the process for two years, I stopped it and returned to my marriage for another six years. I truly understood, but I was very shocked by his revelations and had not seen any of this coming when we began the conversation.

He didn't want things to be this way in a new relationship going forward; he wanted me to know that. He then said, "I will leave now if you want me to – I wouldn't blame you if you asked me to." I didn't want him to leave and at the same time was questioning my sanity for wanting him to stay, despite all he had disclosed. But he had one very big thing going for him: he was a graduate of the Naval Academy, and one thing I knew about those men was they stood above the rest with a badge of honor. It took a higher-caliber person to even get in. And I wanted to believe in Wylie: why would he tell me all this – expose himself and take a risk like this, if he liked me – unless he was willing to stand in his truth and take a better path moving forward. My earlier assessment was probably incorrect; I'm going to guess Wylie could count all of his partners on both hands and both feet, and move into using mine. What was I getting myself into? I was more inclined to run – not from this new information, but because he was just beginning his divorce. In the end, I asked him to stay.

We made out for a little while longer, and then it was time for him to go. He had only been gone about five minutes when my phone rang. I was in the bathroom and missed the call. He left me a voicemail: "Hi, Laurie. It's Wylie. I'm calling to say I had a great day and do not see how it would get any better. Anyway, I called to chat, even though we've been chatting and whatever for the last hour…" When I saw that it was him calling, I thought he might have forgotten something, so I interrupted his message and called him back. He said he had enjoyed our conversation so much he didn't want it to end. We talked for a bit and when I got off the phone I felt the sparkly energy again.

Chapter 11

Is This Love

~song by *White Snake*

https://open.spotify.com/track/3qwnfEm2N8IvD9BaJvOfaW?si=j1MQmwyYSJyDL_dpdGcQeA

Wylie and I couldn't see each other often because of his living situation and because I traveled almost every week for work. Also, he was in the height of his busy guiding season. We talked on the phone but mostly we texted. I sent him the song "I Know You're Out There Somewhere" by *The Moody Blues*, after our second date, to let him know I was thinking of him. Music is such an integral part of who I am. It has its own language, and I was fluent in it. After Wylie told me "We dominated the kissing booth today," I sent him "Your Kiss is on My List" by *Daryl Hall & John Oates*. He texted me:

9-2-2017 4:44

[Wylie] *I love that you sent me songs. I'm gonna make a playlist of them.*

    He sent me my first song, "L.A. Woman," by *The Doors*. Hmmm, I didn't get it. My songs had been rather romantic –I had sent him five by then. I looked up the lyrics of "L.A. Woman" – still didn't get it. He then sent me a message letting me know this was the name of our new playlist – *L.A. Woman* – after me, Laurie Ann. I was laughing. Then he sent me my first real song, "One of These Nights" by the *Eagles*.

    One day when I was shopping with Rachel, Wylie sent me the song "I'm Yours" by *Jason Mraz*. I knew the song but had never really listened closely to the lyrics. I couldn't wait to get in the car to listen to it. Poor Rachel, she was excited for me – but not so much after I made her listen to it on repeat the entire ride home.

    Wylie and I continued to send each other songs back and forth, and I loved it. It looked like I had started something very good with Wylie. He was fun and funny and playful, and he matched my love of music. Our third date took place at my house. I thought lunch would be a good place for me to showcase my cooking abilities. I knew from our previous lunches Wylie liked seafood, so I made shrimp and grits, and a peanut butter – chocolate torte with homemade

~~Once~~ A Cheater...

whipped cream for dessert...or maybe the kissing would be our dessert. Either was sure to satisfy both of our "sweet tooths"!

I needed to dig in deeper and get to know this man I had already begun falling for. I wanted to understand more of his past, and it was easy to direct our conversation there. He told me that his soon-to-be ex-wife had been jealous of two of his female client-friends. One was a woman who had paid for Wylie to climb Kilimanjaro (Killy) – one of the Seven Summits. Wylie explained that she was a big supporter of veterans and that's how he had met her: his best friend owned the International Adventure business, and she had told this friend she wanted to sponsor a vet who could climb Killy and summit on Veteran's Day. Wylie hadn't even known her then, but after he climbed Killy, she became a staunch supporter and had been ever since. There was never, and I was sure would never be, any romantic relationship between them. They were now good friends, and he was also her personal trainer.

His soon-to-be ex-wife had also been very jealous and insecure about the woman he had recently guided on Macha Pichu. Wylie had been a personal trainer for her as well, but again, there was nothing between them but a friendship. I speculated it would be easy to feel jealousy around this man – his entire livelihood was inundated with strong women. It seemed most of his personal-training clients were women, and it sounded like the majority of his guiding trips were either "girls trips" or "couples trips," as guys didn't normally use a guiding service, usually preferring to figure it out themselves.

In addition to a lot of exploratory conversations, Wylie and I had a lot of slow-dances in my living room and hour-long make-out sessions on my couch. I was the make-out queen – to me a make-out session could be even better and more intimate than having sex. My mom always said you would "know" by the kiss if someone was for you or not, and Wylie surely passed that test. In my opinion, kissing is the gateway to falling in love.

Twelve days after I met him, Wylie invited me to watch him perform in a CrossFit competition. I was curious about his world as a CrossFit coach and personal trainer, and the competition was a big part of it. Before I arrived to watch him compete, he informed me several of his friends would be there along with his soon-to-be ex-wife and his daughter. The latter would also be competing. *Well, this should be interesting*, I thought to myself. Wylie met me at my car when I arrived and we had a mini make-out session. We now had enough songs on our *L.A. Woman* playlist that we would play it whenever we made out. Unfortunately, my car was parked out in the open and not in any way hidden; I was rather worried someone might spot us. Wylie left to go get ready.

I chose seats a couple sections over from where the people from his CrossFit gym were sitting. I could see his soon-to-be ex-wife and his daughter. It was odd knowing they had no idea I was there or who I was. I wondered if he got some type of thrill having me there – because of who I was to him and knowing no one knew about me. It made me feel a little like a dirty secret, and I didn't like that.

Wylie was in his element in competition, and he trounced the opposition by a landslide in his age group. When he won, he got up on stage to receive his trophy and there she was – his soon-to-be ex-wife, standing there shooting pictures. I'll bet she would have shot him for real if she had known who I was sitting there watching! Wylie had originally thought she wouldn't be there – or I may never have agreed to go. He came over to my seat and talked to me for a bit, all the while nervously looking around. I asked him via text if we could get ice cream together, and he said that would be nice. Then I saw him walk to the ice-cream cart to get some with friends – that wasn't nice. I began to feel VERY conspicuous and out of place. He had said everyone would be leaving soon, and we would have time for another make-out session in the car. I had been sitting there just waiting and decided to just leave. I didn't like anything about the way this made me feel, and I left.

He called me when I was about halfway home. He was very sorry and disappointed I had left and said that if I had stayed a bit longer, he would have been finished. I didn't care. My departure was the message I sent. I wasn't going to be someone's back-burner babe.

I left on a trip to Austin with my sales engineer and one of my closest friends, LeeAnn. It was so nice to spend some time with her. She still lived back in Chicago where I had escaped from to Arizona almost two years earlier. We had actually contrived this trip for some much needed time together. We did fit in a client meeting too. While I was in Austin, Wylie texted me constantly. He was coaching one of his CrossFit athletes at a competition in Minnesota, and he had listened to our entire playlist on the plane ride there. That told me a lot about how he was feeling about me. He also wanted me to know he had two upcoming trips he would be guiding in Havasupai and wondered if I had any interest in going on either of them. I checked them both out and picked the less expensive backpacking trip (instead of mule supported), where I would carry in my own gear. I would need to buy a bigger backpack, but as a hiker I was up to the challenge a trip like that offered. By the end of the day, I had signed up to go. Stacy couldn't go with me, as she would be out of town at the time of the trip. I thought it would be best anyway to do this trip alone. Wylie was over the moon that I had booked the trip, and I was so excited to journey there with him.

~~Once~~ A Cheater...

Chapter 12

I Want Your Sex

~song by *George Michael*

https://open.spotify.com/track/6QnFHieoch6U9J8zfv6hml?si=V_WZBV56TvGNpAdUquef_A

Exactly one month to the day of our first date, I got an email from the guiding company for my Havasupai trip stating: "Thank you for choosing to rough it with us! We are excited about your upcoming Havasupai trip. Your guide for this trip is Wylie Heartley."

My stomach actually dropped when I read his name. I was super excited for this trip! These trips are sold double occupancy and I was a single traveler, which meant I would be paired with another female single traveler. That was going to be no good. I called and paid extra to have my own tent!

Wylie's divorce planning had begun in earnest. But he still had not made any plans to move out into his own place. They had not even told the kids yet. I was slightly nervous that he might at some point decide not to get divorced after all. It wouldn't have been unheard of – it had happened to me. One good thing he was doing was going to counseling. I thought that was a great idea; it takes a lot to untangle oneself from a 24-year marriage and 28-year relationship.

We met at 5 a.m. for our four-hour drive to the trailhead where the trip into Supai would begin. There were four other people with us on the drive: a young couple from California in their mid-twenties, and two female friends in their late fifties from out east. I got to ride shotgun with Wylie, but he had let me know in advance it was completely unprofessional for a guide with this company to fraternize with clients. He would be on his best, most professional behavior with me; he didn't want to be reported and lose his job. I don't know what I had expected, but this trip had cost me a pretty penny and I was thinking he would be able to just tell people we were a couple. More than anything, though, I was sure he wanted to preserve his tips.

I wanted to charge my phone one last time before we got to the trailhead, so Wylie let me plug it into the van's charger while we were getting gas. When he started the van I heard one of the songs from our *L.A. Woman* playlist, and thought – aw, that's sweet of him. But then I heard another and another – how interesting. I was both shocked and pleased that he was playing our playlist.

When my phone finished charging, I removed it from the cable – and the music stopped. Oops, *he* had not been playing our list. My phone had hijacked the radio – *I* had been playing it! I was instantly embarrassed. Wylie didn't seem to mind at all.

We picked up two more guys for our trip, a son in his forties and his father. We had a very diverse bunch. When we arrived at the trailhead, Wylie had to pack all the food for our group – a total of eight of us. Normally, there would be two guides with this many clients and no mule to carry the extra stuff. Wylie also had all the cooking gear and supplies, as well as his own tent, sleeping bag and personal effects. All that was too much; he literally could not fit it all in his pack. Wanting to help, I jumped in and offered to take the rest. My pack was now *completely* full and weighed close to 50 pounds. Well, that was one way to slow me down; I guessed I would be the fastest hiker there after Wylie. His pack was at least 75 pounds – he was going to be earning his money on this trip!

Havasupai was even more beautiful than I had imagined. There were two very large waterfalls, three medium-sized waterfalls and at least 20 smaller ones – such that if any one of them had been named, it would have been a hiking destination by itself. We set up camp, and I was Wylie's constant helper. I assisted him in preparing every meal and helped with all the cleanups. He was grateful to have my help. We had told the group we were friends.

That night, after playing a few games with the group, Wylie guided me away from the other hikers, in the twilight. We sat on a log next to a raging creek and had a long make-out session. This was our first overnight trip together, and I had set the expectations in advance: I was not ready to have sex with him and would *not* be doing that on this trip. He was completely ok with taking the relationship at my pace, reminding me that I would need to make first the move.

The next day Wylie guided us to the medium-sized waterfalls and into an underwater cave. The air temperature was not very warm and made the 70-degree water feel even more freezing. Wylie had me go into the underwater cave first, after he checked it out to be sure it was safe. We had to stand directly under the waterfall while getting pummeled with a torrent of water, then dive under the water while clearing a one-foot wall, and finally popping up into an air pocket inside the waterfall. I helped guide everyone who wanted to go inside the cave, by pulling them through from the inside vantage point. I was standing in waist-deep water for a long time. My body cannot endure cold temperatures for long because I have Reynaud's Syndrome, which is a circulatory condition that affects my extremities, making my hands and feet cold more quickly than it would for most people. I didn't want to develop hypothermia; I had to let Wylie know about my condition in case my body started to shut down. I really hated exposing any weakness in myself to Wylie, especially this early in our relationship. Despite the cold, it was still one of the coolest things I had ever done. This was such a special and magical place!

Later, as I was having a snack by the waterfall, Peg, one of the women in her fifties, asked me how long Wylie and I had been together. She and her friend said they could tell 30 minutes into the trip that Wylie and I were much more than friends. I confirmed her suspicion, letting her know this was a very new relationship – we had only been together for six weeks. I knew Wylie didn't want to tell the guests about our relationship, but I wasn't going to deny it. Peg was very surprised, thinking we had been together for a longer time. She said our secret was safe with her.

I liked watching Wylie in his guiding element. He was fearless but also projected a more serious persona than he normally used with me; he was more "military." It was interesting seeing all the sides of Wylie. Another thing I noticed was that he used Peg's name 20 times a day! I wasn't sure why he did so. I also observed he would barely use my name – it was as if he was bending over backwards *not* to say my name. Perhaps he was trying not to expose "us"...

While we were hiking back to the campground, I started looking for heart rocks. Wylie had a field day with that. He declared to the group that collecting rocks was the dumbest thing he had ever seen and warned me I would have to hike them out myself. I just laughed at him. Heart rocks were my thing; I had been collecting them for a long time. Wylie declared he would never be caught dead carrying heart rocks out of a hike! I actually thought to myself, *We'll see about that.*

We played games with the group for longer on the second night, and it was dark by the time we finished. Wylie took me on a walk before we snuck into my tent for a private make-out session. One thing led to another and we took our relationship to another level – in my tent, at the bottom of Havasupai. I didn't exactly make the first move, but I did okay it. We had been seeing each other for six weeks now, and I had already completely and utterly fallen in love with this man.

The last night was the warmest, and since there was no rain in the forecast Wylie removed the rain fly from his tent, exposing the beautiful night sky. When everyone had retired to bed, he called me over to his tent. We made love under the stars by the light of the crescent moon. The campsite was situated next to the heavy flow of Supai Creek, so there was no danger of anyone hearing us. – and our tent was secluded enough that no one could see us, either. Afterwards, Wylie said, "Now we have two special places." Wait... I was confused for a minute. Seeing my confusion, he added, "Supai *and* the Grand Canyon! Two very sacred places, according to the Indians."

And he was right. I marveled over the mystical luminescence our relationship seemed to be shrouded under. Who were we *really*? Who meets for the first time at the bottom of the Grand Canyon?! Who has this much chemistry?! Who unites and combines their spiritual energy for the first time in Havasupai?! One thing was for certain: this was no ordinary relationship and I was going to find out who we *really* were to each other.

~~Once~~ A Cheater...

Chapter 13

Moon Dance

~song by *Van Morrison*

https://open.spotify.com/track/6KHNMPZTSif1zFbFKErpNU?si=sbs9C1nnR_GZjBq3uNqbBQ

Wylie and I had such a great trip to Havasupai, and our relationship continued to grow. The biggest issue I had with "us" was how truly limited our time together was. Seeing each other at nighttime was off limits, as he was still living at his house. It seemed like he also had a lot of excuses to not see me. I would get frustrated and would often vent to Stacy or LeeAnn about the amount of time, or lack of time, he spent with me. I couldn't help but feel there was more to it than just him still living at the house, but I couldn't quite put my finger on it. My friends encouraged me to relax and give it time. I often second-guessed myself, drifting back to the conversation on our second date, where Wylie had asked me if we should wait until he was free to begin our relationship. I sometimes wished I had waited to start seeing him until after he was actually divorced. I wondered if I were to pull away from him now, if that would light a fire under him, hastening his moving out and moving him along into his new life with me. Wylie and his soon-to-be ex-wife finally told the kids they were getting a divorce. The boys both said they had known for a long time. His daughter, their oldest, did not take it well. It was going to be a difficult transition for her. She had been the catalyst for Wylie going to therapy, and he had gone at her insistence. I was in love with this man, so I applied as much patience as I could muster. I tried not to take the lead in our relationship for planning when we would see each other, as much as I would have liked to. Instead, I asked demurely when I would see him next. I felt like a fraud.

Wylie had two sizable "girls trips" coming up. He planned to guide to Zion National Park in Utah and Antelope Canyon in Page, Arizona. One of the trips was with a group of women from Canada, and the other with a group of Arizona women. They were identical itineraries and they were HIS trips – all his, not through one of the companies he worked for. When he told me how much he was making on each trip compared to what he would make guiding for someone else, I wondered why ALL of his trips were not *his* trips! He could make serious money doing this. And the clients still tipped him.

A Cheater...

Since his schedule was full and his time was limited, Wylie would ask me to meet him to help shop for the food for the trips, and that would be our date. He planned fabulous menus and was serving gourmet food on these trips. They were also lodge-based instead of tent-based trips – very upscale. After each shopping trip we would retreat to one of our vehicles and talk and make out. That's how we would spend our time together, and it was as much fun doing that together as it would have been going on a traditional date.

Wylie netted $10,000 plus tips on each trip. After he told me about those two trips, my wheels were really turning about the potential income he could make. I could see a vision in my mind of him with this fantastically lucrative hiking business. He had once mentioned doing a full-moon hike, and it gave me an idea: What about a trip built around two nights of full-moon hikes – the day before the full moon and the day of the full moon. He loved the idea. We looked at the upcoming full-moon monthly cycles and discovered we could put our first one together for December. But December, with Christmas and the holiday season, might not be the ideal month to launch our first trip. We weren't sure if anyone would sign up to spend money on hiking – the destination needed to be special and somewhere close enough to be a draw for people.

We settled on beautiful Sedona, Arizona, less than two hours away, with miles of trails meandering through towering red rocks, set under brilliant blue skies. Wylie had lived there for seven years and knew it well. It would be perfect! Also, December was off season, allowing us to find a reasonable airbnb for the overnight stay. Wylie created an itinerary for the trip on a color flyer, to share with my friends. Stacy and Sal thought it looked fantastic and was a reasonable price, and they signed up immediately. They were also anxious to meet this new guy I had been talking about so much. Wylie talked to everyone he knew about the trip and sold it to two women. Now we had four clients, plus the two of us to guide it. We got busy planning some new gourmet meals. Wylie suggested I make the shrimp and grits that had won over his stomach on our third date. I was really excited we were doing this together – as a couple. Wylie was falling for me, but would occasionally freak out about our relationship:

10-25-2020 2:18 p.m.

[Wylie] Shit!!! *You really rock my world!!!* 😍 ♨️ 💯 !! *I really didn't see you coming. I'm really fucking surprised* 🙊 😳

[Laurie] *I know. It's gonna be ok, Wylie – please let yourself go with it. Let's see where it goes...because it's the most amazing thing I couldn't have imagined...*

[Wylie] *I'm trying, baby. Just wasn't expecting this. You are so amazing! I keep pinching myself to make sure I'm not dreaming* 😍

[Laurie] *Baby, I feel the exact same about you – this is really real!!!*

[Wylie] 😳 😳 😳

One night I got dressed up for a Ronald McDonald Charity Event, and sent Wylie a picture of me in my black formal dress. At the moment the picture came through, his son had his phone and held it up to him and his brother, asking who I was. Wylie quickly said I was a friend and confiscated his phone. I just didn't understand why he hadn't taken this opportunity to tell his kids about us. I had *not* been the cause of his breakup, and I understood he didn't want anyone (especially them) to have that perception – but jeez, they were old enough to understand. I continued to remain hidden three months into the relationship.

    Stacy and Sal got sick with the flu and at the last minute had to cancel going on our Full-Moon Adventure trip. Wylie was disappointed and so was I. They let him keep their deposit, since we had already paid for a trip that had been planned around six people going. It was ok – Wylie would still make more money guiding that weekend than he would have working for one of the guiding companies. Plus, I was working as his co-guide for free.

    This was the first trip Wylie would be using his new car. He had already picked up the two other women before arriving at my house. First Jane, who was a long-time personal-training client and who had also organized the Zion trip with the Arizona girls. She took the shotgun position. Jane was about my height, with a slight build and skinny legs. Her thick, jet-black hair bobbed at her shoulders and was pulled back by a pink bandana, with bangs hanging loose and brushing across her forehead. She had chocolate-brown eyes and a pretty face with a very mysterious smile that made her seem sad, as she wasn't showing it fully or generously. Her attire was colorful, almost bohemian in style, and fancier than I would have expected for hiking. Next came Tracy, who was more friend than client. Wylie knew her from a past hiking trip – she had organized the Canada girls for the Zion trip. Tracy was in sharp contrast to Jane, with her tall stature, platinum-blonde hair in pigtails, blue eyes and an easy smile, which she wore often. She looked more like she had stepped out of the Alps than out of Wylie's car. I gave the girls a quick tour of my house and everyone used the bathroom one more time. We weren't going very far – Sedona was less than two hours north of my house. My only disappointment was to be riding in the back instead of shotgun next to Wylie.

    Wylie had told me we had to pretend we were business partners, because both ladies knew he was married and he had not told either of them he was getting divorced yet. He wanted to wait to tell people about the divorce until after he moved out of the house; therefore, we were *not* dating. I wondered when he was going to be moving out. I never pressed him, but when we first met he said September or October. It was now December – great. This might prove to be a challenging weekend...

    When we got to our airbnb, we had to kill an hour before check-in. We all sat in the yard drinking beer; it was a good opportunity to get to know one another. The house had three bedrooms upstairs with two bathrooms. There was a king bedroom in the basement, connected to a living room that had been converted to another bedroom by sticking a queen bed in the middle of the room. Wylie and I had not talked about sleeping arrangements in advance, except for him to say we were *not* sleeping in the same room.

    The girls picked first, each taking a bedroom upstairs. Wylie liked the room with the king bed in the basement and suggested I take the converted living

~~Once~~ A Cheater... 64

room with the queen bed, next to his room. T*hat* wasn't obvious, lol. It was the perfect set up: girls upstairs and Wylie and I two levels below in the basement. The girls never did go into the basement, not even to check it out.

On the day before the full moon, we climbed up on top of a plateau on a big hill with a great view. We were able to watch the sun set at the same time the giant moon was coming up over the horizon. Our hike was a big hit. The weather was perfect, and best of all, our viewpoint was only about a mile's walk from the airbnb. I made dinner after our hike. The weather had gotten cold after the sun set, and we all sat outside on the back porch in a large swing, under blankets. Wylie held my hand under the blanket the entire time. I retired to bed before he did, and about 30 minutes later he came downstairs and scooped me out of my bed, carrying me to his bed. It was so nice to be able to finally sleep together again, and in a proper bed this time instead of a tent. We didn't get much sleep, and when I had finally drifted off the coyote's howling in the yard woke me up. But not Wylie – he was dead to the world.

The next day we hiked to the famed vortex area, and to three hidden arches, only one of which I had been to before despite my extensive hiking in the Sedona area. We had to take Wylie's new SUV on a very rough road, and it was there I learned he had once raced for Range Rover. Was there no end to the skills and talents this man had acquired?

I looked for heart rocks on the hike, as usual, and found a few good ones. Jane made some negative comment about my heart rock hunting. But I didn't hear exactly what she said to Tracy. Jane didn't really talk a lot and was more of a whisper talker. It didn't matter – I still intended to give Jane and Tracy their own heart rocks at the end of the trip, if I could find a really good one for each of them. Heart rocks come in many shapes, some better than others, and I never modified one to make it better. Either it was perfected by nature or I left it behind.

We had an early dinner that night after everyone showered. I also noticed Jane didn't eat very much. She would mostly pick at her food, put a napkin over what I had made, and throw the majority of it away – all the while thanking me and telling me how delicious the meal was. We had vetted the menu with everyone in advance, getting consensus, but she didn't seem to want to eat much of anything. She saved more of her calories for Tequila, and I couldn't blame her – what's not to like about Tequila.

We were all four sitting around the kitchen table laughing. The conversation had gotten louder and more lively, when Jane suddenly stood up, mad at the noise level, and mumbled something about having Asperger's, and then left. It's true that Wylie has a really loud voice, and I'm not exactly quiet. His loud voice was actually something I liked about him – it made mine seem quieter. Tracy wasn't a wall flower, either. We all just looked at each other and shrugged, and Wylie turned the music way down. I don't think any of us had realized how noisy it had become in that small, confined dining room. I felt bad and hoped Jane was okay. She might have been Wylie's friend but she was a client too, and I wanted her to have a good time.

The actual full moon would rise 45 minutes later than it had the night before. We all dressed warmer for the night's hike because we would be out later and the temperature drops quickly in the desert when the sun goes down. Plus, we were climbing up higher than we had the night before. Wylie and I had collaborated on a full-moon Spotify playlist, adding over 100 songs referencing the moon, and he played it all the way up. The hike Wylie took us up on was great but fairly steep. Tracy's back was bothering her, and it would be dark coming back down with headlamps. I was a little worried someone might get hurt – it would have been a fairly challenging hike down, even in the daytime. But the angels were on our side and it would be fine.

We had a magnificent view at the top, and we had it all to ourselves. I pulled Wylie off to an area away from everyone so we could steal a few kisses, with him protesting that the girls might see us. I actually loved trying to steal kisses and being a little risky with him this way, because I really didn't care if they saw us together kissing or knew we were dating. One thing I noticed that day was how often Wylie used Jane's name. Like a lot – a lot! Once I noticed it, I couldn't *not* notice it. The extra name use happened so often I was tempted to childishly count how many times he said it, but I resisted. I started to pay attention to how he used my name – he didn't. He barely ever used my name. Of course, when we were normally together, just the two of us, he called me "babe." Maybe he felt it was safer to *not* use my name at all. But then again, he seemed to use Tracy's name normally...

From our vantage point that night, the moon had to rise higher above the horizon to get above a rock wall, before we could see it. We probably waited an hour and a half for the moon, once we were up there. When we finally saw it, the full moon was perfectly positioned in a peep hole the rocks formed in the distance. It was totally worth the extra wait! We hiked back down the trail with headlamps, and had a nightcap when we returned to the airbnb. Like the night before, I headed to bed earlier than Wylie, hoping tonight he would get the hint and follow me – but he didn't. I was just tired of visiting with the girls and wanted to have him all to myself again. When he finally came to bed, over an hour and several tequila shots later (with Jane), I was starting to feel annoyed at how long he took to come down. He apologized, saying he was just entertaining the clients. We didn't get much sleep that night either, and the coyotes woke me up on cue, again howling – this time to the very full moon.

We hiked to two more destinations the morning of our last day; including another new place I had not been to before. That day I was on heightened alert to Wylie's use of Jane's name. He used her name literally every time he addressed her, and I am not exaggerating. By the time we were driving back home, her name was like nails on a chalkboard to me. I was trying to figure out what could be going on between them, because this was not normal behavior. She was single, as far as I knew, and they spent a lot of time together. Maybe there was something going on between them. But then I reasoned that if there was something between them, he would not expose me to that situation by having us both on a trip together – especially since he slept with me the whole trip. I thought about the CrossFit competition and how I had felt he enjoyed having me there in secret. Was Jane his little secret, too? Would he have slept with me in the same bed in the basement, if he had something going on with her? No, it didn't make logical sense. But this name thing was driving me crazy! I was thinking about it on the way home and remembered how he had done a similar thing with Peggy on our Havasupai trip. He had called her Peg, over and over again. Maybe he liked one-syllable names? Well, I didn't hear him calling me Laur, the nickname all my friends called me, over and over again...

As we got closer to dropping me off first, after our trip, Wylie began telling a story about his soon-to-be ex-wife and her brother. I actually cringed as he used the term "my wife" a few times. I didn't want to hear about his wife or hear him use the word, or even hear him talk in a way that implied everything in his marriage was hunky-dory. It was almost disrespectful to me the way he was throwing this story around, because he never talked like that when we were alone. It felt very much like it was for show – like he was covering the bases. Why was it so important that he keep up this appearance to his so-called "friends"...?

As we were pulling up to my subdivision, Wylie asked me for the gate code. He had been to my house at least a dozen times by now, and he *knew* the code. Oh, ya – he was still busily keeping up appearances. I had to give the code to him – along with a look.

After we unloaded all my gear into the garage, I wanted him to come in the house really quick to tell me goodbye properly. He refused, even though I was going out of town that week and we wouldn't see each other for a while. He didn't want the girls to suspect anything. But I didn't want to end the trip this way. He could have at least pretended he had to use the bathroom – this wasn't rocket science.

By the time I got inside the house after they all left, I was beyond mad. Between not wanting to tell me goodbye, asking me for the gate code, the story about his wife, the use of Jane's name, and me feeling hidden – I had had it!! I walked through my house ranting like a crazy person, yelling, "I'm FUCKING done with this..." over, and over again. It took me several hours to fully calm down. Well, Wylie was going to get an earful the next time I saw him. But before that, I wanted to know what the internet had to say about someone's excessive use of a person's name. Yep – just what I suspected. People use someone's name excessively when they feel affection toward that person – an endearment or a "tell" that someone likes you. The alarm in my gut had been going off the entire trip. At least I felt vindicated now. Good job, gut!

The next time I saw Wylie was almost two weeks later, and my anger had been worn down by several phone conversations and many text messages. We made love that afternoon and were lying in bed together when I first brought up Jane and my concern about her. He of course denied he had used her name excessively and had no idea it had even happened. He assured me there was NOTHING going on between them: I needed to believe him. He reached out to me with his hand palm up and swiped his fingers down my nose in the most endearing way. It was like he was saying, oh, you are so cute to think that. It calmed me and reminded me how into *me* he was – whether or not he used my name as much as he used Jane's. I was also surprised when he told me Jane was married; I thought it was odd spending three days with someone who was married and had not once mentioned her husband. She did not wear a wedding ring, and I had not imagined she could be married. That did make a difference to me.

Tracy and I really hit it off on the full-moon Sedona adventure, and we got together for dinner the week after our trip. Tracy first met Wylie with Jane on the Macha Pichu trip that he had guided six months before. When I asked her if she thought there was anything going on between Wylie and Jane, she told me everyone in her group on the Macha Pichu trip thought they were a couple – everyone except her. The group talked her into finding out for them. She asked Jane directly if she and Wylie were a couple; Jane scoffed and said, "No! He's a pig!" Tracy and I laughed together at that. I was also curious and wondered to myself if Jane might know about Wylie's past. In answer to my question, she said, no, she didn't think there was anything going on between them. But she told me there was a medicine man on the trip who had gone around the circle of hikers, giving each person a spiritual message. When he came to Wylie, the medicine man said he was very sad. It was probably true: that trip was less than a month before Wylie and his soon-to-be ex-wife decided to get divorced.

Tracy also remembered something interesting Wylie had said to her on the trip to Zion that he had guided in October, two months earlier. She and Wylie were hiking along together when Wylie asked her what age woman she thought would be too young for him to be in a relationship with, and whether 28 years old was too young. That made Tracy wonder if Wylie was seeing someone younger. I thought it was a weird question, and in response to what she was wondering, I said, "No, that couldn't be, because *we* were together in October!"

I also had no idea until our conversation went deeper that Tracy and I had so much in common. We had both been on spiritual-growth journeys. She had been catapulted there by the death of her daughter. I could relate, as my spiritual journey had accelerated at warp speed after Mark died. We had a magical conversation. Before the dinner that Tracy and I were planning, I asked Wylie if he minded that the two of us were having dinner together – after all, she was his friend and client. He knew we had hit it off on the Sedona trip, and he thought it was fine – but reminded me that Tracy didn't know we were dating., *What was the problem when he had already told her he was getting divorced?* I did not say a word – I didn't have to. Tracy had already figured out we were dating and had asked me about it in Sedona. Just like at Supai when Peg had figured it out, I didn't want to lie about it. Wylie must not have understood how intuitive women can be about such things. Hmmm, what this man didn't know....

Wylie was going to be leaving on a trip to Mexico with his best friend, who owned the business International Adventure. He would be gone for eight days, climbing two volcanos. While he was away, I would be having a reading with CJ Martes, an angel connector whom I had found in such an unusual way a couple years before. I had been guided to her by both my sister and Mark, and I had no doubt she was truly talking to the Angels. She had brought Mark through in my first reading with her and had relayed information about our relationship that no one in her position could have known.

The day of my reading arrived and I was ready to hear what the Angels had to say about Wylie and our relationship. I had seen CJ in person for my first reading, two years before, but this time I would be talking to her on the phone. I liked to record my readings for accuracy, so I could give my full attention to the message coming through while it was happening, instead of trying to furiously take notes. I sat in my car with my phone connected through the car's Bluetooth speaker, ready to connect with CJ.

She remembered me but knew nothing about Wylie. Our relationship was completely hidden, and there was no way she could have known anything about him – yet she did. She intuited his name began with a W and that he was an Aries. She told me about each of his kids, including knowing their gender and approximate ages. She also knew he was struggling in his relationships with both his daughter and his mother – yes, she was that good. She also connected, with the Angels to find out who Wylie and I were together, as Souls, and also learned that he had been resistant to our relationship. She then talked about our past-life connections, and after a pause said, "He is your Twin Flame" – and THAT explained everything! Twin Flames don't always reincarnate (come to this Earth again) together in the same lifetime, unless they are trying to create something together. They come into each other's lives to work on something they would not be able do alone, but could only do by combining their energy. I knew this relationship with Wylie was a big deal – partly because of where we had met, and also because of our instant magnetic connection. But I also understood the significant challenges that can come with a Twin Flame relationship. It tests you and holds you to a higher standard. If you don't do the work, your twin will hold your feet to the fire until you either do the work – or you burn, or run. I only hoped we had come together *now* because we were *both* up for the challenge!!

Chapter 14

Movin' Out

~song by *Billy Joel*

https://open.spotify.com/track/16GUMo6u3D2qo9a19AkYct?si=yOEFeZXLTAKsOe4oHFJMiQ

Wylie was the most adventurous person I had ever known. He was on a plane now, on his way to Mexico City with his best friend and a small group of guys who were going to be driving five hours outside of Mexico City to climb a volcanic mountain.

The next time I heard from him he had climbed five miles up La Malinche, ascending 4,700 feet on a 14,636-foot volcanic mountain – in under six hours. And that was just the warm-up before the big volcanic hike!

He now had internet reception and was in constant contact with me for a couple days. He was rooming with his best friend, and I was excited to hear he had told him about me. It made me feel more real in our relationship. I was still so hidden in his life; he had not yet told anyone else about me. Ironically, his best friend collected heart rocks, like me. The two of them had hunted for heart rocks together, and he would be bringing home a few surprises. A guys trip was so good for him! I felt he needed that kind of break, especially with everything he had going on in his personal life at home.

We were still getting to know each other. I asked him to share his top three favorite bands. He said the *Foo Fighters* was one, along with the *Eagles* and *The Rolling Stones*. Doing a little research I discovered the *Foo Fighters* would be in our area in October. I bought tickets for us, thinking they'd make the perfect birthday present for him. I was giddy at the thought of giving him this special present, and then being able to see one of his favorite bands through his eyes at a concert together. I gave him plenty of notice to block his calendar well in advance of the concert.

The volcanic mountain turned out to be a formidable opponent for Wylie, with a lot of loose-falling rocks ricocheting down the mountain, mostly due to the careless group of hikers ahead of them. On his way back down, a boulder the size of a college refrigerator only missed him by about 25 feet. It was too close for comfort! They also encountered a scree of rocks that were in constant movement. At the point where the scree field ended their forward motion and Wylie had to step off, he hit the solid rocky ground, and that abrupt movement turned him in a full summersault while scraping his chin on the rocks in the process. He was lucky he didn't need stitches. Mountain: 1, Wylie: 0. It was still a great experience for him.

He had been gone for more than a week, and since we still weren't seeing each other as often as I would have liked, I couldn't wait for him to come back home – I missed him. I welcomed him home with a new song for our *L.A. Woman* playlist: "Kiss You All Over" by *Exile*. And I couldn't wait to do just that!

The day after he returned, I texted him to see what he was up to. He listed several things, but one in particular caught my attention: "Looking for an apartment." As far as I was concerned, he couldn't have his own place soon enough. Until now, we had only been able to meet each other during the day, and the only dinners we had together were on the Supai and full-moon trips. It was an odd way to date someone. He had an appointment to look at an apartment later that day. I hoped it would work out!

One week later, Wylie was moving into his own place. I wasn't able to help him move because his soon-to-be ex-wife and kids were assisting him, and they still didn't know of my existence. Once he was all settled, I was invited over. The place was a disaster! He had far too many belongings for the space, but it was going to have to work. His soon-to-be ex-wife let him leave a few things at her place – thank goodness, or there wouldn't have been room to walk! He had boxes and containers strewn around, in addition to pictures sitting on the floor waiting to be hung. But he was free – and we would finally have no restrictions on when or how long we could meet. It was heaven! I went to Target and bought him a few things to make the place functional – a shower curtain, bathroom rug and garbage cans. I also wanted it to look homey and presented him with a real bedspread, nice sheets and good pillows. He already had these items, but it seemed he had been given all the sloppy "seconds." It was a rather elaborate housewarming gift for him. We had only been together for four months, but to me he was worth it.

I did all kinds of crazy things like showing up in glow-in-the-dark, full-body paint, only visible under black light. I once knocked on his door dressed like Pam from the TV show *Tool Time*, wearing a flannel shirt and cutoff shorts with a tool belt and real tools. Since I was quite a bit more handy than Wylie, I had come to install the bathroom towel bars I had bought him, and to hang all his paintings and pictures. His place looked a little better every time I left it. I would also bring him baked goods so he would have something more tangible to remember me by after I left. He too was stepping up his game by playing our special *L.A. Woman* playlist whenever I came over. We had an absolute blast together, and I was able to be more uninhibited with him than I had ever been with anyone in my life. He really brought out the wild in me!

Wylie had only one trip to the Grand Canyon left before we were to leave for our four-day / three-night trip to Muir Woods National Park, just on the other side of the Golden Gate Bridge from San Francisco. He invited me over to make dinner together so we could see each other before he left. We always had so much fun together, even when doing something as ordinary as cooking and eating.

After dinner, he got out a bottle of sipping tequila that he had brought back from Mexico. While he was pouring it, he made a comment about Jane and him both buying the same tequila. My mind tripped for a second...I couldn't have heard that right. He must have meant he brought some back for her; I knew from our full-moon Sedona hike she loved her tequila. No matter, it was a lovely evening. And it was less than a week before our trip together – I couldn't wait!

~~Once~~ A Cheater...

~~Once~~ A Cheater... 73

Chapter 15

Jane

~song by *Starship*

https://open.spotify.com/track/0fFtudFYi0ZJwGQEZEh6PU?si=wiHJJO64SAGpZs-yBFpA6Q

The night before Wylie's Grand Canyon trip, I was home working on the computer, while music played in the background. The song "Jane" by *Starship* began playing and I smiled to myself because this was a song Mark would play. *Starship* songs were often used by Mark as signs from him from the other side. But this time the name of the song, of course, made me think of *that* Jane. I thought about our Sedona full-moon hiking trip together and wondered if she would post any pictures of the trip on Facebook. I didn't personally use Facebook very much, other than as a gateway to my Soul Heart Art inspirational page, and I didn't spend any time posting personal pictures, or even much time looking at anyone else's posts. I had never even thought to visit Jane's page before.

So Jane *had* recently posted some new pictures, but they were NOT from our full-moon trip. The first thing I noticed was the caption: *Jane is with Wylie Heartly*. There were a series of pictures of her with Wylie and his best friend in Mexico. I instantly remembered Wylie's comment from two nights before about the tequila and he and Jane both buying it. Ah ha! I had *not* imagined what I heard. He had slipped and was probably relieved that I didn't seem to notice what he said, so I said nothing. That son of a bitch!

The day Wylie left for his trip, I spoke to him while he was at the airport and specifically asked him *who* was going on the trip. He named his best friend and a couple other guy names, but he never once mentioned Jane's name. He just made it seem like this was a guys' trip. I also asked him in a text, while he was on the trip, who was with him. He never answered that question – skipped right over it. Guys trip, my ass! I was both furious and confused at the same time. Now all I wanted to do was talk to him. I looked at the clock; it was well after 10 p.m. He would be fast asleep, and even if I called him, he always had the sound off and wouldn't hear it ringing anyway. At that point, I had a full adrenalin rush.

Wylie was leaving around 6 a.m. the next morning for the Grand Canyon, and I would not be able to talk to him about this while he was on a trip working.

I wasn't sure what to do...I just knew it was a blatant withhold! I knew he was accustomed to withholding in the relationship he had just come from. It was a way of protecting his soon-to-be ex-wife from the open marriage situation, so as to not throw his other relationships in her face. Was that what this was – was he involved with Jane?! It would make sense – I had already felt threatened by the way he was acting with her on our trip. But we had had a deep discussion about it and he assured me she was just a client and friend, and that was it. If that was true, why hide her participation in the Mexico trip from me? I just couldn't make sense of it.

My mind began to form a plan. I needed to talk to him before he left on his trip. I was going to need to pay him a visit to find out why he had deliberately kept this information from me, because if he was involved with her I was certainly done with this relationship! I'm sure he thought I would never find out she had been on the trip. But Wylie didn't really understand how my relationship with Spirit worked. Spirit gave me information in countless ways through signs – like the song "Jane" that had just played. And I would sometimes get "hits" of information where I would just know things. It's called claircognizance, when you have "clear knowing" about information you might not be informed of in your normal life. Spirit spoke to me in thoughts that came through like they were my own in my own voice – except, when I tried to chase the origin of the thought, I wouldn't be able to trace it the way I could trace one of my own, original thoughts. You know how that works: you see a cat...and it reminds you of the *Cat Steven's* concert you went to with your friend; then you remember your friend had driven you to the concert in the new car she just got...and you think to yourself, "I need a new car." See, you can trace the thought of wanting a new car back to where it originated – at seeing the cat. But that wasn't always the case with the way my thoughts formed; sometimes they were just there – untraceable. That is how Spirit works with me oftentimes.

I called my friend Angela, who was thankfully still awake after midnight her time. I needed to talk to someone who knew me really well, to help me assess the situation. We'd been friends since our early twenties. She agreed I needed to talk to Wylie – sooner than later. My only option would be to show up early at his place. I couldn't remember if he was getting up at 6 a.m., leaving his house at 6 a.m. or leaving for his destination from the hiking equipment shop at 6 a.m. I would need to be at his house by 5 a.m. to be sure to catch him. I actually dreaded the implication – showing up unannounced so early in the morning could make me look like a crazy woman. NONE of this was my style, and Wylie hadn't known me long enough, or had a long enough history with me, to know that. But I could not let him know in advance that I was coming. I needed his real-time reaction, not a rehearsed reaction.

I wrote out a five-minute speech of everything I needed to say, including several questions I needed to ask him. Angela was my sounding board. After a few tweaks, she approved of my messaging. She then advised me to get some sleep, and wished me good luck.

I was so freaked out, I stayed up all night rehearsing. Around 3 a.m. I took a shower and gave myself plenty of time to get ready, wanting to be at his house extra early just in case I had misjudged the timing and he was leaving by 5 a.m. I left my house a few minutes after 4:00.

Arriving at his apartment by 4:30, I parked close to his door where I could see any comings or goings. I will admit, there was a part of me that was prepared for Jane to walk out of his apartment while I was sitting there waiting for 5 a.m. to arrive. But I didn't see a soul. The thirty-minute wait seemed more like three hours. I practiced my speech over and over again. I was more than ready and tried to mentally prepare myself for the news I didn't want to hear – that they were involved.

At 5 a.m. I lightly knocked on his door and waited. No response. I knocked again, harder. Wylie's sleepy, then very surprised, face greeted me. He was super confused by my presence. I apologized for arriving so early in the morning and also arriving unannounced, but explained that I needed to talk to him before he left and only needed ten minutes of his time.

My knocking had woken him up. He didn't have to get up until 5:30 and was to leave shortly after 6:00. He invited me to sit down on the couch and remarked at how nice I looked so early in the morning. I told him the story of what had happened when I heard the song "Jane," and the chain reaction it had caused. He listened patiently, now more serious and sullen, realizing the topic I was there to discuss. I laid my rehearsed speech on him, telling him I understood that his previous method of self-preservation had been to withhold information, and how that tactic was not only a pattern from his past but completely unnecessary and unacceptable to me. If we were going to be in a relationship, we needed to build it on trust – this was not a good start. He denied remembering telling me who was on the trip – he had somehow erased that episode from his mind. I *knew* what I had asked, and part of my reason for asking was to specifically determine if the trip *was* "coed."

He did admit it may have been possible that on a subconscious level he withheld information from me, and also said something about Jane "activating" me. He then said there was nothing between the two of them except a friendship and he would not knowingly give me something to worry about. He assured me she was just "a nice lady" who wanted to expand her hiking repertoire; he had guided her on Machu Picchu in Peru six months earlier, before we started dating. She was a good client. He had become her personal trainer so she could become a stronger hiker, and they had become good friends in the process. That was it. Period. He didn't want me to devote any more energy thinking about it. Then he reminded me, he had mentioned Jane the other night when he was talking about the tequila – so there was the proof he wasn't hiding anything. He hugged me and wanted to make sure I had heard, loud and clear, all he said.

I apologized for coming over, explaining that I had felt like I had no choice since he was leaving for five days and when he returned we would be leaving on our trip – this just couldn't wait. He did understand it was situational. But then he turned the tables and said I could never do this again to him. He further explained that previously he had had issues in his relationships with boundaries, and that this was specifically something his therapist wanted him to work on. He asked me to respect his boundaries, and to never show up like this

– unannounced – again. I was a little taken aback by this very stern version of Wylie that I had not seen before. I told him I understood, and hoped he understood this was not how I was normally, but was only a result of the current circumstances. We kissed and hugged. He didn't want to be late, so I bailed quickly.

I had an awful feeling of dissonance the entire drive home. God, I hoped I had not just blown this entire relationship with my little stunt. I knew I had been guided to Jane's Facebook page – my gut feeling panned out. I still felt there was some piece of information I was missing, but Wylie had looked me directly in the eyes and said Jane was only a friend. I also connected the dots of who Jane was – *she* had been on the Peru hike, and *she* was the one his soon-to-be ex-wife had been jealous of. Perhaps I *had* overreacted. I remembered Wylie had specifically told me, the day he disclosed his entire past history, that his soon-to-be ex-wife had been jealous of Jane but that there was nothing she should have been jealous about. Maybe, as he claimed, he had mentioned the tequila because it truly was no big deal to him. The only thing I was absolutely certain of now was that he did NOT tell me in advance that Jane was going on that trip.

From: Laurie Majka

To: Wylie Heartley

February 2, 2018 1:01 p.m.

Subject: Some good thoughts after our talk this morning...

Hi Wylie,

I had some more thoughts after this am and I wanted to share them with you...

I am really glad we got to connect on several levels this morning! I am sorry about the timing. If you weren't leaving so early and going to be gone for five days I would have prearranged time to talk to you in person, instead of just showing up. I assure you it will not be the norm with me.

I appreciated your ability to be open and to listen to what I had to say, and to trust me enough to let me in and honestly communicate with me. Communication is something I feel we have been getting better and better with, and I love our interactions. After I left, I was thinking a little more about how you have had to exist in your relationship with your soon-to-be ex-wife...and based on that situation, your method of operation would have been to withhold information. It spares feelings and keeps you from having to deal with hard issues that have the potential to hurt someone. You have been training yourself for a long time to withhold; I think I understand that now. I want to help you find a new way: I want you to feel like you can be open with me and share. I too have been in a past situation where I withheld. I want to feel like I can be open and share with you too. It will help us build a stronger foundation. I can better assess and deal with things when I understand and have enough information to process them. I can't promise I'm going to like everything you tell me, and that telling me things will always be easy – but from the start you shared information with me about yourself that was pretty raw. I didn't run away; I actually moved closer. Remember our second date? You told me so much about yourself, and then you said you wouldn't blame me if I asked you to leave. I've been asking you to stay ever since...

We both have a past and baggage and lessons we have learned from. I love where this is going. I'm excited about YOU. I'm excited about US. I feel closer to you after this morning. I'm feeling more safe being vulnerable and showing you who I am. You said you are a good writer and you love to write, so I welcome your thoughts in return – with no pressure to do so. I understand after your lack of sleep this morning, you may not have the time, bandwidth or energy to do so. So if all you can muster is a ditto 😊 I get it.

Have a great hike down to the bottom of the Grand Canyon tomorrow. I will be thinking good thoughts of you and looking forward to when I'll see you next. I am beyond excited about our SanFran trip – it's gonna be a series of "10" days...

xoxo Laur~~

From: Wylie Heartley

To: Laurie Majka

February 2, 2018 3:21 p.m.

Re: Some good thoughts after our talk this morning...

Hi Laur...

Yes I was a bit surprised to see you this morning. I totally understand your wanting to see me and get clear on stuff before we were out of communication for a while. In the future though, I need you to not surprise me. A part of me was pretty freaked out...so no more unannounced visits please.

Part of me asking this is in the past I've had trouble setting boundaries and keeping enough autonomy for me, and I don't want to repeat those mistakes.

I too love us and am excited about our future, but you are going to have to be patient with me. I don't think I'm ready to move as fast as you are. Please remember that I'm still in a very delicate situation with my family and I need to ensure that I'm as responsible as I can be as I go through this.

I know you have high hopes for our future and I hope I can live up to your expectations. Just try to understand that while I love us, there is also a part of me that isn't quite ready...so hopefully you can be patient.

Have a great weekend. I too am super excited about California...it's going to be so much fun...just one more week!!!

Thank you babe for being so generous and amazing. You are so special and I feel blessed to be in your life.

xoxo Wylie~

~~Once~~ A Cheater...

Chapter 16

I Walk the Line

~song by *Johnny Cash*

https://open.spotify.com/track/7hxZF4jETnE5Q75rKQnMjE?si=P03TgjJ5RB6K1BNtCevV7Q

February 1 had arrived and it was officially Supai season! Time to get the May permits I had promised for my kids' Christmas-present trip there, or I would be sunk. Everyone was queued up to help get the permits. Wylie was back in Sedona with Jane who had assembled yet another group, this time with newbie hiking friends. The way Wylie described it, she had formed this group for the sole reason of getting them interested in hiking so they would go on one of his trips. She had even offered, and paid for, the same airbnb where we had stayed when we guided the full-moon trip, thus offsetting the cost of her friends' trip and assuring they would go. I didn't really like it – didn't understand why she would go so far to help him if she was more client than friend. I wasn't thrilled he was there with her again, but I was happy he booked another trip that was all his.

Wylie texted me a few minutes after the Supai site opened. He had been able to grab the permits he needed on an iPad with crappy internet. Here I was with internet service that I had upgraded for the occasion – and I had not even been able to get on the website! Actually, the Supai site was very primitive. When I was finally able to secure the dates I needed, I put them in my cart and attempted to check out. Except, after spinning for a few minutes, the site would spit you out with no purchased reservation. It was a white-knuckle nightmare. Finally, about 20 nerve-wracking minutes later, I had the coveted permits I needed and Christmas was saved (lol). I had also been able to book trips for June and August.

The following week I picked Wylie up at his apartment to head to the airport to catch our flight to San Francisco. This would be our biggest and longest trip together so far. I had sent him the *John Mayer* song "Love on the Weekend," in honor of our long weekend trip – also adding it to our *L.A. Woman* playlist and playing it on the drive to the airport. I was excited to hike with him and share one of my very favorite hiking places on the planet!

We arrived in Mill Valley, California, before our airbnb was ready. Knowing the area we were staying in was pretty remote, we stopped to get groceries on the way. When we returned to our rental car, I started the engine and the *John Mayer* song "Love on the Weekend" was playing on the FM radio! This was the first time Wylie had ever experienced a synchronicity with me. I thought it was a pretty cool one, and it set a mystical tone for our trip.

Since it was still too early to check in, I guided Wylie on a six-mile hike I knew well, which dropped down into Muir Woods National Park, home of the giant redwood trees. He was in awe of the incredible size of the trees. On the hike back out, I hinted at the specialness of our relationship by first telling him the story of an angel connector whom I had been directed to by Mark several years before. I disclosed that I had recently had a reading with her, discussing *our* connection – and that she had told me we were Twin Flames. I was hoping, at six months in, I wasn't exposing him to too much! This man had only just dipped his toe in the deep waters that are my spiritual experiences. In reply to my revelation, he said, "Ahhh, that makes sense!" I was rather relieved at his response.

We approached a giant boulder I had often climbed up on that exposed a sweeping view of the area we had just hiked. It was lucky timing that we had it to ourselves. We climbed up and enjoyed the view. We had not talked about my surprise visit since our email correspondence, and I wanted to clear the air about it in person. Now seemed like the perfect time. I needed him to know, more than anything else, that a surprise visit like that was not my style. We talked for a long time and Wylie shared something very provocative: He wanted me to know it was okay if I decided, at some point, I needed to see other men. It would even be okay with him if I slept with them. I did not like or understand where this conversation was going! The reason it didn't matter to him was because my revelation about us being Twin Flames had confirmed and strengthened what he had been feeling about me – that this was no ordinary relationship! Our relationship had felt different to him from the start, only he didn't have *words* to describe how it was different. But today, on our hike, he had just received the words – *Twin Flames*. It made perfect sense to him now and connected the dots. The reason he would be okay with me being with another man wasn't because he wanted me to be with someone else; he just understood now that if I did that, I would come back to him. He had a belief in our connection that was so strong he reasoned there was no man who could lure me away. That is how confident he was in who we were. Wow – and I had been worried I was chasing him off! Not a chance. Maybe this man *had f*allen for me all the way, and just hadn't said it yet. He then broached the subject of Jane and wanted me to understand there was no threat; he only had eyes for me and was very excited to see where our relationship would take us.

The airbnb was fabulous, hidden away in the redwoods. We took full advantage of the seclusion – if we weren't hiking or eating we were having sex. Our relationship had gone to a level I didn't know existed.

On the second night we found a sushi restaurant nearby for dinner. Wylie excused himself to use the restroom as soon as we arrived, which was odd because he had just gone to the bathroom before we left the house. Every time he did this my intuition kicked in and I knew he was on his phone either calling or texting someone. Obviously, he didn't want me to know. I just always assumed it had to do with his kids, or more likely his soon-to-be ex-wife. I was sure there were many personal issues to sort out that you wouldn't want your new girlfriend to be privy to. But I didn't like the feeling of mistrust it always elicited in me; there was a big part of me that was still leery of this man's past.

Dinner was nice and I was excited to get back to the airbnb for more alone-time. We were just having a normal conversation on the drive back, when Wylie said he needed to tell me something. He needed me to know that when he started dating me in August, he had already been seeing another woman. She had just graduated with a PhD and in October moved to Flagstaff, Arizona, a few hours north of Phoenix. He assured me it had ended shortly after she moved and they now had no contact whatsoever. WTF – he had been seeing us *both* during the entire beginning of our relationship! There was a definite part of me that wanted to ask him to pull the car over to let me out. My mind had stopped functioning and was spiraling out of control over this new information. In that moment, I almost processed it too quickly, but I finally connected a lot of pieces to the puzzle that I had been missing. Back in September and even October, when we were already dating, I had several conversations with friends about how I felt Wylie wasn't seeing me very often. I felt like it was tied to something I couldn't put my finger on. He had also seemed unusually sad when we would talk on the phone sometimes. I assumed it was due to his home-life situation, but that wasn't it – It was this other woman and the ending of their relationship. Many times at our lunches, I had felt an overwhelming desire to ask directly if he was seeing someone else. But I thought it was ludicrous to mistrust him after everything he had told me, and I dismissed the thought. Unfortunately, I never asked him. Now I understood it had either been my Spirit Team or my Higher Self trying to help me uncover what I may have already known on a Soul level.

When my mind fully recovered, I remembered my conversation with Tracy when she told me about Wylie asking her how young was too young for him. I asked him now, "How old was she – 28?" He was surprised I was able to guess her age but then confirmed she was 28. I didn't say how I knew. I wanted to leave to get away from him! He could see this wasn't going well. He quickly pulled the metaphorical ripcord out of the parachute, and before we could hit the ground, he half-yelled, "I love the fucking shit out of you!" Wait...did I just hear that right? "You love me??" He repeated it, and by then he had pulled the car over at the airbnb. He said he had loved me for a long time and had slipped so many times, half saying it and fearing I might have caught him – but I hadn't. I wasn't happy about him revealing that another woman had existed while we were already together. But I also knew I had no control over whom he had been seeing when I entered the picture. I was trying to be understanding, because he insisted he had ended things as soon as he realized I was the one for him. Instead of me leaving, we made out and then made a run for the house. We almost couldn't get our clothes off fast enough. He loved me!!

On the last morning, as we were getting ready to leave, Wylie confided that if he had known someone like me existed he would have gotten divorced *years* ago. While that made me happy to hear and I understood how genuinely he was expressing this sentiment, there was a part of my heart that skipped a beat – thinking he may believe someone like me was the norm and there were

A Cheater...

plenty more where I came from that he could find and explore. Did he understand, like a few of my friends expressed, that I was a unicorn?! Or did he now think I might be a dime a dozen? I was sure he didn't mean to elicit these feelings in me, but they were my gut reaction. I simply reminded him I wasn't like anyone else and that I was glad we were both available to experience each other in this place in time.

He asked me to follow him to the living room because he wanted to talk to me. When we sat down on the couch he pulled his phone out and said there was a song he wanted to play for me. "Walk the Line" by *Johnny Cash* began playing from his phone. I'm not much of a country-music person, and even though I had heard this song before, I had never really listened to the lyrics. Wylie wanted me to pay close attention to them. He mouthed the words to me along with the song. When it finished playing, he said he would walk the line, and pledged to never stray – with me, he had hope. He felt for the first time in his life, I was the someone who could be enough for him. I was the full package and he understood how rare and special I was. He was so grateful we had found each other at the bottom of the Grand Canyon – which just added to his belief in the magic of "us."

While my heart was soaring at his proclamation, my brain was still busy analyzing the new information it had received the previous night. I was going to need some time to process all that had happened, and I was glad I would have time to hike by myself in Muir Woods. I could mull things over there, after I dropped Wylie off at the airport. I would have time to myself to think, before my business meetings started the next day.

~~Once~~ A Cheater... 83

Chapter 17

Caught Up in You

~song by *.38 Special*

https://open.spotify.com/track/3jYRpwbctfqB77uU7T7K3U?si=zxf_vaNORaCQR_5GY5jwRQ

After he left, I suggested we write something for each other on Valentine's Day. Wylie loved the idea and I couldn't wait to see what he would write. I spent some time writing a special letter for him...

[Laurie] *A dream you dream alone is only a dream. A dream you dream together is reality. So here we are, almost six months in. We have discovered so much about each other, and I'm really in awe of who you are!!! You are strong, physically and mentally – yet you can be so tender with me. I have listened to the* Johnny Cash *song, "I Walk the Line," many times now, and I think of the words you said to me sitting on the couch at our airbnb – that with me you have hope and for the first time you've met someone you feel can be enough for you – and that gives ME hope. I'm willing to take a chance on you – on us – and that's both exhilarating and scary, but now more exhilarating.*

I love everything about you because this is the kind of unconditional understanding I have for you. I love the way I feel in your presence: you make me feel safe and secure and incredibly alive!! When you made me breakfast, you made me feel nurtured and taken care of – something I haven't had in a long time. You make me feel like the most beautiful, sexy woman on the planet. It's a trip for me to see myself through your eyes, because I love how you make me feel about myself. This is something I've been searching for, and I hope you can see yourself through my eyes, too, so you can see how wonderful I think you are. You have captured my imagination, my heart, and apparently you already had my Soul – and THAT connection we have is energizing, magical and amazing beyond this physical World. We can continue in this relationship, day by day, to learn and grow together. We are what we are and I look forward to the exploration of you and of us.

I do have a song for you today, and I want you to listen to the words. It really feels for me like everything in my life before this has been leading up to THIS

~~Once~~ A Cheater...

experience – preparing me for us. The potential for growth and love is something neither of us can fathom because it's beyond this World and all our previous experiences. I love you, Wylie, in a way I've never felt with anyone before, and I'm excited that we are beginning this journey in love, hand in hand, side by side, together. I know that to you I've felt like a dream, but I'm the most real thing you'll ever encounter...

All of my love to you, xoxo Laur

I was in a meeting for work all the next day. Wylie texted me at lunchtime. I had let him use my car while his was in the shop, and he had inadvertently left my keys in his shorts pocket, then washed them. Now all he had been able to do with the keys was to successfully set off the alarm several times. He already had my spare set, and mine were in my purse...with me, in California. I used my lunch hour to run my set over to FedEx. He was having me send them to the soon-to-be ex-wife's house, as it was more secure than the apartment. After I mailed them, I realized that, because she would now know my full name, she would be able to see anything she wanted to on my social-media feeds. Not that she would necessarily look, but I know women, and we are curious creatures who probably wouldn't miss an opportunity to pick up some new information about our soon-to-be ex-husband's new girlfriend.

I participated in a company outing that night. I had just arrived at the event and was visiting with co-workers when I felt the vibration of a text come in. I instinctively knew it was from Wylie. He was so excited about writing me something for Valentine's Day that he had sent me a text telling me he had already emailed it, a day in advance, and was asking me not to read it until I had sent him my email too. I couldn't wait to read it, but I am also one of those people who hates to spoil surprises, so his email would be absolutely safe with me until the next day.

I opened my eyes on Valentine's Day morning with the realization that I could open my email from Wylie. It felt more like Christmas than Valentine's Day! When I unlocked my phone there was already a text from him; he was up early to teach his CrossFit class.

[Wylie] *Happy Valentine's Day baby!!!* 💌 🤍 😍 😘 💯 💋

~~Once~~ A Cheater...

A Valentine's Poem for Laur
2/14/2018

*It began with a question to the park ranger—
and an answer from an innocent stranger...
She had noticed him at dinner,
thought he might look like a winner.
And when they talked the connection was electric,
alas, they lost touch because life was too hectic.
He was married and she had a boyfriend,
but fortunately change for both was the trend.
Persistent she was and reached out about Supai;
is that the extent of her interest, he wondered why?
A simple lunch was enjoyed at the Tryst Café,
can't stop thinking about each other since that day.
A connection like theirs rarely comes along—
an attraction that is incredibly strong.
A flame that has travelled across space and time,
a unifying energy that is a sign—
of the uniqueness of their bond,
cast like a spell with a magic wand.
A spell such as this can never be broken,
as the depth of their love transcends words to be spoken.
And while the future is unsure,
their budding love is a priceless treasure.
That will bring them closer to the promised land,
as they hike around the world...hand in hand.
As twins reunited in Grand Canyon—
forever each other's loving companion.*

[Laurie] *What a wonderful way to wake up this Valentine's day! Thank you, baby, for my poem. I don't have words for what you doing that meant to me. You make me feel worth the effort.* 😍 🤭 💝 💞 ✖ ⭕ 💯 ‼

[Wylie] *I read your letter and I LOVED IT!!! You made me feel so special and desired...I feel so blessed. I LOVE you Laur!!!* 💝 💞 😍 💯 ‼

~~Once~~ A Cheater...

Chapter 18

Believe in Me

~song by *Dan Fogelberg*

https://open.spotify.com/track/3YnoRANvisc9OL9LTjQWYJ?si=JDf8sWN5RjKl9kcoPlltlw

As great as I felt about our trip, Valentine's Day, and the poem Wylie had sent me – I was still crushed by the revelation of "28." I thought about it a lot, and one of the things it did was make the beginning of my relationship with Wylie feel less special.

I had a book printed made from pictures of screen shots of meaningful text messages we had sent each other, from the first text of our relationship right up until Valentine's Day. I had thought of the idea and began working on it a few weeks before. I had had so much fun gathering and re-living the emotions our texts had evoked, and I intended to give the book to Wylie as a special gift for our six-month anniversary. But now that I held it in my hands and reread the messages from my new perspective, I could only wonder what he had been texting "28" at the same time.

She had been transitioning from Phoenix to Flagstaff after graduating with her PhD. So apparently she had begun her move there around October. Wylie had made plenty of trips to the Grand Canyon since we had been together, passing right though Flagstaff on the way – and who knew if he was even at the Grand Canyon like he said. It would have been just as easy to say he was on a trip, then go and stay with her for a weekend. To me, a 22-year age gap felt pretty significant. The way Wylie told the story was, she had been a friend of his daughter's from CrossFit, where Wylie was a coach, and "28" had studied exercise physiology and wanted to become a CrossFit coach and trainer at a gym in Flagstaff.

Because "28" was a friend of their daughter, Wylie's soon-to-be ex-wife gave her a Human Design reading, which is kind of like a spiritual personality assessment. She was intuitive and after meeting with "28" warned Wylie to keep up his guard with her because she could feel "28" was interested in him. He told her he would never come on to "28," both because of her age and because she was friends with his daughter. But in the end "28" had pursued *him*. He admitted he felt flattered by the attention from a woman so much younger. She was a well-educated, smart girl who had a troubled past, but who also had CrossFit in common with him. He let it all happen. He knew his daughter would never accept the relationship, so they kept it a secret. Wylie's wife at the time was aware of it because of their agreement in the open-marriage agreement. So perhaps "28" had been the catalyst for him wanting a divorce. It could not have been me, as we were only having a simple texting conversation at the time. Wylie knew the relationship with "28" could never go anywhere – his daughter would have "freaked out" with the discovery. They kept everything very hush-hush – like he did with every aspect of his life anyway.

    I truly felt I should have been enough for Wylie. Part of me could not fault him for something he was involved in before I came along. But the disturbing part of the story was that it didn't really seem like he had broken it off quickly when he realized what he had with me. As a matter of fact, it seemed like *she* had possibly broken it off with him when he told her about me – if what he told me was even true. At first, he said "28" didn't know about me; then in another conversation he said he told her about me. The only clear part of the story was that he had been very confused and sad when she suddenly ghosted him – "ghosted" in the sense that he had been talking to her via text and she suddenly disappeared, never again answering any of his texts or calls – she was gone. He was confused about someone close to him just suddenly disappearing, and he couldn't understand how anyone could ghost a person. For me, it seemed more like a millennial thing – and I thought he got what he deserved. When he told me about "28" on our Muir Woods trip, they had not been in contact for months. I asked him if she were to send him a happy birthday text message in the future, would he answer her. He said yes, he would. I didn't like that answer at all, as it seemed it could lead to him opening himself to a dangerous game. And I wasn't pleased that he still seemed bothered that she had not responded to him. If he was into me the way he said he was, she should no longer even be a blip on his radar.

    My failing was never *specifically* asking Wylie the right questions when we first started dating. I would be sitting with him at lunch, and the question would form in my mind, to ask him if he was seeing anyone else. Intuitively, I must have felt something because it came up several times for me. But then I would rationalize away what started to seem like irrational thoughts. I didn't want to seem untrusting, considering the fact that this man had bared his Soul about his past transgressions. I reasoned with myself that I must be oversensitive, and that I was just feeling all the pressures he was under of juggling his divorce, his kids and me. He worked three jobs, after all, and still managed to make time for me even though he hadn't been exactly free for the first few months of our relationship. So I never asked the direct question "Are you seeing anyone else?" Instead, I merely encouraged him with my own disclosures to communicate in return. I let him know *I* was no longer interested in or seeing anyone else. I believed he would have followed suit if there had been anything to share. I was dead wrong!

    I needed to see for myself who "28" was. He had not told me her name; I only knew her age, her occupation, her education and that she was now living in Flagstaff. It took me less than 10 minutes to find her on his Facebook page.

Yep, she was 28 years old alright, and she had two very prominent tattoos: a large flower on her shoulder and a lobster on her ribcage.

I would be lying if I said she hadn't gotten under my skin. To combat the upsetting new thoughts, I created a note in my phone and called it *"28's" Got Nothing On Me!* (See **Lessons Learned** in the last part of the book under: "Your Super Power.") I was a grown-ass woman who brought more to a relationship than any 28-year-old ever could have! No offence, I'm sure there are a lot of amazing 28-year-old's out there, but I've done my time! Heck, I had almost 28 years invested in working on myself and my Soul growth. I wrote a list of all the qualities I brought to a relationship that this 28-year old could not have brought. I had spent 21 years as a mother and 25 as a wife. I learned many lessons about sacrifice and putting other people's needs and wants before my own. Lessons like these can only be learned by taking many more trips around the sun than 28. The reminder note in my phone served to take the focus off of her and put it back on me where it belonged. I didn't want her on my mind anymore.

I chose three close friends to vent to about "28." I didn't want everyone knowing about Wylie's past issues; I didn't tell anyone in my family or even a couple of my other super-close friends. I knew they would worry for me. And I was afraid everyone would judge him for it, projecting their values, experiences and belief systems on him – and would likely judge me, too. I needed to keep this mostly to myself, but I'm only human and wanted to have a few sounding boards. I *had* to move past this and find a way to believe in Wylie if I wanted to move forward in this relationship. I *was* willing to take a chance on him. It felt more like a calculated risk based on the hours we had spent in deep conversation about issues from his past, and I was not taking any of this lightly.

Our situation triggered a recollection of the *Dan Fogelberg* story song, "Believe in Me," and I shared it with Wylie in a text.

[Wylie] *Wow babe...that's a really poignant song. I get your struggle. So here's where I'm at...I totally believe in you and I can't believe how fortunate I am to have you in my life. I believe in our love and the feelings I have for you. And it's invigorating and scary at the same time.*

I don't expect you to believe in me but I hope that you will take a chance. I totally get it if you are scared, because I struggle with feeling like I even deserve a chance. So let's take it a day at a time and cherish and nurture what we have. I think we are worth it and what we have is worth it.

[Laurie] *Thank you for that deep response. The thing is, I'll need to believe in you, I can't be looking over my shoulder and wondering if something else is coming. That's the ONLY thing that scares me about you.*

And Wylie, you more than deserve me: You deserve to be in love and to be loved, and I don't mean loved like you have been in all the affairs you've had. I mean loved in the way you can only be in a REAL relationship.

A real relationship between us has the potential to take you to a place you've never been before, and you DESERVE real 📖 💋 💋 true happiness and fulfillment and joy and love. It's your birthright, and at the core you know you DESERVE it all! I am deeply and completely in love with you and who you are and who we are together, and typing that scares me too. But at some point we have to say fear can't win this, fear does not and has not EVER ruled my life or yours. We are fearless!!

[Wylie] *Fuck I love the shit out of you even more and this keeps happening… Just when I think I can't be more in love with you, you defy the impossible* 💯 📖 *Strong work, Laur* 👏 👏 👏

We made plans to see each other. I drove to his place and he drove us to the restaurant. On the way, he made a quick stop at a pawnshop. I had seen them on TV, but I had never been in one in my life. He didn't invite me to go in but suggested I wait in the car, explaining that he just needed to trade in some gold coins. This was the first month Wylie had to pay his soon-to-be ex-wife the agreed-upon $1,000 in child support and $2,000 in alimony. Him going to a pawnshop really freaked me out! We had never really discussed his financial situation, but I felt that when you had to start pawning things you were doing it more out of desperation. Otherwise, you would find a more usual avenue for selling your items, like on Craig's list so you could get more money than a pawnshop would give you. After all, they were in business to make money and had to buy something at a low enough cost to turn around and make a profit reselling it. This stop at the pawnshop made me somewhat worried about Wylie's financial situation.

Wylie took me to his favorite place and treated me to a nice sushi dinner, (even though the detour we took on the way made me feel badly about even going to dinner). We had an easy way of talking to each other, and I never held anything back; I would always try to ask him anything I needed to know, especially after the "28" revelation. I now needed more clarification about her and asked him to share a little detail about the timeline. He obliged but wanted me to understand one thing in particular, by demonstrating it to me with his hands. He began by reminding me that when I came into the picture, he had already been seeing "28." He used his finger to represent her and drug it along slowly across the table. He then said, "You came into the picture," and used a second finger to drag it across the table, very quickly passing the "28" finger. He elaborated: "When you came into my life you were the biggest surprise I've ever had. You passed her so fast and then there was only you." He had never in his life fallen in love with *anyone* as fast as he fell for me. It was so fast and so strong, he had to hold himself back from telling me. He had even slipped a couple times and thought I must have noticed. Nope, I was oblivious – even once googling *How long does it take a man on average to fall in love or say I love you?* The consensus was five months, and since that was exactly where we were in our relationship, I just tried not to worry about it. Actually, Wylie had said to me, early on, "I've already fallen," but I wasn't sure if that meant he loved me – which was what I needed to hear. I did feel like he *might* be in love with me but just hadn't said it yet.

I wanted Wylie to understand he was not going to be able to get away with things with me, the way I felt he had with his soon-to-be ex-wife. So one day when we were having lunch at my house, I told him I had been thinking seriously about getting a tattoo and wanted to know his opinion. He said he was all for it. I said I was considering either a flower on my shoulder or maybe a large lobster across the right side of my rib cage. He almost spit out his food. Yep, I got him good. He instantly realized what I had done. He asked me how I knew about "28," and I just said he shouldn't underestimate my sleuthing abilities.

~~Once~~ A Cheater...

Chapter 19

I'm Jealous

~song by *Shania Twain*

https://open.spotify.com/track/3Sm5TYFgMXyXwgAcY2xweX?si=MgIxwvm9TWOeTieMMDtEew

I hoped I was not making a mistake going on a trip that included Jane again. When Wylie first sent me the itinerary for a three-night/four-day Zion Full-Moon trip on Christmas Eve, I was with Stacy and she was intrigued. Usually we did our own research and planning, never paying for a guided trip. But the advantage of having a guide for this trip was twofold: (1) Wylie was going to take us into a permitted area we had never been before and had been afraid to try on our own. (2) We would be supporting Wylie in his (our) new Hiking Adventure business.

Stacy had been disappointed that she missed our Sedona Full-Moon Adventure trip because of being sick. We both loved Zion National Park in Utah and agreed this would be a fun trip. After we committed to going, Wylie sold the trip to Jane and Tracy, who had both been on the Sedona Full-Moon trip. I was super glad Stacy would be with me this time.

I obviously had an issue with Jane, but at the same time I thought there must be nothing to my suspicions; otherwise, Jane would not be putting herself in this situation, and neither would Wylie. It would be interesting to watch them together from this new perspective. At the eleventh hour, Tracy had to pull out of the trip, and there were now only four of us going. Wylie informed me he would be driving Jane's car, as it would be more economical on gas. That meant Jane would be riding shotgun again on this entire trip, instead of me. He had also decided we were to remain hidden in our relationship because Jane *still* did not know we were dating. I didn't tell him that Tracy knew about us, and I assumed she had probably told Jane, since they were friends.

I had personally paid for and booked the reservations for this trip. We had two king rooms and one queen. The original intention was that Wylie and I would be staying in a room together, but now, to keep up appearances, he wanted Stacy and I to stay in a king room. Jane would be in the queen room. Wylie would take the other (furthest away) king room so I could sneak over and be with him, but not sleep over. I really could not stand all the games we were playing. We weren't teenagers, and this just seemed like pure ridiculousness! He blamed it on his divorce not being finalized, even though he had previously said things would be different when he was living on his own. Now he blamed it on wanting to keep up a "professional" appearance. I still didn't really get it. Was Jane a client, a friend, both, neither? I couldn't wait for the day when I didn't have to deal with all this bullshit. But this was my consequence for agreeing to date him while he was not yet divorced.

Stacy met me at the house at the same time Wylie and Jane arrived with the car. As usual, Jane was more dressed up than Stacy and I, in our hiking attire. I already felt annoyed at Jane. My parents were visiting from Kansas with their four dogs, and were going to watch Storm for me while I was gone. Wylie and Stacy had already met them. Jane was introduced and was very friendly visiting with them; she even took a liking to their dogs. I had to admit, she really did have a sweet demeanor about her. Maybe I had been too hasty in my assessment. After all, the issues I had with our full-moon trip were really around how Wylie had acted, not her.

Jane had been to my house two months earlier, for the full-moon hike with Tracy. I had recently redone my meditation room, in which I had placed a 20-inch round mirror in the middle of one of the walls, and painted sweeping circles radiating out from the mirror. It looked like a giant portal to the Other Side. And if you stood on a certain spot, you could look into the mirror and see the eye of the Buddha reflecting in a painting on the opposite wall. It looked pretty neat, and I took Jane in to see it. She had been a residential interior designer when she was working, and I thought she would really like it. She took one look and said, "Oh, that's something Tracy would have liked." Ok then, I guess I didn't really know Jane and her spiritual beliefs. She was right, though – Tracy would have loved it. I really got the feeling Jane didn't like me much.

Stacy and I loaded our stuff and we all took off on the six-hour drive to Zion. We made a couple stops on the way and even hiked in the Pink Sand Dunes. We had lost an hour due to the time zone change, and now it was getting late. We arrived at the Zion Lodge and quickly checked in, then went on a hike to watch the sun set and the moon rise at the same time. While hiking, we saw a group of bighorn sheep – a rare sighting. This was the day before the full moon. We were saving the actual full-moon hike for the next night on Angel's Landing, a favorite hike in the park. It was off season, at the end of February, and because it was still cold we mostly had the place to ourselves. We left directly from our hiking area to find a place for dinner. The first two restaurants we tried had already closed the kitchen, but we found a pub that allowed us to order dinner from a limited, quick-fix menu – it was a lucky break.

After dinner, everyone was tired. We had a nightcap together in Stacy's and my room; then everyone retired to their own rooms. When I was sure Jane was tucked safely away, I snuck down the hall to Wylie's room. We made love and I fell asleep in his arms. I woke up a couple hours later and dressed in the dark to his slight snoring, then returned to my own room.

~~Once~~ A Cheater...

We all had breakfast together the next morning and afterwards walked around the lodge. Jane kept disappearing, just like she had on the drive up whenever we stopped somewhere. She would walk around and talk to people and come back with their life story. She was waaaay more interested in interacting with strangers than she was in interacting with us. Jane was still such a mystery. In all the interactions I had had with her, I noticed she had not ever mentioned her husband. All I really knew about her was the story of how she started hiking, and that she had two girls. Funny – she could expose people's life story but keep her own story so close to the vest. It seemed an odd game to me. Wylie brushed it off: "Yep, that's Jane – she makes friends wherever she goes."

Wylie took us outside of the park to an area Stacy and I had never visited called Kolob Canyon. I was sitting in the backseat next to the cooler, and as we drove Wylie asked, "Babe, can you hand me a drink?" Stacy and I looked at each other and smiled, both of us catching the use of his pet name for me. Wylie had not noticed it, but I was pretty sure Jane had. We hiked to a cool arch formation and had a lovely picnic-style lunch. It had been very cold on the hike out, with lots of ice on the trail, and Snow covered the surrounding red-rock mountain peaks. It was very beautiful. Wylie and I were faster hikers than Jane and Stacy, and we moved ahead of them. Periodically, we would stop to sneak pictures of us together, as Wylie didn't want Jane to see us doing that either. We took a selfie with the snow-covered mountains in the background, and that became my new favorite pic of us.

The trails traversed up and down hills. The sun had warmed them considerably by the time we got back after lunch, and they had become a muddy, soupy mess! Wylie would be in the lead and suddenly start sliding down on the slippery, muddy hills, uncontrollably, while calling out "Fuck, fuck, fuck, fuck…" It was a hilarious sight! I found several heart rocks on the trail. Wylie picked up a large one and even carried it back for me. He was now heart-rock converted.

After dinner, we headed out to hike Angel's Landing so we could sit at the top and watch the full moon rise. This hike is considered one of the most difficult and dangerous in the park. While it is a 5.2-mile hike, out and back, and climbs 1,500 feet through a series of switchbacks, called Walter's Wiggles – none of that is particularly difficult. But when you climb close to the top, you come to a series of chains that have been bolted into the rocks that take you across ledges that have drop-offs on both sides. This hike is NOT for the faint of heart – and we were doing it at night with headlamps. The temperatures were dropping fast, and near the top it became increasingly icy and slippery. We had been advised to bring our crampons, which are stretchable pieces of rubber with metal grips. We would attach them to the bottom of our hiking boots for extra traction on snow and ice – and we needed them! Jane didn't have her crampons with her, so I took one of mine off and gave it to her. I was so angry that Wylie had not offered Jane one of his. He was the guide we were paying, and I felt it was not only his duty but very selfish of him not to offer his. I didn't say anything, but the more I thought about it the more upset with him I became. Jane was not my favorite person, but I was not going to let her slip – and I would not have wanted to be on those rocks without crampons!

Zion National Park is surrounded by rock walls that the moon had to move above for us to be able to see it on the horizon. We made excellent time – actually too good, because it was very cold and windy at the top and we had to wait an unexpectedly long time. I was freezing even with my extra layers and hand and feet warmers. I started having trouble regulating my body temperature and began shivering. Wylie let me drink the rest of his hot water. We had come this far, and I was not about to miss the full moon rising because I was cold. I toughed it out and we all saw the spectacular full moon that was well worth the wait! I warmed up on the way down by moving fast, and it was so nice to be back at the lodge. We all met downstairs for some tequila shots. Now, that was warming!

I had been watching Jane interact with Wylie on this trip. He was a quick study and had figured out how not to use her name a million times. I never even noticed his usage of it this trip. What I did notice was that Jane was not physically "touchy" with him – like I probably would have been with a close friend or someone I liked. In other words, they didn't seem to share mutual glances, knowing looks, or inside jokes, and she didn't bring up stories of the two of them – she treated him like a casual friend, not even a really good friend. It was good to see, but still hard to understand why she tried to spend so much time with him.

That night, after everyone went to bed, I spent some time in Wylie's room again. The next day, we all had breakfast together before setting out on our longest hike of the trip. We hiked through Stacy's and my favorite areas in the entire park. It was snowy and icy and toward the end of our eight-mile hike, the trail started to get pretty muddy. We were heading for a destination about two more miles ahead, but we all agreed to bag it and just eat our lunch, then turn around and go back. The snow and mud combo had us moving more slowly than any of us was used to. We hiked back through miles of what had previously been soft mud and was now sloppy ice-water mud. It was a mess and it was freezing my feet. I could hardly stand it and tried to warm them with hand warmers, but my feet just couldn't stay dry in those conditions. I was super glad when we were finally back at the hotel to warm up.

I had to return something to Wylie's room and discovered he was in the shower. I saw his crampons and decided to try them on – because, after thinking more about why he had not offered them to Jane, I wondered if they would have even fit her. I put them on and my feet were swimming in them. I have fairly large, size-nine shoes, so they would have been even huger on Jane's smaller feet. Okay, I gave him a pass and was glad he had not been acting selfishly.

Jane showed up for dinner wearing jeans, boots, a flannel shirt, jewelry, and her hair all curled. Stacy and I had just brought hiking clothes had only bothered to shower and change – and it had not even occurred to me to bring a curling iron. True, we were going to town for pizza, and I didn't really know Jane well enough to know if this was how she always was. I still felt it was all show for Wylie. I hadn't even bothered to put on much makeup. When I saw Jane, I said something about feeling underdressed, and she responded with "You look darling." It felt a little contrived and condescending.

By the time we drove home, after all that time with Jane, I *still* didn't really know her much better than I had before the trip. We dropped off Stacy at her house, and she gave Wylie and Jane a tour of the incredible custom home she and Sal had built. Jane visited with Sal for a bit, and then it was time to drop me off at home. I had told my parents nothing about Jane, where Wylie was concerned. My mom commented that Jane had "a weirdness" about her. I asked what she meant, and she said Jane's energy just felt "off" – she couldn't put her finger on what it was exactly.

The next day when I met Stacy to hike, we talked about the trip. The first thing she told me was that Sal said there was something strange about Jane. How interesting – Stacy had never said a word about Jane to him, either. I wanted to know, now that Stacy had spent three nights and four days with Jane and Wylie, if she felt Jane had a thing for him. She agreed that Jane definitely had something for Wylie, even though she wasn't obvious about it. But she added that Wylie would never go for Jane – she was too weird. (I laughed.) Stacy also felt that if he had any interest in Jane, something would have happened there already. I disagreed because Jane seemed like the kind of woman who would need to be chased, and I didn't think she would ever do the chasing. And Wylie wasn't really the chasing type; he was much more subtle. At this point, I decided I wasn't jealous of Jane – but was wary of her. She wielded a great deal of power with Wylie's financial status in her hands. I would be keeping my eyes wide open.

Chapter 20

So in to You

~song by Atlanta Rhythm Section

https://open.spotify.com/track/3Sm5TYFgMXyXwgAcY2xweX?si=MglxwvM9TWOeTieMMDtEew

"There is nothing I don't like about you," Wylie declared to me one day when we were driving back to his place. "I've been trying to find something, and usually by the time I've been dating someone this long I have a pretty long list of pros and cons and deal-breakers. But with you, I can't find one thing." I grinned – that was a pretty big compliment! I didn't have a list of things I didn't like about him either, and inquired, "Isn't that the point? To find someone who brings out the best in you and you in them so that you are better together?" And that is truly how I felt about him! My *only* reservations were related to his past, and were a product of our situation around his divorce not being finalized. That was still holding our relationship back a bit.

One day his soon-to-be ex-wife stopped by to drop off a few things to Wylie. Before he could stop her, she walked into his bedroom and noticed the new bedspread and pillows. She immediately suspected his bedroom had been christened by a woman's touch and that he must be seeing someone new. Since he had nothing more to hide, he told her about me, including the timeline. She asked to see a picture of me and he refused. So she refused to give him the rest of the items she had brought over until he showed her. He gave in, showing her the picture of the two of us with the snowcapped mountains in the background from our Zion hike. She asked my age and was pleasantly surprised I was about the same age as her, instead of 28 years old. She wasn't thrilled he was seeing someone new, because he had told her the main reason he wanted a divorce was to be on his own. Not wanting to get into it with her and slide back into old habits, he downplayed our relationship. She had also noticed the painting I made for him and didn't believe anyone he was seeing casually would have both given that to him and added as many feminine touches as she was seeing, if the relationship wasn't more than casual. **She was not a stupid woman.**

In April, I planned a special birthday dinner for Wylie at a fancy seafood restaurant I loved that was known for their delicious butter cake. It had a lovely low-lighting ambience. We started out in casual conversation but then meandered into a more serious discussion about our relationship. Things had

~~Once~~ A Cheater...

been going well, and we had gotten even closer since our Muir Woods trip when he had declared his love for me. But the thoughts of "28" had still never quite gone away, even with his pledge to "walk the line." I wanted to see where his thinking was now, so I gathered up the courage to ask him a question I needed to ask – but didn't want to know the answer to: Did he think he could ever just be with one person? "No." was his response. I instantly said that made me want to leave!

    He softened. "I hope you don't. I don't want you to leave – and I won't let you leave! I would fight for you and I'm not going to let you go, because this is worth fighting for! This is worth me showing up for you and picking only you. I love you. My love is so strong and so deep that if I didn't see you for an entire year, and if I saw you again, I would love you still and probably deeper than I do now. My love is hurricane proof, tsunami proof, and volcano proof! You need to know there will be times I don't text you, and it has nothing to do with you. It is just that sometimes I'm going to need space. My love is the same; it didn't change or go away. I need time alone in general, but now more so because it's like I'm preparing for the day we won't be separated, and I think that relationship will be Other Worldly."

    Then he said, "But I also struggle with feeling worthy. When you deeply express your feelings to me I feel grateful, but at the same time I don't feel like I am worthy of or deserving of what you say. There is also a part of me that never wants to live with anyone again, because I want to own myself. But you coming along was so unexpected. You are the only one I'm thinking about breaking all of the rules for – that is how strong my feelings are for you. I feel an energy that is so strong and so deep and so connected, that when we are together I feel like everyone around us can feel it – and even feel how I feel about you. When we aren't together it's not as if I don't feel that energy anymore; I'm just so confident it's there I don't need to think about it. Being together feels effortless. I know you like to know when you'll see me next, but I don't need to know because I just know we WILL see each other again. And when I think of us I only think of us in terms of a future. I have never had anyone talk to me the way you do, and I appreciate it on one hand, but I can't trust or believe in it on the other. It's kind of a protection from what I went through with my mom. I struggle with melancholy, and I don't think I've felt that way when I've been with you. I do wonder if I will feel that way if we have more time together, and I wonder how you'll react to me in that state."

    Okay, I was glad I had stayed. But there was more I needed to know. I asked him what he would do if one of his hiking clients came on to him. He laughed and said that doesn't happen, and if it did he would just think they came on to everyone; besides, he would never make the first move. But he did admit he had never thought about it, and he did not have a plan. He also understood how rare I was, and since it took him 52 years to find me, he knew what we had was so special it wouldn't likely come along again in this lifetime. He would not take any chances of losing it. I talked to him about how he needed to have a strategy, needed to be prepared – in advance. He needed a plan. He vowed he would give it some thought. Later, when we were back at my place, he told me he loved me too much – I didn't even want to know what that meant! The only thing

I could really do for our relationship was to live in the present moment and move forward in life, one day at a time.

We had been talking about places in the world we wanted to visit someday. He mentioned Bora Bora as number one on his list. Hmmm – I, of course, had heard of it but wasn't very familiar with it. I did a little research and thought the beauty of it might actually rival the beauty of Havasupai. Wylie was not much of a planner, but I was. I loved having plans to look forward to and thought it was time to plan something big for us to look forward to together. It had been a long time since I had taken a bigger vacation and I felt due for a break. I did a bunch of research and realized I could use hotel points and airline miles if I planned far enough in advance, which would cover most of the trip expenses. My airline didn't have availability that would allow us to travel until January of 2019 (nine months from then). It would be just after Christmas and during the optimal weather window for the islands. I put a little one-page itinerary together and presented it to Wylie at dinner. We had been together for eight months, and the trip would take place nine months from then – more months than we had even been together. I was happily surprised he loved the idea and jumped at the opportunity. He told me he had never planned any event in his life that far out, not even his wedding. But seeing the value in my pre-planning abilities, he decided we could make long-term future plans to see the world together.

The other thing we began building together was the Hiking Adventure business. The lucrative success of his two personally guided trips the previous fall – the first one with Tracy and the second with Jane – had birthed the idea. I then christened the business with a fabulous name. He thought we could add full-moon hiking too, since we had two successful trial-run trips under our belt. It was time for me to set the plan in motion by jumping in with both feet. I built the website, since I had experience in building one for my own Soul Heart Art business. This hiking business had so much potential and earning ability! To start with, we were located within a six-hour radius of California, Colorado, Nevada, New Mexico, and Utah – which all together had more than a dozen national and state parks, and they all had seasonal weather year-round. With Wylie's ten-plus years of guiding experience, this was a no-brainer. We could start small and build the trips up, eventually bringing on other guides he knew and trusted. He could pay them more than they were making anywhere else and still make a nice profit for the business. I could eventually join him as another guide – and this was my exit strategy out of my career into a business of my own making, where I could truly own myself.

My son Ryan had to do an internship for college, and I signed him up to work with Wylie building the business and expanding the website, since he was majoring in computer science. It was an unpaid internship, I wanted Ryan to get something for doing it, so I bought him a plane ticket to Europe in thanks for all his hard work. Even though Wylie expected to get tipped for every hiking excursion he guided, to my surprise he failed to do the same for Ryan's hard work. Hmmm.

I immediately began promoting Wylie and our Hiking Adventure business by doing "commercials" when I was hiking, as people were always asking me about cool hiking destinations – usually at the top of the mountain I hiked most days. Wylie had been able to get a permit for the Grand Canyon from a fellow guide who, as it turned out, wasn't able to guide that trip there himself. Wylie and I were going to guide the trip together, and the two of them would split the profits. The trip was to take place at the end of the month. Stacy jumped into action and was able to recruit two other couples; she and Sal would also come along. Four couples in all would be perfect. I couldn't believe the timing – we would be at Phantom Ranch close to the exact date when we had met, one year earlier. A lot can happen in a year!

My parents had visited me one too many times in Arizona. They fell in love with the area and bought a house five minutes from mine. It was going to be nice having family so close by. They moved from Kansas into their new digs the same day Wylie and I were driving with my kids to Havasupai for their Christmas present. It was also a birthday present to myself, and we would be celebrating my birthday while we were there. I had been planning this for months and was beyond excited to share this most wondrous place with my kids. It was also a great opportunity for them to get to know Wylie better, and vice versa. They would have the long drive there and back, plus two nights and three days in Supai to get to know one another better.

The ten-mile hike in was long for the kids, but nothing for Wylie and me. He guided there several times a season, and while hiking in, we met up with a female hiking guide he knew. He introduced me as "Laurie" and nothing more. I understood why he still couldn't introduce me to his kids, but why did I have to be a secret to one of his fellow guides? I still didn't understand all the secrecy he felt he needed to have in his life. With the exception of that incident, the trip could not have gone better. For my birthday present, Wylie gave me a trip to Vegas that we would take in July, which would include a special surprise.

Even though Wylie was officially guiding us in Supai, it still felt like a vacation to him. We were adventurous – jumping off waterfalls and swimming in the underwater cave. We played games at night and talked under the stars. If I thought I loved Supai the first time, I loved it even more the second, with my kids. And I was excited about guiding my own girls' trip there in one month. When I got home, I picked five pictures of Wylie and me from that trip and hung them in a collage on a blank wall in my bedroom –which would soon come to be known as the Wall of Adventure, highlighting all of our excursions.

Wylie had mentioned CrossFit several times, and one day I asked him about trying it. I was already a fit hiker, but I understood that CrossFit could make me stronger overall. Wylie took me to his gym and gave me my first lesson. We started doing CrossFit together regularly. He would invite me to stay over at his place, and I would take his 5:30 a.m. class. He informed me that since his soon-to-be ex-wife was a member at the gym and so were his kids, he would not be letting anyone know we were dating. We would drive there in separate cars and when I would walk into the gym, he would say, "Hi Laurie, how are you today?" as if we hadn't just spent the night together – or even knew each other well, for that matter. I would roll my eyes at him. At the end of class he would call people's first names to write their results on the board, and he would purposely call my name last – one time forgetting my name altogether! I didn't soon let him forget that. I felt he really took the secrecy of our relationship to an unnecessary level, and it would oftentimes make me feel slighted. He was also overly critical of me during the workouts. He pointed out my flaws to a larger degree than he ever did anyone else's. I would leave class mad at him in one way or another, just about every time. I loved the workout but questioned my own sanity in putting myself in a path to be ignored and made to feel even less a part of his life. I might actually have been living the definition of insanity: doing the same thing over and over again, expecting different results – because, on some level I *did* think it would get better over time. It did not.

At the end of the month, we guided the Grand Canyon Phantom Ranch trip and had so much fun. We took the guests to an amazing waterfall called Whisper Falls and created more fun memories that we later added to our Wall of Adventure. Also of interest, it was on that hike that Wylie told the story of the hiker who died and passed through him.

One night at The Canteen we ran into the guide who had originally gotten the reservation for this trip. He was guiding with another company at the time. Wylie again introduced me as "Laurie" to this guide – never mentioning that we were guiding together, that we were building a business together, or that we were dating. I was mad at him for about 24 hours over that. I felt slighted – every time there was another opportunity to be part of his life, I was denied. I didn't see why it mattered that people he worked with knew about me. It later turned out that this would be the young guide who cajoled Wylie into downloading the Bumble app. I often wondered if he had, in fact, disclosed that we were dating, would that have changed our trajectory? Or, was there something more to why I was so hidden? I was seriously beginning to wonder. The soon-to-be divorce started to feel like an easy excuse to not have to tell anyone about me.

When my ex-boyfriend John and I were together, we often talked about how much fun it would be to rent a houseboat on Lake Powell. I decided to make that dream a reality – only not with John, with Wylie instead. Stacy and Sal were all on board. We picked three other couples to join us – one was the couple who was with me on the night I officially met Wylie at the bottom of Grand Canyon. I made all the arrangements for renting the boat and calculating the costs, and charged each couple accordingly. Now all we would have to do was wait for October for the weather to cool off a little.

~~Once~~ A Cheater...

Chapter 21

Foolish Heart

~song by Steve Perry

https://open.spotify.com/track/6p3HuYPoRBzhyBPErnyNbr?si=ca9w3rKiTr-m3jA6bCXM-g

My brand new mojito-green Jeep Wrangler was finally being delivered. I had been encouraged by Wylie to get it, and I had the courage to order it a few weeks back. The vehicle was something of a splurge for me. It was new and I usually bought used. It was also really green, and showy. I almost didn't do it and might not have if Wylie hadn't encouraged me so much. At about the same time, he paid off a large loan he had just taken out for his own recent vehicle purchase. That really surprised me. We had never fully discussed his finances, but I got the impression he didn't have much money. He had visited the pawnshop that time, and talked about conserving cash. And he let me be the one to finance our Hiking Adventure business and purchase equipment for it. Knowing now that he had had enough money in his account to pay off a large vehicle loan led me to believe he had a lot more than I thought. From now on, I wasn't going to be paying more than my fair share of our dating expenses as I had been doing, thinking he needed help because of his new alimony and child support expenses.

My new Jeep would be coming in while Wylie was on his Supai trip. I decided not to tell him and surprise him with it for our upcoming trip to Vegas. He had made all the arrangements for the trip, since it was his birthday present to me. I knew that he had arranged the hotel, but the rest was a surprise. He did warn me in advance that the hotel we were staying at was part of Holiday Inn's timeshare residence, and that he had gotten a great $99 rate for two nights because he had agreed to attend a timeshare sales pitch. I laughed at him and said there was no way we were buying a timeshare! He concurred.

The summer months in Arizona bring with them monsoon season, with flash floods that come with little to no warning. They hit while Wylie was on his trip in Supai. Luckily, he and his group were on higher ground at the time. They watched as several campsites downstream got washed away. Everyone had to gather their belongings as quickly as possible and hike back toward the Havasupai village to even higher ground. Once there, everyone was directed to the school gymnasium to sleep overnight.

A Cheater...

  The next morning was the day they were originally supposed to hike out, but now were told they would not be getting out for at least two days because the trails had been washed out. Wylie needed to get back for our trip and for my birthday surprise, and he was not going to take no for an answer. Wylie is nothing if not resourceful. He knew a lot of the Havasupai Indians and talked someone into giving him permission to lead his group out. Having guided there at least 50 times over the last several seasons gave him an advantage – and enabled him to easily guide his group out, even though the trails had been washed away. He was the only guide allowed to hike their group out. I was so relieved when he called me to let me know they made it out! He would be home right on schedule.

  My new Jeep was hidden in the garage and I could not wait to show Wylie. But my surprise backfired when he used the garage code to open the door to come into the house. He was surprised, alright, to see my Jeep parked inside, but I missed seeing the look on his face! We visited a bit before hitting the road for the four-hour drive to Vegas. Wylie had been able to take incredible videos of the floods as they happened. When I saw the devastation the muddy waters left in their wake, I was in awe that he was standing in front of me. Very few people could have guided a group out in those conditions. The flood damage was so extensive that no other groups got out for days, and Havasupai was closed for the rest of the season.

  Wylie drove us to Vegas in my new Jeep. The timeshare hotel we stayed at was more like a luxury mini-apartment, equipped with a full-size kitchen that had stainless steel appliances and granite countertops, a dining room, a beautifully decorated living room with a fireplace and balcony; and finally, a large bedroom with a king-sized bed, a huge walk-in closet, and a beautiful bathroom with a steam shower. There were many amenities, and pool areas were lush and beautiful. We relaxed at the pool after we got there, then dressed for dinner, and for my surprise Wylie had gotten us tickets to see a show. It was a really lovely evening.

  We fully enjoyed our time in Vegas. Neither of us is a gambler, but we are foodies and enjoy eating. We went to some of my favorite restaurants and added a new place to our favorites list. The last day was timeshare-pitch day. In the end, we got sucked into a relatively small purchase that still allowed us to travel to international destinations, and to use a website that would allow us access to specially priced deals all over the world. We envisioned being able to let the kids use it, as well as get some use out of it ourselves, and maybe even all of us use it together in the future. I really didn't want the timeshare, but to me it felt like more of an investment in *us*. Wylie had been so resistant to our relationship during the first several months; now it seemed we were finally becoming more a part of each other's lives. And while neither of us planned to get married again, we talked about eventually living together and building a life with one another. The only way I can explain it is, buying this timeshare was almost like getting engaged. We had to sign it as a mortgage, with both of our names attached. I could not imagine him doing this with me unless he believed in us as strongly as I did. I also reasoned that we did have a three-day right of rescission after the purchase, to cancel. Every day I would ask him if he was still in, and every day he still was. Three days later there was no turning back – we were the proud owners of a Las Vegas timeshare. But this time, what happened in Vegas didn't stay in Vegas…

Our relationship got better and better every time we saw each other. He was really letting his guard down and had begun to be more vulnerable with me. One of my favorite things he did was to call me "princess" all the time –it made me feel very special. While we were progressing, his divorce was lagging, in the sense that it was not progressing as much as I would have hoped.

I believe in manifesting my future, and I understand the process: In order for a thing to happen, you need to prepare your life for it by seeing it as if it had already happened, then apply positive emotions like gratitude, happiness, wholeness, inspiration and love to those images. One day I was looking for something in a drawer in my bedroom when I realized all my bedroom drawers were partially to mostly full. I'm not a "things" person, and I don't like having a lot of material items, but somehow, since I had moved to Arizona, I had managed to fill up all the drawers. It made me think about the future and the idea that if your life is full in this way, you are not really making room for someone else to come into it. It was time to do some purging! I wanted to "make room" for Wylie in my life. I cleared out drawers, leaving several of them completely empty. A few days later Wylie was at my house eating lunch, when he made a comment about living together – and then added, "…but I haven't been invited yet." Wow, that was fast! It was just the previous week that I had had those thoughts and had taken action.

Our relationship could not have been going better. His apartment lease was expiring in September, and he had mentioned possibly extending it by three months – but he may actually have been hinting about living with me. We had a timeshare together now, and I had a glimmer of hope. But I also understood his divorce was not progressing as quickly as he would have liked, and he was waiting for it to be finalized before he would tell his kids about me. So until everything was concluded, it was still all wishful thinking.

Even though I was not as much a part of Wylie's life as I would have liked, he was beginning to participate more and more in *my* life. He had met my kids, my parents and most of my friends. Just recently, close couple friends of mine invited Wylie and me to sit at their table for the Ronald McDonald Charity Event coming up. They had previously served on the board and purchased a table every year for six couples. I was really excited to have Wylie go with me this year. There was a silent auction, good food and we would get to dress up and have a nice evening out for a good cause. Wylie excitedly accepted the invitation. I loved how he was becoming more involved in my life and couldn't wait until I could feel the same way about being in his.

Chapter 22

This Kiss

~song by *Faith Hill*

https://open.spotify.com/track/5EYWGM3Ns3iYew8ws0FatB?si=R3gZizHpRKG3xH4IHb4ztw

Talking to Wylie on the phone one day, he told me he had decided to climb Mt. Everest in 2020 – the tallest mountain in the world. I cringed and thought: also the most dangerous mountain in the world! This was a big deal *and* a big decision. Not only is this mountain not for the faint of heart, it is also very expensive to climb – which meant Wylie was going to need to fundraise. He told me about the Vet Charity organization that he had created with a fellow veteran long before, and that he was thinking about starting it up again.

When I next saw Wylie, he told me his best friend had asked him to guide on Mt. Aconcagua in Argentina for the International Adventure business. Aconcagua is one of the Seven Summits (the highest mountains in each of the seven continents) and is the tallest summit in the Southern Hemisphere. Wow, this was a big opportunity for him. He explained that Aconcagua would be great training for his Everest climb. Wait...*guiding*, not just climbing – I immediately asked, "Is Jane going?"

"Yes," he said, sheepishly, "she just put her deposit down this week."

I was instantly mad and wanted to know why he hadn't volunteered this information. "Why do I have to ask to discover what you should be telling me? It makes me feel like you have something to hide." I didn't like his defensive response: "Well...that's what Jane does! Jane climbs mountains!" He then added, almost as an afterthought, "But you asked so quickly I didn't even have a chance to tell you. I was going to tell you."

I wasn't mad anymore – I was now furious. I didn't appreciate his defensive attitude or his tone, and most especially his comment about *that's what Jane does*. It felt like a slap in the face. "Well then, I'm going too!" I said it seriously, but of course didn't mean it. That mountain would be way too cold for me with Raynaud's Syndrome. But I said it to see what he would say, wondering if – half hoping – he might encourage me to go too. Instead, he told me I couldn't go, pointing out that it would be too cold for me. I argued for a while, insisting I *was* going anyway. He actually started to freak out a little at the thought of me going too – which seemed odd. Was he worried about me and my Reynaud's – or something else?

"I'm stronger than she is. I know I can climb it." *I* wanted to be the one that climbs mountains. *I* wanted to be the one spending three weeks with Wylie. Only half joking, I added, "If you are sharing a room with her on that trip, then I'm leaving!" He laughed at me – of course they wouldn't be sharing a room together!

This season, to date, Jane had been on six Hiking Adventure trips with Wylie. I was annoyed at how much she had insinuated herself into his life – and I was getting sick and tired of talking about *Jane*.

When Wylie traveled with Jane to Peru, before we met, he had intended to participate in an Ayahuasca ceremony, but none were available to him then. Ayahuasca is a mysterious plant-based medicine derived from plants found in the jungles of South America. Taken as a tea by mouth, it has been used ceremoniously for centuries to induce an altered state for the purpose of spiritual growth. It has an effect on the body, mind and spirit that can be very healing. Wylie and I had only talked about it one time before. In Peru, his friends invited him to watch a documentary at a college, about a married couple who had both served in Desert Storm and had developed Post Traumatic Stress Disorder (PTSD). Subsequently, they had both taken an Ayahuasca medicine journey. The husband's journey had successfully cured him of all his PTSD symptoms. It took a few more journeys for his wife, but she too was cured. There is now a pharmaceutical company studying DMT (the active ingredient in Ayahuasca) for the treatment of PTSD. When the documentary ended, the veteran couple talked about their experience Wylie was sold (as if he hadn't been already!). He suspected that he suffered from undiagnosed PTSD from his service in Desert Storm. That night his friends introduced him to a shaman named Medicine Woman, who could guide him on his first journey. He immediately signed up with her for the experience.

He began preparing for the Ayahuasca ceremony by changing to a completely plant-based diet. He also cut out all alcohol and sex. He would need to abstain from both for the week before as well as after the ceremony when a person's energy is very open, in order to prevent it from being "contaminated" with anyone else's energy. He would have the ceremony at his friend's house the next week.

I did a little research so I could better understand the process. Certain plants, such as Ayahuasca, are psychedelics – very powerful medicines that can have profound spiritual healing effects. They can also help address issues an individual is having in life that derive from childhood and later experiences. At the time, Wylie was in therapy for issues from his past, and had been since I met him. I knew therapy was helpful, but after more research I understood how plant-based medicine could help him even more. I was super excited for him, but didn't understand the process well enough to know if he could be susceptible to attraction to another woman in that altered state. I had more questions than answers.

Two days before his Ayahuasca ceremony, we met for a CrossFit workout, followed by a late lunch. We had driven separately, and after lunch we walked to the parking lot together, hand in hand. We stopped in front of my Jeep to finish our conversation, holding hands the entire time. Before leaving, we hugged and kissed, then got into our vehicles to head home. About 30 minutes later I got a text from Wylie telling me his soon-to-be ex-wife and his youngest son had been eating at a restaurant that faced the parking lot we had just been in – they saw us walking, talking and kissing. This was bad. Wylie's son was 16 – but he did not know about me. On the other hand, maybe this was good and had happened in order to force Wylie's hand with regard to talking about us with his kids. His soon-to-be ex-wife, of course, had known about us for several months. I hoped this incident was going to somehow be a blessing in disguise. Wylie was definitely freaked out about it and felt sure his son would tell his brother and sister. He especially didn't want his daughter knowing yet, because she was not handling the impending divorce well. I could only wonder what the chances were that in all of Phoenix, we had been at the same place at the same time for them to see us – especially with all of us having an unusually late lunch. Well, it was out of my hands and he would just have to deal with it. I hoped sooner than later.

On the day of the ceremony Wylie sent me a picture of himself dressed in all-white clothing for purity. He was *really* taking this seriously. He would be on a six-hour medicine journey, and then stay overnight at his couple friends' house. The night after, he would meet me for dinner to tell me all about his journey. I was so excited for him and prayed for healing!

The following night, I went to Wylie's apartment to hear about the ceremony. We sat on the couch and I was mesmerized by what he told me about his experience. It brought him a lot of healing. We decided to go out for dinner to continue the conversation. He brought up our second date and reminded me how he had "laid it all out there," and how we could have waited until his divorce was finalized to start our relationship. But he was glad we hadn't, because he loved what we had now and what we'd experienced over the last year. Then he added that at some point he may need to push the pause button on our relationship. My stomach sank and I immediately lost my appetite. My biggest fear was that at some time in the future Wylie would want to experience other women, and I would *not* be okay with that. He assured me the *only* reason he would want to pause our relationship was to be with himself, to feel what it feels like to just be alone – not in order to explore anyone else. He reminded me again: if he didn't see me or talk to me for six months and then saw me again, the feelings would still be there and may be even stronger – we would pick up exactly where we left off.

I said I felt like we already had space – we had autonomy to just be. And I thought we had already taken our relationship slowly enough by only seeing each other once or twice a week for the first six months. He then back-peddled a bit, not wanting me to worry: "Make no mistake," he said, "I know what I have with you – you are absolutely amazing!" But his son seeing us kissing two days before had really thrown him, really made him reflect. He realized he had done things in the wrong order – not logistically, but emotionally. He went from separation to being in a committed relationship.

I couldn't stop crying through the entire talk. I was a crying mess and kept apologizing for how awful I look when I cry. He tried to make me feel better and must have told me half a dozen times how beautiful I still looked.

Wylie wanted to be open and honest with me about his feelings. He didn't want to make any changes right now (repeating that several times); he wanted to continue what we had planned, and he was not going anywhere. He just needed me to know that at some point he *may* need to take a break – and if it happened he didn't want me to freak out about it. He said, "I fell really hard and really fast for you. I let myself fall. It was effortless and I couldn't have stopped it if I had wanted to. You are the epitome of unconditional love. But how do I live up to that?! I wonder if I'm even capable of a love that deep. You make me feel loved!" I tried to lighten the mood by challenging him to take me home and prove it – knowing, of course, he couldn't because of his recent ceremony. I was just going to have to take his word for it.

For the next month after our talk I found myself in a constant state of dread – afraid that he was going to leave the relationship. I had hoped he would talk to his son about us, but it had been a month and he still had not addressed the kissing episode. Our parenting styles were *markedly* different.

Between his guiding and my work schedule, we were about to enter into an almost two-week period of time where we wouldn't see each other. He invited me for dinner and to stay the night, then do CrossFit in the morning. We were having a nice dinner, but I had noticed something important I needed to bring to his attention. Because of my habit of planning for the future, I realized our January trip to Bora Bora was most likely going to coincide with his divorce being final. He didn't have to go to court for it, but I asked him what he thought his feelings would be when the marriage was finally over. I knew that for my divorce it had been a mixture of sadness and relief. He said it would be the same for him, but I wanted him to think about how he would feel being on a big trip when he got the news. Although every part of me wanted to go on this trip with him, I felt he needed to decide in advance whether it was going to be a good idea. My gut feeling, when I brought it up, was that he was going to eventually decline the trip, and I really needed him to decide in advance of the trip if we should go. If I didn't bring it up now, he would not figure it out until it was too late, and I didn't want his lack of foresight to ruin a fabulous vacation. He expressed extreme gratitude toward me for bringing this to his attention, especially since he knew how badly

I wanted to go and how much effort had already gone into planning it. He promised to give it some thought and get back to me.

His apartment lease would expire at the end of the month, and he had decided not to renew it. Instead, he was going to be moving in with – not one of his hiking-guide friends as he had been planning – but with his client and friend who had just moved into a new house. He made the decision based on finances. I had never met her, but I remembered when he was recently invited to her housewarming party that had excluded me. While I understood his decision, I didn't see how this would help him in his battle to "own himself" – and I wished it was me he was moving in with.

The next morning when we got up for CrossFit, he showed me a text from Tracy. She had taken a screen shot of a picture of Wylie with me in Havasupai that I had put on my Facebook page a month before. She was teasing him about us being more than friends because we had our arms around each other in the picture. She, of course, had known for nine months, ever since our full-moon trip together, that Wylie and I were dating. But she had pretended not to know because Wylie wanted to keep our relationship a secret. When he learned I had put two pictures of us in my picture highlights, he made me remove them immediately. I was only friends with two of his friends on Facebook, but he STILL wanted us to be hidden to the world and didn't appreciate that I had posted those pictures. I was pretty miffed. We had been together for over a year! The kicker was, during that same year I hadn't posted ANY picture on Facebook. I really felt it was ok to be public on *my* own Facebook page – it was my life too. I wanted *my* world to see we were together. But his "no" overruled my "yes." In a lot of ways this relationship was very one sided, always defaulting to what Wylie wanted and not often considering my needs.

As long as we had gone down this rabbit hole, I wanted him to know I thought he should tell his son about us. By not saying anything, it looked like there was something to hide, and I didn't understand why he was waiting. He got defensive and said "Don't try to understand it – you can't! *I* can't even explain it. It can't be understood because it's emotional not logical. I will know when it's the right time to tell – it's not. Not everyone in my family knows I'm getting divorced yet." Wow – that was a big revelation. He wasn't even close to standing in his truth. I told him I had almost pulled out of the relationship two weeks before, and if it weren't for the couples houseboat trip coming up, I would have. He joked that he would have pulled out too if I hadn't kept planning so many fun things! We both laughed.

I sat on his lap and told him how much I hated being apart; my feelings of love were so strong. Things had felt so different since "the parking lot kiss," and our relationship felt really difficult now. When we first started dating I never could have imagined we would be where we were now after one year – where I was still completely hidden in his life. Yet it would be dumb to pull out now, when I could actually see the light at the end of the proverbial tunnel. In any case, I would never give him an ultimatum. I still felt like the kids had to come first, and

I couldn't argue about how he wanted to parent them. But I needed him to consider me in the equation too. We said we loved each other, and I left for the airport.

The next time we saw each other was for the *Christina Aguilera* concert. We decided to have dinner first at my place, and Wylie planned to spend the night with me. We hadn't spent any time together in almost two weeks, as he had been guiding and then moved out of his apartment into his new place. I was really looking forward to our time together.

As I was finishing making dinner, Wylie announced that he had made a decision about the Bora Bora trip. I held my breath, because I had already guessed what was coming. He had decided it best that we *not* take the chance his divorce would be finalized during the trip. It would – for him – ruin the trip. Knowing this was coming and actually getting the news are two different things – I could not hold back the tears and had to run out of the room. He came to find me. I was trying hard not to ruin my concert make-up, but it was too late. Even I was surprised at how hard his news hit me. Then he said we needed to hurry up and eat so we could drive his car back to his new place and drop it off before the concert – meaning we would only have to take one car. Wait...hadn't he said he was spending the night at my place? He apologized and said that he had been gone so much lately that he really wanted to sleep in his own bed that night and didn't yet feel comfortable with me staying over now that he had a roommate. I left the room crying for the second time in one night. The strange thing was I already "knew." I had gotten a "hit" of intuition earlier in the day, that he was not going to be spending the night. I returned to the kitchen to serve our food but could not eat one bite. His double whammy had taken my appetite with it. He felt bad about his decision to not stay over and if he had not just moved into his new place would offer to have me stay the night there. This was just ridiculous! He was a grown man. And his new roommate was one of the few people who actually knew about me. I didn't see what the big deal was – he was living there and paying rent. Did he expect from now on to be able to only stay at my place if we were to spend the night together? It felt like he had already ruined the entire evening before it even started. My mood was not good.

After dinner I followed him in my Jeep to his new place. The house was nice, brand new, and in a tiny, gated community in a part of Phoenix that was slowly being gentrified. He had a large bedroom upstairs with an adjacent bathroom. His new room was so much bigger than the apartment bedroom had been, and he made the bed with the bedspread I had given him. At least he had more storage space now, with two closets and an under-the-stairs closet. His roommate had lots and lots of storage space and a two-car garage with not much in it. Wylie took care of that – he had not only moved everything out of his old apartment, but also everything that had been left at his soon-to-be ex-wife's place. And there was still more that couldn't fit. I agreed to let him store the last bit of his stuff in a walk-in closet at my place.

He also had an office downstairs. He had already hung pictures on the walls and put up all his decorations – everything *except* the painting I had given him. I didn't say anything, but I was crushed inside. Everything else he owned was either up or proudly displayed. It was disappointing that even the smallest detail of my existence was still hidden. I was already feeling agitated toward him and this just added more fuel to the fire. At the end of the tour, I finally met his roommate. She was super nice and I liked her immediately. But I sure wasn't feeling like myself and was wishing I wasn't meeting her in these circumstances. Wylie and his roommate would be hosting a pre-Thanksgiving dinner and she personally invited me to come.

Well, he was on his own now – but in my opinion not quite owning himself. I liked it better when he had his own place – not that the apartment was great, because it wasn't. But now it was clear he wasn't even going to be comfortable having me over. Sure, he was saving $300 a month, but I thought he would feel better about himself if, in his 50s, he was completely living on his own. The house was definitely an upgrade, but the situation was a downgrade.

I drove us to the concert, totally annoyed with him by then, and my attitude turned passive-aggressive. I didn't really want to go to a concert anymore. I think my new attitude really freaked him out – he had never seen me like this before. The past 60 days of our relationship had really taken a toll on me. Wylie spent the entire 40 minutes we sat waiting for the concert to start, trying to make small talk and being overly affectionate. He was trying desperately to get back on my good side. I wasn't having it. Finally, he just straight out asked me what he could do to make things better. First, I brought up the hidden painting and asked him why he had put everything up at his new place except for that. He said he still had one last box to unpack; it must be in there. He had not intentionally left it out. I said if he really wanted me to feel better, he could ask me to spend the night. "Done!" he said. See? I really wasn't that hard to please – finally something that took my feelings into consideration. Up to then, everything from our dinner conversation, to driving him to the concert, to cancelling Bora Bora, had been for or about him. By the time the concert started, I was feeling more myself and we enjoyed the show. We got back to his place very late, and I left early the next morning at the same time he left for CrossFit. I don't even think his roommate had any idea I had slept there.

Ten months had gone by since I bought tickets to the *Foo Fighters'* concert. Despite my diligent planning and making sure Wylie put this special event and birthday gift on his calendar, in the end he made the choice to guide a trip instead of going to the concert with me. He didn't even consult me before doing it –and even passed it off as a "whoopsie, too bad I have to work." I understood he needed the money, but it was a shitty thing to do. I just could not imagine doing that to someone. I had given him what I felt was a thoughtful gift, with plenty of advance notice – and the *Foo Fighters* were not in *my* top three favorite bands. Here I was with $400 in concert tickets and no one to go with me.

Luckily, Stacy appreciated the *Foo Fighters* music and agreed to be my "plus one." We had a great evening. But I would not soon forget how many things overall had been skewed to favor what Wylie wanted to do – often to my detriment. Our talks were always slanted to what he wanted and needed. I could not remember one conversation in the previous four months when he had even asked how I felt, how I was doing, or what I needed. It was as if the only happiness that mattered in this equation was his. I had devoted a lot of my time, attention, energy, love and thoughtfulness to *us*. Perhaps it was time for me to step back and observe and think about what I wanted and what I needed, because no one else was. Maybe it was a product of how he was raised; maybe it was self-preservation, but I was seeing a characteristic in him I hadn't often experienced in my life. I like my relationships to be more balanced, yet there was one glaring "con" now on Wylie's list: Selfishness.

Chapter 23

Rock the Boat

~song by *Hues Corporation*

https://open.spotify.com/track/7fu3Tv5rcoGD1PZV7s57WW?si=654dXDU8Q9qwCokbqbL6tw

Boat safety had become my life, as my name and my name alone would be on the $150,000 five-bedroom houseboat we would be renting on Lake Powell. I took two online safety courses and immersed myself in learning every function and feature of the houseboat. Luckily, Sal had a lot of experience around boats, and also RVs and generators, so all the systems were familiar to him. I could rely on him as captain and backup. This trip had been months in the making. I wanted it to be an amazing experience for everyone, and I had invested a lot of time researching and planning it.

Wylie and I left one day in advance of the other couples so we would have an extra day to explore two new hiking places he planned to guide clients on, and neither of us had been to either of them before. We spent most of the day hiking the incredible Petrified National Forest. We were also able to get a day permit to explore the Devil's Playground – a fascinating area that only three small groups per day were allowed to enter. By sheer luck, we had it completely to ourselves. It was supremely beautiful and we had such a wonderful time being there together. At the end of the day we drove to Page, Arizona where we would be spending the night at a hotel and meeting up with the other couples. The idea was that everyone could be up early and have the entire next day on the houseboat.

As we were driving up to the hotel check-in, I suddenly had an interesting thought: Wylie had partaken in so many cool experiences all over the world through his time in the military and his days of Adventure Racing (a team sport involving navigation over an unmarked wilderness course), and it was a rare occurrence when we experienced something new together that he had not experienced previously. With that in mind, I excitedly exclaimed, "I'll bet this is the first time you'll be having sex on a houseboat!" I asked it as a rhetorical question, thinking I already knew the answer.

He laughed. "No...," and with a big cocky smile on his face, he added: "I spent a few days on a houseboat in my Adventure Racing time. I had sex on one then." His answer made me feel like I had just gotten the wind knocked out of my sails. I had not expected *that* answer or I would not have even brought it up. My mind quickly assembled the puzzle pieces: Adventure Racing days = earlier marriage days = *before* he was in an open marriage. It was just another reminder of his sketchy, womanizing, cheating past. Previously, when talking about his past, he had made me feel that the early extramarital affairs were few and far between because he was looking for meaningful connections, not casual encounters. Sex on a houseboat on an Adventure Racing trip would not have been with someone he was in a relationship with. It was casual sex – and it bothered me greatly that he had been like that in his marriage. I was not confident he wouldn't at some point in the future be that way with me. I actually felt sick to my stomach, and all the excitement that had been building, leading up to the trip...fizzled.

I vented to Stacy as soon as I saw her. She reminded me that *I* had not been in his life at that time – he was a different man now, and all that was in the past. I felt a little better but just could not fully bury the new information and let it go. To boot, as soon as Wylie got around the other couples, his personality changed in the sense that he started teasing me more than he ever did when we were alone. He made two comments that night about my age, telling everyone my 50th birthday was coming up and he would need to trade me in for a younger model because 50 was his cut-off age. He was joking, of course, but between the houseboat sex revelation and the age comments, I was not feeling very confident about Wylie.

All five couples assembled early the next morning, ready for our four-night/five-day excursion. Each couple had planned a lunch or dinner to cook for the group. I don't think I've ever seen so much food for a trip in my life! There were both sweet and salty snacks of every kind imaginable. Every couple brought at least one large cooler, and we completely filled the fridge and pantry. Eating and drinking was the goal, while mixing in a little hiking and sightseeing and LOTS of relaxation! I was feeling more myself by the time we all got settled on the boat and pushed off the dock.

Wylie was nearing the end of his busy season and both of us had been traveling for work quite a bit. It was a nice time for us to reconnect for several days. We spent time together, time with the other couples, and we each had some alone time. Most of Wylie's alone time was spent on his phone playing dumb games. I really didn't understand this meaningless game obsession. He also continued to make several more disparaging remarks publicly, directed to me, mostly about my age. It felt like he was purposely trying to push me away. This caused me to go on high alert with him. I also noticed he had not once told me he loved me during this excursion – despite having sex at least once a day. Something was off, and I surmised it was still the residual effects from the kissing incident where his youngest son and soon-to-be ex-wife had seen us. I could not forget that he had previously mentioned he might need to take a break at some point, so I was being observant.

I had a few fun evening events planned. One was a Halloween costume party where Wylie and I dressed up as Wonder Woman and Thor, complete with a long blonde wig for him. It was definitely a picture worthy of the Wall of Adventure, along with several other great shots from that trip. We had a really fun Halloween night, but the highlight of the trip was the glow-in-the-dark party. I regularly painted with glow-in-the-dark paints and loved to use them on my body. When you paint a design, the paint is almost undetectable in normal light but is activated in neon-bright colors under a blacklight. In advance of the trip, I had asked all the women to purchase blacklight flashlights. At the party, I helped each of them create fun body designs on themselves with the paint and paintbrushes I had brought. The guys had been hanging out together entertaining themselves and were very surprised when we all emerged to kidnap our partner. Each couple retreated to their individual cabins to play show and tell with their unsuspecting partner – I turned the music up real loud. The glow-in-the-dark party was a HUGE success and a memorable experience not to be soon forgotten.

Sadly, all good things must come to an end. We spent a couple hours off-loading all the leftover food, and packing up personal belongings. Wylie and I spent the first 30 minutes of the four-hour car ride home reminiscing about the fun trip. That said, his behavior had really been bothering me, and not wanting to repeat past mistakes by keeping my feelings bottled up, I talked about it. I began by telling him a story of what I felt our relationship would look like ten years into the future, with growth and adventures and two people building their lives side by side, and how valuable it can be to have a partner to rely on through thick and thin. I pointed out how if either of us got sick or injured we would each have a true partner to count on. Then I replayed all the hurtful, age-related comments he had made on the trip and explained how they made me feel. He instantly got defensive and said he had been kidding. He claimed that if any of those comments were true it would have been mean to say them – therefore, none of them could have any truth to them. I returned to the 60-year-old scenario, ten years ahead, and talked about how much my body would change in those ten years. I was sure to have more wrinkles, and any beauty I had would certainly fade to some degree. But I believed when two people are good together, none of that should matter! They might actually grow to find each other MORE attractive, because the strength of a relationship would surely increase in that amount of time. He agreed. I then expressed my concern with his many comments during the trip, because it felt like he was telling me my outer beauty was much more important to him than my inner beauty. And in light of the knowledge about the existence of "28," I had a valid concern that he might *really* trade me in for a younger face. He told me again how I was so rare and so special that it could not and would not happen! I also pointedly asked him why he hadn't said *I love you* to me in almost two weeks. He shrugged it off as not even realizing he had been remiss in this way, and assured me he did love me – totally skirting the actual question. In actuality, he had not given me a reason to doubt him, but nothing had felt right since the kissing incident. He agreed it *was* a factor in our situation.

I was just glad I had not let my fear of chasing him away or repelling him stand in the way of asking him the *real questions* that were on my mind. One thing was sure – I was becoming less afraid to rock the boat!

Chapter 24

Spirits in the Material World

~song by *The Police*

https://open.spotify.com/track/4freIkLhC4ATqJH9VGJztu?si=-nlUQ0BQPyZeLvdETyfrQ

Wylie sent me a song by the band *America* for our *L.A. Woman* playlist. I loved that band and wondered if they were currently touring. They were, but not in our area. We had the timeshare now and timeshare points to use, and I wondered if they would be playing anywhere that we could kill two birds with one stone. They were playing in Myrtle Beach, South Carolina, in January. This could be the perfect replacement trip, now that Bora Bora was officially off.

Wylie explored Ayahuasca again and had two more very healing journeys. He would always see me the day after a journey of this kind and tell me in great detail what he had gleaned from the experience. I was so happy these ceremonies were available to him, and for his willingness to tell me about them. He had a lot to heal from his childhood as well as his time serving our country.

The Ronald McDonald Charity Event was coming up, but at the last minute Wylie asked me if he could go to a San Pedro ceremony instead of accompanying me at the event. He acknowledged he had committed to me first and would still go unless I thought someone else could fill his spot. I had gone by myself the year before; Wylie had been invited but was still living with his soon-to-be ex-wife at the time. He had been sorry to miss it, and I was really looking forward to him going with me this time. I knew if he was asking to be elsewhere, my insisting he come with me would take all the fun out of it anyway. But I was also a bit surprised he wanted to do San Pedro again, because the experience had been mild in comparison to any of his other ceremonies. I had a gut feeling he wasn't going for himself – Jane was going. I could just feel it. I asked him directly if she was going and he said she wasn't – he just wanted to do it himself. I wished I was going with him, because I had been wanting to try San Pedro. But pulling out of my commitment was out of the question. I told him to go – go have a good ceremony and I would have my friends find someone else to take his spot.

Truth be told, I don't think the charity event would have been that much fun for Wylie anyway. But I did wish he had made good on his commitment. I was not the kind of person to cancel plans, and he made me look bad by having to call my friends to cancel his spot. On top of it, the ceremony required a sleepover, but since he was not going to the event, of course he would not be sleeping over with me. Instead, he would be going to another event that also had a sleepover. I really hoped I was wrong and Jane was not actually going, but there was no way for me to know. I just had to trust what he told me over my gut feeling, because I didn't think he would lie about it. And I didn't think he would pick her over me anyway.

Jane had "activated" me again – the more I thought about it, the more questions I had about their relationship. I decided it was time to address her again. Sitting in the airport on a business trip, I wrote Wylie a long email asking that we discuss it when we both returned. I waited three days for a response from him and heard nothing. Maybe I had overstepped my bounds.

When I returned from the trip, Wylie came up my way for dinner and to spend the night. We had not yet had a chance to catch up after his San Pedro journey and my charity event. At dinner, he began telling me about his San Pedro experience. After the ceremony he had asked Medicine Woman, who had also guided him on the Ayahuasca journeys, about the topic of possession: Why did people feel the need to be possessive of someone? – he did not like it. My heart sank – it felt like he was talking about me to her and using this story as a creative way to bridge into the email I had sent him about Jane. I needed to brace myself because it felt like this conversation might morph into his again asking to take the break he had been warning about. Before I could ask if that was the direction we were going, he said this conversation with Medicine Woman both did and didn't have to do with me – this was more *his* issue, helping him figure out his energy. He said he didn't want to be my boyfriend. Not the role – he had decided he didn't like the word "my"; that was the distinction for him. He wanted me to introduce him instead as "the man in my life," or "the love in my life," or "the love of my life," or even "the partner in my life."

He admitted he had a long-standing issue with boundaries and thought he finally understood them. He hadn't known he was an empath before I pointed it out to him; he now understood how every aspect of his life played into him being empathic and *feeling* the energy around him that didn't belong to him. This had been a huge revelation! He told me he felt he would not be where he was on his spiritual journey right now – without me. This realization, along with discovering the healing properties of the plant medicine experiences, had moved him forward spiritually! My mind cued in to what he said about not being where he was without ME. That seemed significant! When I indicated that, he said, "Yes. I wouldn't be here without you." And he marveled at the timing of our relationship, coinciding with the breakup of his marriage. He also said he had never connected with *anyone else* on all the levels we connected: in communication, attraction, spiritually, sexually, energetically, and our lifestyle connection – we had it ALL! He then reminded me again, "I still love the fucking shit out of you!"

Wylie also understood how the things he expressed made me want to run in response. These conversations were hard, and he knew they made me feel bad because they were an indication of how he still lagged behind me in our relationship. But he knew I wouldn't run – and he wouldn't let me run. He said, "You can't get rid of me that easily. I will fight for you!" Was he finally getting over the initial issues he had about the timing of our relationship not giving him an opportunity to be on his own? Was he actually seeing how being together benefitted him and finally coming to the conclusion I had – that we were spiritually destined to come together now, in this space and time? I believed the medicine journeys would help him work through all his energy issues and his concerns about needing space. With this new enlightened perspective, he decided that if he could go back in time he would not change anything about us or about our journey.

He said he had thought a lot about our last conversation at his apartment when I told him that if we ended our relationship, I didn't think I would find anyone who would have a connection as strong as ours. He admitted that had put pressure on him and made him very worried he might disappoint me, or that he might not live up to my expectations. Even the mere thought of falling short of my expectations was hard for him. I said I was only expressing my feelings about our bigger Soul connection, and noted how rare it was. I worried that another strong connection might not manifest in this lifetime again for me if our relationship did not work out. It was never my intention to put pressure on him.

He said it had also been hard for him when I shared my deeper feelings in writing, because that too put pressure on him. It made him feel suffocated if he hadn't solicited it and was not in the energy to receive it. He asked me to reach out instead with something to the effect of "Hey, can I share some feelings with you?" Then he could say yes or no, but ninety percent of the time he would say yes. I scoffed, thinking to myself, I was *NOT* going to do that. Instead, I would just stop sharing; I didn't explain it, but I was *not* going to ask permission to express what I was feeling! Especially since many times when I felt inspired to send him a message it was late at night, when he was asleep. If I had to wait for his "permission" to share, that moment would pass for me.

Uggghh, this was going to be hard. I felt like I already had to wait for him to tell me he loved me first. The last three times I said I loved him in person, he didn't even say it back, and the last couple times I said I missed him, in texts, he hadn't responded either. In fact, it greatly disturbed me when I said *I love you* in a text and he responded with a "Thank you" and nothing else. If I thought about it, I felt his communication had really changed since his youngest son saw us kiss. It was so obvious that I went back into the archives of our communications to re-read past texts, and I was correct – I had not imagined it. I was feeling more and more like I needed to pull back for a while with saying I loved or missed him or with sending him songs. It would be hard for me, because I didn't like to hold back or contain my feelings. I hoped he was going to be able to get past the kissing incident and get back to how we were.

I focused my attention back on our conversation where he had said my energy was so powerful sometimes, he couldn't take it, and that he felt he was a very strong man who could take a lot. Not wanting to offend me, he added, "Your energy is amazing, but it's a lot sometimes. I don't think most men could handle you!" He had said all of this to me once before, and my ex-boyfriend John had said it as well. Maybe my ex-husband was stronger than I thought; he seemed to handle it for 29 years just fine – well...as well as he could. We were divorced, but not because of that.

Wylie ended the conversation with these final thoughts: he wanted to be in this "relationship" with me – or whatever we "called" it. He needed me to understand his boundaries and we could figure out together how to better engage so our relationship didn't "freak him out" and cause him to pull back. I can't say I felt better after our conversation – it did have the "run" effect on me. But knowledge is power, and this man knew how to communicate what he was feeling.

Now it was my turn. When we got into the car I finally brought up the Jane email, as it had become obvious during our conversation that he had not read it. He was genuinely surprised and said he never saw it. He had issues with emails and wondered why I hadn't just sent him a text saying "you've got mail." He asked me to read it to him while he drove us home. When we got to my place he pulled the email up on his own computer to go over it in detail with me. He answered all my questions:

First of all, Jane was a friend and a Soul connection; he had no attraction to her sexually and did not think she was sexually attracted to him, either. She really did just book her trip to climb Aconcagua, and he wasn't downplaying it when I asked about it. The question had been out of my mouth so fast he hadn't had time to tell me, but he absolutely would have told me. He agreed with all my points about how I viewed Jane and said he now understood the boundaries he needed to have with that relationship; there was nothing she or anyone else could do to make him cross lines with anyone. He said he would never be unfaithful to me, for three reasons:

1) It would crush me and he wouldn't do that to me.

2) He had too much respect for me and for us to *ever* have our relationship end in that way.

3) He wouldn't risk what we have for someone else.

He was working on his boundaries and putting them in place. He understood now that he needed to have a plan, as I had suggested. I did NOT have to worry – Jane was **not** going to climb Everest. She would simply support his Everest climb financially. Jane did know about me – knew we were together in a relationship. But he didn't talk about it to her, like he talked about it with his roommate, because their relationship was just different. He said Jane had never said anything negative about me, and added, "She's not that way."

I really appreciated the serious attention he had given to all my "Jane questions." His explanations made me feel a lot better, as I had a hard time processing things I didn't understand. I said, "But I *know* my concerns are legitimate: both Stacy and I were on the trip with Jane, and I asked her to observe for me. She does agree that Jane is interested in you – whether you are aware of it or not." With that said, one of two things was going to happen: either I had just awakened a sleeping giant with this knowledge of Jane's interest in him – which now had the potential for him to open himself up to her – or else he would take the appropriate measures to guard himself against her. Either way, it was a Free Will choice, and I had to let him prove to me he was serious about being faithful.

Wylie also told me about Jane's marriage, hoping the information might help me understand that things were not what they seemed. Her husband was now suffering from his second bout of cancer, and it was really bad this time. He was not expected to survive it. Jane had been a caretaker for both of her sick parents, who had since died, and now she was in the same role with her husband. Wylie said the main reason she went on so many trips was because she wanted to support Wylie's business, but she also needed to get away from her situation and spend time healing time in nature. That was all – there was nothing more to it. I really hoped I would be able to put Jane behind us. She was taking far too much of my energy!

The next morning Wylie and I hiked Elephant Mountain, an eight-mile hike that traverses up and over a mountain, with cool Indian ruins at the top. Today's topic of discussion was energy. Now, I'm a good talker, but that day Wylie gave me a run for my money; he spoke the majority of our two-hour hike. Because he was an empath, he said he could feel my energy, and that he felt when there was a "blockage" – it was like a pressure that I needed to release through my words. But my words could sometimes be too much for him. He said it was his issue, not mine, and ever since I had pointed out that he was an empath, he had been studying energy and trying to understand how it works for him. He now realized how much the energy of other people affected him, and he better understood why living with his soon-to-be ex-wife and kids had been a challenge. He needed to be alone and to have his own space, and maybe this had been the reason he was absent so much from the family. I wondered if, perhaps subconsciously, he had chosen professions that led him away from home for great lengths of time, in that the energy of everyone combined was just too much for him.

I asked him if he thought we would be able to live together in the future. He was honest and said, "No, not right now." He might as well have just shoved me into a cactus! Then he added that the plant-based medicines were helping him with his energy – helping him to finally understand it. These new tools would allow him – for the first time – to be able to think about the possibility of us living together. I told him I was not waiting forever for him to decide if he was going to live with me. I said I had been *super* upfront about my feelings, from the beginning of our relationship. I really had only three requirements of him.

1) He needed to be in a monogamous relationship with me.

2) I wasn't looking for someone to date – I wanted someone who was interested in building a future together. It didn't have to be now, but I wasn't going to wait endlessly for him to decide.

3) Building a future, to me, meant living with someone.

It was really hard for me, knowing he could be ok living with his new roommate but not with me – timing aside. He had indicated that her energy was "easy" to live with, but he didn't know if mine would be. He felt my energy was much stronger than hers, and it was just different. I told him I wanted to experiment with this aspect of us and perhaps we could begin spending a few days together, living an everyday life to see how it worked, without a bigger commitment of actually moving in together. He agreed that would be a possibility.

As long as we were putting all our cards on the table, I wanted to talk about his finances. We both had revealed a lot about ourselves in the previous 24 hours, and I had been really surprised when he told me he was paying off his $29,000 car loan. He had been acting like money was tight, and I had been funding most things, which wasn't right. I told him I would pay for the bigger trips together, because many times I would use my American Airlines points for airfare, Marriott points for hotels, and Avis points for rental cars. But he should pay for more of the dinners and outings. He agreed that was fair. I was still going to be funding my concert obsession and would continue paying for those tickets.

Lastly, I wanted to talk more about the medicine journeys. There were parts of the ceremonies I still didn't understand, and I worried about the overnight stay with other people – women, to be precise – and him being in an altered state of mind. Was it like when you were drunk and your inhibitions were gone and you might do something you wouldn't otherwise do if you were in a normal state of being? No, he said it was nothing like that. There were one or two Shamans facilitating and everyone was absorbed in their own journey – absolutely nothing would happen. Good, I could erase the free-love, orgy image that I pictured from the 60s – everything about these ceremonies was done with purpose and was driven by the intention of spiritual growth. That thought made me feel better, but I guess I wouldn't know until I experienced it myself. Wylie suggested we do a San Pedro journey together in the new year. I agreed that was a good place to start.

We spent Thanksgiving with my extended family. I was excited for Wylie to meet everyone and for them to meet him. He had begun to tell a few friends about me and was finally getting around to telling his extended family that he was getting divorced. By now, there were very few people in my life whom Wylie had not met, and there was no one of any significance who didn't at least know about him. I wished he could say the same about me. But we were making progress in beginning to build a future together, and had been collaborating a lot on our Hiking Adventure business. I was most excited for Wylie to meet my cousin, who sold advertising for a big Phoenix TV station. They met and hit it off, and my cousin invited us to come to the station for a tour and to talk about how he could help us promote our business on the morning show. This could be the big break our little business needed.

In December we met with my cousin at the TV station. We got a tour, and then my cousin showed us how we could advertise when our business got a little bigger. But for now he would help us get on the morning show after the first of the year. We filled out some paperwork and just like that, we would be on the show!

Chapter 25

You Can Do Magic

~song by *America*

https://open.spotify.com/track/5dXED6MP1v1qghkaniirb1?si=3ZB5SK9HRB6nXbsfCwNa9g

Myrtle Beach was a poor substitute for the splendor I had planned with Bora Bora, but it *was* a destination. There was an ocean and a beach – it just wasn't exactly what I had in mind. It turned out that Wylie's divorce had been delayed yet again and would not be finalized now until February or March. It seems we could have kept our Bora Bora trip, after all, but perhaps things were unfolding the way they were destined to unfold.

We were about to board the airplane when I realized Wylie had disappeared. I frantically scanned the terminal and suddenly there he was, walking quickly in my direction with a big smile on his face and a diet Mountain Dew in his hand for me. How sweet – he had been on a quest to bring me my favorite drink. Two flights later we were within minutes of landing in Myrtle Beach, South Carolina. We had been in a deep conversation that we needed to wrap up. It ended for the time being with him telling me he might still need to take a break from our relationship. The look on my face made him add, "Not right now, but some time I might." Wow, he sure knew how to begin our holiday with a bang – a bang that burst the cloud that I had been excitedly floating on in anticipation of our vacation.

When we landed, the rental car company upgraded us to a red Mustang convertible, and Wylie insisted we ride with the top down. It would have been perfect if the high for the day was going to be above 50 degrees, which was freezing for me, coming from Arizona. We arrived during the off-season and the town was deserted. We would be spending two nights and three days, which would make this a quick trip. We checked into our timeshare and were surprised that we had been upgraded to a two-room suite, complete with a large, two-person Jacuzzi hot tub. Things were looking up.

We decided to walk the beach and take a ride on the Ferris wheel. After a lovely day, we found a nice restaurant next to the ocean for dinner, that had fantastically fresh seafood. We then retired to our room, where I lit the candles while Wylie filled the tub. I loved our connection, and I wanted to continue the discussion we had started on the airplane. In the tub, we would have complete privacy, and along with the beer and the warm water, complete relaxation. We talked about our relationship. Wylie was still struggling with the same issue he had always grappled with: he had jumped heart first into our relationship without taking a break after his 24-year marriage. And while he loved "us," he knew at some point he was going to need to take a break. It was difficult to decide when and how to do it, because I was always filling up our calendar far in advance. We always had so many fun things to look forward to, and he didn't want to miss any of them. I reminded him of the saying that life was what happened while you were making other plans. I also reminded him how much time we already spent apart. We didn't live together, and he and I both traveled extensively for work, which automatically created a lot of built-in "away time" from each other. And even when he was in town we still saw each other sparingly, averaging every six to ten days. It wasn't a conventional way to do it, but he was still getting his "alone time." We didn't really have consistent contact, often not even texting because he was remote on a trip, with limited phone service. While he could not really argue with any of my points, and he did understand on an emotional level – which could not be categorized or quantified – but he STILL felt like he needed a break from being in *any* relationship, even in one as amazing as ours.

  Then he began to talk about how our relationship might look on a break. He said we already had a phenomenal friendship, which he cherished, and he needed me to know that no matter what, we would always be friends! He elaborated that he had been in many romantic relationships in his life, and he felt they always had an arc – a beginning and an ending to the relationship. He believed the arc of our relationship *did* have the potential to last the rest of our lives. But when every other relationship had ended for him, it was over – he was done with it and he left it behind without needing to ever look back. But he said *things were very different with me* – we had a magical romantic connection that was like nothing he had ever experienced with anyone in his life. There was more depth to our relationship than he could have ever imagined having with anyone. We had stimulating conversations and a deep spiritual connection that he had not known even existed. We also had a business partnership and he felt we could build a business that was more lucrative than we could dream. I was the whole package and he was NEVER letting go! No matter what, no matter if we were in a romantic relationship or not, WE would be friends and connected for the rest of our lives!! I'm not kidding, the energy in the room rose to a crescendo. I could feel his excitement, but just like he had done to me earlier – it was now my turn to burst his bubble...

  I began: "Wylie, I agree with everything you are saying except for one thing. If we are not in a romantic relationship we will NOT be friends – that is not happening." I could see a look of astonishment followed by confusion cross his face. "I am in love with you, and if we are not together romantically, I will not be in your life in any way – we will NOT be friends! I love you so much there is no way I'm going to step back to be your friend, and then sit by and watch you date and fall in love with someone else. Not when I want to be the one you are in love with. It is not happening! Call it selfish, but my heart would not be able to take that kind of pain. When I broke up with my last boyfriend, John, he wanted the same thing – my friendship – and I was not able to grant it to him for the same reason. When Mark and I decided we could not be together because he would not move to Chicago for me, and I could not move to Texas for him (because my kids were little), we tried to be friends. Mark even asked me, "Can't we be friends who think each other is fucking hot?!" And the answer was no – no, they could not!

I then said to Wylie, "I am SO in love with you I would not be able to just turn that off. The attraction would always be there, and the memory of our sex life that catapults me to another realm would always be there. So I'm sorry – we are either *friends and lovers* or we are nothing."

Wylie's face looked like he just lost his best friend. I knew in that moment, his wheels had been turning this way all along. He had banked on having his cake with me, and eating it too. But it was not going to happen. And I knew he didn't believe I was serious. I had the distinct feeling he thought he could sway me and change my mind. But he had no idea how seriously I meant it; I was DEAD serious! He couldn't understand how I could still be friends with my ex-husband. Well, that was a completely different situation. My ex and I had been together for 29 years – a lot happens in 29 years. Mark had happened in the middle of that time, and my relationship with my ex changed a lot. We were a few months shy of being divorced when we got back together for six more years. But I had been more out than in for those last six years. At the same time, I had been forced into a friendship with my ex while we were still married. When we ended our marriage for good, I loved him but was no longer *in love* with him. It allowed me to remain friends with him.

Wylie didn't like that answer one bit, pointing out that it was okay to be friends if *my* feelings changed, but not the other way around. It was true, and there was nothing he was going to able to do about it. I was in love with him, I was in too deep, and for me it truly was – all or nothing.

The next morning Wylie went on a run alone. We were training for our R2R2R trip, and I think he needed time to let our conversation sink in and face the realization that we would not be friends. He had to either buck up and be "all in" together – or "all out" alone. It was going to be his choice. He returned in good spirits and we had a nice day together. The *America* concert was the highlight of the Myrtle Beach trip. They performed in an elegant, southern-styled concert hall, with red-velvet seats and crystal chandeliers. It was ancient, and so were most of the concert goers. In our 50s, we seemed to be the youngest ones there by far. It was a great show and an "easy in" and "easy out," unlike a lot of concert halls at bigger venues. We were back in the car before 9 p.m. We stopped to buy some Krispy Kreme donuts for dessert on the drive back. For a second night, we filled the jacuzzi and enjoyed a much less heated conversation while eating our donuts. Then we went to our magic place again and, as always, it was heaven.

I was very curious about Wylie's medicine journeys, because they had healing aspects I had begun to directly witness in him. He was a changed man who now strongly believed in a higher power that he had not been able to believe in before his journeys. He was beginning to understand and believe in the spiritual experiences *I* had been having, and he was well on his way on his own spiritual quest. I had been on my journey of spiritual growth and discovery for over 20 years, and was ready to add a medicine journey to my repertoire. Wylie suggested San Pedro cactus medicine, which is part of the mescaline family, as is Peyote cactus. He had had a ceremony with a shaman called Medicine Man, who could come to my house to facilitate a ceremony for the two of us. I was excited because Wylie's experience with this medicine allowed him to feel at one with nature. We formulated a plan to do our ceremony outdoors together in January.

When I woke up the morning of the ceremony, I asked Spirit to send me a sign. Then, as usual, I met Stacy to hike up Black Mountain. As we were hiking, I got my sign – I saw a huge meteorite cross the dimly lit sky. It was extraordinary – I had never seen one that big! When we reached the top of the mountain I read Stacy the intentions I had written down for the healing journey, and she prayed with me.

When Medicine Man arrived at my house, we had a chance to visit for a while before the ceremony. We had never met before. He was a younger guy with a lot of experience for his age, who had spent a lot of time in Peru, South America. These medicines and teachings were his only form of income. He also had recently launched a spiritual podcast and excitedly told me about his last guest interview, who coincidentally lived in Cave Creek, the same town I live in. He told me how the podcast had come about for him, and about this most unusual guest who was an oracle.

An oracle is an advanced Soul, a seer who has both medium and psychic abilities and who can also connect to the Akashic Records, to tell you about your past lives so as to further guide you on your Soul's journey. She had built a special room, filled with crystals that are designed to raise the vibration in the room. You could have a reading with her in person or by phone. I was intrigued by the word "oracle," and I listened intently as Medicine Man told me about her gifts. He had also had a reading with her and thought she was the real deal. I began telling him a little bit about Mark, and shared a story about how Mark had once sent me to an angel connector. I suddenly noticed the music on the TV had begun playing "No Way Out" by *Starship*. Then I "knew," without a doubt, Mark was giving the oracle his blessing – because when that song played I had been thinking I could not wait to connect with her to get a reading. I also decided the *real* reason Medicine Man was in my kitchen was not necessarily for the medicine ceremony, but to tell me about this oracle so I could connect with her. That's how claircognizance (clear knowing) works for me.

The three of us sat down in my backyard while Medicine Man explained how the day would proceed. We all set our intentions, prayed, saged ourselves then drank the concentrated San Pedro cactus juice. I had already called a rideshare driver who would take us to a trailhead where we would walk into the wilderness, and then continue our ceremony. After he dropped us off we took two breaks in the canyon and took another dose at each one. The taste was horrid to me, and also gave me a stomach ache – something I rarely experienced.

I had hiked this area extensively, so I led the way. We had been "in the medicine" for over an hour, and now as we walked I could see a visible connection

~~Once~~ A Cheater...   133

between Wylie's energy and my energy. The substance connecting us reminded me of that alien movie where a trail of liquid silver moved together in one long strand that didn't separate. I also saw what looked like white smoke that also joined our energy together as one. It was symbiotic; it didn't matter what we did or where we went, our energy "moved" together. And I felt like it had been this way not just in this lifetime but through our many lifetimes together. I could literally see our Souls' connection. We reached my favorite bench in the park which had the engraved message: *The romance of a thousand lifetimes begins with a single kiss.* What a profound message to find in the midst of what I was experiencing with our energy connection! Wylie and I sat on the bench together and kissed while Medicine Man snapped a picture that I later hung on our Wall of Adventure.

    We spent the afternoon in the desert lying on blankets and communing with nature. I didn't really feel very different on this medicine than I did in my normal life. As I was lying there looking at the bright blue sky, I received a message in my mind from Spirit: *What if what most people are trying to achieve on this medicine was your normal state of being?* Hmmm, it made sense to me, actually. I spent time nearly every day in nature – communing with it, becoming one with it. I had been working on my spirituality for 20 years, and I had done extensive work clearing my energy and raising my vibration. I had honestly been expecting more revelations on this journey, but it did not have any more effect than seeing Wylie and my energy together and getting that one message from Spirit. Plus a good nap. It was interesting that San Pedro had affected Wylie and Medicine Man so much differently than it affected me. But I did understand that you got what you *need* from these medicines, and perhaps I did get exactly what I needed. As an added bonus, Wylie gave me two heart rocks he had picked for me. It was so sweet and his gesture made me feel so special.

    We took a rideshare back to the house after spending most of the day in the desert. Together we had a nice dinner I had prepared in advance, and we each talked about our individual experiences. I mentioned that I had been seeing butterflies all day and had seen at least 50 of them. This was highly unusual, because it was early January when the daytime temperatures were only in the mid-50s – much too cold for butterflies. Medicine Man had noticed several butterflies as well and told me there had also been fairies or wisps (small, mothlike fliers) circling around my head when I was lying in the desert. Receiving that one message and seeing Wylie's and my true connection made the experience good for me. But I was happier that I would be reaching out to connect with the oracle, because I truly believed that had been the real purpose of the day.

    The next morning Wylie sat at the kitchen table with me, working on our Hiking Adventure business. He read me a list of names he was considering for his Vet Charity, and I indicated my preferences. He was really excited. He was going to first set everything up as a charity, then set up a GoFundMe page where he could promote and raise money for his Everest climb. For every dollar he raised for the climb, he would put a small percentage into the Vet Charity. Then he would find vets who wanted to heal in the awe of nature. He would guide them in beautiful locations, and they would receive the experience for free – funded through the charity. I was really proud of him; I think it's important to give something back to this world we live in. He needed to raise about $30,000 for his Everest climb, and that kind of money would also fund a few vets. It would also give the people who donated the chance to win a free trip with him. It was a worthy plan.

Wylie continued to experiment with plant medicines. He had done a couple Ayahuasca ceremonies and a couple San Pedro journeys. But the most fascinating to me were his Toad journeys, also called Buffo, with the active ingredient 5-MEO-DMT, which was in the same category as DMT, the active ingredient of Ayahuasca. The Toad medicine was a shorter-acting DMT that catapulted you out of your body into "the ether," eliciting an other-worldly experience. People reported that their ego completely dissolved as they were reunited with the true essence of who they are as a Soul. Wylie had been shown aspects of the Universe in his experiences, and had been able to feel the vibration of love that IS the Universe. When he described it, I wanted to do it! I was more drawn to do 5MEODMT (Toad medicine) than anything I can remember. I hadn't felt that way when he described Ayahuasca, and had never been drawn or called to do it. Wylie connected me with a shaman he had worked with, and I arranged to have my first session in the early summer. I read everything I could get my hands on so I could prepare – as much as one can prepare for what is described as the "equivalent" of a near-death experience (NDE). I really could not wait for my experience, and I was happy to be doing a medicine Wylie had not already done with Jane.

Chapter 26

What A Fool Believes

~song by *The Doobie Brothers*

https://open.spotify.com/track/0yTnz5LrBAe1IYL0kSovr4?si=HKfiuiZsQQOEjtKDOEIVPg

"Hi, Laurie." I heard a woman fairly far away call out, as I was coming out of Wylie's CrossFit gym after my workout. I wasn't sure who it was at first, since it was early and still fairly dark outside. As she got closer, I finally recognized her. "Hi...Jane." She didn't stop to talk but said, with a question in her voice "I didn't know you did *CrossFit*" as she passed me and continued walking. I turned back in her direction and replied, as I continued walking backward. "Yes, I've been doing CrossFit for over a year now! Good luck on Aconcagua..." If she replied, she was far enough away that I couldn't hear her. Wylie must have had an early personal training session with her that day. I thought it unusual that we had not run into one another in the year I had been periodically working out in Wylie's class. What an odd comment. I wasn't sure if she was playing dumb about not knowing I did CrossFit; it felt like she was playing games with me. If she truly had no idea I was doing CrossFit, then how would she have known so far away in the darkness that it was me walking out of the gym. She knew where I lived, 30 minutes from there, so it wasn't like she would expect us to periodically run into one another around the neighborhood.

    I wondered if Wylie actually never spoke of me and our relationship to Jane. It was strange, because he spent a lot of time with her – personal training with her a few times a week and training her in hiking, plus all the hiking trips she had taken with our Hiking Adventure business over the last year. And yet she didn't know even the simplest things about me. If they were such "good friends," Wylie even once calling her a "Soul Mate," why wouldn't he talk to her about his personal life. I just didn't get it. Or was he hiding that from her because she *did* have an interest in him, and he had something to lose by highlighting our relationship. The encounter left me with more questions about Jane where Wylie was concerned.

    I thought about her comments on the drive home and how she would be leaving soon for Aconcagua, while her husband was fighting his second bout of cancer that was now diagnosed as stage four, indicating he was nearing the end of his battle. Why go now and risk him dying while she was gone? There would be no way to return in time if he took a turn for the worse. I knew it was because she wanted to go on *this* trip. Wylie was guiding Aconcagua for the first time. Aconcagua, she had expressed to him, had long been in her sights as the ultimate goal – ever since she first hiked R2R in the Grand Canyon several years before. What an unnecessary risk, I thought: the mountain was sure to still be there long after her husband left this Earth.

Wylie had tried to talk her out of going, but she wouldn't have it. She explained that they had discussed it, as a family, and her husband was encouraging her to go – to climb the mountain for him, for her and for their family, to make him proud. Even her sister could not talk her into staying home. I knew Jane had been his primary caretaker for months, and I could not imagine the pressure that would put one under, having never been in that situation. The need to get away and escape must have been overwhelming! But her husband's situation was not permanent, and he would certainly lose his battle sooner than later. Why not delay a trip until then? Nothing made sense to me, and I could not imagine making the decision to be away from my dying loved-one under any circumstance. I don't even know if I would want to leave my dog Storm for that long. Truly, who was I to judge; I had not walked in her shoes. It did reaffirm my suspicion that she had strong feelings for Wylie or she would not be going now. The real question in my mind was, Were her feelings reciprocal? Wylie had addressed these questions with me, affirming Jane was a good friend ONLY. I had to believe him, but I didn't have to feel comfortable with the situation.

As I was having this conversation in my mind, I heard the song "What a Fool Believes" by *The Doobie Brothers*, playing on XM radio. I had been fascinated with this story-song several years before. It's about a man who has a lifelong obsession with a woman from his youth. Many years later they meet and he reveals his feelings to her. Sadly, she does not have the same feelings for him. In the music video, as she walks away the song title is heard: "What a Fool Believes." As I heard these words, I realized this song applied to Wylie and Jane, but in reverse of who was who in the song. I believe Jane had long had feelings for Wylie, even if she had not disclosed them to him directly. But she was not thought of in that way by him: she was a money train – why risk derailing that?!

In my mind, I asked Mark, my Spirit guide on the Other Side, if this could be *true*. Songs have served as signs from Spirit for me for many years, often using lyrics to help me solve a problem or answer an unknown question. As I had that thought, the song made a pause that wasn't normally there. When the song ended, it began playing over again from the beginning! I did a double take, realizing what had just happened. The screen should have updated to play a new song, but it still said "What a Fool Believes" *The Doobie Brothers*. When the song ended for the second time, I pressed the replay button feature to see if the song would still play twice in that mode. But no, it only replayed that one time. In my mind, this confirmed Spirit did indeed take over my radio, making the song play twice, only for me. I had my answer. I foolishly kept getting sucked into believing Jane was a threat that she wasn't.

Chapter 27

Gold Dust Woman

~song by *Fleetwood Mac*

https://open.spotify.com/track/1cioTl6lHVmW4UWKEi8ChG?si=ueRdIJfaSNajNX-HNF12tA

Dinner was being served at my house in a couple hours for my extended family, visiting from out of town. Wylie had just informed me he was going to miss the dinner and not arrive until later in the evening. He had decided he needed to go to an Integration Circle meeting, and this was suddenly more important than my family dinner he had committed to. It seemed I was frequently making excuses for him missing something or other. He really made attending this Integration Circle seem so important. I didn't get it. He mentioned something about wanting to see his couple friends before he would be away for three weeks climbing Mt. Aconcagua. I was sure he would have cancelled the whole night, if we had not been planning to try to get Havasupai reservations early the next morning at my house, I had even upgraded the internet and solicited help for him from my dad and the kids.

  I had recently participated in the San Pedro ceremony, and this would have made me eligible to participate in my first Integration Circle in the medicine community. I wasn't exactly sure how the Integration Circle worked, having never gone, but I knew you talked about your journey and listened to other people's experiences. You were there to support each other and ask questions, but mostly you were connecting with like-minded people. I had been excited to go, but then bummed to discover it was on a night I already had this family dinner planned. I couldn't very well join Wylie and miss my own dinner. I wondered if he was going because Jane wanted him to go, but I wasn't really sure whether she had actually done any medicine ceremonies. Wylie hadn't said that she had, but I suspected it – she did everything he did. I would be pretty mad to find out later he had gone to that meeting in order to accommodate her – especially since he was about to be away from me for three weeks and spending every hour with her as her guide on Aconcagua. By the time he arrived at my house, every relative who wasn't sleeping over had gone home. My aunt and uncle, who were staying with me, had already retired to bed; he would have to meet them in the morning. He did get to meet my cousin and her boyfriend and visit with Rachel, who was home from college. We chatted for a bit, and because it was late, then headed to bed.

The next morning we were up early to prepare for the ordeal of getting Havasupai reservations. I was glad I didn't have the pressure of having to reserve a trip on a certain date, like I did the previous year with the trip for the kids. Wylie had sold one of the upcoming trips for June to some of my friends, who had some flexibility on the dates. He also had a trip he needed to book for September, which had a flexible date as well. We called my dad, who would help us increase the odds of reserving a trip by also trying to book it, remotely from his house. So there were five of us working simultaneously to get the two reservations. When the Supai site opened, we all got on online immediately. I was able to grab the June trip in seconds and head to the check-out. But, just like last year, it *looked* like you got the trip, but then it would spit you out of the check-out page without a secured reservation. This went on for what felt like an eternity before I was successful in finally getting the June reservation.

Wylie, my dad, and Rachel had not had any luck getting any dates in September. Desperation began to set in, and Wylie started trying to move his second trip from a September date to any temperate month, like May or June, because all the dates kept getting taken. It was kind of like trying to buy concert seats – once you put it in your cart, it disappeared for everyone else but you still had to complete the payment before someone else could – these reservations were never guaranteed! Wylie was becoming very frustrated. After a long while, he announced he had been able to get what he needed. He found an available date – but it was going to fall on my 50th birthday. He was sorry, but he was taking it to the checkout, and we would just have to move my R2R2R trip to another day. In disbelief, I protested loudly: "*Not* my actual birthday!" He kept saying sorry, over and over, in a way that was more sarcastic than apologetic – like, too bad for you, you'll just have to deal with it. This was business and there was a lot of money on the line.

I was so pissed I wanted to quit helping him. I only had one 50th birthday – it wasn't just any birthday to me, and we had planned months in advance to celebrate it by going on this R2R2R trip together! I couldn't – and didn't want to – do it without him. Not only would we have to move the R2R2R trip to another date, but he would also miss the party on my actual birthday. All for some money?! I swear to God if I had had the cash I would have gotten it and thrown it at him yelling, *Here, take your money if that is more important than me – more important than my birthday and the plans you already committed to.* It would be one thing if we had had tentative plans, but we didn't. And at one and a half years into our relationship, he had a track record now of not putting me first when it was important. Last night's missed dinner was a perfect example.

By the grace of God, he was not able to check out with the May reservation but was ultimately able to get the reservation he needed in September – and thus NOT on my birthday. I was happy we had both succeeded, but not happy seeing the selfish Wylie emerge once again. He never did apologize for the action, or the implication of not caring – as long as things worked out for him, I guessed. When I asked Stacy her opinion, she gave him a pass because she knew he had been under financial pressure. And she didn't place importance on a birth date the way I did. The bigger issue, to me, was honoring what he had been planning with me and making me feel like a priority. Finally, on top of it all, he didn't tell me...but I suspected this trip included Jane, because he did say that the client was her neighbor.

The next day Wylie was heading for Argentina with Jane. There would be six of them climbing Aconcagua, plus the Sherpa (a native guide). I was greatly bothered that he was going with Jane, and I needed something to keep myself busy and my mind off of her. I decided to buy a new couch and found one I liked, with automatic recliners that raise your feet. They were "automatic," which meant they operated on electricity and had to be plugged in. I only had wall plugs, not floor plugs. Battery packs were sold for them, but I really hated even charging my phone and couldn't imagine wanting to kick back and relax – only to find the couch battery had died. Unfortunately, my couch was in the middle of the room. Another option was to run cords across the floor and get one of those threshold covers so no one would trip. But that would look terrible. I called Sal – he was a builder and would know about floor outlets. Yep, it could be done – we could put new outlets in the floor.

I ordered my new couch, and it was to be delivered on Valentine's Day. Wylie would still be gone, and I would be spending Valentine's Day alone while he spent it with Jane. After I ordered the couch I had a change of heart – not about the couch but about the floors. I hated my floors. I had never liked the 12-inch-by-12-inch tannish-yellow Mexican tile that ran through the entire house except for the bedrooms. It was time for a change, and it looked like I would be taking on a bigger project – I would replace my floors. Sal recommended someone for the job, and while we waited for an appointment with him to come give me an estimate, I found the perfect tile that looked like hardwood floor. After getting three estimates, I made my decision to do it. I was glad I would be starting a project to keep me busy.

The day before Valentine's Day I was working in my home office when the doorbell rang. It was FedEx, holding a 1-800 Flowers box. I didn't know who had sent them, but I hoped Wylie... and they *were* from him! I couldn't have been happier. He had also been in constant contact by text since he left and had sent me a flurry of emojis. I could feel, during this trip, how much he missed me – and I missed him. I took a picture of myself with my flowers in front of our Wall of Adventure that was now 40 pictures strong!

Valentine's Day held two special surprises for me. First, my couch was being delivered in the morning, and second, I was having a one-hour reading with Holly Power, the oracle, in her crystal healing chamber. I was excited about both, but more so about meeting with Holly. On the drive to the reading, I was surprised to hear from Wylie's best friend. He was the owner of International Adventure, the company paying Wylie to guide, and was in contact with Wylie by satellite phone, while he was guiding Aconcagua. He wanted me to know the group was doing great and was set to summit in three days. This was great news! I had still never met this man in person but hoped to be invited to the celebration dinner when the group returned.

The oracle reading was amazing! She talked to me about my energy and my life purpose. She then talked about past lives and brought up Wylie, telling me who we were together as Souls. Lastly, without giving her any information, I asked her who Jane was to Wylie. She described them as being what she called a Soul Mate "hairpin" connection:

"She is just one of his close friends from a past life; she wants that strong connection to him, but it has never happened. She's never met anyone like him. She remembers him because of many of their past lives. He has tried to help her on many avenues, but she hasn't accepted it yet. She makes enough of an improvement that he continues to contract with her in this lifetime, saying 'I'll be there for you and we will check in throughout the lifetime.' It's not about her infiltrating, though she would like to. From her motivation, what you are sensing is true. There is no way ever, ever, ever, ever, ever that she is going to infiltrate the strength and the beauty of what you two have created. There is no way. You are the advanced Soul with this. So for you – go into peace and full 100% trust. I'm telling you there is no way, energetically, she can insert herself. So don't allow her insertion in him to be an insertion in you that brings up anything in you, because that weakens it. We are just allowing him to have the contract with another Soul. She has had other opportunities with him, and he is not interested in going there – he's just not." She gave me a lot to think about, and it would take a couple days to absorb all she had advised.

The day after my couch was delivered and set up, I had to disassemble it into parts and move everything off the floors. The bedrooms were now so full of furniture I had to climb over it to get into my bed! Today was demolition day – it would take two days for the guys to remove the existing tile floor. After they were finished, I spent several hours using a shop vacuum to clean up all the dust and residue to make the underlayment as clean as possible for the new floors to be laid. The entire time I was working on the floors, I thought about Jane and my reading and what the oracle had said about my relationship with Wylie. I had already been having a hard time with my thoughts the entire time they had been gone. Now I could barely get Jane out of my mind. My house was in shambles, and it matched my shambled mind. I wondered how I would feel if Jane fell off the mountain. It wasn't that I really wanted anything bad to happen to her; my life would just be easier if she wasn't in it.

I also just couldn't reconcile Jane being with Wylie while her husband was dying. It felt to me like she was just waiting for him to die so she could make her move on Wylie. She had spent a lot of time with him over the last year – going on a total of seven trips with him. Now she was with him on Aconcagua, and I was sure that for her this was a test to determine whether she could climb Everest – so she could spend three months with him. Wylie didn't think so, but I "knew" otherwise. Of **course** she couldn't have waited for her husband to die and climb Aconcagua next year – because the Wylie train would have left. She needed to do it *now* so she could match his pace, since he had already declared he was hiking Everest the next year. To reel my thoughts back in, I began listening to the recording of the oracle talking about Wylie's and my relationship. I needed to focus on that instead of on her. I really had no control over her or over anything she did.

During the time Wylie was gone, I was able to confirm that Jane did indeed participate in an Ayahuasca ceremony, and, based on the timing, she did it together with him. If anyone needed a healing Spiritual journey, it was probably her, especially with her husband battling cancer. Participating in an Ayahuasca ceremony also meant she would have been eligible to attend the Integration Circle meeting. So I may have been correct about the conclusion I had come to before they left, with regard to why he was so intent on going to the meeting. Wylie had once again withheld information from me about Jane – and I caught him. I wondered now if she had also done the Toad journey with him. Even after having my own San Pedro journey, I still didn't like the idea of them doing these ceremonies together – I didn't need them to be tied to each other in yet another way. This was all becoming just too much for me! I also thought back to one year earlier when she had been at my house and I showed her the "portal" in my meditation room. Based on her comment, I didn't feel she had ever been on ANY kind of Spiritual journey. It just seemed like she would do anything Wylie would do. I couldn't brush it all away or reconcile it any longer – there were just too many things bothering me now! Even the comforting messages from the oracle didn't dispel my negative thoughts.

Two days after Valentine's Day, I discovered a voicemail from a strange number – an international number. When I saw that it had actually come in on Valentine's Day, I realized who had called. Then I heard his voice: *Hi babe, just calling to wish you a Happy Valentine's Day from camp two on Aconcagua. I hope you are having a great day. I miss you, love you...take care, bye.*

Wylie did summit Aconcagua – with his entire team! It was an incredible feat, especially when you knew that the group ahead of them and the group behind them had not successfully summited. He let everyone make one victory call with the satellite phone from the top of the mountain. I wished he had called me. He called his kids instead – sadly, they didn't answer. But when I thought about it I realized that, since it had taken me two days to discover the message he had left me on Valentines' Day, I likely wouldn't have answered either. So instead of feeling bad, I was grateful – grateful that the man I loved had thought of me on Valentine's Day when he was in the midst of such a difficult feat. He wanted me to know he was thinking about me – and had even gone one step further and sent me beautiful flowers. I was also grateful for the frequent contact from him and for what we had...even if I still wanted more.

I was able to see Wylie the day after he got back. I wanted to hear all about the trip. We met for a long, early dinner and a movie. He brought me heart rocks from the top of Mt. Aconcagua, and that was beyond special to me! For him, I had compiled my notes from the reading with Holly, the oracle, but instead of reading her thoughts in the order she had shared them, I wanted him to first hear what she said about us. I wanted to play the recording so he could see that what she said was completely unsolicited by me. It was amazing what Holly knew about our relationship. I didn't wear a ring that indicated I was even in a relationship, and because of Wylie's secrecy, we did not have anything on Facebook that tied us together as a couple. Even though we had been together for almost a year and a half, we were still hidden on social media – not to mention in his real life, despite his divorce now being final. I hit the play button and Holly's words began:

"Let's go into the Akashic Record and look at the very strong relationship as someone who is deeply connected, like a boyfriend. I don't see a marriage connection – it's something even higher than a marriage connection. I see him looking at you in a gaze, with no other woman and no other anything in his life, not even work – that's how connected you are. You need to know there is nothing more important in his life than making sure you are okay. So the two of you coming together tells a full story. Instead of both of you being so alike, I love that you bring the whole of one and the whole of the other so together you are twice what you were – rather than half what you were, which is what many relationships are. This is a divine Soul Mate connection with you – I'm going to put it in a Twin Flame aspect."

Chapter 28

Get Outta My Dreams, Get into My Car

~song by *Billy Ocean*

https://open.spotify.com/track/3v8vsQfMQio7ohYqFrEsaZ?si=ipodZZI3QzS-zvOoSPv9iw

Wylie called me one day to ask if he could use my Jeep for a daytrip adventure. He had advertised a Sedona 4-wheeling daytrip and had a client interested in purchasing it. We had vaguely discussed this type of trip when I was thinking about purchasing my Jeep, but we had never formalized any type of agreement. My recollection was vague, and I didn't really remember that he had put an official itinerary together and had been advertising my mojito-green Jeep. He used pictures of it, and since he had advertised mine he couldn't just go out and rent any Jeep. And renting one would eat all the profits, compared to using mine and just paying for some gas. I pushed back because I didn't feel comfortable with the idea. I had recently used my old Jeep Cherokee on a very rough, off-road trip and had broken three motor mounts! I felt that if something happened to my new Jeep while he was using it, I wouldn't be able to discern if it had been from his or from my usage. Then I would be put in the uncomfortable position to determine who should pay for a repair. He suddenly got very passive aggressive, and wondered out loud why I had even bothered to purchase a 4-wheel vehicle if I was *only* going to drive it around on the streets. He said I should have just bought another Jeep Cherokee. I remembered how he had been so "gung ho" about me buying my Jeep Wrangler. He had encouraged me to buy it, even telling me how "hot" I would look driving around in that Jeep – just manipulating me for his own gain. I did not want to believe it.

Wylie had lived and guided in Sedona for seven years and had been a semi-professional 4-wheel driver for Range Rover back in his Adventure Racing days. I trusted his abilities, but I didn't want him to wreck my expensive new Jeep. He talked me into going to Sedona to show me what my Jeep was capable of on the trails.

My Jeep was literally rock climbing. We maneuvered up and up and up, finally playing king of the hill at the top by getting out to enjoy the sweeping view. What goes up must come down, and one steep hill in particular on the trail seemed very dangerous. When presented with the downward slope from the top of the hill, I had a white-knuckle grip and could not speak. Halfway down I became so scared I couldn't hold back tears. The grade was so steep I felt like the tires would lose traction and perilously slide down the hill. Wylie took it real slow, which made it seem like time stopped. It was one thing to feel that way when you were locked into a tried and tested rollercoaster ride, and quite another to be strapped into and risking my own vehicle. He, of course, was never worried for one second and laughed at my reaction. Overall, we 4-wheeled and had a great day and even added a new picture to our Wall of Adventure.

    He took me out for dinner after the Jeep run, and we talked in more detail about how his Aconcagua trip had gone. They had successfully summitted, and he did now feel even more prepared for Everest. Months ago I had expressed an interest in going on the first part of his Everest trip with him; that way we would get to travel there together, and I would climb up to Everest Base Camp with him. It would also reduce a couple of the weeks we would spend apart, since he would be on that mountain for three long months. Wylie had done the Base Camp climb a few years before with his best friend and knew what to expect. When I first brought it up, he had expressed great excitement at me wanting to go with him. But now, sitting in front of me, he drastically changed his mind, telling me he was sorry but I could not go with him. What had changed?! In my mind, even though he didn't say it, it was Jane. I guessed Jane was now thinking of climbing Everest, since she had conquered Aconcagua. Wylie denied she would climb Everest, but I wasn't buying it. I didn't understand how he had gone from really excited at the idea of me going with him, to a firm resolve for me staying home. He explained what a difficult mental task Everest was going to be, and how he would need all of his concentration focused on that climb. I had the potential to be a distraction. There were aspects of Wylie and how he reasoned and thought about things that I was NEVER going to understand! Wouldn't it be awesome to have the support of the person you loved...?

    I disclosed to him a little bit about what I had gone through mentally while he was on his trip, knowing he was with Jane in dangerous situations, and how my mind took me to dark places I didn't like. I shared additional insights from my reading with the oracle, because we had only briefly covered it and had headed to a movie instead. He was intrigued. I shared the oracle's revelations about the past-life connections between him and Jane. It was time for me to put this Jane issue to bed! I felt Wylie had been playing **both** sides and had not been as forthright with me about the relationship as he needed to be. He agreed to let me ask every question I ever wanted to know about her, and we continued the conversation on the entire drive back home.

    Wylie explained how Jane had been such a private person and didn't open up to many people. He shared everything he knew about her relationship with her dying husband, who had miraculously survived her being away on the Aconcagua trip. The two of them had had a great relationship, doing lots of things together like playing tennis and raising their children. She had a hard time with

~~Once~~ A Cheater...

his second bout of cancer, because he was in denial about it and eventually in a lot of pain that caused him to push everyone away – including her. It must have been an awful experience to want to help the one you love, knowing you could only do so much, then having him rebuff you. No wonder she had gone on the trip; maybe the break had been good for both of them. From his standpoint, it must have been very demoralizing to go from a powerful successful lawyer to a shell of a man being ravaged by cancer. I felt more sorry for Jane in that moment than any other feeling. And for me knowledge is power. Hearing these things put certain events in perspective. Perhaps she went on so many trips over the last year, not only to help Wylie but to escape to nature from her situation. But I am pretty intuitive, and I know what my intuition felt on that last trip I took to Zion with her. Her energy and her actions pointed toward an interest in Wylie – confirmed by both Stacy and the oracle. And it made sense, because he had been helping Jane over the last several years to get stronger through the personal training and all the hiking trips. It would be easy to have admiration and feelings of love toward someone who brought out the best in you, made you stronger in several ways, and showered that much attention on you – even if you were paying them well to do it. Even though I now felt better about Jane, I knew the issues around her would never be completely buried.

Wylie's best friend scheduled a victory dinner at the last minute, on the night we already had plans with friends to go to a comedy club. Wylie chose to go to the last-minute victory dinner instead of letting his best friend know he already had plans with me – and I was not even invited. He explained it was more of a "business" discussion than a celebration – his best friend planned to incentivize everyone with special pricing to climb Everest. Just as I had suspected, Jane was planning on potentially climbing Everest, and that would explain Wylie's change of heart for me going on the Everest Base Camp climb. No matter how many Jane discussions we had, I was always left with more questions than answers. Why, after all this time, was I purposely excluded?

I allowed Wylie to take my Jeep on the 4-wheel client trip. He was pumped – and I was nervous. I had only reluctantly agreed to let him use my Jeep for this *one* trip. BUT I requested he **not** take it down that steep hill with his clients, especially since there was another less risky route down, and that section of the trail was optional. I bargained that they would still have a great time without that part, and I would feel better about letting him use my Jeep.

A few days later Wylie returned my Jeep from the successful 4-wheeling adventure. I asked him if he had skipped the part I had requested him to. He got a sly grin on his face and admitted he *did* take the clients on the one and only part I asked him not to. He was continuing to do whatever he wanted, as long as it served *him*, regardless of what I had requested. It seemed that the more generous I was, instead of appreciating it, he just pushed the envelope. One thing was certain, he wasn't going to be using my Jeep again for clients, and to his credit, he never put me in that position again by asking.

~~Once~~ A Cheater...

Chapter 29

Magic

~song by *Olivia Newton John*

https://open.spotify.com/track/56BSwBKWHYIdQOgYLHiehs?si=6RA-gieRTv2jTciNzwNVfg

Wylie had been talking to me about his recent experiences with psilocybin, the active psychedelic ingredient in mushroom medicine. He had taken this very seriously, the way he had with San Pedro and Ayahuasca. They were medicines designed for self-discovery and Spiritual work, and he suggested we try it together. I wondered if I would have a better experience with this medicine than I did with San Pedro, which didn't seem to have much effect at all. We agreed to do it at my house.

Wylie arrived with the psilocybin on St. Patrick's Day, and we were going to celebrate the mushroom instead of the four-leaf clover. I did make corned beef and cabbage in advance, because I doubted we would want to make dinner when we finished. I had already saged the house to clear out any negative energy, and to be fully prepared for the ceremony we would also need to sage each other as well. We talked first about our intentions, and at 3:30 p.m. we took the small, infused dark chocolate with sea-salt truffles, cheers'ed each other and ate it.

Since Wylie had already experienced a few journeys, the medicine began to take effect more rapidly for him. He also took a slightly higher dose than I took. We laid outside on lounge chairs, staring at the bright blue sky while listening to Wylie's Medicine Music playlist. I looked intently at everything around me and could feel nothing unusual. I wondered if this was going to be a dud, like it seemed to be last time with San Pedro, because I never really felt much of an effect. At some point I noticed the colors had become a little more intense, and Wylie could tell I was beginning to feel the effects of the medicine. He was already well on his way. It seemed like his music got louder, and I heard a lot of Indian chanting and drumming. I didn't like it. Couldn't stand it. Hated it! This was not normal for me, and I was beginning to feel strange feelings. I had previously read that under the effect of this medicine, music was supposed to be enhanced in a good way, so I couldn't understand my reaction. I actually had to hold my hands over my ears like a little kid. It was so awful and intense, I needed to close out every bit of sound. I sat like that in my lounge chair for a while, and thought *this is crazy, I need MY music*. I got up and Wylie asked, "Hey, where are you going?" I mumbled something and went inside to get my headphones. I felt a little "off." My intention was to just use the music on my phone and sit outside where I had been, using my headphones. But now that seemed dumb. I went back outside, told Wylie his music was bothering me, and moved to the hammock.

My next door neighbor was outside and I prayed he wouldn't see me; I didn't want to engage in conversation. I quickly lay down, hiding my body in the hammock like it was a cocoon. I was about to pick my own music, and it seemed like Wylie turned his music volume down. Then I noticed the birds were *really* loud. I had more interest in connecting with nature anyway, so I just closed my eyes. I saw an image in my mind of a person's upper body made of each continuing color of the rainbow. Like a kaleidoscope, it would just rotate over and over in swirling colors. Then it seemed to get more intense and move faster, like the image itself was having an orgasmic effect, rising higher and higher to a single point of orgasm – until I decided I didn't want to look at it anymore because it was nonsensical to me.

When I opened my eyes the world around me was so much more intense and defined than it had ever seemed before, as if all the colors were deeper and brighter and the edges were sharper. I felt like I had suddenly acquired hyper-vision. The stucco on the side of my house was fascinating! My mind wanted to connect the shapes in the stucco and make pictures of them somehow. The stucco moved and was very three-dimensional, not like it usually is – flat with no pictures. Then I noticed the smells! My neighbor had an outside fire going, and it smelled like smoke and maybe pot. It was so strong and intolerable – I couldn't stand it. I had to get away. It seemed just awful. This medicine had heightened all of my senses beyond what was normal.

I entered the house and was utterly blown away by the color and depth of the TV screen, and also by the movement of everything in the room. The light made my living room seem so beautiful. I realized how important aesthetics are to me, and I was happy that I had redone my floors to make the house beautiful. I looked at the wall my TV was hung on, and it seemed really, really close. Then I closed my eyes and when I opened them again the wall seemed quite far away, then up high, then down low, and so on for quite a while. The entry into my bedroom seemed like it was the entryway to a basement. Then it seemed super close to me. All these thoughts made me think about how our common reality is formed in the mind and contingent on how the mind is conditioned, because I knew how the entry to my room was "supposed" to look. These new perceptions were not the norm. The background screen of the TV displayed waves of the most beautiful violet-purple hue. There were squares on the screen and each had a single vivid color in the brightest shade of yellow or green or red, etc. Everything was SO sharp – I was seeing with pure clarity, like it had all been dull all my life. I was reminded how putting glasses on makes your vision crystal clear – only I didn't need glasses.

Wylie walked into the house to use the bathroom and caused me to notice the time was 5:24 p.m. We were already two hours into the ceremony! My mind freaked out a little, because it didn't seem like more than a few minutes had passed in the hammock, and I had only been in the house a short time. I pointed out to Wylie how late it was and he was shocked too. We walked outside together and each of us lay back down in our own chairs. I felt an overwhelming need to lie with him, and I asked him to hold me. He obliged, moving us to a little sofa under my covered porch. I noticed how vivid the mesquite tree looked – how beautiful, how defined, and how bright the sky was too. Everything looked so much prettier than it did in "normal" life.

He told me to close my eyes, and I said I couldn't. I wanted to, but I wouldn't do it. Every once in a while he would tell me to close my eyes again, and I would say I couldn't. I kept thinking, *When he comes out of this, he's going to be mad at me because I'm ruining his experience by being so close to him.* I wondered if he would be mad because he didn't get to be separated with no interaction. His previous medicine journeys had been experienced alone, without interruptions from anyone. He began sloppily caressing my face – kind of hitting it, then missing it, and resting his hand in an odd places. It annoyed me slightly. He would stroke my face, but then his hand would block my eyes and my view. I would let it rest there for a minute because I didn't want to disturb him – but I finally moved his hand away. Then he began breathing so heavily – half snoring, half making really weird loud noises, almost moaning. I asked if he was ok. He answered me like normal and not in some heavy dream state like it seemed he was. But he was so loud I kept thinking my neighbor was going hear us. These noises could *not* sound normal to anyone!

Then I wanted to close my eyes and reluctantly did so. This time Wylie began to caress my face normally, but he was still breathing very heavily. I started following his breathing, and I felt like we were both in sync, and we were loud. For a moment, I thought about the neighbors again – but then I didn't care anymore. Wylie said, over and over, very softly, "Laurie, it's okay. You are safe. I won't let anything happen to you, trust me..." I started feeling tears streaming down my face. Then I "let go" and we were somewhere else – I didn't feel my body. Wylie seemed slightly above me – but then he WAS me, and I WAS him. Our breathing was the same – we had merged into one, and I could talk to him in my mind: *Can you feel this? Can you hear me?* It seemed like we were one Soul together, floating in a space somewhere. And it felt normal and natural, more real than "real life." I was more me in that place than I ever had been in my own body. We were like that for what seemed like a long time, but time did not seem to exist there.

Somehow I came out of it. I felt his body next to mine and started sobbing. I cried harder at the realization of the enormity of what we were *together*! I now had a knowingness of our true connection, our true state of being. I could feel tears on my face. (Wylie later said he didn't hear or feel me sobbing, and I realized I may not have even done that out loud – or for real.) I could hear the neighbors again, and *they* were loud but also seemed so far away. I followed Wylie's breathing again and noticed the song "Magic Carpet Ride" playing in the background. It felt perfectly placed. Then I heard Wylie say softly, over and over again, "Just let go, just let go Laur...just let go..." And I let go. I went back to where we had been before. (Wylie told me later he was "holding space" for me to join him – he was holding space both for himself and for me.) We were one once again. I told him how much I loved him, as I was coming back out of it again. I felt an overwhelming feeling of pure LOVE, and my mind became my own again. My first thought was, *Did that just happen?! We were one!!! Oh. My. God. I cannot believe what just happened – was that real?!* Wylie suddenly got up and said, "Yes! Wasn't that wild?! I have to pee." (Later, I chuckled at that.)

I was still out of it, almost couldn't feel my body and I was conscious of watching him move to pee outside, and I told him, "Don't pee outside, the neighbors will see you!" Then I said, "We were one." He said, "We can go back there again if you want..." He laid back down and told me I was generating heat, but my body was only a vague sensation of tingling to me. I could not feel any part of my body. We went back "there" again. After a while, I heard him talking out loud like he was far away. He was saying, "This is real!! THIS is why nothing matters, why the bullshit of boyfriend and girlfriend is an insult – NO! We are far, far more than that. Do you see now? Do you see what we are? That is true, unconditional love; that is the true space of love and how living together or not living together doesn't matter. That experience was better than any sex, better than any orgasm!" We had experienced, as Souls, what it was like to be ONE in a pure state of unconditional love.

He still sounded far away to me because I wasn't fully back in my body. And when I started to slowly come out of the medicine I heard him talking normally. He said, "Wasn't that wild?!" I could only feel my body in tingles of energy, waves of energy. I opened my eyes and hugged him so tightly like I couldn't get close enough. I looked at the sky and it was dusk and the stars were already coming out, and all the stars I could see in the sky were moving. I asked him if he saw all the stars moving. He said he did, and then said, "But they aren't really moving, except for that plane." I didn't see a plane. He told me we went back in again one more time to that space where our bodies dissolved into nothing, and then it was almost like we separated. Again, I slowly felt my body coming back and I realized one of my feet felt really cold. My whole body should have felt freezing, as it gets cold in the desert quickly, but I hadn't noticed any temperature sensation until now. Then I felt the pain in my finger from where I had cut it earlier while making dinner, and it really hurt. I realized I hadn't felt my throbbing finger or my body for a very long time – for hours. Then Wylie declared he had to go to the bathroom again, and as he got up I noticed the song "White Rabbit" by *Jefferson Airplane* had just begun playing. It was the song I had been hearing in my mind all afternoon, before we took this journey, and I had meant to play it but had run out of time. Not only did the lyrics fit – which were about mushrooms and how your mind was moving – but it was also a *Starship* song that Mark had played in every concert I had ever seen him in, so it felt like a confirmation at the end of our experience since it was Wylie's music, not mine, that was playing.

I got up to go in the house and I was just laughing at the song and the timing and the enormity of it ALL! And my overwhelming feeling in the house was of awe and amazement and total disbelief about what we had both just experienced. All I could do was stand there and look at Wylie with my hands over my mouth and my eyes wide, and say "I can't believe it!!! I cannot believe what just happened!" Then I had to go see my face in the mirror... I just had to look at my own face in the mirror. Wylie called out behind me, "Where are you going? I'm eating – I'm starving!!" It was my face in the mirror all right. I grinned at myself, still in total disbelief – also noting my pupils were huge!

The corned beef was totally ruined from an extra four hours in the oven. When it had finished cooking earlier, I had turned the oven off but just left it in there. It was all dried out and more like beef jerky. My diet Mountain Dew tasted really sweet – too intense. As we ate dinner we both compared our experiences and Wylie said his "*Lion Caté*" came out to take over – he couldn't help it, he always come out in his medicine journeys, and that was who was coaxing me to just let go. Then Wylie turned very serious and said, "Also, this is why if I were to never see you again it wouldn't matter, we are *always* connected – no matter what!"

~~Once~~ A Cheater...

Chapter 30

Waiting for a Star to Fall

~song by Boy Meets Girl

https://open.spotify.com/track/5J6dMtMyhaNCBojLxpdbzb?si=1qRJeCDnQKCbif8qpZ8LOQ

My cousin contacted us as expected to let us know we had been scheduled to appear in April on the Arizona Daily Mix, a morning TV show on KAZT-TV/NAZT-TV. I was really excited about the timing because we already had several permits and reservations for hikes in the Grand Canyon, Havasupai and Zion that we needed to sell! I had recently completed the website listing the various itineraries we offered, and the logo was being designed by a graphic designer. We had just received the final design copy, and everything for our thriving little Hiking Adventure business was falling into place.

Wylie had been able to sell some big lucrative trips over the last several months. Several of them were funded by Jane. She had contributed a lot in helping Wylie get this business off the ground. (I don't know that she would have been so anxious to help if she had understood my true involvement.) He was still supplementing his income by guiding trips for two large companies, but sooner than later, he wanted to be on his own where he could earn what he was worth. I thought this TV exposure had the ability to catapult our business to the next level.

Unbeknownst to me, Wylie had different ideas. He informed me that he had already spoken to my cousin, who had helped him submit an interview agenda to talk instead about his Everest climb and his Vet Charity. He felt raising money was his biggest need, and for now it took precedence over the Adventure Hiking business. While I understood where he was coming from and knew he was under pressure to raise this money, I was more than a bit miffed. He had not even mentioned one word of it to me before setting that ball in motion.

On Thanksgiving, I introduced Wylie to my cousin so that we – together – could promote our Adventure Business. We even talked about how we would go on the air together to promote it, maybe even wearing shirts made with our new logo. I wasn't quite sure if his change of heart had to do with his need to raise money – or his need to still keep me a secret. I felt like he had gone behind my back instead of facing me head on, because the real reason was that he didn't want to be seen with me on TV. Come on! Lots of people partner in businesses together – we didn't have to walk on set holding hands and kissing. The way he did it seemed underhanded to me, and he never made any kind of apology or even acknowledged that he had taken away *from us* the opportunity to showcase and sell the Hiking Adventure business. I had invested a lot of time building the website, I had paid for equipment for our business, and I had financed permits for trips a year out. I had even been doing daily "commercials" on whomever I happened to cross paths with, to help him find leads for our business. I also helped design itineraries and come up with trip ideas around full moon adventures and hidden gem adventures – and in the end, he took it *all* away from us. The irony with the TV promotion was that through fundraising he was looking for people to support him by donating money, and even though his Vet Charity was itself a worthy venture, if he had instead promoted our Hiking Adventure business, it could have generated significant revenue and endless referrals. This would have brought in enough money for him to earn what he needed for his Everest climb. Not only that but it seemed to me that for someone who talked a lot about wanting to "own himself," funding your own Everest trip with money *you earned yourself* would be a nice step in that direction.

    I was seeing a more self-centered side of Wylie and it wasn't my favorite part of him. I didn't say much because he had already set the wheels in motion and made the decisions, and it was too late to change. I did go with him for moral support while he had his interviews for Everest and the Vet Charity – which were great. They were so good in fact he was later invited to be on another show to talk in more detail about the Vet Charity. As for me, I was starting to doubt that my investments in our business were going to pay off anytime soon. I had not taken one dime from the business, and chances were looking slimmer that working for it would be any kind of exit strategy from my current career into this one in the near future, if ever.

Chapter 31

Silent Lucidity

~song by *Queensrÿche*

https://open.spotify.com/track/6OSyCAmXT4Gkd3OQ2aPOaF?si=eHRLZvOqRJSEnMeOJWYvDA

After Wylie returned from Aconcagua, our life together became more normal. The talk we had in Sedona calmed a lot of my fears, and I felt it had brought us closer together, as had our mushroom journey. Wylie also started to become more accepting in general of our relationship. I had recently met a longtime friend of his and his wife at an Integration Circle. He had told his friend about me long before, and I assumed the wife knew as well. It wasn't until I met her that I realized from the questions she asked me that she had *no* idea we had even been dating, let alone that we had been in a relationship for almost two years. That was disappointing to me and very telling. But Wylie suggested we all get together for dinner, and I felt he was finally beginning to see things through my eyes. When they came to my place a few weeks later, we had a lovely evening together. I genuinely liked them, and it was nice to feel like Wylie wanted me to be more visible in his life.

Wylie's spirit medicine guide, whom he called *Lion Caté*, had given him an idea. He had been toying with the thought of getting a tattoo for almost as long as I had known him. He had several ideas, but none ever seemed to resonate enough for him to make the idea permanent. One day, close to his birthday in April, he accompanied his roommate when she went to get a tattoo. It was then he realized he wanted to get a tattoo of a lion's head on his shoulder to represent *Lion Caté*. He would have a large four-leaf clover inlayed on the lion's face to make it his own unique design. After the tattoo artist drew up the design, Wylie scheduled an appointment to have the idea made permanent on his birthday.

To support his more than six-hour tattoo application, I worked half a day and had plans to meet him so I could see the last hour or two. Unfortunately, the tattoo artist had worked more quickly than anticipated and I arrived just as he was finishing. The lion was in full color and beautifully done, with gorgeous blue eyes. It was also much larger than I had anticipated. I loved it, although I also loved his body without anything on it, so it would take some getting used to. I took him out for dinner to celebrate his birthday, and afterwards we went back to his place to initiate *Lion Caté. Rooaarrrrrrr!*

The month of May brought with it my 50th birthday party, our R2R2R Grand Canyon adventure, and some very cool event opportunities. My sister Stephanie called me one day to tell me she had just watched a YouTube video she thought I should watch. When she mentioned that it was over two hours long I laughed, because I didn't really have that much time to sit down to watch it. I was juggling a few projects around the house as usual. To entice me to watch, she added that it was the *Joe Rogan Show* and he was interviewing a man who was talking about medicine journeys – specifically, DMT. Now she had my attention. I was doing a landscaping project, so I pulled up the video podcast on my phone and listened as I worked. At the end of Joe's interview with author and journalist Graham Hancock, he mentioned that Graham was touring the country. I was curious and looked up his tour schedule and discovered he would be speaking in Sedona – less than two hours from my house – in just two weeks' time. And as a bonus, Dr. Rick Strassman – who had studied DMT for years and had written a book called *DMT, the Spirit Molecule* – would also be speaking, on the night before Graham was to speak. Tickets were available and I purchased one for Wylie and one for me. The talks were on the two consecutive days after we returned from our R2R2R hike. I was excited that I would have more time with Wylie, who was also very excited about seeing these two speakers. I also marveled at the timing of my sister having seen the interview, and my luck that the event was so near to me and I could see them in person in a very short time. It seemed divinely orchestrated, especially since I would be having my own DMT journey the next month.

We were not disappointed by the speakers. They were super informative and helped me to better understand, spiritually, the healing powers these medicine journeys offered – especially those involving DMT. DMT is the active psychedelic ingredient in both Ayahuasca and the Toad medicine. It is produced in the brain only two or three times in your life – when you are born (Soul enters the body), when you die (Soul leaves the body), or if you have a traumatic experience like a Near Death Experience (Soul both leaves and re-enters the body). In fact, many people describe their journey on these medicines as near-death experiences and come away enlightened in various ways. It is referred to in that way not because your body clinically dies (it doesn't), but because these are the closest words to describe the experience. By contrast, an out-of-body experience is your Soul exiting your body in a way that it then "sees" or perceives the body from a different viewpoint; alternatively, you might view other locations on Earth or elsewhere. With these medicine journeys, you leave your body and also your ego dissolves, such that you don't in that state even identify with who you are in your body. You leave the physical earth plane and cross the veil to the Other Side, often having experiences with angels or entities or even God, in a place that is not this earth plane. That had certainly been the case multiple times for Wylie.

After each talk, we were able to personally meet the speakers, Dr. Rick Strassman and Graham Hancock, even getting our pictures taken with them. In many ways I felt my life was becoming more mystical, and I loved the direction Wylie and I had gone together as a couple.

Wylie was going to be guiding a trip over the Memorial Day holiday, and a girl from the CrossFit class asked me if I wanted to partner with her for a big workout at Wylie's gym. It was called Murph's Challenge, a workout that a fallen Marine used to do, and it was named in his honor. Murph's Challenge was done at CrossFit gyms all over the country. I had heard about this workout the year before but had not tried it, and having nothing else going on, I agreed to do it with her. I arrived at the gym before her and was standing around waiting for her when Jane walked in. I was very surprised to see her there, because the thought of her doing this workout had never entered my mind. I walked up to her to say hello and she greeted me with, "Hi, Laurie. Of *course* you're here, where else would you be today." Wow, not only was that a super weird comment, but from her tone of voice it seemed kind of rude. Knowing she had Asperger's Syndrome, a condition associated with difficulties in social interactions, I just smiled at her. About that time, my friend walked in, and to my surprise we all three did the workout together.

My friend and I did the full workout, less the 20-pound weighted vest that some people wear while doing it. Jane did a more modified version using pull-ups with rings instead of bar pull-ups, and she did a shorter run. I thought that amusing, since she had been taking CrossFit classes and had been personal training with Wylie all those years. Plus, hadn't she just climbed one of the Seven Summits two months before? I assumed she would have been stronger than me. As it turned out, the joke was on me, because after doing 100 banded pull-ups, 200 pushups, 300 squats and a one-mile run, I was so sore over the next two days that I could barely bend my arms. It was probably the most sore I had ever been from a workout in my life. Admittedly, with Jane there watching me, I had stepped up my workout. Actually, I'm so competitive I probably would have done the workout the same way had she been there or not. Anyway, I never did mention Jane's comment to Wylie.

Right before I left for a business trip to Colorado I heard a song I had not heard in many years called "Silent Lucidity." I became obsessed with this song and spent many hours while driving around Colorado playing it on repeat. It has a very mystical, other-worldly aspect to it that was in total alignment with where my life had been heading. My life was changing in many ways.

I would often have dinner with Wylie, then stay over at his place and go with him in the morning to take his 5:30 a.m. CrossFit class. Wylie always started his class by asking some question like, *What are your plans for the weekend?* Everyone who wanted to share could answer. But this day he became very stoic and announced, without making any kind of eye contact with me, that Jane's husband had passed away the day before. I think I was the most shocked person in the room! Not because he died – he had cancer after all, and I was expecting his death – but because Wylie had known since the day before and had not breathed a word of it in the 12 hours we had just been together. It felt like a slap in the face! I asked him later why he didn't tell me and he said we were having such a great night he didn't want to put a damper on the evening. Then I asked him why he hadn't told me when we got up, before class. He said he hadn't been thinking about it until he got to class and one of the girls wanted to announce it. He added that he was unhappy about announcing it to the class because Jane was such a private person – which just seemed like such a ridiculous statement. I don't think many things are as public as a funeral or a memorial designed to have as many people as possible celebrate the life of the person who just died. I asked about the funeral arrangements and he said the family was only planning on doing a memorial in September. When I asked him if he would be going to the memorial, he shocked me for a second time by saying no, he would not attend.

  I still could not wrap my head around the strangeness of their relationship. Jane spent on average over $1,200 a month paying Wylie for personal training and the many trips she went on with him over a year's time. He told me over and over again she was his "good friend," once even calling her a "Soul Mate." They had also done several medicine journeys together. And yet he was not going to attend her husband's memorial?! What was I missing? It really made me wonder if there was some sick, twisted, hidden sexual relationship between them. Was there something to feel guilty about that would keep Wylie from wanting to go – if not to pay his respects to her husband, then to support his good friend? No matter how hard I tried, I could not reconcile this very unusual relationship. I voiced concerns of a twisted relationship between them to Stacy, who laughed at me and told me my active imagination was working triple time....

  The day of my Toad medicine journey had finally arrived. I was beyond excited for this special healing experience when I greeted the shaman who would be guiding my journey. She knew I had been recommended to her by Wylie, who had had two experiences with her. I brought her a heart rock I had hand-picked specially for her from my collection. She smiled and said, "When Jane did her session with me she brought me a heart rock too!" *You have got to be kidding me – double whammy!* I asked the shaman if Jane had done her Toad journey recently, and she had not. I remembered asking Wylie if Jane participated in a Toad medicine journey at the same time he did. He said she had not. Yet it was obvious by the shaman even referencing Jane to *me* that the common denominator could only be Wylie. Secondly, didn't I remember Jane snickering at my finding heart rocks on both the Sedona and Zion full-moon adventure trips? Yet I find that she herself is now looking for, finding and giving away heart rocks! Here I was trying to be mentally prepared for this incredible journey and now I instantly felt anxiety at both of these new pieces of information. No matter how hard I tried, it seemed I could not escape Jane.

  By all rights, Jane should have been inconsequential to me. But it did hurt knowing that over time Wylie had lied and withheld information about her – why? In any case, it did not matter today; I needed to get back to center. I shared my new song obsession with the shaman and we listened to it together. The song put me back in a better state of mind. I talked about my intentions and we said a prayer. She saged me and sent me on my journey.

  I would like to describe my heavenly journey, where I left my body for 20 earth minutes and was reunited with who I really am: the true essence of my Soul. I was in the place of pure LOVE and at one with the light. Unfortunately, I do not have human words to describe the power of our Soul, the vibration of our Soul, or the Love we truly are. All I can say is this was the single most profound experience of my entire life. I experienced the true essence of me, of who I am as a SOUL. And I was allowed to carry that information back to my human memory. It was life-changing and one of the greatest gifts I have ever received. I will say, there is nothing but light and love when we leave our human bodies. We are here on this Earth to learn lessons and to learn about love from this human vantage point. No lessons are ever wasted and if we can send more positive than negative ripples into the world, we have had a life well lived....

The end of June brought with it the first trip where Wylie and I would be guiding together in over a year. Two of my friends had gotten a total of four couples together for the Havasupai (also called Supai) trip. Since they knew Wylie and me as a couple, we would not have to be hidden or pretend we were not together. I had gotten and paid for the permits for the trip, found the clients for him, and was going to help him shop for the food, cook, clean up and co-guide – all the while letting him take the profits. Our Hiking Adventure business was still in its infancy, and I was helping get it off the ground. The intention was that as it grew I would eventually leave my job and become the CEO or CMO, taking a salary and guiding trips when I wanted. I had heavily invested in the business by paying for many of our large trip permits that would book sometimes a year in advance. In addition, I had invested over a thousand dollars in equipment. This was also allowing Wylie to get the business going so he would both own himself and make a lot more money than he was making with other guiding companies. I was banking on it paying off for us both.

Havasupai is the most heavenly location I have ever visited on Earth. It was so much fun to share it with my friends, and to return to a place that held so many special memories for Wylie and me, as this was our third trip there together. Wylie was in rare form on this trip; he was almost borderline obnoxious, telling the group several private matters about me very few people knew. It wasn't like there was a lot of drinking – there was some, but not enough to justify his behavior. I brushed it off as him feeling so comfortable with my friends and with me that he was just showing off a little. I also noticed one strange thing: when we were making out in the tent one night, I felt Wylie was kissing me differently. I could not put my finger on what had changed, and I almost said something, but chalked it up to my active imagination and the fact that we had been so busy since my birthday that we had not had much alone time together.

The end of this trip also marked the first skirmish Wylie and I had ever had. After each Supai excursion we would treat the group to lunch in the first major town outside of Supai. Wylie had one place he always took clients. He had made arrangements with the owners such that when he brought a group in, they would comp his meal – it was a neat perk. I was fully aware of this, and as the person at the head of the line I let the staff know we had two guides on this trip. I placed my order, then let the guests order their food. I moved toward the back of our group and asked Wylie what he was going to order. He harshly told me not to worry about it and to just order my own food. It was a rather abrupt response and I was taken aback by his unfamiliar attitude. He said it loudly enough to elicit the attention of several people in our group. A moment later, he pulled me aside and in an aggravated whisper told me I was messing things up because he was supposed be getting his food for free. Now I understood – he didn't realize I remembered the game and had already set those wheels in motion. I let him know that not only was *his* meal free but I had already alerted the staff that we were co-guiding and *both* of our meals were to be free, which was the usual arrangement with two guides anyway. He softened slightly with that realization but exerted no effort to apologize.

When we returned from the Supai trip we spent the night at Wylie's house and took a mushroom medicine journey together the next day. I was amazed at being able to return to my Soul's vibration once again and to be in that space of pure and unconditional LOVE. We had our own separate journeys this time, but every journey offers opportunities to heal and this one was no exception. Later that afternoon, Wylie and I sat down to talk about our experiences. Once again he brought up his feelings of our relationship being so intense and my love for him being so strong, and how he is a strong man but seems to be no match for me. He mentioned again how he might still need to take a break at some point in the future. I was getting sick and tired of this same old discussion. I just could not understand how we were back in this place again. This time I took great offense to his comments and became defensive. I pushed back – either he liked and accepted who I was and I made his life better, or he didn't. He acquiesced but it was too late. His comments put me in run mode, and I left. We had spent quite a bit of time together on this trip and Wylie had not been his normal self. We needed a break from each other for the next few days at least.

Wylie spent a couple of consecutive days with me at my house around the July 4th holiday. I really tried to relax and be present while he was there, and to imagine how it would feel if he and I were actually living together. For the most part, we had not experienced the normal nuances of being together in life, instead of just dating. Most of our time together was spent meeting for lunch, going to dinner or making dinner, seeing movies and concerts, or attending friends' parties on occasion. We had been on several trips together over time and occasionally did still grocery shop together for trips. But we were rarely "just together" for any amount of time – doing normal day-to-day things like working from home, doing projects around the house, or even just watching TV together. We were still very much in more of a dating relationship and still only seeing each other on average every five to eight days. It was a product of Wylie not making an effort to see me more than that – I always wanted more. Even after all this time, we hadn't progressed into a more everyday relationship.

That July 4th holiday, we spent a lot of time just hanging out, and I noticed how much time Wylie spent on his phone, especially at night. One night, as I was getting ready for bed, it seemed like he was texting someone. He seemed amused and I got the distinct feeling at that moment that he was texting a woman. But I brushed off my gut feeling as being paranoid. After all, he was here with me and just a few weeks earlier had written my special birthday poem.

We watched fireworks together for the first time, and I just loved having the opportunity to spend time with him. We were invited to my parents' house the next day. My dad and one his neighbors were having "battle ribs," and about

~~Once~~ A Cheater...

20 neighbors would be there to eat dinner potluck style. By this time we had been together for nearly two years. Wylie introduced himself to several of my parents' neighbors as "Laurie's friend." One neighbor, who was a good friend of my mom's and knew Wylie and I had been dating for a long time, made fun of Wylie's "friend" reference when I walked up. The two of them bantered back and forth, joking, but I was just pissed. I knew full well Wylie didn't like the term "boyfriend," several times stating that it diminished who we were together. Well, if "boyfriend" diminished it, "friend" took us down to a level that made me feel small and insignificant to him. What the heck happened to "the love of my life" term he had suggested we call ourselves? Seriously – friend?! We talked about it later, but he wasn't receptive to the conversation and was kind of an ass to me. Why did I always feel like we took one step forward in our relationship and two steps back? I was already looking forward to my reading with Thomas coming up the next week, and now even more so. I was hoping to get some type of clarification. And I did....

It's hard to believe six days after Thomas met with me at my house and said, "It's really not about other women for Wylie," that I got the text from my good friend Shannon alerting me to her potential "match" with Wylie on Bumble. Blindsiding him at his house the night before with my Bumble-Gate discovery had been a living nightmare for me. I had hardly slept after I got home and had read his "sad, sorry and confused" email the moment I woke up. My only response had been an accidental reply meant for my friend in reaction to his omitting the "e" in the spelling of my name by mistake. I wrote: "The smart ass in me wanted to say, 'Is that for me? You didn't even spell my name right...'" Oops! I had actually intended NOT to respond as my response. A few hours later there was a new email from Wylie in my inbox:

~To: Laurie Majka

From: Wylie Heartly

July 22, 2019, 11:28 a.m.

Subject: Initial Thoughts

Dearest Lauri,

This morning on my way to CrossFit a line from the original Blade Runner movie popped into my head. It was a narration from Harrison Ford toward the end of the movie. He comments on a dying cyborg and notes that a star that burns twice as bright lasts half as long. So I'm not much one for hypothetical scenarios but that line triggered the following as I thought to myself, if two years ago I had been presented with a crystal ball showing only two choices in how our relationship would go, which would I pick?

Scenario #1) You and I would connect on many levels and have an amazing friendship that would last a lifetime. We would partner to create awesomeness and leave the world a much better place having known, grown and flourished together.

Scenario #2) You and I would connect on every level, have amazing adventures and a wonderfully passionate relationship that created a magic that you had never felt before, and it would end within 2 years.

Which would be the pick?

Now I know you would create a third scenario that would be the combination of the two, ending in growing old together. I think that was our dream, but that is not what the crystal ball shows.

Whether we wanted it or not, scenario #2 is what became our reality. If I had been capable of the third scenario, then we clearly wouldn't be in our current situation. With hindsight as it is, I would have chosen scenario #1.

Wylie~

      He was right. I would have picked a third scenario, and it was utterly and completely his fault we were where we were. All the energy I had been putting toward the new project that Mark wanted to work on with me was diverted to my relationship issues. I could barely eat. I felt sad and confused and just couldn't reconcile what had happened. Luckily, I had a much-needed vacation planned four days after I walked away from the relationship.

Chapter 32

Hold the Line

~song by *Toto*

https://open.spotify.com/track/4aVuWgvDOX63hcOCnZtNFA?si=Q7wEPr4fTQW3h-zCjJ_iNQ

I took a vacation to the cabin I had once owned with my ex-husband, in the Upper Peninsula of Michigan. In Chicago, I rented a car and began the six-hour drive. I was looking forward to listening to my two favorite FM radio stations once I got close to the cabin. The radio worked fine in Chicago and all the way to the cabin, but once I got there the only station that would pick up was 102.5, a country station. I was able to scan through all the stations, but that was the only one that would connect. Even when I manually typed my stations into the radio they wouldn't stay tuned in. Reluctantly, I listened to the country station. Not that I don't like country music, but I was looking forward to listening to the music on the FM stations. On Sunday, they didn't play music at all but broadcast the NASCAR race instead. I decided I was going to have to play my own music. As I pulled up the options to connect my phone music to the car, I saw the XM radio options. I should point out that XM is a $13.99-per-day option, which I had not activated, and only two times in all my years of renting cars has the XM option ever even worked. I pushed the button anyway and to my amazement the XM stations came to life! I set up my favorite stations – The Bridge, '80s on 8 and Yacht Rock. I was getting my "fix" of the FM radio stations inside the cabin, and now I at least had music I liked in the car.

  I went on one of my favorite hikes near the cabin. I hung my hammock by Fish Lake to read a book and take a nap. When I woke up, I was staring at the lake. At that moment, I felt compelled to pray about Wylie and me. It had only been one week since I left our relationship, and I was having a difficult time with the situation and the complexities around the break. I needed guidance and prayed out loud to God, and asked my Spirit team to gather to help me get through this time. I played some songs I had previously included on a new Spotify playlist called *Twin Flame Choices* and loudly sang each of them, especially the song "*I Still Believe*" by *Mariah Carey*. I then packed up to leave.

  When I started the car, I heard the song "Hold the Line" by *Toto*. I thanked Mark for listening to me pray and responding so quickly. My last contact with Mark before he died was at a concert where the band played there *Toto* songs along with the usual *Starship* lineup. "Hold the Line" was one of the three

~~Once~~ A Cheater...

Toto songs. I looked at the screen and noticed it indicated: XM Yacht Rock, *Looking Glass* "Brandy (You're a Fine Girl)" – except the *Toto* song was playing instead. The entire song played and when it finished, the screen flashed and updated to "Diamond Girl" by *Seals and Crofts*. I have long said this is God's song to me, and I felt like this was a double message from both Mark *and* God, answering my prayer. But only when the lyrics *"Hold the line, love isn't always on time..."* really sank in, did I *FREAK OUT*! I thought the message was that love *wasn't* on time and *wasn't* going to work out. I felt sad. I felt let down, because usually when Mark communicated to me he was sharing something good. I had never really pondered this song's lyrics before.

I drove for a while and then changed the station to '80s on 8. "Africa" by *Toto* was playing – another one of the three *Toto* songs from the concert long ago. This song prompted me to begin talking to Mark in my head, asking if what I had just heard was true, and proposing that if Wylie and I were *not* going to work out, to please move Wylie to email me and give me an answer – let him verbalize whether we were or were not going to work out. Have him answer this question.

Later, I googled the dictionary meaning and song meaning of "Hold the Line," and I saw it also had a military term meaning: do NOT give up – hold the line – maintain your current position – stand firm and do not retreat. I also viewed a website where people were commenting on the song lyrics. Many of them were saying that when love wasn't on time, if you were patient and gave it time it would eventually work out. With this new understanding, I began to have hope again.

The next day I spent three hours in the car with Ryan and decided to tell him what was going on with Wylie and me. Ryan was super supportive. I also told him about what had happened a couple days before, when the song "Hold the Line" had been playing while the screen indicated a completely different song. I was still talking to him about it as we approached a tiny town. I wanted to stop at a store there, so I pulled over but noticed a sign in the store window that said they close at 5:00. I glanced at the clock in the car and realized they were already closed, as it was 5:30. In a lull in the conversation, I noticed the song "Hold the Line" was quietly playing in the background although the screen said "Make It with You" by *Bread*. – once again what the screen said was not the song playing. This time Ryan was my witness. He could not believe it! To top it off, when we got back to the cabin I had an email reply from Wylie in my inbox, saying he did not want our relationship to be over. The time of the email: 5:30 – the exact time my screen froze.

Stacy and Sal drove their RV from Arizona to the Upper Peninsula of Michigan to spend part of my vacation with me. On their first full day there, Stacy and I were supposed to meet at the cabin to pick blueberries at 7:30 am, but as her phone was on Central time and mine was on Eastern, she showed up an hour later than I expected her. Having extra time, I sat down to respond to Wylie's email from the previous day. The response just flowed out of me, and I quickly sent the email to him.

Ryan was there at the cabin too and we all left for our kayak trip. When we got there, I had to wait for Sal and Stacy to unload their kayak. I sat in the car re-reading the email I had sent Wylie, now panicking that my response had been too hasty. While reviewing it, I heard the song "Hold the Line" begin to play on the radio. The screen said Yacht Rock: *England Dan & John Ford Coley* "Nights Are Forever Without You" – again a repeat song from earlier, and again it was not the song playing. Stacy and Ryan both walked over to the car in time to hear the song and see the car screen as well. Double witness! They were both shocked. I was shocked too, because each time this has happened I felt Mark was telling me to stop worrying about all this: Spirit had me covered.

On my last day at the cabin, I was running out of time to hike Bruno's Run, a ten-mile trail, so I had to run it. When I finished, I only had twenty minutes to relax in the hammock next to the lake. I decided to use my time playing four songs from my Twin Flame Choices playlist: "Lessons in Love," "With a Little Luck," "Truly Madly Deeply," and "I Still Believe." I sang each of them passionately, sobbing the whole time. I then packed up my hammock and headed to the car. When I started the engine, the music didn't begin playing right away, and I thought to myself; "Hey Mark, what do you have to say to me now?" The XM station The Bridge then came to life and began playing a song I didn't like, so I switched the station to Yacht Rock. The screen indicated *Doobie Brothers* "Minute by Minute" was playing – only it wasn't – the last verse of "Hold the Line" was streaming from the speakers. This time I was truly dumbfounded, because never before had these incidents happened with such frequency – and, once again, this was on the heels of a very intense time for me with Wylie. I snapped a picture of the screen and later wished I had taken a video instead. The crazy thing was that as I drove back to Chicago I remembered the radio-freezing episode with Wylie back in June after telling him about the reading I had received at Thomas's show, and I was able to connect the final dots that tied all the "Hold the Line" songs together. For confirmation I had taken pictures of the screen that day, and luckily they were still on my phone.

A few weeks after my vacation, my sister Stephanie was in town for our Dad's 70th birthday. My parents got us all tickets to see Chris Isaak in concert. Stephanie and I decided to drive separately and meet my parents at the venue. On the drive home, we talked about the concert and how musicians are spiritually open. I mentioned Mark and then started talking about Wylie – and at that exact moment "Hold the Line" began playing on the radio. The screen said *Boz Scaggs* "Jojo" was playing – but it was not. This time I didn't miss the opportunity to videotape the screen with my phone.

Watch video on YouTube: www.youtube.com/watch?v=BvTnrw3T4Jo

~~Once~~ A Cheater...

Chapter 33

What You Won't Do for Love

~song by *Bobby Caldwell*

https://open.spotify.com/track/7dL8FCLzEaWC2A3qWQuz1q?si=ZFNrjOXXSOyvWlrCPBauCw

August was going to be a very difficult month. Stacy, Sal, Wylie and I had planned an incredible couples trip to Washington State. We had planned it four months earlier, and I never could have imagined then that I would be in this situation. Of course, I couldn't let Wylie go with us now. Unfortunately, I had purchased his ticket, and he got to keep the credit for future use. I was disappointed in him that he didn't offer to reimburse me – doubly so since it was entirely his doing that we were where we were now. But I was more upset that he wouldn't be by my side hiking, walking the beaches, splitting meals, and spending time with me. Now I was destined to be the third wheel on a couples trip. A huge part of me wanted to cancel as well, but Stacy and I had been planning this trip in our minds for over a year. Like her sharing the Upper Peninsula of Michigan with me, Washington was her special place, and we were excited for the getaway.

I had a lot more downtime on the trip than I did in my normal life; it was more thinking time than I needed. Wylie and I had been sending each other deep email communications many pages long, back and forth. Email was a place where we could gather our thoughts and be reflective and contemplative about what had transpired between us in our relationship over the previous nearly two years. It was a safe place, where we both felt comfortable sharing real thoughts and feelings. We were, in a sense, getting to know each other now on a deeper level. I received a long email from him on the day I left for the trip. While on the trip, I would stay up late every night creating a thoughtful response to him. Here are a few of the thoughts we shared with each other:

[Wylie] *What was not to love about our relationship – we do always have an amazing time together regardless of what we are doing, and that is a unique gift. It was a dichotomy that I struggled with – how much I love you and being with you versus needing the time to own myself and take a timeout from being in a committed relationship. And I certainly did not want to disappoint or upset you (double fail there).*

While we connect on an amazing number of levels, I do think we have one underlying difference in our energy/desires that is significant. I believe that your desire to be in a committed relationship and build a future within that construct is far stronger than mine. I feel like you have a clear idea of how you want your relationship with me, or whoever is your boyfriend, to look. I think you are completely attached to how it will look, and I think you don't have much wiggle room in that. I'm not saying this like it is wrong. You just have a deep knowing of what is correct for you. I wish I had a similar knowing, but I don't have the depth of your commitment or clarity of your vision. And that is the main thing that I am working on in myself. What is it in me that resists being a "boyfriend" or whatever other relationship label that is so common and seemingly necessary in our society? Why don't I have a deep desire to find "the one" and build a future with someone? These are aspects of myself, especially in the context of relationships, that I am examining.

What I know about myself is that I tend to be an "in the moment" person who enjoys fun, adventure, romance, deep conversation and a meaningful connection. I don't like to be labeled. I don't like making promises, I don't like being manipulated or controlled. I do not like feeling responsible for the happiness of someone else. To me all this feels like "pressure" and it's not a pleasant feeling. Is this immature of me? Is it "how I am wired" and I have to accept it? Can I change, evolve, outgrow these feelings and ideas I have about myself and relationships? These are all VERY SIGNIFICANT questions that I must find clarity around.

There is much to this life of ours and I like the directions we are going. You are writing a book, building your challenge to help many people and developing your power to positively change the world. I am going to climb a mountain (or 2 or 3...) and learn the lessons they offer me. I am going to help as many people as I can broaden and explore the natural world around them. We are connected in an inseparable way, we just need to figure out how to best support each other and love each other and be with each other. It's not rocket science, but at times it can be challenging.

For now, my mistresses are the mountains. As I prepare for them and build myself physically, mentally, emotionally and spiritually, I will be focused on answering the questions I have about myself and how I hold relationships. The better I know myself, the clearer I am about my wants, desires, fears, strengths, weaknesses, etc., the more solid a foundation we will have to build our relationship. I know you are doing the work and I pledge to you that I will as well.

[Laurie] *You said you don't want to feel responsible for someone else's happiness. I truly get that. You can go back to my Soul Heart Art and read what I wrote about exactly that subject from 2013 to 2017 – I painted several paintings and I probably addressed that at least 50+ times out of 400 paintings. It is similar to my message of self-love – you have to feel love from yourself or happiness from yourself before you can feel it from someone else. I have never said I can't be happy without you, or I couldn't have left in the first place, right? I don't have that fear.*

*But let's talk about this a little and put some perspective on it. Does having you in my life make me happier – yes it does!! and I hope it feels the same for you!!! Isn't that mostly (outside of family) how we pick who we spend our time with? We become friends with people who make us feel happy when we are around them. Just because I feel happier with you in my life does not mean I get my happiness FROM you – I still get it from me. I get happiness from my outlook on life and my positive glass-half-full nature and from the people in my life – from my kids and family, friends, Storm, from my time in nature, from my hiking, from being in my beautiful house, from living in Arizona, from my trips to see this amazing World of ours, from eating fabulous food, from my job and making money, from my daily interactions with others, from what I am sending into the World – just from living, Wylie! If I died tomorrow or we didn't have a relationship anymore, would your happiness have decreased because I am no longer in your life? I hope to God that answer is Yes – because that is a yes for me if that happened to you. But does that mean that I was **responsible** for your happiness? No! Because you don't have just one basket you keep your happiness in. Just because you are in a relationship does not mean you have put yourself into a position of pressure to make someone else happy. I think **You** feel pressure more because you don't want to let someone down or disappoint them – but for God's sake, if that stops you from being in a relationship you might as well never enter into ANY relationship with anyone ever – family, kids, friends, lovers. It is inevitable you are (or I am) going to disappoint, not live up to or let someone down – that is life and that is going to be a part of any relationship, and that is because no one is perfect. So take the pressure off of yourself by looking at this differently.*

Lastly, your label of "boyfriend". You will not get around labels in our society – you are a man, a hiking guide, a dad, an ex-husband, a son, a brother, a coach, a friend…and no matter what you think, if you are in a relationship with me people will see you as the label boyfriend. What I am hoping in addressing all the above issues is that by you being my "boyfriend" you can view this in a better light – less possessive/less owning you – because of how I view my expectations, as above. I do think you need to let these thoughts go as they are not serving you.

I was devoting significant time to my correspondence with Wylie; I wasn't ready to give up on our love. I do believe in manifestation being created on a Spiritual level, and I was doing my part in that way to bring us back together; that was how I would use the songs from the Twin Flame Choices playlist. I would play a song and concentrate on all the wonderful parts of our relationship, then send that energy to Wylie. I had also created one specific ritual: every Sunday night at 7:20 precisely, I would play the song "I Still Believe" by *Mariah Carey* and imagine the two of us dancing in his office, passionately making out, as we had done at that exact time just before I exposed my knowledge of Bumble-Gate.

The saddest day since Bumble-Gate for me was August 22. This would have been the official two-year anniversary of our first date. Anniversaries are very special to me because they celebrate the significance of who a couple are together. I had planned a very memorable surprise anniversary trip months in advance for the occasion, and had only given him the dates for him to block his calendar. He knew nothing else about our trip. I purchased the plane tickets, and we were to leave for the East Coast the morning after we returned from Washington State. We were going to have an anniversary dinner in the Boston harbor, then drive to our timeshare in Vermont where we would spend several days relaxing and exploring three states neither of us had ever visited before. More significant than what we were doing was that we would have ten full days together with the two trips. That would have been heaven, because there was *never* a time when Wylie and I did not have fun together. Instead, on the anniversary date, we were relegated to texting.

On the 22nd Wylie sent me a "Happy Anniversary" Bitmoji message and we spent part of the day texting each other. One thing was certain: I was willing to do a lot to save this love. I only hoped it would be enough....

Chapter 34

The Flame

~song by *Cheap Trick*

https://open.spotify.com/track/528CAH5pTLq86oZ52fHifA?si=WmUW7776R3-TntNoFOV2Rg

Even though my sister was in town for our Dad's birthday, it was a rather sad day for me. Wylie and I were still on our break, and months earlier I had purchased tickets for us to see *Cheap Trick* and *ZZ Top* together. I also realized it was our last scheduled event on the calendar. Wylie had been super-excited about this concert; now Stephanie was going to be my plus one. While I was getting ready for the show, I texted him a picture of my tickets with a crying face emoji reminding him of what he would be missing. He expressed his sadness at not being able to attend and wished me a good time with Stephanie. I sent him a song link of my favorite song from the set list: "The Flame" by *Cheap Trick*. He agreed it was a good one, and added it to our *L.A. Woman* playlist.

Stephanie and I were driving to our second concert of the week. Many times in the past, during and after concerts, Mark had made his presence known with various signs. Since his death, I had seen 64 bands perform, and there had been many signs around those concerts. On the way to this night's concert, just ten minutes from my house, I noticed the license plate on the car in front of us said "SOULM8". Wow – I told Stephanie about a very similar license plate – "SOLMATE" – that I had seen after a concert several years before, not long after Mark had died. The two of us continued travelling along for about fifteen minutes with the "SOULM8" car still in front of us. Just before getting onto the highway, both our cars caught the red stoplight. A car on the cross street to our left ran his red light while turning left onto our street, then quickly got into the far right lane in front of us. As our light turned green, the "SOULM8" car pulled ahead and for about fifteen seconds was right beside the car in the far right lane, whose license plate said "GO BVRS." The "GO BVRS" car then quickly made a right turn into a high school parking lot, disappearing from sight. Now, Mark is not only my Soul Mate but vowed to send me beavers as signs – it was a double sign! What are the chances those two cars, "SOULM8" and "GO BVRS," could exist in the same space at the same time *with* me right behind to witness it – on the way to see a concert, no less. I realized then that this night was going to be special – but even I could not have anticipated the event to come....

When we arrived at the concert my sister got into a thirty-minute line to buy a tee shirt. I got us drinks and arrived at our seats ahead of her, just as the opening act was ending and they were beginning to set up the stage for *Cheap Trick* to play. Something made me look behind me at the stairs, and I immediately saw him – Wylie was walking toward me with a giant smile on his face. He had found me in the crowd and was coming to say hello. It was the first time we had seen each other since the Bumble-Gate incident that ended our relationship. Stephanie arrived after purchasing her tee shirts and offered to sit in Wylie's seat so he and I could sit together for the concert (a generous gesture on her part).

Wylie couldn't get enough of me during the show. We made out and danced together – it was a truly joyous reunion. There was an intermission after *Cheap Trick* and before *ZZ Top* started, a good opportunity for us to catch up, as we had not had much time to visit before the first band took the stage. Wylie was excited to share with me that he was going on a training expedition in Asia on a mountain called Island Peak. It had several similarities to the Everest climb and would be a good training ground. He would be leaving in a month. I asked who was going and he named his best friend, and a woman he didn't know whom he referred to as the hair dresser – and Jane. My heart sank to my feet. Then my brain fired, instantly connecting the dots: training hike plus Everest. I knew it – she was planning on going, just as I had predicted, seven months before! I asked the question out loud, "Is Jane planning on climbing Everest?" He said it was still unknown at this time, but potentially, yes; it would depend on how she did on this hike. My brain scrambled and I was at a complete loss for words. Sensing my instant unease, Wylie changed the subject and told me he had adopted a cat. Well, that was dumb – he was gone more than half the year and for long periods of time. He said he really missed having a pet of his own, and his roommate had encouraged it, adding to the fray of three dogs she already owned. Life was moving on for both of us...

When the second band, *ZZ Top,* took the stage Wylie resumed his public display of affection toward me. You would not have known from how we acted that we were not completely together! When the show ended I offered to give him a ride home as he had taken a rideshare car to the show. It was the perfect opportunity to meet his "dumb" new cat.

I wondered if this would be the start of a new beginning for Wylie and me. Clearly, we had missed each other, and it was obvious our chemistry had only increased over time. We had been disengaged for five weeks that felt more like five months to me. It really wasn't enough time for Wylie to get his shit together and address the internal issues that had caused our demise in the first place. But we had learned a lot about each other with the 20,000 words of email correspondence that would have filled 60 pages of a book. There was no part of me that didn't still think we had many more pages to fill with our story.

Two days later he was at my house fixing dinner with me. He needed my help with a Grand Canyon issue for our Hiking Adventure business, and instead of talking on the phone had made an effort to stop by. He later admitted it was the perfect excuse to see me. It was a welcome visit and we kept our conversation lighthearted.

Our texting picked up over the next week and we were in contact with each other nearly every day. He suggested we get together again and I invited him to have dinner with me. We had a serious talk this time, and I voiced my concerns about Jane going on a trip with him yet again. He patiently listened, then explained he knew exactly how I felt because he had had a similar experience with feelings toward me and Mark. I was shocked at the comparison, because Mark was dead and would not be rising from the dead to come back into my life again. On some level I did understand: it must have been intimidating having a man from my past sending me messages of inspiration from the Other Side. Not everyone would be able to handle that. Wylie explained that he was a strong man mentally, but my connection with Mark *was* unnerving and still something he could not fully comprehend. I wanted to reassure him and told him how I was fully and completely in love with HIM; how if Mark came back to life and stood next to Wylie, making me choose between the two of them – how Wylie is the only man I wanted in my life and I would choose him! About that time Wylie suddenly stood up and headed to the back door, beckoning me to follow him. The sky was unusually dark and ominous for Arizona, and off to the east was a beautiful rainbow! It was a sight to see and it felt like a sign. It was all the sign I needed – we made love for the first time since our break. As if to prove the rainbow really was a sign, the next morning the rotating screensaver picture on my laptop featured a large, bright rainbow. I will never fail to be amazed at the ways Spirit finds to send me signs of confirmation.

We were now primarily communicating by text again. I shared with Wylie some of the roadblocks I had been experiencing in my new project that Mark was supposed to be helping me bring into the world. Wylie wanted me to know that he was there to support me, as he had voiced in our last talk. And to prove it, he reached out by text to ask me questions and offer his support and advice. He also wanted to see how I was feeling after the more serious conversation we had had. One of the things that had been bothering me was, when I expressed my concerns about Jane he never addressed them – turning the tables, instead, and the attention toward Mark. He apologized, saying he thought he had addressed it. Then he sent this text:

9-18-19 10:03 a.m.

[Wylie] *I hope you don't worry about it anymore. Jane and I spend a fair amount of time training and getting ready for the mountains. That is all there is to it. Please try not to worry. She is a close friend who has been through a lot and that is it.*

But I had asked Wylie a very specific question regarding Jane, and I still felt like his text message was avoiding the full answer. I asked for more. He replied as follows:

[Wylie] *I understand. Jane is a close friend. Period. You are one of a kind to me, babe. Our relationship is so special I would never try to compare it.*

Chapter 35

Insecure

~song by *RaeLynn*

https://open.spotify.com/track/1Cz73d6PqsQwSxXhfLrP0k?si=DmYTVlvMRIO2wpx_L0xTUw

Jane was going on yet ANOTHER trip with Wylie and I just couldn't overcome the dissonance and insecure feelings this brought up in me. He hadn't exactly come right out and told me she was going – I still had to ask *who* was going, even though I "knew" before her name left his lips she would be on the list. Yesterday's phone call had caught me off guard. I was usually pretty measured with my words and would have had an idea of what I wanted to talk about before having a conversation. But I had clearly buried some unresolved feelings about his trip with Jane that had unintentionally spilled out. I knew the minute I disclosed my true feelings I had said more than I wanted to say, and hoped I was not chasing Wylie away. Luckily, I had a work call I had forgotten about that caused me to suddenly end my call with him. I disconnected the phone with a feeling of unease. I felt mad more than anything and I just couldn't shake it!

Getting ready to leave on another business trip to Kansas City was a welcome distraction. I called Stacy on the drive to the airport to vent some of my pent-up feelings to someone who knew all the parties involved. Stacy listened patiently as I described my concerns about the phone call with Wylie. She said she understood why I felt this way, but that in the scheme of things, Jane was just a speck. She was nothing to Wylie, and if I pulled out of the relationship because of her it was like throwing the baby out with the bathwater. That image made me laugh, until a disheartening thought popped into my head. In a flash, I realized Jane was NEVER going away. There were Seven Summits, and although a plan had never been mentioned, Jane had completed one summit and if she climbed Everest, that would be two, leaving five more to conquer. Her attorney husband had just died bequeathing her a lot of money, and she had nothing but time, as she didn't work. I didn't think I could stomach the thought of her spending that much time training and traveling with him over the next few years...I got cut off from Stacy in mid-sentence. Then my radio crackled back to life and was playing the song "Hold On Loosely" by .38 *Special*. I wondered if Spirit had done that on purpose!

I called Stacy back. She was also traveling in her car and Sal had been listening to our conversation over the car speaker. He too knew all the parties

~~Once~~ A Cheater...

involved and added his two cents: "Laur, she is just a client!" Stacy then offered, "The only way you are going to be okay with Jane is if you can get to know her better. If you could spend some time with her socially, all these feelings would go away." It was something to consider, and I thought about it some more at the airport. I was also curious about the song that had interrupted our conversation. I looked up the lyrics for "Hold On Loosely" and was surprised and intrigued to see the chorus of the song had been created by purposely turning the chorus of "What a Fool Believes" upside down. Interesting – that was the song that had been played on XM radio twice in a row last February, when I was having similar "Jane feelings." I seriously couldn't make up what happened to me through Spirit, and I had no previous knowledge of this song fact about the chorus.

Feelings of jealousy were not a normal part of my nature. The last time I had felt jealous of any woman in relation to a man was over 32 years earlier. I was 18 years old when my boyfriend's ex-girlfriend began pursuing him hot and heavy – giving me a legitimate reason to feel that way. Feelings of that type had taken a 32-year sabbatical, and I had never expected emotions from the least mature part of me to rear their ugly head again. But if I really thought about *why* they had materialized, it was because they were connected to how Wylie had handled the entirety of the Jane situation.

I needed perspective about my relationship with Wylie. Part of the purpose in having a relationship break was to gain perspective while we were out of it. I had written many notes to myself over the course of our relationship that I had stored in my phone. Whenever Wylie and I would have a deeper conversation, I would document pertinent parts of what we had discussed so I could go back and read what he had said to me. It helped me to stay in my heart-space with him when my head was overanalyzing things. So I spent most of the plane ride re-reading the notes I had written to myself. Unfortunately, reading them did not have the intended effect of making me feel better; instead, it illuminated some patterns I had not previously noticed.

I didn't get to my hotel until after 2:00 a.m. but I still forced myself to get up early the next morning for a much needed run in nature. I had slept longer than I should have and was feeling rushed as I needed to get back for a work call. But I still took an extra few minutes to send a very long text to Stacy, sharing my observations from the notes...

9-24-19 7:24 a.m.

[Laurie] *Rereading my notes on the plane did not have the intended effect, as I realized Wylie had been telling me for a long time that I was too intense and he needed a break. He has acknowledged over and over again that he doesn't know if he can live with someone, yet I have not listened to what he was trying to tell me.*

After reading my notes it made me wonder what I'm doing in this relationship, as he might never come around! So much talk over time about me being too much for him to handle. A year ago April, at his birthday dinner, I asked him if he thought he could only be with one person – he actually said "No." I had forgotten about that, but then he also said over and over he didn't want anyone

~~Once~~ A Cheater...

but ME in his life! He said he wouldn't find someone better than me – and yet when our relationship was at its pinnacle he wound up on Bumble! I don't know, I'm starting to harden my heart (lol that song played on the radio today). I know Spirit has told me to hold the line – but I'm so much in my head! I'm heading out to my five-mile forest run. Maybe I'll feel better/different in nature. I just feel mad about everything right now. I feel like I want to take down our Wall of Adventure when I get home and tell him when I land on Wednesday that it's over – he is free...I am done!

[Stacy] *I am sorry you are so mad and frustrated. I wish I had words of wisdom for you. I thought Wylie had changed his stance over time, and recently said a few times he could not imagine his life without you and that he was starting to think differently about you being in his life more permanently...*

[Laurie] *He has, but re-reading our journey was NOT a good experience, especially since he said he wanted a break so many times. It's like I never even listened to him! So am I not listening when he says he doesn't want a relationship this intense? He said I'm the only one he would consider in breaking his rule of not living with someone.*

Spirit chimed in by playing the *Starship* song "We Built This City" as soon as I got in my rental car. Then, as I was pulling up to the trailhead, the radio station advertised the *Toto* concert here in Kansas City this coming Friday. I heard snippets from the songs "Africa", "Hold the Line" and "Rosanna" – all songs Mark had played at a concert the last time I saw him alive. Those are pretty specific songs for me, all of them played in one short 15-minute period. Clearly, Spirit was reminding me to get back to my heart-space. I realized that if I had not delayed myself by typing those long texts to Stacy in the hotel, I would have gotten to the trailhead before those songs played. Timing!

After my workday finished I needed some more time in nature. It was a beautiful day and I hung my hammock by a lake. I had not finished rereading all the email correspondence the night before and wanted to do that. One thing was for certain: when I ended contact with Wylie after Bumble-Gate and we were *only* emailing each other, I was in a much better place than I was now that we were seeing each other and sporadically texting again. I felt like I had begun slowly spiraling downward, and a large part of it had to do with the new information about Jane going to Asia and potentially being away with Wylie for three months the following year climbing Everest. I couldn't think anymore; I needed to pack up and go because I had plans to meet my sister Stephanie for dinner.

I went back to the hotel to freshen up, and as I often do, I turned to Spirit for comfort, venting my feelings and questioning Mark. I challenged Mark and joked with him that he should send the *Starship* song "Jane" to me on my drive to see Stephanie. Stranger things have happened...

I began the 30-minute drive to meet my sister. About ten minutes into the ride I heard a song by *Supertramp* on the radio that I had not heard in many years – the song "Goodbye Stranger." The chorus repeated the name "Jane" over and over again, nine times, bidding her goodbye. I laughed at the thought! Then, as her name played from the speaker, a car passed me on the right with a license plate reading "F8THFUL." Knowing how Spirit has communicated with me in the past using license plates and songs, this was NO accident. Spirit was acknowledging that Jane was *not* a threat as far as Wylie was concerned. It felt like Spirit was trying to guide me out of this situation, and if I wanted to stay in the relationship I was going to have to find a way to beat this insecurity.

Stephanie had long been my confidante, but I didn't talk to her about my Wylie situation at dinner, because there was a huge part of me that had given up on us already. Wylie was taking his time and I had no idea if and when he would be capable of resuming a normal relationship. Jane was never going away, and I didn't know if I wanted to deal with that. Finally, even if Wylie did come back, we had not addressed the fidelity issue. I didn't know if I was ever going to be able to trust him. I was actually thankful he had not reached out to me on this trip, and maybe it would be best if he pulled back contact and dealt with his issues on the mountain. I would have three weeks with no contact and I could pretend we were finished. I could get back to feeling like myself again, instead of feeling like this crazy person I didn't know.

The next day I checked out of the hotel after my business meeting finished and had a few hours before I had to leave for the airport. I used the time to take a long walk around the lake. When I finished I hung my hammock next to the lake. I was watching YouTube videos about Near Death Experiences in an effort to raise my vibration, because my thoughts during the hike had once again been consumed with Jane and Wylie being away together for three weeks. He still had not addressed my email and I had not heard from him in two days. I could "feel" he would be reaching out to me soon, but I was on the fence about seeing him if he asked me to. Whether I would or not was going to depend on *how* he asked me. I was concerned he might just want me to stop by his place on the way home from the airport. I had no intention of being anyone's booty call – not that he had ever really treated me that way.

Moments after those thoughts I heard the familiar custom ping of a text from Wylie. He was inquiring about my day, my return, and my schedule. He asked me on a real date to see a movie and to have dinner with him the next evening. He was making an effort, but my gut was giving me strange feedback that I could not put my finger on. I agreed to the date and decided I would share at dinner the insights I had uncovered from our correspondence, and the best way to do that was to put together a timeline of our relationship. In going over my notes, the biggest epiphany I had was that in a small way I could see how Bumble-Gate may have been a product of him, as he put it, needing to take a break. I didn't want to make excuses for him, but I had definitely uncovered some significant patterns in our relationship. This date with him was going to be important, and I had to address the Jane issue once and for all.

An hour later he texted me again as I was packing up to leave:

9-25-20 5:24 p.m.

[Wylie] *If you think about it, can you do the Phantom Ranch lottery submissions? I think today is the cut off.*

~~Once~~ A Cheater…

[Laurie] 🤭 *Is that why you really reached out to me today?*

[Wylie] *No. I was just going thru emails and ran across one that reminded me.*

He was hard to read. It felt like he was making a request with an ulterior motive. I didn't want to believe it, but, when I analyzed the patterns, things were feeling pretty one-sided in his favor. Of course, I helped him with the lottery submissions anyway. Then I watched the trailer for the movie he suggested we see together. It had several very attractive women in it, and I had only one request: he was *not* to tell me, albeit kiddingly, that he wanted to put any of the actresses from the movie on the "Free Pass" list. He didn't acknowledge my request but simply responded: *Get a good sleep and see you tomorrow* 😍 😍

~~Once~~ A Cheater...

Chapter 36

Little Lies

~song by *Fleetwood Mac*

https://open.spotify.com/track/08o75xMKmGrKny6GsXrNJW?si=IHitLM9ITIasmZ6I7vgmSQ

In the morning, Wylie texted me wondering if he could ask me a favor: Would I be willing to load up and bring the rest of what he had left in my closet to him, as long as I was coming over. He said he had a few items he was missing that he would be needing for his upcoming trip to Island Peak and thought they might be there. Seriously?! When we had ended things over Bumble-Gate I had requested he remove all his stored belongings from my place within 60 days. It was approaching the 60-day time period, and instead of making the effort to get his own stuff, he had trapped me into doing it. There were still quite a few large bins and random items – his "not much stuff" filled my entire Jeep! How shitty to ask me to bring it to him. Shitty, because now instead of feeling like he wanted to see me, it felt more like our get-together had been contrived so he didn't have to make the 35-minute trip up to my place to retrieve his stuff! I was so aggravated I called Stacy on the drive to meet him. Boy, if I was already irritated, she sure fueled the fire with her reaction, confirming what I had suspected – that he may just be using me yet again.

When I arrived at his house I was in a rare sassy mood. My attitude toward him was not very warm, but passive aggressive and slightly on the mean side. I said several things out loud that I would have normally left in my head. I had gone past the point of wanting to be helpful and finally voiced my feelings to him. He apologized, assuring me he had not intended to ask me to bring anything when he originally invited me out. Then he shared that he had had a fairly shitty afternoon himself. He had not seen his ex-wife in many weeks, and she apparently had "let him have it." He didn't elaborate on what the "it" was, but as we were unloading all the remaining items from my car, he declared that he had been trained to beat lie-detector tests. I didn't respond verbally but every alarm bell went off in my head at that moment – my brain was having a five-alarm fire! Wylie had never disclosed anything like that to me before. Sure, I knew of his military background as a Marine intelligence officer, and he would, of course, have been trained for work like that. But alluding to his ex-wife in the context of lying made me realize the only person who says something like that is someone who needs to use such an ability. Sure, everybody lies once in a while. I read that the average person tells 1.6 lies a day, but I think most lies are white lies designed to keep from offending or hurting other people's feelings. At least that had been my own personal experience with lying. I had a pact with myself to stand in my truth whenever possible. But this was certainly not the type of lie that would be needed to "beat" something. My mind went back to Bumble-Gate and half a dozen other incidents I had wondered about over the past two years. This new information left my mind reeling, and my heart didn't know how to recover.

On the drive to the movies I told Wylie we would need to have a more serious conversation at dinner to address my two emails he had avoided responding to. And I added that it was going to be a good talk that had the potential to make us stronger. I wanted to share with him the observations I had made from reviewing my timeline. He laughed at me and told me I could never play poker because I couldn't hide how I felt – at all!

The movie was entertaining, and when it finished Wylie needed to use the bathroom. I didn't need to, so I waited for him...and waited...and waited. He had to have been in there for over ten minutes, which felt like an eternity. I was keenly aware that he was either texting or talking to someone, and by doing so in the bathroom, it made me feel like, once again, he had something to hide. The lie detector comment earlier had not left my thoughts. Since we were still on our Bumble-Gate break, I was feeling braver in voicing my opinions than I might have been if we were fully together. When he finally emerged, I immediately called out the long amount of time he had spent in the bathroom, expressing how uncomfortable he was making me feel. He apologized, referencing an issue he was having with his oldest son that he had been taking care of. That was an odd response, since he had been telling me earlier how his kids often didn't answer him or text him back. It seemed like he regularly used his kids as his excuse regarding texting communication, and now I secretly wondered if he had kept up with any of the Bumble women. I had no idea, as I had only looked at those conversations briefly – and if he had, he was technically well within his rights to do so because I had broken up with him! The only caveat was that I had also told him I was not interested in even entertaining the idea of getting back together with him if he wanted to move toward seeing other women. He assured me in many emails that his intention was *solely* to work on his own issues and to experience what being *alone* – and not in any kind of relationship – felt like.

We went to our favorite pizza place for dinner and ordered our usual. I presented my timeline to him, complete with realizations. I talked about how much "28" had bothered me; and after that Jane, and how his deceitful past and lack of disclosure to me had made me feel supremely uncomfortable about her. I told him that reviewing my notes and seeing how many times he said he needed a break made me realize I had not been listening! I should have let him have the break when he first brought it up. Reviewing our timeline made me feel bad because it uncovered patterns I had not noticed in linear time.

Next we addressed the last two emails I had sent him that got no reply: I wanted to know whether or not – if he knew in advance he would die on this trip, or if I died while he was gone – he would regret our Bumble-Gate time apart. Wylie really had a distain for hypotheticals: Why speculate about what could never be known? he argued. I explained how it was more about getting him to look at our situation with a different perspective, to see how he felt deep down inside. I was trying to help him get clarity and see things in a new way. My perspective on life and relationships was different than his because I *had* experienced someone close to me dying before their time, and I was keenly aware of the regrets that come with that event. With my explanation, he better understood why I wanted him to entertain the hypotheticals, and from then on we had a more productive talk. He agreed that, yes, if one of us were to die, he would regret the time we didn't have together. But he strongly felt everything was unfolding in the way it was meant to unfold. He then talked about his kids and how they hadn't really been contacting him and making time to see him before he was to leave on this trip. They knew the dangers associated with mountain climbing, and he decided that if something happened to him they were meant to have those lessons.

I told Wylie how I had been on the fence about meeting him that night. He said he would have been sad and confused if I had declined, because in his mind our last conversation was so great, and that we were okay. Funny – I had thought that last conversation went badly, but he didn't see it that way. He told me again that he is not a runner, and that he is *not* going to run from us – not once had he wanted to run! So interesting – I had never understood that before. I had been thinking his wanting a break was so he could decide *if* he should stay or run, but he was telling me he had no intention of leaving. All he wanted was a break, to regain his footing. He said I was the one who had been the runner! Wylie was a very good listener and stayed completely engaged, not once interrupting me. I talked and cried, and he validated all my points and took responsibility for how I was feeling because of his actions.

After listening to me, he had an insight about us that he shared: he made a W with his fingers and the middle point of the fingers represented us as two that came together as one – this is us, when we are in our heart-space. But when we are both out of our heart-space and back in our head space, we are separated and become each side of the W as two individuals again. He continued, "When you are in your head-space you see how you want our relationship to go: you want us to live together and grow old together. But if you can just stay in your heart-space, then we just ARE, and we unfold perfectly. Even when things seem hard, it will feel okay – like this talk – and it will all just unfold as it is meant to."

When Wylie was in his head-space, he said he didn't understand my energy or our relationship. He was afraid he couldn't live up to the ideal of who he needs to be for US. He was trying to move back to his heart-space because he realized he needed to get back to us being together again, even though he didn't know what that would be like. This seemed like a real breakthrough for him, and his thought process brought me back to Jane. I needed to understand why time and again he had withheld information about their activities together. It had eroded my trust.

He admitted that he knew from the beginning something about her "activated" me, and he had done his best to not throw their relationship in my face. This situation was his own fault because of how he had handled things in the past. He agreed to answer any question I asked where she was concerned, but he would not initiate telling me things about her. I told him he *needed* to take responsibility and at least tell me the big things. He then admitted he didn't know for sure if Jane would climb Everest, and he didn't really want her to.

I needed to know one more thing. If something happened on the mountain and if Jane came on to him, what would he do? He was silent for a long time – too long. I was instantly mad and felt I had my answer before he said one word. He claimed he wouldn't answer because he didn't want to entertain my hypothetical. He said he could not see any scenario where she would come on to him, because nothing had ever happened between the two of them. I reminded him that her situation had changed: she was now free from marriage – her husband was dead. He said no matter what, he would never ever let any situation happen while he was guiding. And if she crossed a line, he was not some scumbag who would take advantage of a widow. I pushed back because he would *not* be guiding the Everest trip. He then admitted there was some remote part of him, that if the situation was right, he could be with Jane.

All I wanted to do was to leave – to run. We had had this conversation before and he had always taken the stance that he would **not** do anything with her – ever. His admitting it was a possibility was the fear I had always known; I had always felt. Since I had nothing to lose now, I asked him if he had ever done a mushroom ceremony with her. He said they had. My gut already knew the answer before I asked the question, but my head still reacted. I just didn't know what to say. I asked if he had had the same experience with her that we had with the mushroom medicine where we became one Soul. He laughed at me and reminded me how that single experience was the most profound of his life, and no one could ever touch where we had been together.

He grabbed my face and said he had never been more **in love** with me than he was now, at this moment. He appreciated who we were together, and the ability for us to have these hard conversations just made our relationship grow stronger. He expressed that when we're together we are pure magic! And then we proved it in bed. The next day my brain wrote this email…

Wylie,

I am super thankful we had time last night. When we are together it is pure magic!!!

I've been writing my notes from our convo and as I typed them I have to address the one sticky part that came up.

~~Once~~ A Cheater... 185

First, I appreciate you taking responsibility for me being in the place I am with my thoughts about Jane. But last night you did move from your previous position that I had nothing to worry about with you and her – and how you would not EVER do anything with her – to last night you saying that you would/could never have with her what you have with me, but that there is a remote but real possibility you could be with her.

You realize, that one statement alone kills me, and I will now never be able to feel secure where you and she are concerned. It's like you decided in that moment to give yourself an out because you stated there is a remote possibility – an excuse to NOT act in complete integrity where I am concerned. If I have misunderstood please correct me.

I'm not one for ultimatums and would leave you before I had to ask you to exclude anyone from your life. So if there is some remote possibility, as you stated last night, then I am now going to make one request of you. I am asking you to not do any more psychedelic ceremonies with her where the two of you would be alone. She has met people in the medicine community so she can find someone else to do that with if it's outside of a group activity. And I ask the same of any heavy drinking in the same situation – alone. She loves her tequila, as we know. Notice I only requested "alone." Why put yourself in an altered state with her if there is ANY part of you that doesn't know??? And for the record it FUCKING sucks that you said now you didn't know. I'll be honest, it has the ability to be the undoing for me with us. The only reason it isn't is because of Spirit and how they have been guiding you with me. In my heart-space I don't believe it will ever happen – but my head-space thinks I'm a fucking lunatic for believing what my heart thinks.

*You have said you would not do something with her because you know how I would be devastated by that. You even said if anything ever changed with your feelings for anyone else, you would talk to me first before doing anything physically – but you have less control doing that in an altered state. I feel pretty pissed that you did a mushroom ceremony alone with her – that's just not ok. Look, I'm not trying to own or control you, but this relationship has to be for the good of **both** of us and you need to be thinking about me and not just yourself, Wylie.*

If this is too much to ask just let me know. I really think it is fair based on the situation you have created here.

       In the end my heart would not let me send it, but my heart let me send this text instead...

9-27-20 1:09 p.m.

[Laurie] *I have one request from last night. I ask, based on what you disclosed about not being sure, that you don't do any psychedelic medicines or heavy drinking alone with Jane. She can find someone else to do those things one on one with – she has the medicine community. Why put yourself in an altered state and risk us when you are not 100% positive? I hope you take some time to*

~~Once~~ A Cheater...

think more about what we talked about. If I misunderstood what you said, please correct me. I did hear you loud and clear that you know you would never have with her, or anyone, what you have with me and my heart sings when it hears that. I just really hope after last night you know what we have and how otherworldly it is, and you do your part to protect my heart and not risk us. 🌈🦁👩‍🦰🦁🏳️

[Wylie] *I hear you loud and clear. I do cherish what we have and last night was other worldly* 😍 😍 😍 😚 😚 😚 💯 !!

[Laurie] *I love you, babe, utterly and completely* 😍 😚 😚 😚

[Wylie] 😚 😚 😚 😚 😚 😚

Three days later he sent me a song. It had been a very long time since he had done that. The song was "Nights in White Satin" by the *Moody Blues*. It is a very haunting song that says "I love you" over a dozen times. Receiving that song sent my heart over the moon. It was just what I needed from him. To top it off he also sent the song "I Won't Give Up On You" by *Jason Mraz*. In all he sent me three songs and I was flying high. He would be leaving on an airplane to China the next night. I had a friend in town and would be driving very close to Wylie's house on my way to meet her the next day, so I asked if I could stop by to kiss him one more time before he left. He texted back...

[Wylie] *That would be lovely. What an awesome surprise* 😚 😚 😚

When I got to his house the next day, the first thing we did was christen our new songs. We slow-danced and kissed for a very long time. Being in his arms took me to a place I can't describe, where it felt like we melted into one again. I brought Wylie a tiny heart rock to carry with him on his journey, so he would have a piece of me with him. I had infused my energy and love into it by carrying it with me on a hike.

We didn't have much time because I was meeting my friend for dinner, but there was one more thing I needed to do before he left on his trip. I had to read him the thoughts I had written. I expressed my concern for what he had disclosed the evening before about there being a possibility, no matter how remote, that he could somehow respond to an advance by Jane. He needed to know that any action in that direction was not alright with me. He expressed again that he had no interest in her and didn't want me to worry about that while he was gone. I still asked him to be observant on this trip; he was going to have three weeks to spend with her. I wanted him to think about his feelings toward her and his real motives where she was concerned. She was a friend, yes, but more a client. Had he been playing both sides and possibly sending her signals of slight interest in order to keep up and even increase the financial support? One of the things Wylie had expressed in our break was wanting to own himself. Did he really own himself where she was concerned? She was a huge part of his income, between the personal training and all the Hiking Adventure trips she had contributed to. I secretly wondered if she was financing this Island Peak hike as well. Wylie had been fund raising to climb Everest, so it didn't make sense in my mind to spend $10,000 on a trip when he still needed to raise $30,000 for the Everest climb. I kept that thought to myself.

      I kissed him goodbye, as promised, and as I drove away I hoped my frank talk had not caused him to feel upset with me. Moments later I had my answer...

[Wylie] 😚 😚 😚 😚 😍 😍 😍 😍 😍

[Laurie] *I deeply love you and I do believe we are getting stronger and things between us are unfolding perfectly* ✖ ⭕ 😍 😚 😚 😚 😚

[Wylie] *You are welcome. I'm glad you share with me. I love you deeply as well and it is perfection* 😚 😚 😚

~~Once~~ A Cheater...

Chapter 37

I Won't Give Up

~song by *Jason Mraz*

https://open.spotify.com/track/05pKAafT85jeeNhZ6kq7HT?si=xORCQgjcSvCQnSHw44JqqQ

I still had only told a handful of people about Wylie and our breakup, but I tried to keep up my social calendar during those difficult months after I ended things with him. It was especially important for me to connect with people I could have deeper spiritual conversations with. I had gotten close to Medicine Woman, whom Wylie had engaged to explore Ayahuasca. She and I had last gotten together after my full day with Thomas, when we talked mostly about the big project I was bringing into the world with Mark's help. I had also shared the information Spirit had relayed about how the medicine was still working in Wylie.

I invited her to my house for dinner and afterwards we sat on the couch and talked. We talked about Wylie's mountain climbing trip on Island Peak, and I shared with her that Jane was considering climbing Everest next year and was using the Island Park climb as a test. She knew Jane through the medicine community, as Jane had participated with Wylie and with her in an Ayahuasca session. Of course, he had not disclosed that to me; I had found out another way. I also shared what had happened with us, ending our relationship. But I didn't tell her about Bumble-Gate out of respect for Wylie, since she was friends with him, and not everyone would understand the complexities of our situation.

I was honest with her about the feeling I had that Jane was interested in Wylie. We talked about the medicines, and I asked her about the San Pedro ceremony Wylie had attended many months before, instead of honoring his obligation to go with me to the Ronald McDonald Charity event. I knew Medicine Woman had been there, because Wylie had talked to her about the topic of possession relating to being labeled boyfriend and girlfriend, and he shared their conversation with me at dinner months before. She surprised me by confirming Jane had indeed participated in that ceremony – I knew it! I instantly felt betrayed when I realized Wylie had blatantly lied to me about that event, and I voiced my concerns to Medicine Woman. She said it made no sense that Wylie would have attended the ceremony to support Jane, since Jane would have had her and other people she knew there, besides Wylie. Regardless, I still felt Jane had asked Wylie to go with her, although perhaps he had done it to preserve their

~~Once~~ A Cheater...

financial arrangement. It didn't matter; my gut had *always* told me he had gone in order to be there for her first time experiencing San Pedro – he had chosen her over me, and I knew it. I had called it out, and he lied about it. I felt like Medicine Woman wanted to tell me something more about Wylie and I wanted to ask, but was too afraid of what might be revealed. So I didn't pursue it.

 Despite hoping earlier for no contact with Wylie while he was gone, that was not how things unfolded. He was in constant contact with me during his entire trip. I had made significant plans of my own while he was gone: it had only been five months since we completed our R2R2R Grand Canyon hike, and while I was still in top shape I wanted to conquer a new hike called Cactus to Clouds, in Palm Springs, California. It was a 19.8-mile hike climbing 10,459 feet to the top, and like the Grand Canyon, it passed through five eco-systems. I wanted to achieve something similar to what Wylie was doing, and this would be a significant challenge but without the cold and inclement weather. My challenge was going to happen in just one day versus his two weeks of actual climbing, and I would only be climbing to 10,459 feet vs. his 10,922-foot climb ending at 20,000 feet in elevation! But mine was still considered a big hike.

 Stacy and Sal had agreed to accompany me on my crazy journey. I was to climb the first 8,000 feet by myself while they took the tram up to meet me. Then Stacy would climb the remaining 2,500 feet to the top with me while Sal hung out waiting for us to summit and return. Unfortunately, the tram had maintenance issues the weekend we planned to go. Since we had already arranged to be out of town, we all piled into the RV and made a diversion to Utah to visit Arches National Park and Canyonlands National Park to hike. I continued to be surprised every time I heard from Wylie. He even asked me to send him pictures and expressed disappointment that we had gone without him.

 Wylie's trip to Island Peak was very different than his Aconcagua hiking trip had been. They acclimated to the elevation change starting at 9,383 feet in the town of Lukla by next ascending to several villages in Nepal and staying at hostels every night. The four of them shopped, hung out, and ate in these villages while exploring and going on daily group hikes to further acclimate. He posted lots of pictures on *our* Hiking Adventure Instagram account, even though this was neither a Hiking Adventure trip nor one he was guiding. Stacy followed this account and would show me the new posts. I could not help but feel a jealousy at seeing him posting pictures with Jane next to him – they looked like a couple. And it was on *our* Hiking Adventure business site, to boot – the business I had named, co-partnered, financed, and built a website for. It was that day that I discovered there wasn't a single picture of me on that page – not one! This was despite the fact that I had guided five trips with him. And he had posted several pictures of personal adventures we had been on together – but not any that included me in the picture. It was like I was invisible and completely hidden. But not Jane – she was in several of the posts, and I was greatly saddened at this new discovery. With this recognition, I dug a little deeper into the social media posts that I had ignored over all that time. It was interesting that – although I had tagged Wylie in two Facebook posts, which would have been added to his own personal Facebook timeline – he had hidden them. Imagine being in a relationship with someone for over two years and knowing they had not only kept you from meeting their kids, but there was no public evidence you were even in their life – which made me wonder why he was really hiding me. Was it so he could be with other women and preserve the appearance of not being in a relationship at all? My mind went to the worst places. I wanted to reply to him saying how slighted, sad and crushed I felt that I didn't even exist in his world, and that he could contact me when he wanted me to be a real part of his life. But I didn't, because texting was not the place to address any of these concerns. This would have to wait for his return.

Riding in the RV between Arches and Canyonland while and looking out the window at the beautiful scenery, an epiphany when I realized the strong contrast between the scenery and my own ugly thoughts. I did not like the person I had become since my breakup with Wylie. I didn't like the conversations I was having with people, in that my life did not usually include any drama or many negative expressions. My conversations were normally more upbeat and fun and even inspirational. This negative spin had pulled my vibration way down – that was clear. I had had nice texting convos with Wylie the day before, and I had been feeling better about him – but now I felt like I had lost my *real* self and didn't know how or if I could get myself back...and still be with him. Serious doubts were creeping back in, and every part of me wanted to stop all communication, erase all my connections to him on social media, and take down our Wall of Adventure when I got home so I could harden my heart and get ME back!

Stacy noticed my attitude change and we talked about it. I voiced my social media concerns and how hard it was for me – knowing Wylie was having these great experiences with Jane. She already spent more time with him, and they saw each other more frequently. Here she was, traveling with him for three more weeks, and for the second time that year. I had never even spent two consecutive weeks with just the two of us. I didn't know how I was going to survive this trip! Stacy did her best to put things back into perspective for me, reminding me of the effort Wylie had been making lately. She pointed out how the songs he had recently sent said a lot about how he felt about me. Jane didn't get songs from Wylie – at least not that I knew of.

The next weekend the Cactus to Clouds tram was up and running once again. It was a challenging 8,000-foot hike by myself up to the tram, and it gave me lots of thinking time. I made a *Cactus to Clouds* playlist on Spotify that featured every song Wylie had ever sent me during our two-year relationship. Meanwhile, I kept thoughts of Jane at bay, and just made a plan to direct my thoughts to the amazing things I was creating in my life while trying to make the world a better place. It worked – I killed it!

Stacy and I summited Cactus to Clouds about four hours before Wylie summited Island Peak. Of course, Jane stood next to Wylie at the summit with her traditional pose – holding both arms above her head, as she did in *every* picture. I mimicked her stance in my own summit. Ya, it was petty – but it sure made me feel better; I am still human, after all!

Two days later I was in Kansas again on a business trip. It was late at night and I couldn't sleep. I was scrolling through some of the new summit pictures Wylie had posted. So many people commented, giving him congratulations. But one message in particular caught my attention:

Mom here. [She didn't have an account and had posted though someone else's account.] *Good on you, son! So proud of you and Jane! Give my love to Jane.*

My heart stopped. GIVE MY LOVE TO JANE! Wylie was *not* close to his mother, who lived a state away, and he barely talked to her. But apparently he had told her Jane was going on the trip, and apparently she knew about Jane and felt enough of a closeness to want to send her love. What was I missing here??! Wylie's best friend was also on the trip and there was no call-out or sending her love to him, even though Wylie had known him much longer than Jane. I felt a mix of confusion and fury as I felt my vibration tank once again. I just couldn't get that message from Wylie's mom out of my mind. I tried to justify it, because I knew she desperately wanted to be a part of his life. Maybe this was just her way of asserting herself into his life and the comment actually meant nothing, but instead put her in a light of being a more active part of his life than she really was. The whole situation definitely rocked me.

I didn't show my hand to Wylie or voice any concerns. He "liked" the comment from his mom, so he had definitely seen it. If it was really something to worry about he would have hidden it, like he had hidden my two posts on his timeline. I could not control what anyone posted, or all the women I didn't know who sent him "like" and "love" responses to every one of his posts. The only thing I could control was me – so I officially banned myself from looking at any more of his social media. It was poisoning my mind, and social media was only partial reality, at best. I never looked back again and went to work watching more spiritual videos to once again raise my vibration.

Wylie called me shortly after he was back in the country and suggested plans to see me the next day, which was surprising, considering his jet lag and lack of sleep. I felt like he was really making an effort again where I was concerned. We met for an early dinner that turned into just sharing beers and appetizers. His trip was really good. He had spent a good amount of time with his best friend, but interestingly had not told him about the current situation between us – interesting because his friend had been the first person he ever told about me and our relationship. Also, my suspicion about Jane paying for Wylie's trip was incorrect – his roommate had paid for the trip. She had paid for several trips for him in the past and had generously sponsored him as a vet. She also helped the International Adventure business, owned by his best friend, who was a very dear friend of hers.

When Jane was mentioned, I brought up the loving comments his mom had made about her – wondering aloud if his mom even knew about me, since his kids still didn't. Wylie said she did indeed know about me and our relationship. I then broached the social media topic and shared all the observations I had made since he was gone. He denied that I was not in any picture of our mutual Hiking Adventure business, and to prove it pulled his phone out to show me. But he was wrong – there were none. And I made sure to point out the ones that included Jane. He got a sheepish look on his face in realization and quickly put his phone away, not wanting to further open that can of worms – too late for that!

As long as we were on the topic, I said that not only was I hidden on his deceptive online life – I was still hidden in his *real* life as well. He had never let the CrossFit community know about me as more than a friend, despite my participation there for well over a year. I cried a little and said how hurt this made me feel, and how I felt insignificant and unimportant in his life. He acknowledged my feelings, wiping the tears away, and said he had not felt he was hiding me, or realized that I felt hidden. I pointed out that he had not been standing in his truth and asked him if there was any place in his life where he was 100% truthful? I knew he hid parts of his life from his kids and from his friends, and I reasoned this could not feel good. I added that it seemed like he had created dual lives with me and Jane.

"You don't tell her about our activities, and I have to ask you about your activities with her. Why isn't what you share with her more like your relationship with your roommate? What are you actually afraid of? Are you just using Jane – "playing her," in a way, for financial gain? I can no longer feel like you do things to protect HER. And when do *my* feelings matter? Why am I not your number-one concern? If you truly believe Jane has no feelings for you, how could there be anything at risk financially? Instead, you are severely damaging US. All the hiding makes me wonder what you are hiding."

Rhetorically, I asked, "Have you been in some sick, twisted game with me? It's really hard knowing you spend ten times more time with Jane than you have EVER spent with me since we've been together. I have not even had two consecutive weeks with you. And the Bora Bora trip we planned together last year got taken away from me because of the timing of your divorce. And then there were the two trips we had planned but couldn't take because of the Bumble ordeal. It all makes me feel insignificant and "less" – like you can't tolerate being with me for longer periods of time, but you can with Jane. It makes me question if we should even be together. We either remedy this, where we are back together, or if you are not ready I'm pulling back all communication, because I can't do this back and forth – half in, half out. I cannot be hidden anymore! Not at CrossFit, or at our Integration Circle, or online. I won't be blatant about the relationship online, because of your kids, but I should no longer have to censor things about us." To myself, I reasoned this had been his MO in **all** his past relationships; it was an old pattern he needed to correct.

Finally, I read to him again the compilation of notes of Thomas' reading concerning our relationship, and reminded him how Thomas said we needed to build a stronger foundation. Now we would need to work on **re**-building it – because, according to Thomas, we were going to have a "test" in our relationship, but by December things would be better. We were still officially on a break and had not made an explicit decision to come back together yet. I wanted to know how he thought we were doing, and where he thought we were going in the relationship. He didn't answer but directed my attention back to dinner and asked me to just enjoy this night together. I shifted the conversation back to less threatening topics like work, travel and activities I had participated in when he was gone.

Even our difficult talks still had the effect of bringing us closer together. It was a magical reunion, and it felt like our relationship *was* slowly coming back together, even if we hadn't made specific decisions. I spent the night with him for the first time in months, but woke up in the middle of the night in a dreamlike state: *I saw circles that were all interconnected, and each one had a light outlining it in muted but beautiful colors on a black background. Even more than what I saw in my mind's eye, I felt the vibration and love I have only experienced on my journeys to the Other Side. My instant reaction was a joyous feeling of being in that state once again. Then, in the upper left-hand corner, I saw a flash of white and I saw Mark's face, mostly his smile.*

It had been a long time since I had seen Mark, and I had almost forgotten how beautiful his smile was. Joyous tears instantly formed in my eyes and ran down my cheeks. Then, as suddenly as it was there, his face was gone. It was not a dream but something else – Other Worldly. And I felt nothing but gratitude for the extraordinary experience. I knew I was being reminded of the vibration I was.

After Wylie's and my reunion, our texting resumed a more normal cadence – more like it was when we were fully together. He was back to wishing me a good morning and goodnight in text, and everything in between...even asking me to see him again.

We met for breakfast and afterwards I helped him shop for his upcoming Hiking Adventure trip. We kept the conversation pretty lighthearted and just enjoyed spending time together. But when he went on his trip, I didn't hear a single word from him in the three days he was gone. I got really worked up, not understanding how we could have gone from such a great, intense connection that ended with him thanking me for the time together – to absolutely nothing! By the time I heard the custom ping of his text message, when I was hiking with Stacy, I was too pissed to even respond. I waited seven hours to send him a non-typical, one-word answer to his question. I just couldn't stomach the inconsistencies with him! I asked him to call me later when he was unpacked from his trip. I needed to have a real discussion – not a texting conversation.

He called me while I was eating dinner at my parents' house with Ryan. I let everyone know in advance he would be calling, so I left to take the call in another room. I had the conversation already planned out in my mind, and I launched right in. I had experienced another profound Toad medicine journey while he was gone, and while I was on the Other Side, Spirit had showed me the true nature of the love I had for him. I was shown that, aside from the relationship with my kids, there was no one on this planet I had more love for than him, and I felt he needed to know I was coming from a place of love. Next I expressed my frustration at our complete lack of contact over the last few days, and I explained that I could not be in a limbo relationship with him. I was ready to come back together as a couple, and asked him rhetorically if he needed more time to figure things out. From our contact over the past several weeks, I believed he *was* ready to resume our relationship. He didn't answer the implied question, which itself was an answer, because if he had been ready to come back together the answer would have been a simple yes. He explained that he was at the car wash and not in a good place to talk, but asked me to meet him the next day to discuss it.

I was done waiting and was not about to wait one minute longer so he could string me along – just to tell me later he needed more time. So I asked him to share his thoughts with me now. He said he had been thinking a lot on this last trip, which was why he had not been in contact. He had been deeply affected by the difficulty of the Island Peak climb in Asia. He realized that if he was going to make it off Everest alive, he was going to need to divert ALL his time, energy and attention to getting ready for that mountain – and although he loved me, it might be best if we delayed coming back together as a couple until *after* he completed the Everest climb. My mind quickly made the calculations, and I realized he was talking about next June – more than seven months from then! I was done waiting and being in limbo. He had tested my tolerance and patience to the nth degree, and I needed to be all in or all out! I told him I was pulling all the way out and asked him to contact me if and when things changed. And just like that I had given up!

~~Once~~ A Cheater...

~~Once~~ A Cheater...

Chapter 38

I Don't Want to Be Your Friend

~song by *Nina*

https://open.spotify.com/track/75AKFZo2Dc58GXc8fCKFmx?si=xL3WI4VJSy-jktB0_5f7cQ

The next day I felt severe regret in ending my relationship with Wylie on the phone without a real, in-person, conversation. Did I jump the gun? Was I too harsh? Were my expectations of him too unrealistic? He had a real point about his anxiety around Everest. Maybe there was another way we could move forward and still be together. All these thoughts cascaded through my mind, building on one another. I remembered Thomas had warned me that Spirit was working on my patience; perhaps there was more work to do in that area. I finally relented and texted him...

[Laurie] *When we last spoke you said you wanted to talk in person and I didn't let you. I've been thinking about that, and I would like to see you in person. You really shocked me about asking to not be in each other's lives until June – I wasn't expecting that on ANY level and I feel numb about it. I'm open Wednesday to Sunday. Would you like to come up here for dinner one of those days?*

[Wylie] *Let's do lunch at Tryst. Does Thursday work? I too was shocked by our conversation and the outcome.*

[Laurie] *I want to have hope, Wylie. My greatest desire is for us to be a part of each other's lives. I don't want to be afraid of this anymore.*

[Wylie] *Perfect. Me too.*

He had picked Tryst Café, the location of our first date. Although I would rather have had a dinner meeting, I was encouraged by his wanting to meet at our special place. I had hope again, and I excitedly arrived first in my Halloween costume. I wore a long, flowing white dress and put two tiny devil horns on the top of my head – I was two parts angel and one part devil. He walked into the restaurant and I began playing on my phone the verse from the *Eagles* song "One of These Nights," which referenced my costume. It was also the first real song he had ever sent me for our *L.A. Woman* playlist, but I doubted he remembered that anymore. He laughed at my clever gesture, and as I stood up he hugged me – no kiss. It was suddenly platonic and that set the tone.

We sat down and ordered our usual. The energy was not good; it felt chaotic. He said our phone conversation had wrecked us, because I had pulled away again, making it all or nothing. He couldn't understand, with the way we felt about each other, how I could go to nothing. He had been reflecting on the Everest climb and explained again how doing it was such a big task that he would need his full attention on it. I was like crack cocaine to him. He had never felt anything like this before from anyone he had ever been with. He said it was like I was an addiction for him. He had never in his life felt so attracted or drawn to anyone, EVER. And this was why he picked the restaurant where we had our first date. He still loved me, that had not changed, and he wanted me in his life. He couldn't bear to NOT have me in his life. But then as he was walking into the restaurant to meet me, this profound thought suddenly "dropped in" for him – he needed to stay connected as friends until his Everest climb was complete. We could still support each other and talk and collaborate, but not be romantic... I cut him off with a harsh "NO!" It was like he was trying to resurrect the conversation we had had in the jacuzzi tub in Myrtle Beach, when he broached the conversation about us still being friends if we were no longer together romantically.

I was instantly pissed and started gathering my things to leave. It was NOT happening!! He begged me to stay to finish the conversation. My anger flashed at him, and I said I could not imagine supporting him in this way so he could just meet someone else, I didn't think he would remain unattached during that time. He defended his proposal, explaining it had nothing to do with wanting to be with anyone else! He didn't have the energetic bandwidth to be with me – let alone be in *another* relationship. He felt like he was almost going to have to become a monk during this time so he could survive the mountain.

He went on to say he had just come from a meeting with his best friend, who owned International Adventure business, where Wylie had to officially declare his intentions to climb Everest in 2020. He also shared that Jane had had too difficult a time on Island Peak and would not be joining him on the Everest climb. At least that was good news, and I was happy he had shared it proactively. But I pushed back hard on being just friends, because I was in love with him and would not be able to be around him without being physical. I suggested we could be together and hold hands and kiss without having sex if he wanted to retain his sexual energy.

I then told him he had wrecked my confidence in moving forward with someone new in the future. He had made so many comments about my age over the past year that I had begun to doubt myself physically. He had even made an age comment at breakfast a week before, and it had made me feel supremely uncomfortable. He made me feel like he put so much stock in my physical appearance – as if it even mattered on *any* level. It was odd, because he said he thought I was by far the most attractive person he had ever been with. I asked him if he valued my outer beauty more than my inner beauty. I also resented how he had made the Bumble app cutoff at age 49 – when I was 50. I wouldn't have

~~Once~~ A Cheater...

even matched with him! He denied it all – not that he had not said it, but that he thought any of what I had expressed was actually true. He said I was the most attractive woman my age he had ever seen. And if he lined up ten people right now and asked them to guess my age, not one of them would guess I was over 45 years old. Some might even go to the early 40s or even as low as 39 – that's how young he thought I looked. He promised he had only ever *joked* about my age – and if he had meant it. that would just be mean. He wanted to assure me none of what he had been bringing up about age had to do with his feelings or his attraction to me – and every word he said in my birthday poem was still true.

He declared he had made his decision. We were at a standstill. I told him he was selfish and how it's always been about him! He agreed it WAS selfish – mountain climbing IS selfish. I said yes, but that he's *always* been selfish in his life – because his Adventure Racing was selfish too in terms of the amount of money and time spent away from his family. I didn't say it, but he had been completely selfish where his kids were concerned, and I could see why the relationship with them was strained. Everyone makes sacrifices in a relationship, but it was me making all the sacrifices in ours! I then got mad all over again about Bumble. He said he hated the fact that Bumble ever happened and that I had found out. My instant response was that I didn't think I would ever, *ever* be able to trust him again. He said he couldn't even begin to address that issue until after the mountain climb.

I tried to imagine how things would look in his proposed scenario. Did he think we could just be reduced to friends and then later, after his climb in June, resume a romantic relationship. He was not a planner by nature and declared he couldn't think even 48 hours out, so he knew he couldn't begin to think about June.

We sat there in silence for a long time just staring into each other's eyes. He rubbed my arm and then I held his hand. I told him just the feeling of holding his hand was better than anything I had ever had with anyone else. He felt the same. Then I started negotiating and fighting for us again in earnest. How would we go to events at friends' houses and act like we were just friends – it was a ridiculous thought. Would we not be holding hands? He said he could hold my hand, and I added that I would at least want to be able to kiss him too. We decided to think about it some more and meet again later to talk about it. He paid the bill and we walked out to my Jeep where we hugged. He kissed me one more time before I got into my Jeep and drove home.

He had ***forever*** ruined the specialness of our first-date restaurant and all the memorable lunches we had had there! How dare he use our place in that way – I would never have done that to him! He could have picked 15 other restaurants within a one-mile radius of that one. Tears began to cloud my vision. Our relationship felt really, *really* over this time, because my heart already knew being friends would never work for me! The longer I drove, the more indignant I became. How dare he push me out of his life right when he was attempting to achieve the most difficult task he had ever taken on. When the going gets tough, isn't that the time that you cling to the ones you love and care about more than ever? He was the most selfish person in my life – I toggled between being mad

~~Once~~ A Cheater...

as a hornet, exasperated, and Soul crushed. I realized as we left the restaurant that my heart had been hemorrhaging – and he had put a band-aid on the wound as he told me goodbye at my car. I bled out before I got home.

I called Stacy and asked her to meet me at the house. Lucky for me she was available. We arrived at my house at the same time. She immediately hugged me and we went in and sat down on the couch to talk. I told her the entire story, not leaving a single detail out. By the end of the discussion I knew that my heart could NOT accept less for itself than it deserved. I knew my value and my worth, and I was not going to dispense one-sided friendship for him to use up and throw away later. I had one thought, and it brought me to sobbing tears... When I recovered enough to speak, I told Stacy I needed her to help me do something; I stood up and beckoned her to follow me into the bedroom. I turned to face the Wall of Adventure, and without even turning to look at her, I asked if she would help me take it down. She agreed to help, and said it would be best to not stare at it every day. I sighed, then left to get the ladder and an empty box, thinking to myself: Take Down That Wall!! Within minutes, our two years of adventures were relegated to a cardboard box on an empty shelf.

I should have known better – known that things were headed in this direction. The signs were there in the music that had been playing while I was getting ready to meet Wylie – none of them good signs. I should have known when I invited him to have dinner at my house and he suggested a lunch meeting, that something bigger was up. But I believed what I wanted to believe...

Later, we traded emails back and forth with me trying to "sell" him on the value of remaining in his life, and him explaining that he had to honor his "download" (from Spirit) of us being friends, and how he felt it was out of his hands. I cried for 24 hours straight. The next morning my eyes were red and swollen, just in time for me to host my first ever Facebook live session, talking about my new spiritual project. I didn't even feel I looked like myself when I saw my reflection in the mirror before going live. Wylie showed up on Facebook in an effort to prove how committed he was to being my friend. I was grateful for the support, but being friends was absolutely and completely out of the question.

Twin Flames

We are twins reunited for purpose and growth

Of one thing I'm certain, we've taken this oath

To uphold and uplift one another in LOVE

To put no others above

It's a choice we made before we came,

a birthright for us both to claim

To learn and grow with each other

through space and time

Forever in your heart,

Forever in mine ♥

~~Once~~ A Cheater...

Chapter 39

She's Gone

~song by *Hall and Oates*

https://open.spotify.com/track/5dFoWIiJ2814hRwMYDcFiU?si=6FWRvoeMQkak0zP4U7c7Bg

I was feeling pretty sad and downhearted, and like I was in limbo with my life. I missed Wylie. I never wanted our relationship to be over, but I was done accepting less for myself than I knew I deserved. To ease the pain I pulled up our *L.A. Woman* playlist for comfort and was surprised to see a new song there. "She's Gone" by *Hall and Oates* had been added to the list by Wylie! Just two days earlier I had heard this very song on the way to meet Stacy to hike, and I told her about the lyrics and how the man in the song regretted losing the woman in his life. I joked with her about wanting to send that song to Wylie, as I felt it mirrored the loss he would be experiencing, but I didn't do it. Amazingly, we had both heard the same song and had an inclination to send it to one another. Clearly, Wylie and I were still connected energetically – yet another confirmation of our powerful Twin Flame affinity.

December became the month of my quest to find answers. I was failing miserably on my own in uncovering answers to the future of my relationship woes. As I have often done in the past, I turned to Spirit. Not only was I praying myself to sleep each night, I was talking to Mark and my Spirit team constantly. It wasn't enough. I needed more help, so I turned to my spiritual books library. I was drawn to a man who had written a book about auras. Dougall Fraser was a gifted medium but had been more inspired to help people understand their own gifts to the world through interpretation of their aura. I loved his book but had never had a reading with him. I found his website and scheduled an appointment for a video reading in the first full week of December. I also decided to book a reading with Moriah, a medium whom I trusted, and with whom I had had much healing through her insightful connection with Mark. We had not spoken in over two years – I was definitely due to talk to her again. The reading would take place right before Christmas.

About that time, I unexpectedly received an email from Wylie. Over a year before, I had been successful in procuring a Grand Canyon lottery reservation for our Hiking Adventure business, which I had done as a help to him and the business. As his trip approached, the weather took a turn for the worse, morphing into a blizzard that caused the National Park Service to cancel the trip.

He had accepted a refund instead of rescheduling, and since I had been financing our Hiking Adventure business by paying for lottery permits, the credit went back on my credit card. Even though he had previously reimbursed me for it, he still owed me a significant amount of money for our timeshare, but he asked me to send him the credit anyway. In hindsight, the timeshare had been a foolish idea. I did have three days after agreeing to it to rescind the deal, and had been on the verge of making that choice every single day. But Wylie had stood strong in our commitment and I went along, because in my mind him making a commitment like that was almost like proposing. That purchase spoke of his belief in the strength of our relationship – otherwise, how could he have taken a gamble with that much money. At the time we made the purchase, I could *never* have imagined we would be where we were now...

From: Wylie Heartley

To: Laurie Majka

December 3, 2019 4:07 p.m.

Subject: Touching Base

Hi Laur,

I hope all is well with you and your book is on track and moving toward publication. I hope you had a restful and relaxing Thanksgiving with your family.

I've been thinking about you quite a bit lately. Thanksgiving especially so, since I spent last year with you and your family. I cherish those memories and am very thankful that we shared so many good times and made so many wonderful memories.

Because of the weather, my Thanksgiving trip cancelled. Phantom Ranch actually refunded the money because of the weather. I'm not sure which credit card they refunded it to — it may have been yours since that might have been the one the original charge was made out to. If so, let me know and we can sort it out.

My Everest plans took a major hit today. The Chinese Tibetan Mountaineering Association raised the fees by $10,000. So instead of owing $30K, I am now essentially back to square one and owe $40K for the trip. If the company I'm going thru doesn't get at least four clients, the trip will cancel and I'll have to wait until 2021. It was going to be a stretch raising $30K so with the increase, it puts it even more out of reach. Either way, it should sort itself out within the next week or two.

Please know that if you ever need to touch base, I am here for you. I so want you to fulfill your dreams and I know sometimes challenges can be hard to overcome. You have amazing friends to support you and I hope you count me as one.

~~Once~~ A Cheater...

XOXO Wylie~

From: Laurie Majka

To Wylie Heartley

December 6, 2020 8:42 a.m.

Subject: Touching Base

Hi Wylie,

Even though we are not together, I will always wish the best for you and I really hope you are finding what you are looking for in life now. Yes, we made Lots and Lots of amazing memories in 2 short years. For me there is a cloud over those memories and I hope someday I will be able to look back at them and smile and cherish them as you do. But as the fog of loving you is lifting, I'm exposing such a deep imbalance in our relationship that I didn't see before. I gave so completely and fully without expectation – but I gave so much more than you did. I can now see how my love felt much too intense for you. I don't know how to love someone less – but the lack in where you met me should have been a guide. I think, as I wasn't getting what I needed from you, I just thought: I'll give more and that will make it better. But it seemed to have had the opposite effect and sent you looking for someone else. I feel so bad looking back at how hidden you kept me for so long, and how I accepted someone who would want to see me as little as you did. I just couldn't see it all until now – perspective has a way of doing that. I will be more ready for my next relationship so I do thank you for your role in that.

I too have been working on something big in myself, and that is being in my heart-space not my brain-space (remember our restaurant discussion?) – it is getting easier to do and is making me happier.

Let me know when you want to discuss the finances. I'm assuming this moment is not the best time for you, but we will need to wrap up the loose ends as we both move on in our lives...

Love, Laur~

     My reading with Dougall was different than with any other intuitive I had had before. He was also warm and open and insightful, and saw the world in "full color." Upon seeing me, he said my energy felt like he had put his finger in a light socket! I laughed at the imagery. He said that I had every color of green around me, including a color he could not describe with human words because we don't have that color on Earth. That color even has a distinct sound to it. He said when he sees my Soul he sees a little girl running around so excited, wanting to wake everyone up to raise their vibration. After talking about my aura and my future as he perceived it, there was time built into the reading for questions. I only had two for him: I wanted to know what he could foresee regarding my relationship, and what he felt the "hold the line" signs had been about.

He asked me to say Wylie's full name three times and to say his birth date. Then he concentrated for a minute before explaining that when he connects with a person's essence he hears a word that describes that person. Wylie's word was *inconsistent*. Well, no surprise there – nailed it! Dougall went on to say, "Wylie plays with wanting to be spiritual, but he can't quite stay there. He can't really meet you where you are." He sighed and revealed more. "I'm sorry, I don't think he will get there with you." My heart sank in my chest. I knew how hard Wylie had been trying with the medicines, and I remembered again how Thomas had said, "The medicines are still working in him." But Thomas had also said things along the lines of Wylie needing to do a lot of work on himself to meet me where I was. I had been so confident he would be able to get there with me. Of course, Bumble-Gate had been a forewarning of things going downhill between us. Dougall's perception gave me the feeling of holding a full, untied balloon between my fingers with the air slowly escaping and the balloon gradually losing volume. I wasn't ready to hear it. He then said the only thing I could really do was to connect with Wylie's Higher Self and tell him what I wanted and expected – and he warned me, "Do NOT accept less!" But he told me not to worry, because there was someone else out there for me who was already spiritually *there*. He then added: "'Hold the line' is about you holding the line for what you will accept for yourself."

I thanked Dougall for his words of wisdom and we disconnected the video session, leaving me alone with my thoughts as I transcribed the session into my journal. I still did not want to fully accept what I had just heard and how I interpreted it.

The next morning I went on a trail run with Storm. I couldn't get Dougall's words out of my mind. I knew it was very important for me to not accept less for myself than I deserved, but I also knew how much love I still carried for Wylie in my heart. There were so many aspects of our relationship that had been wonderful, and part of me wanted what we had, at all costs. The further I ran, the more distraught I became at the thought of how Wylie had not shown up for me. I speculated and wondered: if he came back to our relationship many months or years from now, would I want the relationship then? About that time I had come full circle on my run and arrived back at my Jeep.

When I turned the Jeep on, the volume of the radio was barely audible and I left it that way. It was time to talk to Mark – this was serious! I spoke to him out loud. "Mark! I think Dougall might be right about 'hold the line.' I feel like I really should move on from Wylie. So unless I hear from you, I will believe I should move on. If I am to wait for Wylie to "show up," I need to hear from you! You need to send me 'Hold the Line' or I will believe otherwise."

Even though I said all that, my heart was winning over my brain – I did not want this relationship to be over. I held my breath and turned up the volume of the radio. The station was on XM Radio, The Bridge. I had never heard the song, or the group that was playing. The lyrics said, "Give me a sign so there is no chance of changing my mind. There will be no chance of changing my mind." Wow, ok – but it wasn't "Hold the Line." That gave me some hope!

~~Once~~ A Cheater...

I drove to the grocery store to pick up a few things before going home. When I returned to my vehicle, I was deep in thought again about all Dougall had said. I began pulling out of the parking space, when the song on the radio suddenly caught my attention. The car screen said *Ambrosia* "How Much I Feel" – but that was not what was coming out of the speakers. "Hold the Line" was playing! I had to re-park my Jeep because I had instantaneously burst into tears of joy at the realization that *this* song was playing – in answer to my request! In the seven years since Mark had died, only on one other occasion had he sent me a song "on demand." I really didn't expect him to do it! But while I was running I had finally, albeit half-heartedly, made the decision to move away from the idea of having a relationship with Wylie. Before that, I was still convinced that "hold the line" was more about waiting for the relationship to come back than holding the line for myself. But I had made a very specific demand: "You need to send me 'Hold the Line' or I will believe Wylie and I are done!" Sending an "on demand" song was not Mark's style in life or in death, but today he had obliged. Spirit had answered me – without a doubt! Apparently, Wylie's and my story was still not finished.

The Christmas season was in full swing and I had been invited a month earlier to a party at the house of some close friends. Wylie had attended the same party the year before with me. That party had an "ugly Christmas sweater" theme, and I had gotten really creative. I custom designed matching sweaters in the theme of a childhood favorite Christmas Special, *The Year Without a Santa Claus*. We wore Heat Miser and Cold Miser "ugly" sweaters for the occasion. It was such a special outing that I even added a picture of the two of us to our Wall of Adventure. This year I RSVP'd for two, with the hope that he would make an appearance again with me. But as the party loomed, that seemed less and less likely, and I didn't invite him. I had been skirting the news of our breakup to my circle of friends – which had been easy all summer, since there was a legitimate excuse that Wylie couldn't attend several get-togethers due to his guiding schedule. But it was now time to rip off the band-aid and stand in my truth. Wylie and I were *not* together and I didn't know if it was even a possibility in the future. I spent the entire party trying to half explain why he wasn't there with me. Sadly, I learned that night that several people thought Wylie wasn't right for me. But I couldn't truly stand in my whole truth because I didn't want to tell anyone the real catalyst for our breakup was his Bumble-Gate blunder. Only four close friends, my sister, and the kids knew the truth. It put a huge damper on what should have been a fun evening.

I could not wait to connect with Moriah again, and the day of our appointment had finally arrived. I was in need of answers more than ever. The sound of her voice made me smile. From the other end of the telephone line, Moriah gushed, "I'm so excited I get to talk to you!" She jumped right into the reading, bringing my maternal grandmother through with an important message. After delivering it, and before I could respond, Moriah paused for a moment, suddenly more serious, and asked, "What's going on in your relationship now?" I replied simply how trying my life had been since July, and noted this was one of the most difficult times I had faced in my life. She asked, "Are you still in love, or not?" I said, "Yes, 100 million percent!" My grandmother returned with more words of wisdom from her perspective on the Other Side. She acknowledged the qualities I brought to the relationship, stating that I was an 11 on a scale of 1 to 10 (not that she was biased, lol). She told me through Moriah I needed to see myself as the prize, and she admonished that "Someone better fight for you, for once! You can't have this 'lack' feeling – it just seems like you got hit by a train." I agreed.

Then Mark chimed in, noting he and Wylie were very similar in their relationships with me. He said, "When you got too close emotionally, we both ran the fuck away." (Yep, that sounded *exactly* like Mark, expletive and all.) As long as Mark had shown up, I asked if he could answer my question about the "Hold the Line" signs. Through Moriah, he responded:

"He wants you to know you have an intense burning desire and you are going to overcome what is holding you back – and the greatest single obstacle of all for you right now is this selling yourself short. You are still settling for far less than you are capable of. So this is his sign to you! And you already know that whatever you think about grows. Only *you* can want something for yourself – and not because you think your partner wants it for you... So this has to be your own goal. *You* have to be absolutely clear about what you want it to be, and that's what you are doing. But the problem – and the reason he's sending you signs – is that **you have to have complete faith that you deserve this!**"

"I *did*," I said – at least that had been what I was saying out loud. But was it really true for me? Something for me to think about later. Then Moriah noted, "If it's any consolation to you, I think by this time next year the two of you are back together." I groaned and asked if it was really going to take that long. She said, "Yes, because he is being a putz." We both laughed. Then Moriah offered: "I could help Wylie, you know. Do you think he would be open to a reading?" I knew without a doubt he would be, because he had wanted a reading with Thomas.

Moriah continued with her own words of wisdom: "You need to put it out to the universe and forget about it. Imagine if your kids were standing outside of your window asking for something over and over again, saying, 'Mom. Mom. Moooom.' You would be like 'Shut up!' See, you are overfilling your swimming pool." She was right – I had been pretty obsessive with what I had been asking for. She said, "'Hold the Line' has to do with you feeling like you can't ever really have utopia – like you can't ever really have what you want, because when you do you are always disappointed. Even though you live a very spiritual life, and you tell other people to hold the line for themselves, you think it doesn't apply to you, because you already know this. But you are still human, and you still have that opposite voice in your head. So now you have to let go of it and let it go to the wind. And I have a feeling it's probably July or August that this relationship turns around. But here's the issue..."

She abruptly stopped mid-sentence and said, "God – why, Mark? Why? Oh, Mark..." Then she continued with what she had been saying: "...by that time you might have someone else fishing around for your attention, and you are going to have to make a decision about which relationship you want – because you can't do anything easy," she kidded me. "Here's the problem: Who the hell do you know who's still a rocker, who's still famous, who is in a band?" I said, "Nobody." She then realized: "Oh shit! This person that Mark's talking about is somebody who's still pretty prevalent in the industry – and would remind you of him [meaning Mark]. How the hell would you ever meet someone like that," she wondered out loud. "This is like by this summer." She sighed and said, "Just be prepared to meet someone," then added "I really don't know what you are gonna do!"

Somewhat at a loss, I changed the subject: "Is Wylie my Twin Flame?" Moriah replied, "Yes, but you have more than one. Mark was your Twin Flame too." Wow – that was a quadruple confirmation: Moriah, CJ (the angel connector), Thomas, and Holly (the oracle reader)!

Moriah concluded the reading by stating, "Mark needs you to know one more thing: You need to be number one in the universe – you need to be *everything* to someone! Mark wants to bring the greatest love to you. He knew you needed to have the Twin Flame connection as a bridge to get you where you need to be next. So now the energy to fix things is on *Wylie, not you*!! Because this is Wylie's life-lesson – and you can't take it away from him! Right now you are Wylie's teacher, and he will need to be vulnerable, not emotionally verklempt or emotionally constipated. He needs to be doing the grownup work of letting somebody in. He needs to love you in a very intimate way." I added to that: "He has told me several times he doesn't feel like he is ready for or deserves my love." Moriah softened a bit. "Yes, that's why this is about him." I got emotional and tears started to fill my eyes. "You know, I have loved him with my whole heart. That's what makes everything so difficult for me." She replied, "That's 100% correct."

It was time to pull the focus of Spirit back to my life-lessons and the spiritual work I was here on this Earth to do. As always, Moriah was very insightful in all areas of my life. Our exchange lifted me back into a higher vibration from where I had been at the start of the session, while talking about Wylie again. I fully trusted in her connection to the Other Side, and especially to Mark. One thing was clear: my lessons with Wylie were to be continued…

Through the generosity of Moriah, Wylie received a free reading from her the next day. He even sent me the recording so I could listen to what she had shared with him from Spirit. Wylie and Moriah were both veterans, they had both served in Desert Storm, and she recommended a book for him to read that she thought would help him with some of his struggles. I hoped he would take to heart the messages he had received from Spirit, and that he would read what Moriah recommended. I was for *anything* that had the potential to put us back on the same path together – in a relationship again.

Later that day I received a wrapped package. Wylie had sent me a present with a Merry Christmas note attached. I opened it on Christmas morning and sent him a picture of the book he had given me, next to the breakfast I had prepared for myself. I was all set to read…

[Wylie] *You are welcome. I think you'll enjoy it. Enjoy a relaxing day.*

[Laurie] 😘

Wylie didn't respond to my kissing face emoji, and that just sucked! I had a Christmas present for him too, but had not made an effort to deliver it before Christmas. On December 30, I decided to drop it off at his place. I sent a text message letting him know I would be leaving it outside by the door. I had no desire or intention to see him because I still felt slighted by him not responding to my emoji. I left it on the porch, wrapped and inside a bag with a note.

The next night was New Year's Eve, and I had made plans to spend it with some very close friends. We were all having a good time eating and reminiscing when I heard the familiar custom ping of a text coming in from Wylie. He had waited 24 hours before even responding to having received my gift. He sent a text picture of the ceramic toad (a reminder of our medicine journeys) I had given him, which was now sitting in its new home on a table in his bedroom.

[Wylie] *Happy New Year! Thank you so much! Very cool.*

I didn't reply. A response from him 24 hours after dropping off a gift felt more like a slap in the face than a thank you. He sent me a second text the next morning on New Year's Day, saying "Happy New Year." I didn't respond to that text, either.

Chapter 40

Love's a Hard Game to Play

~song by *Stevie Nicks*

https://open.spotify.com/track/6kV3WnGRt8RAxpFC4rl8Ni?si=MLfusMt7TZeZnQCVjI9B5Q

This was not the way I had envisioned bringing in the New Year, I had fantasized we would be together kissing each other at midnight. Thomas had said, "Spirit wants you to know *predictively,* over the next few months – like by December – you should feel more like 150% on more solid ground in your relationship." But Wylie's Free Will had certainly thwarted that prediction.

I'm sure Wylie was shocked that I hadn't answered his New Year's well wishes – it was very much unlike me. A week went by and I had resisted the urge to look at any of his social media posts – I didn't want to keep tabs on him. One day I was on my Spotify homepage and I noticed they had compiled my music year in review. It was interesting to see which songs I had played the most, and it was no surprise when the top ten were all songs from my *Twin Flame Choices* playlist that I had created over the summer. Music has such significant healing powers. Hmmm...that made me wonder what music Wylie might have been listening to. I searched for his name and paid a visit to his Spotify homepage. He had created a new playlist called *2020 New Music*. Although I didn't know most of the 283 songs, I wanted to understand *him* better – what better way than through his music.

I began listening, and the more I listened to his songs, the more intrigued I became. There were a ton of blues songs about being sad and downhearted and disappointed in yourself. But over and over again, a significant number of songs were about love and loss – and still being in love – and about waiting for someone (perhaps me) to come back. Each time I heard a song I felt could be about us, I added it to my *Twin Flames Choices* playlist. By the time I was finished there were 75 new songs added to my list. I felt in my heart that these were significant songs. And I could not forget how I had specifically asked Mark back in December to send me the song "Hold the Line" – if I *wasn't* supposed to leave the relationship with Wylie. With us apart now, that memory and these new songs gave me a small glimmer of hope again. They also took away some of the animosity I had been feeling. I could see he was hurting, and that softened me.

~~Once~~ A Cheater...

Around that same time, I received two pieces of mail at my address that belonged to Wylie, even though he never lived with me. I reached out by email to let him know I had received them and that I would be dropping them off to him on the way to the airport. I also mentioned I had found his *2020 New Music* and I had followed his list on Spotify. I told him I could understand from the songs he had included on the list how he was feeling, and that I had a new glimmer of hope for us and our relationship. I felt the first and last songs were the most significant, and I guessed he had picked them intentionally – well, hopefully so.

When I arrived at his house to drop off the mail, I was disappointed he was not there. He was on a trip, but his roommate was there and we were able to talk for several minutes. She told me Wylie had talked to her about what he did to ruin our relationship with regard to Bumble, and that she thought he was a jerk for doing what he did to me. But she said he didn't as a rule talk to her about his personal relationships, and it made me sad that he didn't have anyone close to him he felt he could confide in. But it was a nice validation hearing her thoughts about Bumble, and it felt good to connect to her because, as his roommate, she was connected to him.

Since my business trip to Kansas gave me quite a bit of downtime on the airplane, I created a new project for myself. I would listen to each song from Wylie's list, then write down the significant lyrics so I could see them on paper. It took me the entire plane ride there to barely begin recording the lyrics from his playlist, and it hardly made a dent in documenting all the songs in my journal.

Then the signs began. I was in my rental car on the way to my hotel when one of the songs from the list began playing on the FM radio station. Although there were 75 significant songs that I was documenting from Wylie's playlist, there were only one or two that would have played on this 80s-themed radio station – and what was playing was not an 80s song. Actually, twenty percent of his list was older than the 1960s era, another twenty percent were in the blues category, and the rest were all current music I had never even heard of. I was very surprised to hear one of his songs on that station – and if it had played five minutes later I would have already arrived at the hotel and would not have heard it.

Next, I pulled into the hotel parking lot and saw a car with a license plate that had Wylie's name on it! That sign blew me away. Spirit had been using license plates to communicate to me for many years, but seeing his name on one was pretty specific and unusual. I hypothesized there might be spiritual guidance working behind the scenes to bring us back together. At least it felt that way to me...

I continued to work on documenting the song lyrics in my journal during the next two nights at the hotel, as I felt compelled to include them all. I finished the last of the song lyrics on the airplane ride home. When we landed, I got into my parked vehicle in at the airport lot, and as soon as I started the engine I heard the last verse of the only other song on Wylie's list that could have played on one of the XM radio stations! The timing was incredible. I had been upgraded to first class on this trip, which allowed me to exit the airplane more quickly. The upgrade had been a catalyst in delivering me to my car just in time for me to hear this special song. I am always in awe of the way Spirit is able to send me songs with such perfect timing.

The next morning I got in my Jeep to go hike, and when I started the engine the song playing on the radio was the same song I had heard at the airport the night before. It seemed like Spirit was letting me know – unequivocally – this relationship was NOT yet finished...

~~Once~~ A Cheater...

Chapter 41

Can We Still Be Friends

~song by *Todd Rundgren*

https://open.spotify.com/track/5iMGkgvuX8bLLzVuZPAv79?si=bouaRgO-SOmeyjonQuUJ3Q

The songs from Wylie's New 2020 Playlist served as an impetus to opening up a crack in our defunct communication. One day, I was watching a video on YouTube and decided this video would be helpful to Wylie in his spiritual journey. I sent him the link, urging him to watch it. It had been nearly two weeks since he sent me the text wishing me Happy New Year, which I had ignored. He responded an hour later, thanking me for sharing the video, and expressing interest in watching more with that type of content. Although I had already broached this topic via email, I decided to ask him again about his playlist – specifically, about a few songs I felt he had chosen in honor of us. He replied that he had not consciously chosen any of the songs with us in mind, but agreed he could have been adding them subconsciously, perhaps from a Higher-Self state of consciousness. I also gave him access to the Twin Flame Choices playlist that I had created after Bumble-Gate, and told him about the Mariah Carey song "I Still Believe" being my most played song of the year.

Then I pressed play and listened to Mariah's song again. The lyrics took me right back to the feelings I had had all summer and brought me to sobbing tears. All of a sudden, the clock made a loud clicking noise, momentarily tearing my attention away from the song on my phone. The time read 11:11 – wow, such a spiritual message! I was inspired to throw all caution to the wind and ask Wylie what my heart *really* needed to know. I texted: *If I shouldn't "still believe" that we will love again, you need to tell me, Wylie, because as hard as I've tried in all this time I still have not hit the bottom of us.*

I didn't expect him to answer me right away, but I did expect him to respond – but he didn't. It seemed I had asked him a question he couldn't answer.

The next day I was standing in my bathroom, just out of the shower, when my phone rang. I was surprised to see it was Wylie calling. He was equally surprised when I actually answered. He explained that he was "in the neighborhood" and had been visiting an old friend, who was staying with a friend in my town, and since he had just passed my street, he took it as a "sign" to call me to see if I wanted to have a drink with him, or dinner, or both. My text question from the day before came to mind, as it had not yet been answered, and I realized this meeting might turn into a repeat of our conversation on Halloween. Maybe he needed to tell me in person our relationship was completely over and I should not "believe" or have hope. I agreed to go to dinner with him, but still had a foreboding about seeing him – afraid of what he might disclose.

He arrived at the house 15 minutes later. I was still getting dressed, so Ryan entertained him while he waited for me. We had not seen each other for a couple months. With him looking handsome as ever, we awkwardly hugged one another. On the drive to a nearby restaurant he showed me the book he had ordered and was reading at Moriah's recommendation. I was glad to see he had followed through and was taking her advice to heart.

We made small talk while ordering drinks and an appetizer. It was still rather early for dinner, and we were the only customers in the restaurant – at least we had privacy. Wylie shared that he only had a couple of weeks to make his final decision about climbing Everest, before he would lose his large $25,000 deposit. I then revealed that I had had a premonition back in December about his Everest trip and saw in my mind that he would not summit if he went this year. I have claircognizance – that is, clear knowing as a psychic – and I knew something would happen that would not allow him to summit. I'm not always right, but I felt sure I was right about *this*. I explained to him that I didn't see him getting injured, but there was something about him not being able to summit – it could even be a matter of the weather, or something else. I also saw that if he waited until 2021 to attempt the climb, he *would* summit. I could tell he was intently listening and taking it all in. He also said he felt Jane would not be going on the Everest trip. At that point in time, I almost didn't care anymore whether Jane did or didn't go. Besides, I didn't think she had it in her – it would be quite a feat for a 57-year-old woman, with or without Wylie. He didn't want her going anyway, in that he felt he could possibly be distracted from his own calling to summit if she went. He had been working on discouraging her since their trip to Island Peak in October. But he was doing it in a less obvious way so it didn't seem like it was all his idea for her not to go.

I had a couple of thoughts that had been bothering me since my reading with Moriah. She had told me Wylie's ex-wife was undermining our relationship. Until she mentioned this, I had not really spent much time thinking about Wylie's ex-wife, although I did feel sorry about the relationship she had suffered in with Wylie. But from everything he had said about her, she seemed like a really nice, decent person, I suppose if you looked at it from her perspective, the reason he wanted to exit the marriage was because he wasn't in love with her anymore, which he had expressed to her. He also told her he wanted to be on his own – free of being in *any* relationship. Of course, I hadn't known at the time that he was seeing "28," but thinking about it now, she could have been the catalyst for their breakup, not me. I was just an accelerant who set a fire under him, helping him to move on with his new life. It must have been a slap in the face for his ex-wife to realize he had now been in a two-year relationship with me, when he had earlier declared he didn't want to be in *any* relationship. I had probably been naïve to take her off my radar – perhaps Moriah was right that she had been undermining us. Wylie admitted she had not done me any favors, and I deduced that when she saw us kissing those many months ago, this single event started a snowball effect that changed the course of our relationship for the worse. He agreed that her seeing us together that way had flipped a switch in her, and that perhaps I was correct in my deduction. So Moriah had been correct, and at least I was finally getting honest clarification about things I had long suspected. Making matters worse, Wylie had recently let his ex-wife know our relationship was finished, and as a result they were in a good place again. Now I felt like he had slapped me in the face, too. Ouch – all this time I thought we had been trying to find a way back to each other. Had he just been trying to find a way to be completely out...?

I worked up the courage to bring up the text from the day before about the Mariah Carey song and how I needed to know if I should no longer have hope of us continuing a relationship together. He shared that he had almost written an email to me that morning, but then decided to sit on it. Ironically, after that decision, the visit to my town came up and he had taken it as a sign. He really debated whether he should call me while he was in town, and when he finally decided to, he didn't think I'd answer. He wanted me to know that our relationship not coming back together now was purely because of timing. When we met, it was like a bullet train – he had to hop on. But it was always so intense for him. He didn't think I understood how intense it felt, because I was used to my own intensity. He had fought it at first, but after the Muir Woods trip in San Francisco he decided to let go and just run with it, and he could clearly remember when that happened. He said if he had met me after his divorce, our relationship would have taken off like a rocket and we would probably be married by now, even though neither of us wanted to remarry – that's how strongly he felt about us. But once his ex-wife and younger son saw us kissing, it changed things for him with his family, and he felt himself pulling back more and more. I felt that too.

He went on to say that right now he felt his energy needed to be 100% focused on his kids, and especially on fixing the broken relationship he had with his daughter, which was still bad. His daughter was still so mad at him that he was not allowed to be in the common areas of his ex-wife's house when she was home. Earlier that week, he had had to hide in a bedroom until she left. The story made my blood boil – they were treating her like a spoiled princess, letting her get away with bad behavior instead of facing the situation like the 23-year-old adult she was. I expressed my sympathy, but part of me couldn't even feel sorry for the situation he had put himself in. I was sure the reason his daughter was so angry with him was that she had discovered his unscrupulous behavior in the marriage to her mother. I could only imagine what she knew in detail that I did not.

He then took both of my hands in his and said the short answer to my text question was yes – yes, I could believe in our love. He talked about how his feelings for me had not changed one bit, but that he still had so much work to do on himself. He was not ready to come back together yet. He asked me to stay with him in my heart-space, to live in that place of love with him, where I could feel it and believe in it and draw on it for inspiration. But if someone else were to come into my life with whom I felt I could have a stronger love, he didn't want to hold me back from that. He knew I was all in and ready to be with someone who was in the same place I was. He assured me it had nothing to do with me. I had done everything right – this was all on him. He just didn't know what his future was going to look like. But he did know one thing for certain – he wanted me in it! He could not bear the thought of me not being in his life. He felt we fired on so many cylinders outside of just our love interest, and he implored me to reconsider being his friend. He said it would take all of his will power to keep me in the friend zone.

The tears that had pooled in my eyes while he was talking now found their way down my face in a hot steady stream. I could not bear the thought of *not* being in a romantic relationship with him. He gently removed his hands from mine to wipe the tears away. I was silent for what seemed like a long time for me, and finally responded: "I'm sorry, I just can't, Wylie." It was way too much to ask of me. I was in too deep to sit on the sidelines supporting him in friendship – knowing he couldn't *not* be in a relationship for long. He said he wanted to be on his own, but I knew he had no idea how to do that. He had never been on his own – been alone – for any significant amount of time in his entire life! I could not stand by in friendship and watch him enter into a new romantic relationship with someone else in the future – when this was all I had ever desired with every fiber of my being. It was a hard NO for me!

On top of it, he got a lot of benefits from being friends with me – I was his confidante, his cheerleader, and a sounding board for his business – but what was in it for me? I already had what I needed in those areas; I already had a life rich with deep, meaningful friendships, both male and female, as well as incredible relationships with my parents, who were my biggest cheerleaders and advisors. What did Wylie really bring to the table? Sure, I loved to share my world with him, and he was often the first person I wanted to tell when something significant had happened to me, but that was all in line with being in a loving relationship. What I needed was a romantic relationship – I didn't need just another friend.

He expressed his sadness at seeing me cry and didn't want to be the cause. He asked me to remember the feeling of love we experienced together in the mushroom ceremony, because our love was other-worldly. He believed we could have love together again, but that we needed to have it without attachment – without attachment to how it would look. He felt I had gotten too attached to how I wanted the relationship to work, and it led to me being frustrated with him most of the time. If we could continue now as friends, perhaps we could begin to build a better foundation. He assured me he was not interested in anyone or in meeting anyone, and was not open to anything other than working on himself to fix what was wrong there. He asked me to take my time and really think about it. By then, I had lost my appetite, and when the buttercake we ordered for dessert arrived I could only pick at it. I should have known getting together was not going to result in what I wanted and needed.

He drove me back home and walked me into the house. Ryan wasn't home; he was at my parents' for our Monday night ritual of watching *The Bachelor* together. That was where I was supposed to be too, but I had decided to skip it that night because I needed answers to my relationship with Wylie.

He hugged me goodbye, then kissed me. We made out for five minutes and I asked him if we could dance. I cued up the song "I Still Believe," and as we had done so many times before, we slow-danced in my living room. Our bodies melted into one. We kissed, softly at first, but as the intensity of the song rose, so did the intensity of our kissing. This was our magic place – it had not faded but remained in that space where it had always been. It was as if nothing about our romantic connection had changed. He played with my hair, pulling me closer and closer to him as if we were melding into one person – one Soul. And just as we had been in our mushroom ceremony, we vibrated at a level that felt electric. It was as though we were merging into one. He lifted my leg off the ground and held it, and we danced so close I hardly had the strength to remain standing. But the fierceness of his strength held me in place until the fervor was so great that neither of us could take any more. We pulled away and the fog lifted from my brain – reminding me he wanted to be friends, not lovers. Well, we sure as hell were not going to be "friends with benefits"! I did NOT play *that* game!

We had been dancing and making out for 45 minutes, but it felt like an eternity and a moment, all at the same time. It was time for him to leave. I announced I was kicking him out. He looked a bit surprised because of how the last several minutes had built in intensity. I needed him to leave. And I had to leave to go to my parents' to watch the last half of our show together.

Before he left, I took his hand and pulled him into my bedroom. I wanted him to see what I had to look at every day – the empty Wall of Adventure that had once held so much joy and happiness for us. After he expressed his regret in not seeing it there, we walked outside through the garage, hand in hand. We had one last embrace that lasted slightly longer than it should have. While looking deep into each other's eyes I wanted to say "I love you," but stopped myself. I could feel he loved me too, but I wanted to hear the words from him. It was a battle of wills, and neither of us spoke the words.

We got in our vehicles to leave, and as he led the way out of my subdivision, he called me on the phone. It brought me back to memories of when we first started dating. He would leave my house and call me within minutes. I didn't know if he just needed to hear my voice again, or if he didn't want our time together to end. The gesture always made me feel special, and wanted, and loved. And there they were, the feelings from him that had been missing over the past few months. Maybe they weren't buried – only tucked away...

In any case, I had some serious deliberating to do. To friend or not to friend – that was the question. I did not have the answer.

Chapter 42

Promises, Promises

~song by *Naked Eyes*

https://open.spotify.com/track/5yZT3gqgZNBkTPX6G3XDTL?si=KztNQhQhRi2R4CGSeTcaoA

For the next several days, I thought of nothing but Wylie's friendship request. There was a part of me that wanted to have him in my life always, but there was a greater part of me that knew the only relationship I would be capable of having with him was a romantic one.

  A week later I suggested we meet again to talk, and he offered up lunch; I knew this could not be a rushed conversation, and I could tell he was hesitant to meet again. But he agreed to dinner at my place. I asked him to come at 5:00, but he texted me that he was on his way and arrived at 3:00.

  We had a mini make-out session in the kitchen as soon as he arrived. Clearly, our attraction and passion for each other was as strong as it had always been. With us still standing there in the kitchen, I told him I had had an epiphany after our last talk: What if our time apart had nothing to do with him? What if we had experienced this time apart because Spirit was giving me the time to get my book, *Signs Surround You, Love Never Dies*. ready for publication? In our time apart, I had done a significant amount of work in marketing my book, and I now planned to release it in February or as soon as I received the final lyrics permission for it. There is no way I would have been in a position to send my book out into the world if we had stayed together. I had used every spare moment to do this special work, and as much as I wanted a relationship with him I felt this time might have been carved out for this purpose.

  My book had many spiritual components to it and had the potential to help a lot of people heal from their losses. Thomas had predicted it would be published in the beginning of the year; and also said there was a lot of spiritual excitement around the book. My motivation to send it to publication had sort of taken on an energy of urgency. Wylie appreciated that concept, and I think he rather liked the idea of being taken off the hook for his dumb Bumble-Gate incident. His being out of the picture for a while had also afforded me extra time with Ryan, who would be leaving a few months later for his pilot training. It gave me more focused time than there would have been if my attention had been divided between the two of them.

We poured two beers and moved our conversation to the couch in the living room. Sitting next to each other, our bodies touching, we turned slightly to face each other. Wylie admitted he had not been sure if we should get together when I suggested it, because he wasn't sure if we had anything more to discuss. Over time, I had gotten better and better at interpreting his feelings and emotions from afar, and I had accurately felt his resistance. He had sat with his thoughts for a few days, then finally surrendered, to see what might come up in meeting with me. He had absolutely no agenda and was open to whatever came up. I was relieved to feel his open energy. But on the other hand, I had two very specific things I wanted to discuss – also with absolutely no expectations.

Wylie started off by telling me that when I didn't answer him on New Year's Eve or Day, he had gotten a "hit" that I had begun seeing someone else. I couldn't hide my amusement at his assumption and I began smirking in response, as I was in no way, shape or form open to starting a new relationship. He had been pretty sure about it until I shared the signs I had received relevant to his music playlist. I reminded him of the comment he had made to me when we were in Muir Woods, when he said it wouldn't matter to him if I dated or slept with someone else. He was so confident in the strength and power of our relationship that he knew no one else would compare, and that I would come back. I asked him if he felt this was still true for him, because it seemed to me that it may no longer have been the case, from what he had just disclosed about thinking I might be seeing someone new. Was it possible he would be jealous of another man? In response to that, he said he never let his thoughts go to that place, the way I did. But he did realize in our last conversation that he had unfairly asked me to be friends, and he had since realized that (a) we would never be able to be *just* friends, and (b) "friend" was yet another label he had tried to put on a relationship that was much too intense and special to label. He had thought about it a lot and realized being friends didn't "feel" right, and he had been "stupid" to request it. He also understood now why I had so vehemently resisted – it didn't feel right to me either. He said the only place our relationship belonged was in the heart-space, where we had become one in the mushroom ceremony. Our relationship was indefinable and it could not exist outside of that mystical place of love.

I felt a relief wash over my body and I leaned over to kiss him passionately, while simultaneously getting tears all over his face. I was so completely moved by the depth of this man, and I could feel the unwavering love he had for me. I agreed with everything, but we both felt neither of u was fully ready to resume the relationship in an "all in" manner. He still had the task of working on some issues, and on his relationships with his kids. And I needed to bring my book to fruition and focus my attention on Ryan before he left for the Air Force. We agreed that we would just have to "be" and take it one day at a time.

But before we could end the conversation, there was one more area I needed to address. I asked him if he was still talking to anyone he had met on Bumble. He said he wasn't and that he had long since deleted that account and had cut all ties. I went a step further, remembering that I had to be both very specific and also very broad with Wylie so as to cover all possible bases. He had, in our past, answered very specific questions…but they had not been the right questions for me to fully uncover what I *really* wanted to know. So I asked him if he was currently talking to or seeing ANY women. He said he was not and that he had learned a lot from his past. He now understood that when we met our attraction was undeniable, but even though he was in a relationship at the time, his energy was open to other people. He now understood that being open or closed was an important aspect for him to be aware of.

I said I was willing to take our relationship as it comes – one day at a time – *but* I had absolutely NO interest or desire to be in any kind of open relationship with him! If he thought he could still be open to seeing or meeting anyone else – like on Bumble – then I would not move forward with him.

I talked again about how devastating it had been for me to find out about "28," and how that had tainted things for me – and he had again hurt me badly with Bumble. I didn't want to feel hurt in that way yet again. But at the same time, by me even bringing this up and asking him not to see other people, I feared he would feel I was just putting pressure on our relationship again. His response was "I'm not open to anyone else!" He *assured* me his energy was **not** open to anyone, and he said, "Please, do not worry about that!" I believed in his sincerity when he looked me directly in the eyes and spoke those words. My line of questioning, and his answers had left no room for interpretation. I felt euphoric! And at that moment all I wanted was for us to become one with one another. We moved to the bedroom and turned on our Spotify *L.A. Woman* playlist and did our best to become one once again.

Later that night he texted: *Thank you for a wonderful afternoon and evening. I smile as I think about it. Sweet dreams.*

Chapter 43

Stop Draggin' My Heart Around

~song by *Stevie Nicks and Tom Petty*

https://open.spotify.com/track/66LhCsc06aTa2Ig7iYPDSP?si=tfH6WQUpQ4GDfj3c56MW9w

We had seen each other exactly one week before he was to leave on his trip to Argentina, where he would be guiding four men up Mt. Aconcagua. I still held out hope he would want to see me one more time before he was to be gone for three full weeks. But as the date of his trip inched closer, the chance of that seemed to slip more and more.

I was sitting on an airplane waiting to take off for Kansas City, when I received this text: *My latest text exchange with my daughter... "I'm heading to Argentina on February 1st for 3 weeks. I'd like to get together this week if you are up for it." This was her response: "No thank you, no thank you."*

I felt sorry for him; that response had to hurt. But I could feel my own annoyance creeping in as I saw that he was making an effort to see her – and, while she had no desire to see him, here I was longing to spend some time with him again before he left, yet he was making no effort to try to see *me* again. So it wasn't really that he couldn't make the time, because with this new piece of information there was clearly now a gap in his schedule. Did he just have no desire? My brain tried to talk my heart into thinking he didn't want to see me because our last encounter had been so special – anything else would have just been rushed and could potentially diminish the connection we had just experienced. My brain wasn't buying it but my heart held on to the hope that he would suggest a rendezvous over the next few days, after I returned from my trip.

I was driving home from the airport, and Wylie had two more days to make a reunion happen before leaving for Argentina. I was feeling it was less than likely, since he had made no inquiry in my direction. I spent the drive home talking to my good friend Gina. We used the first half of the ride to talk about what was going on in her life, and then she lightly inquired about Wylie, knowing it could be a sore subject. I briefed her on what had happened over the last few weeks, bringing her up to the present moment.

~~Once~~ A Cheater...

I told her one of the things that had been bothering me about Wylie not making an effort to see me before he left, was a similar incident from the previous year. Wylie had been getting ready to guide the same trip to Argentina, and we had made plans for dinner at my house so he could meet several members of my extended family who were in town. Earlier that day he let me know he would be arriving very late for dinner. He planned to stay overnight at my place because very early the next morning he would need my help in obtaining some hiking permits for our Hiking Adventure business. He had known about the dinner plans for quite a while, but at the last minute altered *our* plans so he could instead attend an Integration Circle at the house of a couple who were close friends of his. Wylie had many times expressed *not* enjoying these Integration Circle meetings, but made a *huge* deal of going to this one, stating that he needed to see these friends, as he would not be able to see them for several weeks because of his Argentina trip. It seemed so odd to me at the time (and still did now), because he made his attending that meeting seem almost urgent. The odder part was that I suspected Jane had recently participated in a medicine ceremony and I wondered if he was going to the Integration Circle at her request – not for the reason he had stated. She was newer to the medicine community, and may not have wanted to go by herself, I reasoned. But that was silly – she was a grown woman, fully capable of attending a meeting without a "sponsor." Besides, she had known the hosts for several years! By this point, my intuition about Jane had so fully convinced me this was all true. I remembered trying to uncover the real reason he was going – but again, he made it about connecting with these friends.

The Integration Circle was located close to his house but about 40 minutes from mine. He assured me he would only "stay for a bit," but ultimately he arrived at my house at nearly 9 p.m., well after dinner had ended and after my relatives had left. I remember how slighted I felt that he had picked his event over mine. It seemed when there was something he needed to do, it always won out over any of my priorities – or his prior commitments to me. The kicker was that when he returned from his guiding trip, I carefully observed to see *when* he would see his couple friends again. It was over a month after he returned from his trip before he saw them, with me, at another monthly Integration Circle. So much for the urgency in not seeing them for three whole weeks. I never asked him about it then, but the entire story had re-entered my mind, because when Wylie really wanted something, he made it happen.

Clearly, he was not applying ANY of this type of effort in my direction, with regard to seeing me again before his trip. As I was saying those words to Gina, a white car passed me on the right with large words written in cursive on the back of the car...

...and the license plate also read BELIEVE. I was only about five minutes from my house by this point in the conversation, yet I had never seen that car before – and for that matter, have never seen it since. It very definitely felt like a sign from Spirit. I got the message loud and clear and assumed it meant *believe in us*, but it could just as well have meant to *believe in my gut feelings*. Either way, I was going to need to find a way to let go and be without attachment, as Wylie had urged when we last saw each other.

Wylie still hadn't made an effort to even text me after I returned from my business trip, until the night before his trip. My annoyance toward him had begun to turn to exasperation because his lack of communication had, once again, left me feeling slighted and on the back burner of his life. This left me feeling really sad, and the only way I could express my emotions was through tears. I resisted the urge to text him or email him my feelings, choosing instead to vent when my sister called. She advised me to somehow make peace with all these feelings, because it would not be healthy for me to keep experiencing them over and over for the next three weeks when our contact would keep diminishing the further he climbed up the mountain. She also gently reminded me Wylie and I were still not "fully" back together, and I was putting expectations on the relationship as if we were "all in." She was right, and I spent some time reflecting on my own perhaps unrealistic expectations.

The next day I had a Reiki session scheduled with a new friend. She was very spiritual and wise and had been in a Twin Flame relationship herself, so she understood my plight. She tried to perform some healing to help me let go of my feelings of not being "picked" by the men in my life. By the time I left, my energy was feeling much more grounded. I had ordered a pizza to pick up on the way home. After paying for it, I got back into my vehicle to continue the drive home. The radio screen said the song "Ventura Highway" by *America* was playing. But it wasn't – "Hold the Line" was streaming through the speakers. This particular sign never failed to flabbergast me! I recorded a video of the last minute of the song, just as it ended and the car screen reverted back to its normal state, once again matching the song that was playing with what the screen said was playing. I felt Spirit was again sending me comfort and advising me to "hold the line."

Wylie and I had discussed getting a permit to return to Havasupai, the sacred place of our first physical union. The day he left for his Argentina trip I was able to snag a coveted reservation for us to experience the coming summer as a mini getaway. Wylie had guided there many times but had never fully vacationed there. We had both expressed great anticipation and hope in me securing a reservation for us, and as luck had been on my side, I had successfully gotten one! These reservations went on sale once a year and were sold out within minutes. It was a hot commodity and I knew many people who had tried for years, unsuccessfully, to procure one. I texted him, excitedly letting him know we got the golden ticket! He called me a few minutes later from the airport. He was in a long line to check his gear and was clearly annoyed with the situation. The call was choppy and curt, as he was too distracted to give me any real attention. It felt like he had called me to "check a box." After a minute, we said our goodbyes and both of us awkwardly paused again, as we had done in person when we last said goodbye. Each of us seemed to be again waiting for the other to say "I love you," but neither spoke the words. He had been on speaker phone,

~~Once~~ A Cheater...

with my friend Stacy sitting next to me since she had assisted me in securing the Supai permit by adding more "people power." Stacy gave me a knowing look as a single tear escaped and ran down my cheek.

I couldn't shake the feelings of frustration that Wylie had stirred in me as a result of our call. But I decided that climbing the largest mountain in the Southern Hemisphere was a formidable task which held a measure of danger, and that his coming back home was not a guarantee. I gave myself permission to communicate what I was feeling, remembering my situation with Mark where I didn't stand in my truthful feelings. I shared these feelings with Wylie, not wanting to have any regrets later...

2-1-20 10:10 a.m.

[Laurie] *When we talked on the phone today I knew u were in travel stress mode, and when we ended the convo I paused, both wanting to & wanting u to say I love you. But I hesitated b/c there is a part of me that is afraid you won't say it back. My ego is still rather fragile n I've been protecting it. But tomorrow is not guaranteed, so I need you to know in writing that I love you Wylie* 😊

[Wylie] *I love you too babe*

Thank you for sorting out Supai, it will be very special to return there.

I felt so happy – I hadn't let my fear stand in the way of sending him a message. It was the first time he had called me "babe" since we had been back in whatever it was we were now calling our relationship.

A few days later I was finishing climbing down Black Mountain, my daily hiking spot, when I had thoughts about Jane and how crazy my emotions had been when she was on that trip climbing Aconcagua with Wylie a year earlier. It would have made more sense in my mind for her to wait for her husband's passing, so she could have had those three extra weeks with him in his time of need, rather than following Wylie across the planet. Yep, the mountain was still there; it hadn't gone anywhere – but her husband had. I really shouldn't judge her, but I don't think I would have made the same choice in her situation. Thoughts of her rarely entered my mind anymore – things can change drastically in a year. But I was glad she had not gone on the Aconcagua trip again this year.

I let Storm into the Jeep and started the car to head home. The song "What a Fool Believes" by *The Doobie Brothers* was playing on the radio. I remembered how this time last year Spirit sent me that same song to help ease my mind about Jane. Interesting timing that just moments before I had her in my thoughts. That song was followed by "Goodbye Stranger" by *Super Tramp*. Wow – I got goose-bumps all over my body! The second song had caught my attention when I was in Kansas City the previous summer – it used the name Jane over and over again in the chorus. This was a double Jane reference from two very specific songs I associated with her and *only* her, playing in consecutive order right after I had thoughts of her. Spirit was precisely acknowledging me where she was concerned. Then, to make sure the message was clear, the last song that played as I pulled into my driveway was "Guitar Man" by *Bread* brought to me, of course, by my guitar man on the Other Side. I don't think I will ever stop being in awe of the workings of Spirit communication.

Wylie continued to communicate with me while he was traveling to South America. He sent me pictures of himself with the men he was guiding and texted me a lot – several times nearly every day and even from the first few base camps. He was engaging and informative and sent me more 😊 than he had in a long time. I had had no expectation of when I would hear from him over there, as I knew not only that the Wi-Fi connection was likely limited but that he was also limited to solar battery power for his phone. Every time I heard from him it felt like a gift, and I tried to stay in a state of gratitude. I used this time to practice remaining in my heart-space. I would reel my thoughts back in when my brain would try to run away with them by making all kinds of assumptions and wild speculations. During the middle of the trip his communication dried up, and this time he let me know in advance that would happen. Besides, I was actually busy with my own life too.

He had now been gone two weeks and it was Valentine's Day. When the doorbell rang, I didn't even want to hope for anything – after all, it could just be an Amazon delivery. I opened the door and was handed the familiar, long rectangular box from 1-800 Flowers. My heart skipped a beat. My head told my heart to relax – they had to be from him since my dad was the only other person who would send me flowers, and he had already hand delivered some to me. I thanked the delivery driver; then took the box into the kitchen to see what he had sent me. There was a note included inside along with the profuse buds of stargazer lilies:

Thinking of you today. Hope you have a special Valentine's Day.

Love, Wylie

~~Once~~ A Cheater...

Chapter 44

Man on Your Mind

~song by *Little River Band*

https://open.spotify.com/track/4LzdgN6x9EHyE8MDjrq4lq?si=rEPms-riSZqDVTGLOenZXg

Wylie was on his long travel day back from Argentina. For the whole trip, he had been in contact with me more than I would ever have expected. But until yesterday, I didn't have *any* information about his return travel plans – which had completely blown up, as they had missed a flight. This caused them to get home 12 hours later than planned. Originally, tonight was the night he was supposed to land, but as usual he hadn't asked me to pick him up from the airport. I never fully understood why my face wasn't the first thing he wanted to see upon his return from these long trips, because if the roles were reversed his would be the first I would want to see.

It was actually a lucky thing he didn't need me to meet him at the airport, since I had plans of my own. Dawn and Dale were back in town; their return at this time had been arranged many months before. In the fall, I had received an email notification that pre-sale concert tickets were available to purchase in advance of the general public. I was so excited because this 1970's easy-listening rock band had a bunch of hit songs that I loved, and I had never seen them in concert. When I clicked on the special email link, I was shocked to see there were tickets available in the second row! Usually, the front rows are sold out within minutes of a concert going on sale. In the 115 concerts I had seen in my life, only a few times had I been fortunate enough to have tickets in the first few rows. I quickly bought two tickets and decided it would be the perfect Christmas present for Dawn, my beautiful friend and fellow concert lover. I called her husband Dale and asked him if he could make arrangements for them to be in Arizona on the concert date, as they spilt their time equally between Illinois and Arizona.

We were all meeting at the concert venue for dinner before the show. I arrived only minutes before Dawn and Dale, and met Dawn while Dale was parking the car. The venue was both a concert hall and a casino – and the casino was a zoo because many of the 2,000 concert goers had arrived early to gamble, and eat at the various restaurants. None of the eateries were allowing advance reservations, only first come, first served, so we quickly made our way downstairs to one of the less popular restaurants. We passed a few other restaurants along the way, and they all had long lines of hungry people waiting to get in to eat. Dawn and I waited in a short line to put our name on the reservations list. We heard the hostess tell the people in front of us that the wait to get a table was 90 minutes! At that rate, we would be lucky to be seated, let alone eat our meal, before the concert started. The restaurant manager walked up just as Dawn and I stepped forward to put our name on the list. The manager flirted a little and offered to let us order our meal at a table that had just become available in the bar area. Evidently, two apparently attractive ladies had an advantage over the long list of people who had already been waiting. We thanked him for his kindness and explained that we were attending the concert. Just as Dale arrived, we were promptly seated at a small tabletop in the bar area, which just happened to have the needed three chairs. "Lucky" became our theme for this concert. First the great seats, now the available table. I wondered what else this special night might hold...

After a delicious dinner, we walked around with Dale until he found his favorite Raging Buffalo card-game machine, where he planned to entertain himself while we watched the concert. Dawn and I entered the giant ballroom where the show had been set up. We had fantastic seats in the second row, slightly off center but directly in front of one of the lead guitarists. I remarked how it felt like old times, when Dawn and I had attended many *Starship* concerts where we sat in this exact position in front of my love, Mark Abrahamian, the lead guitarist. Then I remembered Moriah the Medium's prophecy about me meeting and connecting with a man who was in a relevant band. He would remind me of Mark and in the future would vie against Wylie for my attention. I chuckled a little at the impossible thought of meeting someone in *this* band – it was my first concert since her prediction.

I hadn't looked up any of the band members in advance of this concert, except one. The keyboardist was married to a member of *Starship* whom I knew, as she had played and toured with Mark when he was alive. I was really happy she had found love. They had just tied the knot in Hawaii two months before.

The lights dimmed and the band took to the stage, assuming their positions. The lights went up and they all began singing in their signature harmony style. The lead guitarist was handsome, and he looked down from the stage directly at me – our eyes locked and his face lit up. He gave me a huge grin and I smiled back. I felt a rare but instant electric connection. I took pictures of the band and a couple videos, until an usher singled me out and asked me not to record any more videos. At least 20 other people around me were doing the same thing. Very embarrassing...

The lead guitarist would periodically look at me and smile. I looked him up on my phone and learned his name was Kirk, and showed Dawn. He was 52 but looked younger than his age. He had dark hair and dark eyes, and with a guitar in his hands did in a way remind me of Mark. He even had a similar stature. He was not only the lead guitarist but was also the lead singer for several of the songs. He had a beautiful voice that was unbelievably close to the original 70s singer who was no longer with the band. Dawn turned to me and asked if I had noticed the guitarist kept looking at me; I now had confirmation it wasn't just my imagination. I responded, "Yes, and I don't know how, but I "know" I will be meeting Kirk after the concert." Dawn nodded and smiled in agreement. Kirk would throw his guitar pick to someone in the audience after nearly every song. He had twice tried to throw it to me but it was deflected away each time. The third time was a charm – he perfectly lobbed it into my open hands with another special smile for me. He continued looking at me occasionally when he was singing, and I would sing along with him. I knew every word of every song.

It was a high-energy concert, and after 13 songs the band left the stage. The crowd continued to clap and make noise, encouraging them to come back out for an encore. They took to the stage one last time, sang their final song, and assembled in one long line across the stage and took a couple of bows. But then, instead of leaving the stage as most artists would, they made their way across the front of the stage bending down to shake the hands of fans. They also announced that the band would assemble at tables outside the ballroom, where fans could buy tee-shirts to have signed, and get autographs and pictures with the band members.

I stepped over the row of chairs in front of me so I was now pressed up against the stage. Kirk made his way toward me. He smiled a huge smile, then, kneeling down, took my hand in both of his. He asked me, and at the same time motioned, to meet him out front after the show. I nodded in agreement because it was still really loud in the room, making it difficult to talk or hear anything.

Dawn and I left the concert area to go find Dale, who was happily winning at his machine. Dawn found a card-game machine she likes to play, and I sat in the empty seat next to her to watch, since I don't enjoy gambling. We talked about the concert and about Kirk. Dawn said he reminded her of Wylie. Hmmm, that was interesting. I didn't really see the resemblance.

After 15 minutes I wandered back to the concert area by myself to see what kind of progress the band had made with the crowd. There was still a fairly long line. I stood back by the wall and watched the band interact with their fans. Kirk was pretty friendly and seemed genuinely interested in meeting the people that so wanted to talk to him. Kindness is a quality I highly admire. He looked up and locked eyes with me again, and we smiled at each other. I knew he was still going to be a while longer, and I had no plan or desire to wait in a line to meet and greet with the others – that seemed too much like a groupie move. When he turned back to talk to a fan, I slipped back out of the room. I worked my way through the casino back to Dawn. I gave her the update and watched her play for a while. Then after ten more minutes I decided to head back to check on Kirk's progress; I didn't want to wait so long I missed him. It seemed like the band really took their time getting to know the fans and were not in a rush to be done. I peeked my head in the room again and saw there were fewer people waiting.

To kill time I visited the ladies room, and when I returned the line was only a few people long. I decided to park myself up against the wall about 20 feet back from the band's table. Kirk noticed me again and this time made a comment to the other guitarist and motioned to me. There was a little back and forth banter between them. I thought about Wylie, knowing he was on an airplane on his way back through Los Angeles. If his travel plans had worked out for him he would be landing at home about now. I turned my attention back to Kirk, and about that time he stood up and walked over to greet me. I met him halfway. He reached out to hug me, then looked me in the eyes and told me I was beautiful. I felt myself blush slightly at the compliment. I thanked him and suggested we get a drink.

I ordered a beer and he ordered a glass of zinfandel. He reached in his pocket to pay but then realized his wallet had been left behind in his room. I remembered how Mark never carried his wallet with him at a show, either. Kirk was genuinely embarrassed, but I didn't mind paying for our drinks. We walked away from the concert area and found a seating section that was partially open to the outside. It was a cool night but sheltered enough that I wasn't cold. A DJ nearby was playing mash ups, where two songs are mixed together.

Our conversation was effortless, as we instantly connected through music. Kirk confessed he had tried not to keep staring at me during the concert. I joked with him that he did a lousy job! We talked about where we grew up and where we had lived, and how music had shaped our lives. He was an accomplished musician who had written many songs and had played with several well-known bands. He had joined this band only two years before, and was a one-fifth owner. He shared that when he was younger he had owned the band's "Greatest Hits" album and had played it until the record wore out. I remarked that it had been an omen of things to come, for sure, and took it as my cue to go deeper with the conversation. I was really enjoying the talk with him. We bonded over our admiration of singer/songwriter Dan Fogelberg. We agreed he was one of the finest story-song writers, and I lamented that I had not been able to see him in concert before his death. Kirk had seen him, and lots of other artists.

Kirk saw one of his band members walk by and excused himself, letting me know he would be back in about ten minutes. It was perfect timing because I had not looked at my phone for quite some time, and I assumed Wylie would be back in Arizona by now. I texted him and he texted back at 11:11 pm. To my surprise he was still in L.A., stuck there with mechanical issues and waiting for a new aircraft. I was texting my condolences but was interrupted by the DJ who had walked up to me, leaving his music momentarily unattended. He asked if he could buy me a drink. That was surprising, as he seemed at least 15 years younger than me. I was flattered, but more anxious to finish my text conversation with Wylie before Kirk returned. Luckily, the beer the DJ had gone to fetch for me was sold out; I am a one drink person and I had already had a beer with dinner and then one with Kirk. I'm a lightweight when it comes to drinking and it doesn't take much to make me tipsy. I needed to keep my wits about me, so I thanked the DJ for the gesture. He asked to connect with me on social media before running back to his station to play the next song. About that time, Kirk had returned, and I was starting to get cold. The DJ began playing louder techno music as the casino nightlife picked up. Kirk and I decided to find a quieter and warmer place to continue our chat.

  We found an L-shaped couch in a private area and resumed our discussion. Kirk disclosed he was unhappily married. I didn't mention my relationship with Wylie, even though I could have since he had encouraged me to keep myself open to other men. But I had no intention of being open to someone new, including Kirk. I had made a promise to myself long ago that I would not start something new with someone if I was already in a relationship – and I intended to keep my vow. This was a harmless conversation between two people who, for whatever reason, had enough of an energy connection to want to meet and talk. I did talk about my ex-husband and the mistakes I had made in our marriage. Kirk said in the two years he had been in the band, he had never cheated on his wife; ours was the first deep conversation he had ever had with a woman he met at a show. He marveled at our magnetic attraction, and I took the cue to dive into the topic of Soul Mates and Soul Contracts – none of which he was familiar with. It was an enjoyable conversation with lots of questions from Kirk, and I was once again assuming the role of spiritual teacher, the way Mark had done with me years ago...

  Kirk turned our conversation back to music and told me the band was recording a new album that year; he had recently recorded and written and co-written two new songs. He was really excited about them and asked me if I wanted to hear them. I felt honored that he wanted to share them with me. He stood up and suggested we go to his room to play them. I hesitated, because I thought he was just going to play them on his phone from where we were sitting. I agreed to go with him but set the expectation up front, that *all* we would be doing was listening to music. He agreed, and said that was his only intention as well. We continued talking all the way to his room.

  He was essentially a stranger to me, but I didn't feel I was in any danger. Kirk's energy actually felt very safe. In the room, we both took off our shoes and propped up two pillows on one of the double beds. Then we lay down, side by side, and he played his songs. I was super impressed – they were really great! He told me I was the very first person to hear the recorded version of the songs. He had not even had time yet on this trip to share them with the band. He was really excited to be a part of the band's next album; it was going to be an honor and he couldn't wait to perform one of his own original songs on stage.

  Next, we turned our attention back to Dan Fogelberg. Earlier, I had told Kirk a story about one of Dan's songs, and he requested I play that song for him. He immediately recognized "Believe in Me." As we listened, I mouthed all the words along with Dan's vocal. He wanted to hear every one of Dan's songs I had saved on my phone. I had five in total and played them in order. Kirk reached his arm across my body and rested it on my stomach, then cuddled in a little closer to me as the music played. I didn't mind, but I didn't return the gesture. I was not about to start something I couldn't finish. We enjoyed the songs and he serenaded me while playing his favorite Dan Fogelberg song from his own phone: "Same Old Lang Syne."

I glanced at the clock on the nightstand and it was nearly 3:00 in the morning – wow, time really does fly when you're having fun! Kirk mentioned how far it was past his usual bedtime of 11 p.m. and that his time zone was two hours ahead of ours. I put my shoes back on and thanked him for the privilege of being the first person to hear his new songs. Before I could even stand up, *he* thanked me. He told me that nine months earlier he asked his wife to listen to some Dan Fogelberg songs in bed, the same way we had tonight. She made it through one song, then declared she didn't want to listen to more and got up and left the room. I felt instantly sorry for him. I understood the intimacy and importance of sharing what feels like part of your Soul, when the music is significant to you. I secretly smiled inside, realizing *I* had been the one to bring up my love of Dan Fogelberg, having no idea he was one of Kirk's top-three all-time favorite artists! Wow, we truly were Soul connected. But how and why, only time would tell...

We both stood and hugged goodbye. I thanked him for the conversation, and he walked me to the door. I didn't offer my phone number or indicate when or how we would be in contact again. He was married, after all, and if he had any interest in me, he could find me when he untangled himself from the situation, and not a moment before – that is, if I were also available. He had several ways to find me. I had given him my business card for my recently released book, *Signs Surround You, Love Never Dies,* which had my website address where he could reach out to me. He knew my name, so he could also find me on various social media platforms. If all else failed and he lost my card or forgot my name – and if he was really resourceful – he could ask the keyboardist's wife how to find me. She and I had been connected on Facebook for years. As Mark always used to say, *time will tell*. I was very curious to see if Kirk's and my meeting had been a fluke or part of Moriah's prediction.

Stacy met me the next morning to hike. As we drove to the trailhead, I told her about the concert and about Kirk. She asked to see his picture. I had disclosed nothing about how he looked. She took one look and said, "He reminds me of Wylie." Hmmm... curious – just what Dawn had said. In the end, I only told LeeAnn, Stephanie, Ryan and Rachel about my encounter with Kirk, since they were all privy to the information Moriah had given me. It would be interesting to see if anything evolved...

Chapter 45

Taken In

~song by *Mike and the Mechanics*

https://open.spotify.com/track/2JzPnd5bmNBHri3hBBEXZF?si=hW6fNhqqQl6feqS1d71h7Q

I hadn't heard from Wylie since the text exchange the night before, and had assumed he was finally back in Arizona and already up and running. He was to guide a trip and likely would have already left early that morning. I casually texted him, asking if he had made it back. He answered right away that he was back and already with clients on his way to Sedona. I didn't hear from him again until 10 p.m. when he let me know he had had a good trip and was heading to bed.

It had been exactly one full month since we had seen each other. Wylie emerged again, explaining how long he had slept in, and asked me if I wanted to have lunch with him the following day. I was puzzled as to why he would again want to just have *lunch*, and not see me at night so we could have some real quality time together instead of a rushed lunch. I declined, partly because I was NOT settling for lunch, but also because I had breakfast plans with Dawn that day. It was, after all, a workday, so I couldn't spend half the day doing personal things on the company's dime. Feeling slightly annoyed, I challenged him with, "Why lunch?" Instead of answering, he asked me to have dinner with him that night. I already had dinner plans with Ryan and my parents. (Seriously – he had had ***four*** weeks to make plans to see me when he returned, but as usual he had not thought ahead.) It was Monday, and he suggested we "shoot for Wednesday." I sent a kissing face emoji in enthusiastic response, but then realized I may have jumped the gun. Had I misunderstood his intentions..."shoot for"? Did that mean maybe? In the end, we made plans for dinner Wednesday night at my place.

He arrived empty handed. I had been hoping he would bring me heart rocks from this trip as he usually did. It was a magical reunion anyway. We slow-danced, ate dinner and made out a lot. Then we relaxed on the couch to watch a movie together, which we had not done for a very long time. His presence in my house felt like home. He didn't spend the night, because he had an early class to take the next day. I would be leaving for San Francisco to attend a memorial in

~~Once~~ A Cheater...

two days. Between my travel schedule for work and his busy trip schedule, there was no telling when we would see each other next. We parted ways without any future plans.

Two days later, I was on an airplane on my way to San Francisco, where I planned to hike for three days in Muir Woods. The giant trees in the dark redwood forest held a special place in my heart. It had been two years Wylie and I were there and he had declared his love for me. I was bummed he wouldn't be on this trip with me. We had discussed his coming along, but he was scheduled to participate in a three-day Wilderness Responders refresher course for work. As for me, besides hiking, I had plans to see a medium and also attend the Memorial Service of Mark's aunt, so it was best that he not come. I was excited to connect with Mark's mom and family, and Wylie's presence would have made that awkward.

I woke up early the day of the Memorial service and climbed 2,500 feet up to the top of Mt. Tamalpais. I didn't see a soul on the trail, and I relished the solitude. I showered at my airbnb, then navigated through the city to meet with Alan, the medium.

When Alan answered the door, I noted he looked just like he did on the YouTube video where I first saw him. Through a series of coincidences, my sister had been guided to that video of him, and she was sure that I was supposed to watch it. I was surprised when I began watching, because I had already found this very video on my own over the summer when I was working through *Bumble-Gate* and trying to raise my vibration. When I first watched the video, I had been focused on the story of Alan's near-death experience. But when I watched it again, from my sister's recommendation, I was more drawn to the story of him developing his mediumship. I felt certain I had been directed to him to have a reading. But when I tried to schedule one through his Facebook page, he never responded. Next I emailed him a request – no response. I was anxious to arrange a reading in advance of my trip, not wanting to miss the opportunity to meet with him because of a glitch in scheduling technology. I decided to "go old school" and call him on the phone – I was surprised when he personally answered. He explained that he was no longer conducting readings and no longer monitored his Facebook page. He asked me why I felt I needed a reading. I explained that I would be traveling to San Francisco and that I had been led to him specifically. I was accelerating my spiritual journey and wanted to see what messages Spirit had for me through him. He asked me when I was coming to town, then said he would make an exception and grant me a reading.

Now at his door, Alan invited me into his nautical-themed office. He talked for a while about his background, explaining that he had been trained to hear his Spirit Guides and had honed his abilities over many years. Then he wanted to hear a little bit about me. After a quick "synopsis," I asked him if he would mind if I recorded our session, and he obliged. Then to further connect us, he asked to hold my hands. He prayed to his Spirit Team, then got right into it. He connected with two of my relatives, even getting my Aunt's name, Lois, correct. I am always so amazed when a medium can hear a name, because it imparts a greater degree of evidence to the reading. My aunt had been gone seven years and there was nothing that would connect us to each other that one could have researched in advance. In any case, he didn't need to prove his abilities to me – he had already passed double-blinded, stringent tests that certified him as a statistically accurate medium.

Lastly, Alan connected with Mark – the one person I had been waiting to hear from. It took him a minute to figure out what Mark was showing him about his profession, by making a point of telling him it was "intellectual." In my head, I admonished Mark because I knew his comment had the potential to lead Alan astray. Intently listening to something he was hearing in his head, Alan suddenly turned to me asking if Mark's profession was intellectual like an artistic artist. I enthusiastically nodded in agreement, amazed at the association he had made. He then asked, "Does he play guitar? Because he made my fingers feel like they were playing a guitar." He said that while making a strumming gesture with his hand. "Oh, he has long hair – I can see him now. And he took his music *very* seriously." Yep, nailed it!

Mark had several messages for me about my spiritual journey and how he was assisting me from the Other Side. I inquired about the multiple signs he had been sending me by playing "Hold the Line" over other songs. Alan replied, "What you are doing is holding the line. He loves you from over there, and you know that. You have love from Mark from across the veil – you have that if you will hold the line. Eventually, you'll find someone on this side you can love who is worthy of you. In the interim, he loves you and you can hold on to that – you don't have to let go. At some point he'll say 'Don't hold the line.' So wait for that – it comes eventually. It will suddenly come. Be satisfied with what you already have. The rest will be brought to you – you will know. He'll tell you when the time is right. It will be revealed to you."

At that point Mark disclosed that Wylie was jealous of him. Alan elaborated: "He may not even be consciously aware that he is, but until he can let go of those feelings he is going to feel stuck. Things will open up for you in your relationship when Wylie can let go of those jealousies." Wow, Wylie himself had never revealed any feelings of jealousy toward anyone, where I was concerned. But he did once compare Mark to Jane...

I wrapped up the session with Alan – paid him, thanked him, and hugged him goodbye. I got back in my rental car and plugged in the address for the location of the Memorial, to navigate through my phone. Just as I started the car, the beginning notes of "I Still Believe" by *Mariah Carey* played on the FM radio station. This was my number one, most-played song from the previous year on Spotify, and in many ways it was the song that had brought Wylie and me back together just a few weeks before. It was also a song that could *only* be attached to Wylie. My reading had run 20 minutes over, even though it had begun on time, and I marveled at the timing of hearing *this* song as soon as I started the car – especially since the last message I received from Mark was about Wylie. That song was followed by "Nothin's Gonna Stop Us Now" by *Starship*. Mark was making sure I knew there was *no doubt* he had delivered these incredible messages through Alan!

Seeing Mark's entire family after hearing from him in my reading was a special treat. The memorial for his aunt was more of a celebration of life. And, of course, it was a celebration for them both – as Aunt and nephew were now reunited on the Other Side. I had a chance to visit with Mark's mom, dad, brother and cousins. I felt so blessed to be close to his family.

The next day I decided to do some work at the airbnb before leaving to hike. I intended to stay through lunch, then head out. I prepared my lunch but realized when I sat down to eat it that I had frozen my diet Mountain Dew by mistake. I decided to pack up earlier than planned, go get another drink, and take my lunch with me on the hike. I could find a place on the trail to eat.

There was a store a few miles away. I picked up a few items there and got in a long checkout line. It was a crowded Sunday morning. I waited patiently to pay for my items but now wished I had gone to the convenience store instead of this busy grocery store. I got in my car, annoyed by the delay. As I was driving to the trailhead a car turned in front of me. I gasped at the license plate – MO**MARK**Y. The car was only in front of me for a couple minutes before it turned onto a different street. I was astonished at the timing and the turn of events that caused me to be in this exact "right" place at the right time in order to receive this special sign.

During my entire trip, I noticed Wylie's texting seemed "off". It wasn't the frequency as much as the content – or lack of. I was keenly aware he was using far fewer emojis than usual and did not respond in kind when I said I missed him, etc. Again, something was "off" and I just couldn't put my finger on it. I spent a good deal of time turning those thoughts over and over in my mind during my 17-mile hike.

I returned home from San Francisco around midnight that night. Timing was not on our side, because Wylie had already left for a trip earlier in the day, and I was scheduled to leave for Kansas City before he returned. Work was unusually busy, but it still was not enough of a distraction to keep my thoughts off Wylie and our most recent disconnect. It seemed we were constantly taking one step forward – toward each other – then two steps back.

Wylie returned from his trip while I was still in Kansas City. Now that he was back home, texting should have resumed a more normal cadence – but it had not. We exchanged a few texts back and forth during the day, but I was tired of texting. I had scheduled dinner with a friend who lived 45 minutes away from my hotel, so I decided to call Wylie during the drive. Hmmm – no answer. He had not shared that he had any plans. I rarely called him, usually letting him take the lead to call me. He texted me back...

~~Once~~ A Cheater...

3-4-20 5:56 p.m.

[Wylie] *Hope your day was good. Doing dinner and a movie with my younger son. Let's connect tomorrow* ☺

[Laurie] *Hope you had a good time with him. What movie did you see?*

    No answer. I had sent the text early enough for him to respond before bed, if he didn't want to respond while he was out. Something did not feel right to me. I didn't know what it was. It wasn't really that I didn't believe he was with his son, but why not reply? I tried to ignore my thoughts but couldn't. I was up late working and went to bed late. Now tossing and turning, I could see this was going to affect my sleep. I finally relented when I couldn't stand it anymore; I decided to express my thoughts and feelings...

3-5-20 1:19 a.m.

[Laurie] *Everything about how you've been communicating with me for a while says you don't care as much anymore. I call you, you don't answer. I text you, you don't respond much. I say I miss you, you don't say it back. I get you didn't want to talk tonight, being with your son, but you can't even answer my text about what movie you saw? That takes 10 seconds. Am I not worth 10 seconds of your time? You didn't answer me in this a.m.'s text, either. What am I supposed to think and feel? I've always made a lot of effort with you. Your lack of effort is an energy and I feel it...I just don't understand. Help me understand...*

    Getting the text out of my mind and onto my phone didn't help me sleep. It was over an hour before I finally fell asleep, mentally exhausted.

    When I woke up, the first thing I did was check my phone. No text response from Wylie. But it was still early in Arizona. Instead of being bothered by his lack of response, I was now worried about the pressure a text like that was putting on our "relationship" – or whatever the heck it was we were calling ourselves these days. My state of being could be summed up in two words: FREAKED OUT. One thing was certain – I did not know how to be halfway in a relationship. For me, it really needed to be all in – or all out.

    I had no scheduled work calls early that morning, so I planned on going on a quick five-mile hike in the woods. Wylie's actions had caused me to get less sleep than I had hoped, and I tried to make it up on the back end by sleeping in. Now my whole day was behind and it was only 7 a.m. I was ready to leave the hotel but remembered I didn't have any water in my room and the faucet water at this hotel in Kansas City tasted terrible. I walked down to the lobby to buy a bottle of water, then walked to the rental car. As soon as I saw the sun, I sneezed twice in reaction to its intense brightness. Uggghh. Sunglasses – I was going to need them for my walk. I ran back up to the room to grab them and was finally

~~Once~~ A Cheater...

ready to go. When I started the car, the Jack FM radio station came to life and began playing the song "Nothin's Gonna Stop Us Now" by *Starship*. Interesting song for this station to play, in that they played a mix of songs from the 80's to today. There was such a low chance of hearing one of the *Starship* songs, compared to the chance of it on an all-80's station. I just couldn't believe I was hearing this song – Mark was sending it to me for sure! Look at all the delays that caused me to leave later than I had planned. I felt it had happened so I could receive *this* song as soon as I got in the car! It was also the very same *Starship* song I had heard three times on my San Francisco trip the previous weekend. I felt not only a comfort in knowing Mark was with me, but as I began to listen I felt the lyrics were telling me Wylie and I would be ok. I felt somewhat consoled.

3-5-20 4:46 p.m.

[Wylie] *Hope your trip wrapped up well. I sent you an email.*

My heart sank. I didn't know if an email would be good or would be bad. Either way, it was a more thoughtful response than a text. I really wanted to talk to him in person, but I wasn't getting home until later that night, and he would be leaving again on another guiding trip in the morning. We didn't have plans, which had become our new norm, and I didn't get that he was going to make an effort to see me. I read his email:

Hi Laur,

I'm in trip prep mode, but I wanted to take a bit of time and respond to you. I'm not sure where to begin, so I'll just get straight to it.

We have an amazing time together. Our chemistry is off the charts. We have similar interests. We spent a good chunk of time apart and shared our feelings, perspectives, and views of each other and our relationship. We reconnected and it was as if nothing had changed. And therein lies the rub.

While all the great aspects of our relationship remain the same, apparently so do the aspects that were found wanting.

You texted me and asked me to help you understand. One question came to the forefront of my mind...

Have you ever considered that I'm not the one? That I'm not the one who is going to make your dreams come true? That while I may have most of what you want in a partner, I don't have it all?

You shared with me about your spirit guides seeing 360 degrees and if you go it alone you only see a small piece of the whole. Maybe you are so focused on me being the one, that you are being blind to the entire picture.

You know I love you and have only the best of wishes, intentions and hopes for you. But I cannot unequivocally say that I am the one for you and that you are the one for me.

I wrote this a few hours ago and went to do some shopping before re-reading and sending it.

The bottom line is that I don't know how to do us. We've tried a full-on, committed, romantic relationship. That blew up. I tried to draw the line and say I only wanted a friendship and not a romantic connection. That was a big fail. I don't know what other options we have.

I do know that I had a very challenging experience on this last climb in Argentina and since that time, I have been questioning everything, and I mean everything...my work, my relationships in general, my commitment to my family, my commitment to growth and evolution. I alternate between being hopeful and frustrated; content and restless. I thought I had made a lot of progress going into that trip, but it really shook me.

Unfortunately, I do not have time to deal with my doubts and restlessness right now. I have a job to do this weekend and the next. I have people counting on me to deliver them a great experience.

I don't know what else to communicate other than what I have. I know you want more. You always have. And you deserve it.

I'm gonna get back to trip prep now. I look forward to your thoughts and perspective. You are always very insightful.

XOXO Wylie~

    Of course I had considered he was not the one for me, but not because he was missing qualities I desired. My biggest struggle with Wylie was that I didn't believe he understood what a relationship truly was, and he certainly didn't know how to be in one completely. He always seemed to have one foot out. He didn't grow up with examples of healthy relationships to emulate into adulthood. His marriage had been compromised for the last 23 of the 24 years. He had never learned to stay. And it was happening been compromised for the last 23 of the 24 years. He had never learned to stay. And it was happening again with me. I knew I scared him. I was the one holding his feet to the fire, asking him to hold himself accountable to a higher standard, which he had never come close to achieving in ANY relationship. Not with his ex-wife, his family, his children or his friends. I felt like he was looking for excuses to escape doing the work. Was depression a symptom of that? I worried he would use it as an excuse to let himself revert to the old habit of cheating in every relationship he had ever been in. I knew he was hanging on by a thread – and if he dropped, I didn't think I could be his safety net. He was going to need to rally and find the inner strength I knew he had possessed in his military life but had never come close to in his interpersonal-relationships. The email made me want to run again – my inner alarm bells were screaming for me to exit before it all blew up...

Thirty minutes later, after I had more fully processed his email, I had an overwhelming feeling of complete and utter, unconditional love and understanding for this man – the way we had felt during our mushroom ceremony. There it was, the part I was missing – he had been struggling with internal issues since his trip and had not shared his plight with me. Finally – something I could attach logic to! I hoped he would be open to seeing me, as this was not a texting or email-reply conversation. We hadn't seen each other for eight days.

3-5-20 5:58 p.m.

[Laurie] *I land at 8:15. I would like to stop by on my way home from the airport to share my thoughts in person, would that be ok?*

[Wylie] *I would like that. How about let's meet at Helton Brewery? Just shoot me a text when you have an ETA.*

An instant agreement saying he would like to see me was good, but it was also odd he wanted to meet me out, and not at the house. Why meet in public to have a private conversation instead of at his place, where it was more intimate? That didn't make sense, but nothing Wylie had done lately reconciled with how things had been in the past.

I couldn't wait to get on the flight so I could land and talk to him in person. I reached my gate as an announcement over the loudspeaker ended which started a commotion with the passengers waiting to board my flight. All I needed to hear was one word: CANCELLED. At that moment, I also got an alert on my phone from the airline about contacting them to make alternative flight arrangements. Instead, I had someone from my work travel office on the phone within seconds. I learned a bird had hit the windshield of our incoming aircraft, which had compromised the windshield and it would need to be replaced. The plane was officially decommissioned. Seeing as this was the last flight of the evening, there was no replacement plane available, and I wasn't going to be able to leave Kansas City until the morning. As soon as the realization hit me about not making it home to meet Wylie, I burst into tears. The intensity of my emotions caught me off guard. I was, after all, still at the airport and under normal circumstances didn't cry in public. I couldn't help it. All the stress in dealing with Wylie's communication, and now not having the chance to connect with him before he left for five days on his trip to Joshua Tree National Park, proved too much for me. A phone call was going to be a poor substitute.

I booked a room at the airport Marriott a few minutes from the terminal. I had talked Wylie into doing a video call with me instead of a traditional phone call. We had never done anything like this before, but I used video calls for work almost every day. I knew that it would at least give us the feeling of really connecting. I got settled in my room, grabbed a snack and a beer and placed the call.

Wylie began by telling me in more detail what he had experienced on his mountain climb. He explained how, on the day of the summit, he "wasn't feeling it." He didn't have any desire to climb that mountain, and he had never experienced anything like that before. I wondered if the 22,000-foot altitude had had anything to do with it, as altitude can affect your mental well-being in many ways: The atmospheric pressure is 40% that of sea level pressure, which means your body is taking in far less oxygen – less oxygen to the muscles and less oxygen to the brain. But I kept those thoughts to myself, just wanting to let him express himself. On the climb up, he had wanted to turn around multiple times but resisted the urge, as he was the guide and clients were counting on him. He had also been dealing with a very challenging client, even declaring this client to be the most challenging he had ever had. That spoke volumes, because I had many times witnessed the infinite calmness Wylie possessed under pressure. When they finally reached the 22,837-foot summit, he hugged the Sherpa and came close to breaking down – not even feeling happy to have summited, only relief in reaching the top. It was his second summit while guiding there two consecutive years – a monumental accomplishment since summit achievements on this mountain only happen in 30-40% of all attempts. He truly was a mountaineering rock star. He then had the arduous task of climbing back down – which he realized he didn't want to do, either. Through shear will power he pushed those thoughts aside and made the descent back down.

His thoughts were now a jumbled mess, as his mental fortitude had broken down on top of the mountain and had slayed the way he saw himself. He was questioning everything in his life! Did he even want to climb Everest in the future? Did he really want to continue guiding anymore? Who was he, and what was he going to do with his life from this moment forward? He also examined all the relationships in his life and was only left with confusion. This was why the depression had set it.

I watched him wipe a tear away. This was most raw emotion he had ever shown me. I felt sorry for him – perhaps it was more than just the altitude exposure he had experienced. I knew he had been searching for more meaning in his life through the medicine ceremonies, and he had been praying for answers. Perhaps he *had* received the answers without knowing what he had asked for. It is my understanding that sometimes, in order to understand, you must first be broken open before you can face yourself. Be careful what you ask for.

The conversation turned to us, to our relationship. I had a question I had been wanting to ask him – his answer would tell me what I needed to know. Was he still drawn to me? He answered by saying he was more drawn to me than any other person he had ever been with. But it was an overwhelming feeling of being drawn and connected, with a backlash of feeling overwhelmed because the strength of our love was too much for him to handle. He explained that he deeply loved me, but the intensity of the love also made him feel like running. Interesting, since I remembered him telling me he wasn't the runner – I was. But, he added, our connection was so strong he had been unable to leave. I really couldn't relate to how he felt. Songs and poems and books have been written by men pleading and praying to find a depth of connection like ours. Why was he so resistant to just letting my love fully in, accepting it, then reciprocating it? Maybe he had not evolved enough...

In the end, we hadn't made any inroads to solving our relationship dilemma. He acknowledged his recent disconnect from me but made no promises to improve. All he could assure me was that his love for me was as strong as it had ever been. But also just as scary.

To alleviate the pressure of our heavy conversation, he told me a little bit about the structure of his upcoming trip to Joshua Tree National Park. It was the first time he would be sponsoring a vet with his Vet Charity. Although he had been looking forward to showing this vet the "awe of nature", there was a part of his heart that wasn't in it and he didn't want to go. It had been almost a year since he went on the TV program promoting the Vet Charity. In that time, he had raised a significant amount of money for his Everest climb, and a portion of that money was to go into the charity. I was surprised that this was to be the *first* vet excursion he sponsored, as I remembered him talking to a vet who asked to be put on the waitlist last May, when we were on the R2R2R trip. That was nearly ten months earlier. I also thought it strange he was only taking one vet, but also taking two random women in their 40's. Once again, something just didn't feel right about this trip. It wasn't going to be his usual Joshua Tree trip in the wilderness, where they would stay completely off the grid. This was going to be less of a hiking-centric trip, with more reflective meditative activities and a medicinal-mushroom ceremony built in. I wondered if the women knew what they were getting themselves into on this trip and how well Wylie *actually* knew them.

3-6-20 7:28 a.m.

[Wylie] *I hope your flight today went smoothly. Btw I'll be going offline during this trip so if you don't hear from me, that's why. Have a great weekend.*

[Laurie] *When are you back? I'm in Dallas now. I love you, babe! I really hope your trip is everything u want it to be* 🍀 🐨 🙏 😌 😌 😌

[Wylie] *Thank you. Back Monday night.* 😌

Despite our call the night before, which had made me feel closer to him again, all progress was lost when he failed to respond once again to my declaration of love for him. I knew I was still missing a piece to this puzzle. What else was he not telling me...?

~~Once~~ A Cheater...

~~Once~~ A Cheater...

Chapter 46

Lost in Love

~song by *Air Supply*

https://open.spotify.com/track/6MfVSA5iKBPHzo6RGARjL0?si=EjCUC3RiQ1ufeR6Y3zL0vA

Wylie disconnected from me, as promised, and we had had no contact whatsoever since he left for his trip. One morning, after hiking with Stacy, I got in my Jeep to drive the 12 minutes home. It had now been 12 days since Wylie and I had last seen each other. He would be driving back with his three guests from the Joshua Tree trip later in the day. I was halfway home, deep in thought about our upcoming concert, when a song caught my attention. Wow, it was an *Air Supply* song, the very band we were seeing in four days! I snapped a picture of the car screen and sent a text to Wylie...

~3-9-20 7:59 a.m.

I can't wait, babe...

I figured I wouldn't hear from him until after he returned home from his trip late that afternoon. In the evening, I had the Monday-night ritual at my parents' house, watching the TV show *The Bachelor* together. By dinner time, I still had not heard from Wylie. I reasoned he was busy de-rigging from the trip and may have returned later than normal. He still had not replied to my early morning text about our upcoming concert, but was probably waiting until he could send me a more thoughtful text. By 9 p.m. I *still* hadn't heard from him. A sadness washed over me, and a few tears welled up in my eyes, spilling out at the thought of being in the same place I had been with him for weeks. It seemed like he just didn't care anymore; he was so unmotivated with me. An hour later he finally texted...

3-9-20 9:45 p.m.

[Wylie] *Me too! Is it going to be Maddie or Hanna Ann?*

A fucking "me too" text?! Well, I could see why he had taken 13 hours to craft that carefully written, thoughtful text to me, I thought sarcastically. I could not believe it. He could have texted that five-second response at any time in the previous 13 hours. I was certain he had taken time to respond to *other* people all day long. But then at that moment I understood why he hadn't responded to me earlier in the day. Wylie's phone, when paired with his car Bluetooth system, would announce every incoming text message. I always suspected he didn't text me much during trips because he didn't want to explain to whomever he was with who "Laurie Majka" was that kept sending him messages. With his disdain for the label "girlfriend," how would he explain who I was without using that word? I had always purposely restrained myself from sending him texts when he was driving with guests, for that very reason – out of respect for him. I was no longer sad; now I just felt pissed. I didn't respond at all to his inquiry about Maddie or Hanna, referencing the final contestants on the TV show I was watching. Wylie didn't ever watch the show, and I was sure he had gotten sucked into watching it with his roommate.

Twenty-four hours later I still had not responded to him. He sent me a similar text the next evening when I was again with my parents watching the season finale of the same show. This time, I sent a curt reply and we had a very short volley back and forth.

He had stopped mirroring *any* of my expressions of loving him, and would instead reply "Thank you." Once again, every alarm bell was going off in my head, alerting me that something was very, very off. I had crafted two emails over the last couple weeks, expressing my concerns and ending each by stating that he was making me feel like there was someone else in his life. In the end, I never pressed the send button. I knew how much more productive an in-person conversation could be than a one-sided email.

It was now just two days before the concert, and we hadn't even spoken live. The Joshua Tree trip had been his first ever Vet Charity–sponsored trip, where he hosted a vet to "give them the gift of awe in nature." It was his charity slogan, and he had been very excited about this trip. It wasn't as if I had been even peripherally involved in his charity. But the year before, I had helped him narrow down names for it and had gotten him the connection to promote it on TV. I would have thought he would be excited to share more about it with me. There was a time when he would have called me as soon as he was away from guests, to tell me all about his experience on the ride home. But again – nothing.

3-11-20 7:31 p.m.

[Laurie] *I really thought you would have wanted to tell me about your trip by now.*

[Wylie] *When we see each other.*

[Laurie] *Just so you understand, you are making me feel very unwanted. I feel like an afterthought to you, and that makes me very sad. I'm happy to wait to hear about your trip 'til we see each other, but these are the feelings that have come up. I don't like feeling like I'm not important to you.*

[Wylie] *I'm sorry you feel that way. Let's talk about it more when we see each other.*

[Laurie] *Is this all still related to what we talked about the other day, with how you've been feeling since the mountain trip?*

I was still constantly reasoning and trying to make sense of what I couldn't quite put my finger on. Only saying he was sorry I felt that way and taking no responsibility for his part in it, put me on heightened alert.

[Laurie] *I wasn't looking for a big serious discussion before the concert. I spent a lot of money on these tickets, and I really just wanted a fun night on Friday. I don't want to have a discussion where you are going to make me cry before the show. So if you have something heavier to tell me, call me now.*

I called him. No Answer.

3-11-20 7:44 p.m.

[Laurie] *I knew you wouldn't answer.*

[Wylie] *Let's talk tomorrow. I'm with my youngest son.*

I only partially believed him, because he usually didn't text me very much if he was with his kids – yet he had texted me quite a bit that night. I decided I could not put off any longer sending an email expressing my thoughts. I needed him to hear and understand my position *before* the concert.

To: Wylie Heartley

From: Laurie Majka

3- 12- 20 12:19 a.m.

Subject: Thoughts to help you understand me

Hi Babe,

I'm not trying to make you feel bad, as I know you are not in a good place right now, but neither am I. We've talked a bit about where you are, but not really much about where I am.

I've felt so disheartened lately. I've been burying myself in work for hours and hours on all my projects. I have so much to do and it feels like so many obstacles.

~~Once~~ A Cheater...

I think I feel disheartened for a lot of reasons. I'm not making much headway with my personal projects. Work has been SUPER challenging. I don't feel like I have any control over the deal I've been working so hard for a year to close.

*And I feel like you are pulling further away. I was hoping after our talk last Thursday you would return from your trip and call me like you always used to. Or ask **anything** about how I am. All I got was a "me too" text at the very end of the day last Monday, and that just made me feel like I'm only an afterthought to you. I wasn't worth the effort of replying earlier in the day, or with any substance. It was like, I texted you something thoughtful – me being so excited to share the concert with you – and you didn't care to reply. I figured you were busy traveling back from Joshua Tree, and I didn't even expect to hear from you until after 4 p.m. But you've been busy in the past and still made time for me. It's not like I don't have something to compare this to. It was like, at the end of the day you remembered I had texted you and then quickly replied, and it made me feel like I'm not even top of mind. Can you see how it felt that way to me? Plus, I know you are on your phone a lot, so I'm sure you were sending text messages to people all during the day and night, but I didn't make the cut.*

I just feel really sad about a lot of things in my life at the moment, and like nothing is going my way. I NEVER feel like this. I always have a lot of areas that are good, and, yes, I still have areas of my life that are good – but right now it feels like so much is going wrong. I cry really easily and I don't feel like myself.

I get it: we are not fully back together, and now we don't know how to navigate "us" in this state. But why are you so different with me? Even when we were apart during your entire trip to Island Peak, you engaged and texted, and you texted me a lot on your last trip to Aconcagua. You wanted to know what I was doing and how I was. Lately – nothing. I don't know how much is still related to what you shared last week about your depression, but I will tell you, to me it has the feeling like there is someone else. I don't really believe there is, but something is very off and it seems like I'm still missing part of the puzzle.

I would like to talk to you. I want you to understand where I am too. I just need help understanding you. Is this just temporary, and are you needing space and taking a break from everyone?? Or is it just me you are pulling back from? Knowledge is power, and I feel like there is still something I don't know...

On a happier note I put together my Soul Whispers posts and I'm working on April. I'm also publishing the painting I made for you on your birthday. Tonight I had to create the Soul Whisper for it and wanted to share it with you:

What are you made of? When you really want something, do you back down, or do you go all in – fear be damned! On a Soul level, we cannot forget the inner power and strength we possess. Never let fear win or you will live your life with regrets. I believe in you, you ARE fearless...xo Laurie *(Written with you in mind.)*

This week has been so super shitty for me. Between all the rainy weather and the "cluster" work has been, everything seems off for everyone, not just me and

~~Once~~ A Cheater...

you. But the one bright spot is that I've been so excited to share the Air Supply Concert with you!! I've only had front row at one other concert in my life. I feel like this will be such a great night for us, and we both need it. Just to have a nice dinner, nice conversation and enjoy each other's company and a great show, would be the bright spot for me right now.

I do love you, Wylie, with all of my heart. I do believe LOVE is the most powerful force in the Universe – and we have that in spades. I do believe love will see us through, and I don't want to – can't – give up on love or on you. I do believe this will all have been worth the effort in the end, and we will look back with hindsight and say – yep, that was why we had to go through all that. Maybe it will turn out to be the cement in the foundation we are building...

xoxo Laur~

  The next morning, after reading my email he texted to invite me to lunch. Feeling slightly suspicious of his motives, I asked him if he still planned on attending the concert with me. He responded immediately that he intended to go and expressed his concern it might be cancelled because of the COVID-19 pandemic. People had begun distancing from others and limiting their everyday activities by quarantining in their homes to help further curtail the spread of this deadly disease. Other states had mandated shutdowns of large gatherings, and our state could follow suit any day. For the time being, it was mostly business as usual.

  We made plans to meet for lunch at 11:30 at a restaurant near my house. My phone rang an hour later. It was Wylie letting me know he was on his way two hours north to tend to his older son, who was sick with what seemed like a stomach virus. His ex-wife was concerned but unable to make the trip and had requested Wylie go instead. He wasn't the best father, but he did on occasion put his kids' needs ahead of his own. I was still somewhat surprised as his son was *20 years old*. Something about the whole thing didn't feel right.

  All morning, I had been thinking about what I wanted to say to Wylie at lunch. I felt he had been minimizing the impact his depression was having on him. He and I were very connected, and lately I could feel sad feelings that I didn't recognize as my own. It occurred to me that I might be picking up on a psychic level what he was feeling. Instead of lunch, we talked on the phone, and I was able to elaborate on my thoughts. I shared with him the sadness and feelings I had been having of almost a longing to exit this world. That was not me; those were not my feelings.

  He admitted he had been having his own feelings and thoughts like that, and perhaps it was true that I had been picking up his emotions. He then assured me this was all systemic of the depression he had been experiencing, and that he didn't want to give up on us. In turn, I assured him I was there for him and had no intention of abandoning him during his time of need. My request was that he communicate with me **more**, when he was in this very fragile state. He graciously thanked me for my understanding and for my support. He said he loved me and was excited to see me and spend time with me at the concert. I wished him luck with his son, and as I hung up the phone the dark cloud that had been hanging over me lifted. I sent him an emoji that expressed "love you tons" to which he replied, "Thank you." Whoa…the lack of hearing him say "I love you" back felt like happily listening to a great song on a record and the needle hits a scratch, jumping and momentarily interrupting the song. Something was still amiss…

The next day Wylie was on his way back to town, leaving his son feeling better and on the mend. He assured me he would be on time for dinner and would meet me there at 5 p.m.

I put in some extra time perfecting my appearance, wanting to look especially nice for Wylie that night. I had chosen a restaurant I had never been to that was close to the venue. I wanted to avoid the overcrowded restaurant issues we had experienced at the casino, at the concert with Dawn. It was a Friday night and I found it difficult to get a reservation – the only available time was 4:30. It was a rainy drive, but just as I was approaching the restaurant the rain cleared and a beautiful rainbow lit up the dark-gray sky. It seemed like a positive sign!

Wylie arrived. I had not seen him for 16 days. I saw him before he saw me, and he was handsome as ever. It felt so good to hug him. As soon as we were physically together, it was as if no time had passed between us. I had been seated at a huge private booth. The restaurant was busy but, save for the waiter interruptions, it felt like it was just the two of us. We ordered drinks and appetizers and began talking about all that had been going on in each of our lives. We talked about our work and our kids, and the crazy pandemic that was changing the world around us. Communication, when we were physically together, was truly our strength – and I could feel all of the chemistry and love was still there that had felt missing over the past few trying weeks. He several times reached across the table and stroked my nose with the back of his hand – it was something he did that made me feel he was so present and still so into me. We ordered another beer to share, then dinner.

Over dessert, I let the conversation go a little deeper and we dived into what I had been feeling recently. He apologized for how he had made me feel, and assured me it had *nothing* to do with me. These were all *his* issues – he was still dealing with the pressures of our relationship that had plagued him over the past year. He felt very bad for his part in how things were now, and he expressed that he acknowledged his issues were going to take more time. He was concerned about me because he knew I wanted more out of our relationship, and that I deserved more – but he wasn't capable of being all in. He worried that more time would pass with him being in this state, and at some point I would realize I had been wasting all this time with him and would resent him in the end. He took both of my hands in his, leaned closer and in a more serious tone looked me in the eyes and said, *"I need more time. I promise I won't string you along."* Then, in case I had missed it, he repeated himself. He told me he deeply loved me and had so much respect for me. He actually had tears in his eyes, a rare sight. I felt relief wash over my body. I had no desire to be with anyone but him! I understood what he meant about time passing and not wanting to waste it, but Wylie's assurance was worth its "weight" in gold. I remembered how in the beginning of our relationship he had expressed that he did not like to use the term "promise," because in the past he had used it loosely and it had ultimately caused him to let someone down. I knew what a big deal it was that he had said *those specific words* to me. His last sentence, about the word *promise*, echoed in my mind on a loop.

On the short drive to the casino resort, he followed behind me in his own vehicle. My phone rang, and I was surprised it was him. I laughed that despite spending the last two hours talking, he wanted to connect some more. His interactions with me felt more like they had in the past. We parked next to each other, and I invited him to get into my car. We used the extra time before the concert to have our own little make-out session. I played some of the slow songs we would be hearing at the concert. It was a great way to kill 20 minutes.

We headed inside and found our seats. We had not been seated for longer than two minutes when Wylie announced he was leaving to use the restroom. My spidey senses went off immediately – he had used the restroom less than 30 minutes before. I instantly "knew" he was lying and was going to make a call or text someone – I could feel it. Part of me was tempted to follow him just to see what he was doing. But then again, I reasoned I was being ridiculous and had nothing to worry about. If he needed privacy for something, I would just need to trust him. He wasn't gone but a few minutes. When he returned he suggested he buy us a drink.

Once back in our fantastic front-row seats, we still had a few minutes before the show. I remembered his birthday was coming up in a few weeks and I wanted to make sure I was on his schedule, so I offered to take him to lunch or dinner that day. He blew me off with a *"We'll figure it out later."* I instantly felt like there was someone he would rather give first dibs to. I hoped it was just his kids.

The lights dimmed and the band assumed their position. I was sitting one row up and 12 seats over from where Dawn and I had been sitting three weeks earlier. I couldn't help but remember the special smile Kirk had given me when the lights went up. I smiled at the thought of him, but was more than glad I was here with my handsome date. The lights went up and the lead singer walked near where we were sitting. While singing the first song he looked down at me and blew me a kiss. This seemed to set into motion something within Wylie. Perhaps even the thought of another man being interested in me triggered him, because from that moment on he didn't take his hands, lips or eyes off of me. We might as well have been the only people at the concert. He sang to me and made out with me, and when a fast tempo song came on, he held me from behind and puppet-danced me. It was one of the best physical times I had ever spent with anyone in my entire life. It was better than sex, because it was in ways more intimate and lasted longer – throughout the entire concert, since it was intertwined with the live music. The feelings I had had of us together at the *ZZ Top* concert we had attended, came flooding back to me – remembering how deeply we felt for each other. You can fake words, but you can't fake how someone makes you feel when they deeply kiss you.

~~Once~~ A Cheater…

Then the band played the song "Two Less Lonely People In the World," and I felt like the only woman in the world to Wylie. I wondered why he still wasn't able to fully embrace our relationship and be with me as frequently as I wanted to be with him. So many songs are written about love and wanting love and regret at losing love…what was it that kept him from wanting to fully reciprocate the love I had for him? Well, he had certainly shown up tonight. I actually felt sorry for the people around us, because I had once witnessed a couple acting the way we were at a concert, when Wylie and I were apart during *Bumble-Gate* – I had felt jealous of them. I wondered how many people we were having that effect on. I don't mind public displays of affection, but we certainly took it to another level that night.

When the concert ended, he walked me to my Jeep and gave me a very sensual kiss goodnight and thanked me for the wonderful evening. I drove away realizing we once again did not have any future plans. He was also leaving on another trip in the morning. But it didn't matter in this moment – I was on cloud nine. And to prolong those feelings I listened to *Air Supply's* song "Lost in Love" on repeat the entire 30 minute drive home.

Storm greeted me at the door, happy to see me and ready for bed. My phone pinged and it was a text from Wylie…

3-13-20 10:37 p.m.

[Wylie] *That was a perfect evening. Thank you so much. You looked so beautiful tonight and I was really happy you shared this evening with me* 😘 😍 💋

I love you. Please don't forget.

Chapter 47

Keep on Walking

~song by *Kate Usher & The Sturdy Souls*

https://open.spotify.com/track/0IN3ZpxOSXNB34pppys87F?si=uiSKCCBpSJ6d6zxuvSE1NA

Communication with Wylie had been stagnant since our amazing concert date. I found myself not being able to reconcile his words with his actions. He loved me, "don't forget," but had no intention of spending much time with me. It didn't help that he was now scheduled to be away on a weeklong hiking trip in the McDowell Mountains, with a group of high school seniors from Chicago, who were flying into town with chaperones. The fact that this trip was "sticking" was pure luck, as the majority of the United States had begun reacting to the COVID-19 crisis with lockdowns. A couple of Wylie's personal hiking trips had already cancelled, and my business flight that week to Kansas City had just been postponed, also due to the pandemic.

Wylie informed me he would have little to no cell service on this trip. It was not uncommon for him to go "off the grid" during a trip, but it had been occurring with noticeable frequency on his last several trips, including the previous week's trip to Joshua Tree when he changed the trip lineup to be more mellow, less hiking-centric. Which meant they would *not* be setting up camp out in the wilderness where *literally* would be no cell service, but would instead be in an area that *had* service. Yet he made it a point to tell me he planned to have no communication with me when he was gone. I rationalized it was because this was the first trip where he was sponsoring a vet for his Vet Charity – except he was hosting others in addition to the vet. This lack of contact would have been fine if it had been the norm throughout our entire relationship. But it was not the norm. Wylie had on many, many occasions shocked me by contacting me either by text or by phone from *very* remote locations, when I was least expecting it. But I didn't really give it that much thought, as I always tried to be very understanding of him needing space and at times needing less contact – although, if I was honest with myself, it was not what I desired. I even wondered, on some level, if he was really going on a trip at all. In any case, I was ready for more, not less – I was ready to either be all in, or all out. It was those thoughts that had my mind toying with the idea of leaving the relationship.

Wylie returned from the wilderness five days later to a new world...

3-20-20 7:00 p.m.

[Wylie] *Wow! Has everyone lost their minds? How are you?*

Uggghh, another *text* from Wylie. There was a time when he *always* called me on the drive home from his trip. Now all he did was text me. He also would have arrived at home several hours ago, depending on when he had returned from de-rigging. Again I had the feeling of being last on his list. Strangely, I was, at the same time, happy to hear from him and had to keep reminding myself that we were not fully back together in our relationship. But I was having great difficulty navigating in these unchartered waters. When he texted me I was also at the moment indisposed to speaking to him live, as I had my parents, both kids and their respective boyfriend and girlfriend over for dinner. I alerted Wylie to the situation, and he asked me to call him when they left.

I didn't wait for everyone to leave to talk to him. We were playing some card games after dinner and I excused myself, explaining I would sit this hand out, and took my exit to call Wylie.

He sounded tired and downhearted. Earlier in the day he learned his CrossFit gym would be shutting down due to the COVID-19 pandemic. Although he was no longer coaching CrossFit classes at the gym, he was still conducting his personal training sessions there. He told me he had had to run to the gym first thing after arriving back in town, to grab his personal weights and training equipment. He would now be setting up a personal gym in his garage in hopes of persuading his clients to train there until the gym could reopen. I silently wondered how many of his clients would even be comfortable leaving their homes, now that much of the U.S. had begun to "shelter at home," except for strictly essential needs. Time would tell.

Wylie then told me he would be leaving the next morning to partake in a San Pedro medicine session at a shaman's home in the Superstition Mountains. This was news to me. Generally, these sessions were planned fairly far in advance because you needed to prepare your diet and mental health, to get the most out of a session. Wylie had participated in various medicine ceremonies over the time we had been together, and he always took them very seriously – always changing to an all plant-based diet and even abstaining from having sex during the week leading up to and the week after a ceremony. I couldn't help but remember Thomas' omen from last summer, when he said, "Spirit needs you to know, the medicine is still working in Wylie." I took his prediction as good to know that the universe was personally assisting Wylie in addressing his issues.

I knew who the shaman was that Wylie would be staying with, because he had been to this location a couple times before. The shaman was a bit of an "odd guy," and Wylie reminded me he would not be in any kind of contact with me because the house rules stated no cellular devices. This shaman was a techy and had written papers on the danger of cell phones and the radiation they emitted; I had forgotten all about that, but it did raise a vague recollection – since it provided yet another great excuse for Wylie not to be in contact with me, even though it was true that the nature of the ceremony would tend to preclude one wanting to be on their phone. I knew Wylie was in good hands there, so hearing from him could wait until the following day. These sessions generally began in the afternoon, and then the group would spend the night and eat an early breakfast together. Wylie, not being one to stay long the next day, would be home early. Still, I felt puzzled that he had not ever mentioned this session to me, and I got the gut feeling he was not going alone. It was the same feeling I had had about Jane many months ago when Wylie skipped the Ronald McDonald Charity event to do the same ceremony at the same location. But Jane was of no concern to me now, and this felt like someone different from her...

    I woke up the next morning in better spirits than I had been in the day before, while waiting all day for Wylie to contact me. I had both of my kids home, which didn't happen very often anymore, and I reveled in their presence while happily making breakfast for everyone. My thoughts would drift to Wylie and I would wonder how his ceremony had been. I really hoped he was getting the healing he needed from the recent depression (or melancholy, as he liked to refer to it) after his incident on Mt. Aconcagua. I assumed I would be hearing from him sooner than later, since he always shared his ceremony revelations.

    By midafternoon I *still* had not heard a peep from him. No text, no call. My emotions started to slide toward sadness, despite being with my kids. I had planned to take Ryan, his girlfriend Brittni, Rachel and her boyfriend Marlon on a hike to a waterfall. Everyone was really excited to go, but we kept pushing up the time to leave while Rachel was finishing her college homework. When everyone was almost ready to go, Ryan pulled my Jeep out of the garage so we could all get in more easily. I always listened to XM Satellite Radio, which Ryan was not a fan of, so he had already changed the radio to an FM station. Everyone was finally loaded into the vehicle, and as I started the Jeep the beginning of the song "Nothin's Gonna Stop Us Now" by *Starship* was playing. I did a double take. Hearing the song, I wondered if the music from my phone had been connected to the radio by mistake. Then I noticed the station had been changed. Wow! Here I was thinking about Wylie, and this song came on the radio – the very same song I had heard on the radio station in Kansas City when I was having similar misgivings about him. What message was Spirit sending me today? There was absolutely no accident in the timing of the receipt of this specific song. Was it an attempt to comfort me, or was Mark just saying hello?

    After the hike, we all hung out at home. I had a few things to do around the house, and for once I didn't hide my sadness from everyone. Ryan voiced his concern, asking me if everything was ok. I said I was still upset about issues I was having with a big deal we were trying to close at work, trying to throw him off the trail of what I was really sad about. He asked me if I wanted to talk about it; I declined the offer. Later that night, after eating dinner, we all sat down to watch a movie. I heard the familiar ping indicating a text message from Wylie had arrived on my phone. I noted the time...9:28 p.m.

[Wylie] *Hey how was your weekend? Sorry I didn't connect sooner. Things were a little hectic today.*

I answered him and we exchanged a couple of texts before I expressed that I thought he would be calling me, not texting me. Immediately after I sent that message, my phone rang. We talked about his ceremony for a bit, but he didn't go into deep detail like he usually would – which again made me feel like he was withholding. Then he inquired about the kids' visit. I told him I didn't want to spend much time on the phone; I wanted to spend my time with my kids. He asked me what my schedule looked like. I said I would be working from home all week, since my company was on a travel moratorium. Rachel would be leaving in the morning and Ryan would be heading back to Tucson with his girlfriend, so I was home and completely free the rest of the week. Wylie's response was "We'll figure it out" – even though the idea of us seeing each other was his. I felt stunned again at his resistance to making any specific plans with me, and I was instantly angry but didn't express it to him. WTF – he hadn't seen me for nine days AND he wasn't guiding or working, yet he could not make an actual plan to see me?!! In fact, why not see me Monday *and* Tuesday *and* Wednesday! I hung up the phone feeling both sad and completely annoyed.

The next morning I met Stacy at the trailhead to hike. I usually did the talking on the way up the mountain, so I started right in about Wylie and all that had transpired over the weekend. I told her that the only choice I thought I could make to keep my sanity was to exit the relationship. Stacy had spent a lot of "couple time" with us and, like me, could see potential in the relationship. She said, "If Wylie would ever actually show up for you, I think the two of you would have a fabulous relationship." She was right, but I was beginning to doubt he could "show up" – even after almost three years together, and I wondered if *"IF"* was worth waiting for...

On the way down the mountain, Stacy talked about her current real estate deals. As we were nearing the end of our hike, I observed, "You know, no man has ever really fully shown up in a relationship and actually *picked me...*" My voice trailed off...and I thought to myself, *"not picking me" was the primary relationship obstacle I had realized in psychoanalyzing myself.* And then I remembered ...*except for Mark T.* Mark T. had been a short, one-year relationship ten years earlier, shortly after my affair with Mark Abrahamian had ended, and just after filing for divorce from my husband. Mark T. had been my truest example of what it felt like when someone **did** pick me. I was going through a divorce at the time, and the timing of our relationship and my attraction to him was "off" for me. Ultimately, *I* didn't pick *him*. We parted ways as friends over ten years ago. We didn't talk often, with two exceptions: we spoke yearly on each other's birthdays. His would be coming up in a month.

I bid Stacy goodbye, loaded Storm in the Jeep, and climbed in to begin the 12-minute drive home. About three minutes into the drive, my cell phone rang. The car screen announced the caller as "Mark T." – the very person I had spoken of mere minutes before! I answered the call proclaiming incredulously, "What the heck are you doing calling me when I just said your name out loud less than five minutes ago?!" Mark laughed and said how we would always be connected. He then explained he was calling me because when there was a world crisis he felt like I was the voice of reason who could help bring him back to equilibrium. He had been concerned about the COVID-19 pandemic and wanted to hear my take on things. I shared my thoughts; he said my positivity always made him feel better. The conversation turned to our kids and what was happening in our lives. I talked to him a little about what had been going on in my relationship with Wylie, and I explained why I had mentioned his name shortly before he called. He said, "Laurie, you are an amazing woman who deserves a man who matches what you bring to a relationship. It sounds like Wylie isn't doing that. Don't settle for less than you deserve!" We had a great 30-minute conversation. To me, it could not have been a "fluke" that Mark T. thought of me and chose to act on that thought by calling me mere minutes after I had spoken of him.

Adding to the intrigue of the timing, while still on the phone with Mark T., I stopped at the mailbox before I reached my house – a small package was waiting for me. Inside was a ring I had ordered with a glass bee on it. When Mark T. and I were dating he gave me a beautiful matching necklace and bracelet set for Christmas from the Coach store. Each piece featured a glass bee. There was a matching ring he had not bought at the time. I always liked that ring and wished I had it to complete my set. A few times over the years I had searched for one for sale on eBay. About a week earlier, for unknown reasons, I decided to look online again for that bee ring and, to my surprise, found one for sale that was also just the exact size I needed! Ironically, the bee ring had arrived and was in the mail I just so happened to be picking up at the very moment I was speaking on the phone to the very person who had purchased the matching jewelry set for me! The universe was truly working overtime that day.

When I walked into the house, Ryan was up and eating breakfast. It wasn't long before the subject of Wylie came up. Ryan began, "Mom, Brittni and I were talking about how sad you were this weekend. Was it because of work or Wylie?" I admitted it was both. I was actually frustrated with work, and I really was sad about the way Wylie had not been showing up physically or emotionally in our relationship. Ryan continued. "You know how much Brittni admires you? She thinks you are one of the most accomplished and strongest women she has ever met. But she has noticed since you and Wylie started to get back together how much that relationship has affected you negatively, to the point you don't even seem like your strong self. We don't think he's right for you. Things haven't been good for the two of you for eight months, and you are so upset – and the two of you aren't even completely back together! I hate seeing you like this; we both do."

Wow. Those words really stung, and I could feel the sting of tears begin forming in my eyes. I became defensive: "It's sad that I'm not allowed to show my true emotions to anyone. In my life, I am almost always happy and rarely sad. Yes – I've been on a rollercoaster of emotions with Wylie since Bumble-Gate, but it's not fair that when I decide to show my true feelings, you are making me feel like I have to hide them." Ryan said, "Mom, I don't want to hurt your feelings, but it's been more than you just being sad…it's almost like this relationship changes you and has become an immature relationship. It's been going on for months. I don't like seeing you getting hurt over and over again." Then he gave me a huge hug. I thanked Ryan for sharing his thoughts. He let me know he was there for me.

I went back to my computer to do some work, but my mind kept wandering to the thoughts Ryan shared with me. What kind of example was I setting for my kids?! It reaffirmed my resolve to begin pulling out of the relationship. I prayed for strength and asked that I be guided toward the highest and greatest good. With Mark T.'s words still ringing in my ears, I began writing an email to end the relationship with Wylie…

Chapter 48

Misled

~song by *Kool & the Gang*

https://open.spotify.com/track/1TTRvU5OO7CUZQlj3ujFce?si=CMd2FNTiQO6T9udEfAL9JA

Wylie texted me around 5 p.m., asking me how my day was going. I answered but wasn't very engaged with him as I was sick of all his superficial nonsense. After a couple short volleys back and forth, I didn't give the conversation anywhere to go and it stopped as quickly as it had begun. Around bedtime he hit me up again and asked me how the rest of my week was looking. It was now Monday night and we *still* didn't have plans to see each other. I told him I was wide open, except for one night that Ryan and I were going to look at engagement rings for his girlfriend. I remarked how different things were with all nonessential commerce shut down because of COVID-19. He responded:

[Wylie] *It's definitely a strange time. I wake up in the morning and remember the bullshit and get a sense of dread.*

[Laurie] *Well maybe you are just feeling me.*

[Wylie] *Why do you say that?*

[Laurie] *Because, I know it's what you are feeling.*

[Wylie] *Hmmmm. That's interesting, maybe we can connect on Wed or Thurs?*

[Laurie] *Maybe.*

    This was an atypical response from me, and he knew it and responded instantly with...

[Wylie] *I can come your way. Think about it. Hope you have a restful sleep. Sweet dreams.* 😘

[Laurie] *Night, Wylie* 😘

  I knew he could feel through my responses that things were "off" with me. It was interesting that as soon as I sent my cryptic response he immediately threw out the offer to see me. His response felt manipulative to me, and I wasn't playing games by saying *maybe*. I was truly considering sending him the email to end things and let the amazing concert date be our last contact. I knew our next interaction had the potential to cause more harm than good, because of the way I had been feeling about him and also because of his lack of enthusiasm toward me.

  The next morning I continued honing the email that would put the final nail in the coffin of our relationship. I texted LeeAnn, disclosing my plans and asking her to call me when she had time. She called me a few minutes before a work conference call I had was to begin. I began reading her the email, but soon realized I wouldn't be able to finish reading it and discussing it before my next scheduled call. She was about to commence with her own series of work calls that would keep her tied up for the rest of the day, but she promised to call me back later so we could finish our conversation.

  My sister called me in the afternoon and I read her the now-completed email. She agreed it was time to let Wylie go and urged me to send the email now so *I* could let him go and get back to feeling like myself. I felt a renewed strength and decided there was no point in waiting any longer. But as soon as I hung up with my sister, I remembered I had not finished the conversation with LeeAnn, and I reasoned that waiting a few more hours to send the email wouldn't make a difference. Before LeeAnn could call me back Wylie reached out via text while I was weeding in the backyard. He asked me how the big deal I was pursuing at work was going, and I asked him if he had any takers to do the workout in the new garage gym. Since I planned to send the email anyway, I decided to throw all caution to the wind and ask him a few pointed questions.

[Laurie] *I am curious about something. I haven't seen you in 11 days. Why did you want to wait to see me 'til Wed or Thurs? Why not Sun or Mon or Tues?*

[Wylie] *Because I'm trying to get my business stuff sorted. On Friday I found out my guiding company had canceled all planned trips and that I wasn't going to be able to use the CrossFit gym for my personal training. And you have a shit ton going on with your work deal, and I want you to hopefully have more clarity on that.*

[Laurie] *Ok, that makes sense. Would have been a good thing to communicate to me, you know? Otherwise it feels like I'm last place on your calendar and in your life. Hasn't felt good.*

[Wylie] *I'm sorry. My communication hasn't been consistent lately.*

[Laurie] *No it has not!!!!!!!! I'm in run mode.*

[Wylie] *I don't blame you.*

[Laurie] *I've spent two days writing a long email describing it all from my vantage point.*

[Wylie] *I'll look forward to reading it when you feel like sending it.*

[Laurie] *No, you won't want to read it. Always feels like you have some reason to put me on the back burner of your life... It's not mean in any way, but it is an ending. That's why seeing you is a maybe. I don't know that I can anymore. When things are falling down around me I want to grab on tight to the ones I love for comfort and support. You seem to want to push the ones you love away. I don't get it.*

[Wylie] *I understand where you are coming from and you are correct. It's a disconnect in how we deal with stress.*

[Laurie] *Most men would be finding ways to see me, I feel like you try harder to find reasons you can't see me. Stress will never go away. Is that how you deal with your kids and your friends? It's not, from what I've seen. Just me.*

[Wylie] *I'm sorry if that's how you feel.*

I sat there for a minute, supremely annoyed that he had *once again* pushed it all back on me, taking no responsibility for his part in *why* I was feeling this way – almost making me feel bad that I did feel this way. Before I could respond, LeeAnn called me back. Since I had already read most of the email to her earlier, I did a quick synopsis of it and read her the text exchange I had just completed with Wylie. Her response surprised me. She sided with him, reminding me of the completely vulnerable place Wylie had just been in with his mountain encounter followed by depression. And he was now facing the very real prospect of little to no income for an unknown period of time, as COVID-19 was not only wreaking havoc with people's immune systems but was simultaneously taking the economy down along with it. Maybe now was not a good time to leave the relationship. What if the communication issues were a symptom of what was going on in his life? She reminded me of the phenomenal time we just had at the concert when we last saw each other, and how much he loved me. He was really struggling, she said, and recommended I call him before doing anything rash like sending an email to end it all.

The compassionate side of me dropped my thoughts back down into my heart-space, ripping them out of my analytical, judging head-space. I knew she was right. I needed to see him in person, to talk to him, to sympathize with his current plight and make him feel better. This couldn't wait! I almost couldn't get off the phone fast enough. It had only been 26 minutes since Wylie last texted me. I called him. No answer. I headed into the house to shower and called him again. No answer. Impatiently I called him a third time. Still no answer. What in the world could he be doing to not answer, since his phone was never far from his grip? I hadn't left him a message. I decided to try to call one last time. No answer. I jumped in the shower, then dressed quickly and decided a talk could *not* wait. I needed to see him *now*. If I hurried I could be to his place by 6 p.m. Surely, he wouldn't have plans, since restaurants and most other places had been shut down due to the virus. Yes, going to see him was going to make everything better!

Chapter 49

Alibis

~song by *Sérgio Mendes*

https://open.spotify.com/track/5t8YfppCGP89RcJrjs4Ybj?si=Y3ToJeR-SoiKGDYqAInwmQ

Pulling up to the gate of his subdivision, I pressed the code to open it and felt an surprising anxiousness to see him. The house was on a cul-de-sac, and as I passed it I felt relief at seeing his car in the driveway. There was also a white car parked where I would normally park. I remembered the new garage gym setup and thought the car must be his roommate's, so I parked on the street two houses away. I rang the doorbell and his roommate came to the door. She greeted me with a very puzzled smile and I reached over to awkwardly hug her before remembering we were in the COVID-19 era now, when most people were in a quarantine state. She was in a bit of a frenzy because, as she explained, she was on a video call with her daughters while baking cookies. I saw the video screen and waved hi to the girls, whom I had met a year earlier at the pre-Thanksgiving dinner. She quickly hung up with them and then asked me if Wylie knew I was coming over. I explained that I had called him four times but he had not answered, and I decided since we had just been texting I would come over to cheer him up. She said hesitantly, "He's...not...here..." I was puzzled and replied, "But his car is in the driveway?!" She said he was on a bike ride and asked me if I wanted a fresh-baked cookie. Then she offered to call him. He didn't answer her call either, so she offered to text him to let him know I was at the house. She set her phone down on the kitchen island and motioned me to have a seat on the couch in the adjoining living room.

She seemed genuinely surprised to see me and asked how I had been. I hadn't seen her for several weeks, not since I had dropped off mail for Wylie. That was before Wylie and I had our talks in January, when we decided to resume our relationship. She had been a sounding-board for him back then, but told me Wylie didn't talk to her about his personal life very much. I asked her if he had told her about our concert date 11 days before. She seemed surprised by the news, saying excitedly that, no, he hadn't mentioned it – which I thought was really odd, and I realized she had no idea we were seeing each other again. We continued to make small talk, and since Wylie was still not back 15 minutes later, I let our conversation go a little deeper. I asked her if she had noticed Wylie seemed depressed after his Aconcagua climb. She had noticed he seemed a little sad, and she talked about her own bout of depression that required medication. She said it had really taken its toll on her last fall. She mentioned how kind Wylie had been to her during that time, and I was truly glad he had been able to help her through that experience.

Finally, more than 30 minutes after I had arrived, Wylie walked through the front door looking absolutely disgusted. Then, instead of walking over to greet me where I was sitting on the couch, he walked to the island and bent over it, resting both elbows on the granite countertop and cradling his face in his hands. I was really confused by his reaction to me. Turning toward me with his face still in his hands and, in an annoyed tone, he asked me what I was doing there. I decided I was going to need to use a little levity. I rose from the couch and began walking toward him saying, "I stopped by hoping we could have a make-out session, and maybe I could give you the virus and you could give me the virus..." At the end of my statement, I was slightly giggling at my clever reference to a video he had sent me earlier in the day. He was not amused and took a sharp breath in. I suddenly realized he wasn't annoyed; he was angry – an emotion he had never before directed toward me. My mind snapped back to the memory of the last time, over two years earlier, when he had been upset at my unannounced dropping by. But we had been together over two years – surely he wasn't mad that I had just stopped by?! I put my hand on his back, giving it a quick rub, and asked more seriously if we could talk, while also referencing I had called him several times before coming over. He immediately straightened up and said sternly, "Yes, let's go talk outside." He threw me off by marching me out the front door – this seemed really serious! In the past, whenever I had been at Wylie's roommate's house, we had always talked in the open or in the backyard. And if we needed privacy, we would talk in his office or his bedroom. Wylie offered none of those options. His treatment of me scrambled all my thoughts, and I felt like I was in a fog of sorts and didn't quite have my wits about me. This was NOT how I had imagined our conversation would go.

I sat down on the porch stoop, thinking I was settling in for a conversation. I didn't plan on having our conversation standing up. Wylie did not sit down but began pacing near me, and in a very abrupt voice said, "This does not work for me!" I was momentarily confused, until he began explaining. "You cannot just drop by. I have to maintain boundaries. We discussed this. This does not work for me."

"My brain began to clear, and the first emotion I felt was indignation. I retorted, "Wait...are you kidding me?!" My voice went up an octave and at least two decibels. "That happened when we had only been dating for six months, when we hardly knew each other!" I raised my voice a couple more decibels, on the verge of yelling now. "**WE** have been together for over two-and-a-half years – and I'm not allowed to stop by unannounced?! Are you fucking kidding me?!!"

He responded back calmly but sternly, "I have never stopped by at your house unannounced." To which I replied, "YOU are welcome to *stop by my house unannounced any time you want!!*" Again he repeated, while raising his voice and taking a step, then spinning on his heels, *"This does NOT work for me."* I was full-out yelling now: ***"I don't get it!"*** Then questioning: "So I'm not allowed to stop by, even though we have been together for over two years??!!" He babbled something about how he had issues with his boundaries and I needed to respect them. He then reverted back to **"LAUR-IE!"** enunciating each syllable. *"**THIS DOES NOT WORK FOR ME!**"*

I thought I was dealing with a strong man, but I realized at that moment: weak people push other people down to make *themselves* feel stronger. I had finally had enough, and I stood up. Taking a step closer to him, I asked rhetorically, *"So, you don't want to talk!"* He answered my rhetorical question anyway: *"NO!"* I pushed past him, having to walk around him, then walked awkwardly between the two cars parked in the driveway. As soon as I was past the car barrier I quickened my stride, half walking, half stomping to my car while muttering under my breath, *"I cannot fucking believe this."* I was shocked he let me walk away.

I didn't look back. I opened the door to my Jeep, climbed into the seat and, slamming the door shut behind me, screamed, *"I AM FUCKING DONE WITH THIS!!!"*

~~Once~~ A Cheater...

Chapter 50

How Long (Has This Been Going On)

~song by *The Players*

spotify:track:3MzBt3xxpdptFlSpBw1Ua6

That was it! I was utterly and completely through with him and all his bullshit. I was absolutely furious with the way he had reacted to me. As I drove back toward the highway, thoughts began bursting into my mind. OH, MY GOD...he had someone there?!! I racked my brain trying to remember what his roommate's car looked like, but couldn't. Was it white? I didn't think so. I think it might have been red. Her car was an SUV, just like the white car in the driveway. I just couldn't remember.

Then it all came together for me. He hadn't answered his phone because *she* was there doing god-knows-what upstairs with him. He must have been pretty surprised to see the message from his roommate announcing I was there... Then I realized I didn't remember seeing a bike in the driveway, either! I know for sure I never heard the garage door open, so he couldn't have put it away. And I remembered he only rode his bike on trails. It wasn't a street bike; it was a mountain bike that he would place in his car to drive to a trailhead. The house was in the heart of Phoenix, and there were no trails within many miles. Of course he *wasn't* on a bike ride! That was why his roommate hesitated when telling me he wasn't home. She had faltered as she tried to make something up. She knew exactly where he was, and she was covering for him. I was disgusted. Woman to woman, I was someone she knew, and I didn't think I could have done the same. But I did believe she wasn't aware we were still seeing each other. I must have blown up that perception when I disclosed we had been at the concert together recently, and what a great time we had had.

She had a full-blown liar living under her roof. What a surprise I must have been, showing up! He came in the front door, yet he wasn't on a bike ride. And wait...he must have been upstairs the entire time and climbed out a second story window to make it look like he was coming back from a ride! He must have told "her" he would be back and left her in the bedroom, and then gone to another bedroom window to get out. No wonder he was so pissed when he came in. I remembered the strange look he had given his roommate; it was a glance like, look what I just had to do!

~~Once~~ A Cheater…

Then my heart kicked in and told my brain to go fuck itself – he wouldn't cheat on me! He promised he would *never* end our relationship by being with someone else behind my back – he had too much respect for me! Besides – he had said, 11 days earlier, "I promise I will not string you along." And he made me feel so loved when we were together! But my brain reminded me of how he had gone to the bathroom at the restaurant that night, then again within minutes of arriving at the concert venue. I had gotten the distinct feeling he was not going to the bathroom again but calling or texting someone. I had almost followed him to see if I was right. But on second thought, he did have a ten-minute car ride without me and could have called or texted then, so why would he wait – it didn't make sense. Ok, nothing was making sense now!! I was just second-guessing myself.

I noticed the radio volume was turned all the way down; I turned it up and the *Hall and Oates* song "She's Gone" began playing. I was dumbfounded, as this was the song Wylie had placed on our *L.A. Woman* playlist in December when he thought I was gone. I took a picture of the screen, typed the word "Perfect!" and in anger sent both to Wylie's phone. At that moment a car passed me on the right with a license plate that began with the word "CRY." I felt instantly sad and humiliated and mad and confused. I called LeeAnn for comfort and to vent, but she didn't answer. Then I called my sister Stephanie and she sleepily answered. I felt bad for waking her up.

Stephanie and I talked for the rest of my drive home. I replayed every detail and talked about all possible scenarios. I was so completely confused!! As soon as I hung up with Stephanie, I decided I needed to talk to Wylie. I really only had one question for him. Surprisingly, he answered on the first ring. I skipped all formalities of greetings and went straight to my question, "Were you really on a bike ride?" to which he answered, "Yes." Then he said, "I don't think we should talk on the phone because we will wind up saying things we might regret." But it was too late for that for me. "The way you talked to me and treated me is absolutely unacceptable! In over two-and-a-half years I have never said or done one unkind thing to you, Wylie. I have been nothing short of amazing to you. *No one* treats me like that!" I revealed that I had written an email over the last two days and would be sending it to him in a few minutes. Then I said, "Good luck to you." And without saying goodbye, I hung up. I was still really, really pissed.

As soon as I walked in the house, Ryan asked how it went. I told him everything and my theories, and read him my pre-written email. Then, before pressing the send button, I added a new first sentence.

From: Laurie Majka

To: Wylie Heartley

3 24 7:41 p.m.

Subject: The winter of our relationship

I have not changed one single word of this email since I got home…

I would rather be doing this in person, but I need you to understand what happens to me in person, and why I just can't see you.

The last eight months have been very challenging, some of the most stressful and unsettling of my life. This summer felt so much different than things have felt since the end of October. I felt you a lot more after the Bumble thing – you were still "there." I could still feel how much you loved me and how much you **cared** *and I felt like you wanted to work through things and come back – it was ONLY a matter of timing. At least, that is what you led me to believe.*

You say in words now that you want our relationship still, but your actions don't support that. For the past few weeks I have felt like an afterthought, an inconvenience, unimportant, and like you are just not that into me – with the exception of the flowers you sent me on Valentine's Day. That did make me feel very special!! I have done nothing but make excuses for you in my mind about why you are treating me this way. I do believe we teach people how to treat us in what we accept as treatment from others. Being aware of this, I have a few times expressed my feelings of not feeling important to you lately. Despite my expressions to you, it has not gotten better. Even Sunday, it would have been nice when you got done with your San Pedro overnight if you had just sent a quick text, "I'm done, I'm good, I've got a bunch of things to do and I know you are with the kids. I'll reach out later." That takes what, like 30 seconds. You can't tell me you did not text anyone else between the time you left the ceremony and 9 p.m. that night. If you really did care about me I would have heard from you before 9 p.m. – in part because you know from the expressions on my face that I've been sensitive to how you've been relating to me. So I would think you might have taken that into consideration, which again typing this leads me to believe I am nowhere near top of mind for you; and also just because when you are into someone you WANT contact with them. As I've said, I know how you were with me before – it's not like I don't have a lot of past history with you. I can feel how it feels when someone is into me and you just aren't. This is also why I asked you if you were feeling better now. I understood when you were feeling depressed how you just couldn't reach out to me, but now you are through that and things should be a little better. **I truly believe if we were living together you wouldn't downward spiral as much when you go into a depression.** *My energy/vibration level would lift you up and help your overall mood – much like the effect of being with me at dinner and the concert.*

I could even feel your "absence" in the way you said you wanted to see me this week. You asked if I had plans. I said I was wide open (me being receptive feminine energy), and it wasn't like you were like: I can't wait to see you – and put yourself on my calendar. You said, ok we will figure it out and see when it works. So you were going to figure out your calendar and place me there after everything else is scheduled. Fit me in after other things that are more important in your life – I'm the last thought, the last consideration, the whenever it works, because you really don't care that much. So last night I mentioned that the feeling you have of dread, might be the feelings you are getting from me – and you immediately threw two dates out to see me. The part I can't wrap my head around is your empty schedule. This is the only time in the history of knowing you where you have almost nothing on your calendar.

*No trips, no trip prep, no scheduling to do for the gym or for the people you coach cuz they can't go to a gym. The only thing you have right now are the few personal trainings to do in your garage. My point is there is NOTHING stopping you from seeing me. You could have seen me Sunday, Monday **and** Tuesday and you pushed me off to Wednesday or Thursday (no urgency) and not even more than one time seeing you this week. The thing is I would see you every day if I could and you can't even get excited enough to see me soon or more than once. Not into me – AT ALL!! Get it? Do you really understand how this has made me feel? Ok, we are not **fully** back together – I do understand that – but I'm sorry, Wylie, I don't half-do anything in my life and I'm not good at "hold on loosely." This being "partially in" brings out the worst in me; it's not good for me at all.*

I talk to my kids about relationships and one of the things you want in a partner is someone who brings out the best in them and the best in you. I am no longer the best version of myself with you because of how you make me feel when we are not together. I'm a sad version of myself and that is not who I am – sad. It is no longer acceptable for me to be in this relationship. I also know you have not been doing this to me out of any malicious behavior by stringing me along, etc. I really do feel like you have been in a battle with yourself – pick her, don't pick her. Maybe you don't know what you have or maybe you just don't know what you want. Maybe you think you don't want anything.

All that being said, I DO KNOW without a doubt you love me!! You can't fake or hide the feelings of love with someone, and I keep thinking back to our Friday concert. The way we talk and communicate, the way you look at me, the way I feel your energy with me, the way you kiss me, the way we were together at the concert – it felt like you couldn't get enough of me. You made me feel so incredibly loved and full, and how amazing it was being with you. So for this reason I don't want to see you. I would rather our last contact be the memory of that incredible evening.

I get these are trying times, but I was feeling this from you before the world went crazy, before you knew your livelihood was at risk – and I'm super sorry for those changes for you. I would love nothing more than to be the person you turn to as a sounding board as you go in new directions. Someone to help you brainstorm and to cheer you on. There will always be changes and reasons you can give me as to why you don't respond to me, distance yourself from me, etc. Love is a choice, Wylie. A choice to love someone is sometimes a leap of faith. No one is ever sure if they are picking the right person, but if you want someone they need to know it, need to feel it and not just sometimes but always. The laminated heart I gave you said "When someone loves you, you won't have to question if they do, because they will show you in every way how they feel about you." I think the idea is twofold: partially because they love you, feel attached and want to be with you; but also because they don't want to lose you. I feel like you really don't care if you lose me. You have totally taken for granted that you won't because you know how strong our connection is and how strong my feelings are for you. But you are wrong. You are losing me now.

~~Once~~ A Cheater...

I told you how much I love you and how you can count on my love, and none of that has changed. You know how I feel; you know my heart, my effort, my level of commitment and energy. But I just can't continue doing it all by myself. You know where to find me, you know where I live. If you decide you want to be with me, you will find a way. I know what Spirit has been telling me. Yesterday when Ryan moved my jeep, he changed my radio station from XM to FM. I got in to take the kids hiking, I had been feeling sad about you all day, and the radio began playing "Nothin's Gonna Stop Us Now" from the first note, just like it did after I texted you in Kansas City. Stacy said "If Wylie really showed up for you, the two of you would be a phenomenal couple." She is right, we would. I think we both know the potential. But I don't know if you are capable of showing up. You don't fight for things like I do. You say to yourself it will just sort itself out. But nothing of value happens on its own. This is the attitude you've been applying to our relationship – it will just work out – as if you don't have to do anything to have it, to keep it. Relationships don't work that way. They take energy and love and nurturing. Although our connection happened magically, the relationship doesn't just magically sustain itself. I can't be the one doing the majority of the work.

When your birthday comes around I wonder if you will remember how much I wanted to be a part of your day, to celebrate you and to let you know how amazing I think you are. I offered to take you to lunch or dinner. You couldn't even commit to either, telling me without words it wasn't really important to you if I was with you or not. I bought this beautiful square redwood box for you in Muir Woods that says "The mountains are calling..." and I wrote beautiful things about you and about fun memories we shared, to put in that box. I'm sad I won't be able to give that to you. I want you to pay attention to that day. Do you have anyone else who will make you feel that good about yourself in your life? Anyone who wants to celebrate you the way I do? Who do you have in your life that really counts, who you can REALLY count on? Food for thought.

You have committed to pay for your part of the timeshare which is due May 1 – $8,203. It will begin accruing interest on that credit card after that. I hope you are still able to pay it.

I don't know what will happen with our Supai reservation but if they open up again I do plan on going. I need my tent, sleeping bag, sleeping pad and small collapsible bowls with the plastic matching silverware, etc., please. I thank you again for letting me keep the paintings. They mean a lot to me – I will never sell them or give them away – and they will in a sense be hope for us, reminding me that we are in the winter of our relationship. But unless there is an ice age, spring might come again someday. I have never lost hope that we are meant to be. "I Still Believe" will always be our song of that hope. I just feel like I have done EVERYTHING and I mean everything in my power to make it work and I just can't do it alone, Wylie...

I love you forever,

Twin Flames Eternally,

Laur~

Then I texted him: *"Email sent. I will always love you no matter what; that will never change for me. My love was about as pure as it could be."*

Shortly after sending the text alerting him of my email, LeeAnn called me back. As I often do when I'm talking on the phone, I began wandering around. I headed outside into the now-dark backyard and began circling the outside perimeter of my pool as I explained everything that had transpired; including feeling like Wylie had jumped out of a second-story window, and my theory about there being someone else in the house with him. His last trip to Joshua Tree, which was the Vet Charity trip, had been suspicious to me because he took two random women in their 40s along, Plus, he told me that he, the vet, and one of the women had done a mushroom ceremony together, and when he described it, I got the feeling she was someone he was seeing romantically. I also suspected he took this same woman on his recent San Pedro journey – which would explain why he had not told me about the session in advance. I concluded he had probably spent the entire next day with her and that was why I hadn't heard from him until late that day. His contact with me had changed drastically while I was in San Francisco, and I now guessed this mystery woman was the reason. LeeAnn agreed it was suspicious, and she expressed how proud of me she was that I would not allow anyone to talk to me the way Wylie had. She noted that he would really need to soul-search and fix what was wrong with him. I continued the conversation, walking round and around in circles; the combination of my body movements along with LeeAnn's soothing words made me start to feel a little better. The fact that my relationship with Wylie was over for now was really beginning to sink in. I thanked her for the call and wandered back in the house, which seemed super bright in contrast to the dark night sky.

Ryan asked me if I wanted to watch a movie. I actually didn't want to do much of anything, but I thought a movie might help take my mind off my thoughts, and that would be a welcome escape. I grabbed a beer and joined him on the couch. It wasn't long before I was sound asleep – partially because of my low alcohol tolerance and partially from needing an emotional escape. I woke up as the movie credits played. I kissed Ryan goodnight and headed to my bedroom, with Storm leading the way; she jumped into bed ahead of me. All I really wanted to do was sleep, and I almost skipped getting ready for bed, but instead I hurriedly brushed my teeth. After setting my alarm to hike in the morning, I was sound asleep again in minutes.

At 11:29 p.m. I was awakened from a sound sleep by a single tone from my phone. It's interesting that I needed three loud rock songs set as alarms to wake me in the morning, all set at full volume – and even then, many times the entire song would play and I *still* wouldn't hear the alarm. But *this* special tone, assigned to Wylie's texts, could easily arouse me from a sound sleep. My immediate thought was that it was very late for Wylie to be texting me since he rarely went to bed much past 10 p.m. My second thought was that he had reconsidered our earlier, horrible conversation and was apologizing for his part in it. I was about to be wrong on both counts...

~~Once~~ A Cheater…

3-24-20 11:29 p.m.

[Wylie] *I've given my love to someone else.*

Please forgive me for not telling you sooner.

Here's a song for you…"Bridges" by Fifth Harmony.

    I felt an immediate rush of adrenalin and my head began reeling in response to what I had just read. I read it again, unnecessarily, as the text would forever be ingrained in my memory…"I've given my love to someone else"??!! I was furious. All the pieces to the puzzle I had been trying to put together suddenly and completely formed the full picture I had been missing. *Of course!!* The white car in the driveway *had* belonged to someone else, not to his roommate. He *had* jumped out of a second story window! I now understood it ALL!!

    Wait! Had I missed the weather report? Did we just have a hurricane, a tsunami or an earthquake that was larger than Wylie's love for me? He had proclaimed many times, his love for me was stronger than any one of those natural disasters. It had taken him less than three years to fall off "the line" he had been walking: I was remembering his promise that he would be true to me and would "walk the line." It took less than three years for the rarity of me to fade and for him to already be forgetting his self-proclaimed astonishment that someone like me existed. My fear had come true that he might believe I was a dime a dozen, and that he would go off in search of another woman who didn't already have any qualities he didn't like. In sheer anger, shaking, I immediately sent him a series of five texts:

I fucking knew it!!! That's why the overreaction. Was she there?

I will never forgive you for that, Wylie.

The reason you were so mad is because you had to climb out of the fucking window. There was no bike. I figured it out on the way home.

You have absolutely NO integrity AT ALL!!!

Fucking coward, couldn't even look me in the eyes and tell me. On text – really? I have lost every ounce of respect I ever had for you.

    The pedestal I had put him on in my mind came crumbling down as if it had been made of chalk. He fell to the ground and turned to dust as well, because the man I knew, or thought I knew, was made of truth and strength and goodness, but he was none of those things – only a figment of my imagination. He *never* really existed.

    There was an irony that we would now refer to each other as *ex-boyfriend* and *ex-girlfriend* – when he was never able to fully embrace the boyfriend and girlfriend labels in all the time we were together. I finally understood why – he had probably NEVER been faithful to me. And calling me girlfriend made it harder for him to cheat on me. If he didn't use the label, then maybe he could rationalize that he wasn't *really* cheating. I also understood that what we once had...could never ever be again. So to seal the wounds of my heart, I began putting into motion all the necessary measures to begin building a fortress around my heart – to protect it from Wylie, so he could *never* get back in to hurt me again.

First I blocked his phone number on my phone. The answers to my last text messages need not ever be revealed or known to me. I already had **every** answer I needed. Was he a good man? No! Therefore, he no longer belonged in **my** life.

Next I turned to my phone loaded with social media applications and began erasing him from my life. I opened my music-streaming application, Spotify, and found the playlist Wylie and I were collaborators on – the *L.A. Woman* playlist that Wylie had created for us many months ago. I erased all 117 songs, leaving it completely empty. How sad; we had spent a lot of time finding and sending each other beautiful songs to commemorate our journey of love...and now that journey had abruptly come to a screeching halt. I then unfollowed it so I would not be tempted to go back to it later to add mean songs. It was a private list between just the two of us that I now no longer allowed myself access to. I also could not stomach the thought that he would use *that* list to set the ambience to make love to the new woman, the way we had done time and time again. I hoped he had not already used it in that way – and I cringed at the thought. But I also secretly smiled a little at the thought of him reaching for his phone to use it, then discovering the list was empty. I was tempted to erase a few other song lists he had made me a collaborator on, but decided to take the higher road and just unfollow them – releasing him more and more from my life. I also deleted every playlist of mine that he had been following, because I couldn't bear the thought of having him be any part of my life. Next I unfriended him on Facebook and blocked my own Facebook page by adding his name to the list of blocked people that now included him – actually, only him – which prevented him from seeing *anything* on my personal page. I had never had to or wanted to unfriend anyone in my 13 years on Facebook. It felt very sad, and it gave me that strange feeling of dissonance. I also "un-liked" our Hiking Adventure business page on Facebook. He had been following me on Instagram through his personal page, our hiking business page, and on his Vet Charity page. I clicked "unfollow" next to his name on every one of them. There! We were done – disconnected – if only on paper.

Then I remembered the song "Bridges," the song he had just sent in the last *ever* text message to me. I could already tell by the name what it was going to be about. How DARE he suggest to **ME** that I not burn bridges??!! I had no desire to listen to the song, but I did pull up the lyrics on my phone. Yep, sure enough – build bridges, not walls. It was laughable. Well, it was much too late for that.

I took screen shots of the messages from Wylie and sent them to LeeAnn, who was the last person I had spoken to. She surprised me by calling me back at nearly 3 a.m. her time, and within seconds of receiving my texts. She had stayed up late working and was brushing her teeth while thinking about me as my

A Cheater...

message came through. We talked for several minutes, and as usual, her words had a soothing effect on me and made me feel slightly better.

    I lay back down in bed after our call and tried to sleep, but I was still sooooo angry I could feel the adrenalin coursing through my body. I knew sleeping was going to be nearly impossible. The revelations began flooding in as I remembered actions and slight nuances of conversations that suddenly made sense. There had been a lot of ideas I couldn't reconcile until now. I felt played! But I did realize that on some level he had tried to be something he just wasn't capable of sustaining, and he had been struggling for months – maybe even for our entire relationship.

    I didn't cry; the tears weren't even near the surface – unusual for me. The only emotions I felt were betrayal and anger. But then my thoughts began to shift to someone else instead of myself. They shifted to my ex-husband, who had been on the receiving end of betrayal – perpetrated by me. I felt a camaraderie with him in this moment, knowing my feelings would have been feelings *he* would have felt...dealt by me. A sadness began to wash over me...not for myself but for him, and tears began to stream down my face. I knew that situation was entirely different than Wylie's and my situation, since I had never *set out* to betray him – but the results were the same. I lingered in those thoughts and feelings for a while before making peace with them and letting them go. That episode of my life had happened long ago. My ex had forgiven me, and I had forgiven myself. Would I now be able to forgive Wylie? That question would have to be addressed later. What I really needed was to attempt to clear my thoughts so I could get some much needed sleep.

    My bedroom clock projected red numbers on the ceiling, and I watched hour after hour pass by. All I could do was toss and turn, think and think and think. My mind was a hamster on a wheel. The adrenalin finally subsided around 4:30 a.m. and I fell into a fitful sleep. The loud rock song streaming from my phone woke me at 6 a.m., urging me to get ready to hike. I had probably slept less than two hours, and I felt that familiar sick-tired feeling. It was time to get up and face Stacy, to tell her the bad news...

~~Once~~ A Cheater...

Chapter 51

Someday

~song by *Mariah Carey*

https://open.spotify.com/track/6TSM5vkz0WzyZsNAKKYDcw?si=zDFFdXZBTAutkM3gNpD7fg

After removing the rose-colored glasses I'd been wearing, the feelings of love faded a bit more, and I was finally able to see through him – to see who Wylie truly was.

I was in desperate need of closure and words were my ammunition. I spent a good chunk of the morning carefully crafting an email to him. I now had time to assess and process, and I had a few things I needed to get off my chest. First, I needed to send my thoughts to the people in my life who cared most about me, all of whom I sent the following email about my breakup with Wylie:

If you are reading this it is because I know you love ME and you will not judge me for this relationship. I am sending this to you for closure for me, because I WANT to send it to Wylie, but I know how much "no contact" keeps my power with me instead of giving it away to him. I am taking the high road by not sending it to him. Obviously, Wylie and I are over, and the way it ended will not leave me pining for him. It will allow me to move on without comparing everyone I meet to him. I am strong, and I believe in love and that an incredible Soul Mate will come in for me when the spiritual timing is right.

Wylie did have a lot of really great qualities. He is much more than he is living up to. I can't help but see not only the person, but their potential. And for a long time Wylie did make me feel so special and so amazing. Despite everything, I believe he did love me in the weak way he is able to "love"...

The following is the email that I'm sending to you my loved ones, but that will never be sent to Wylie.

~~Once~~ A Cheater...

Subject: The ice age of our relationship

Wylie,

I mentioned in my previous email that we are in the winter of our relationship – but an ice age has unexpectedly fallen upon us that will last for the rest of this lifetime...

*When I arrived at your house, it was actually to comfort you. I was feeling I had not been sensitive enough to your recent depression episode followed by the blowing up of your livelihood re the COVID-19 scare. It's funny: when I arrived I was encapsulated in complete innocence. I did notice the white car in the driveway, but I just assumed it was your roommate's car since you told me you had set up a training gym in the garage, and that she would now have to park outside. I don't really remember seeing or knowing what her car looked like, because it was usually either gone or in the garage. Of course, in hindsight, it must **not** have been hers.*

*Wow, what a shock for you to have me stop by unannounced for only the second time in our relationship of two years and nine months. I must have been moved by Spirit. I still don't think you understand who I am spiritually, and I know you have not connected to who **you** are spiritually. From all the "signs" I've gotten from Spirit over the last year, there must have been a lot of what I will call "contractual obligation and excitement" around our relationship. In other words, I believe we both had committed to come to this Earth to perform some "work" that only we could do together and that would help change the energy in the world. I believe there was a lot of excitement from us and from Spirit that we had agreed to come together to do this! But you kept trying to sabotage it – and congratulations; after months of trying, you succeeded! You have broken our contract and it will not be completed in this lifetime. Perhaps we will have to try again in another lifetime. But you are going in the wrong direction, spiritually – and I mean wrong, because you don't grasp the importance of the ripple effect. All your thoughts and all of your actions contribute to this effect. I am so incredibly sad for you when I think about the damaging, negative ripple affects you have been sending into the world. You truly DON'T GET IT! But you will. You will understand when you have your life review, and you will be so disappointed in many of the choices you've made. You will realize that I had come along to help you, to love you, and to lift you up, to raise your vibration and to hold you to the higher standards you wanted for yourself. But there was only so much I could do.*

As I mentioned above, I arrived at your house in innocence, and I was absolutely shocked by your reaction to me. It was completely over the top and sent me into a state of confusion and shock. Only after the blanket of confusion lifted while I was driving home, did I realize: wait...I didn't see a bike...and I would have heard the garage door open for you to put the bike away. Was that white car in the driveway even your roommate's car...? OMG, you must have had to jump out of a second-story window and come in through the door to make it appear like you were coming back from a bike ride. I know you only trail ride, so you wouldn't really leave from the house to go on a bike ride. YOU panicked, because you were doing something wrong. All you had to do was walk down the stairs and say, "Hey, I didn't leave for the bike ride yet," or "I was already back from the ride. I just got out of the shower." But I really think you climbed out of a second-story window instead.

   You ushered me out of the house because, of course, "she" was there. Wow, wonder what she heard, what she was thinking, or what you had to tell her. I had NO ulterior motive in coming over. I wasn't checking up on you in any way – I guess I should have been. Disappointing thing to me is that you sat on my couch a mere eight weeks earlier and told me: "My energy isn't open to anyone else." And then you added, "I don't want you to worry about that." Then, 11 days ago at our fabulous dinner, you said, "I have a lot of issues I'm sorting through. I promise I won't string you along." Then, to top it all off, later that same night you sent me a text that said, "I love you, don't forget!" You promised me long ago that you had so much respect for me you would **never** end our relationship by being with someone else behind my back. To quote your own saying: "Big fail" there.

Well, guess what. YOU didn't end our relationship by being with someone else. I – ME, not you – ENDED OUR RELATIONSHIP, because of you treating me poorly. For the two days before that, I had already been writing the email to end things. I'll bet I'm the first person in the history of Wylie's universe to end a relationship with him (you). All you brought to our relationship was lies and deceit. You did teach me a lot about trust and further trusting my own gut – so I thank you for that. You won't miss me for now; you'll have your new shiny penny. But she won't fulfill you, at least not for long. No one will, because you will need to first look inside your own self and fix what is broken there.

I'm not sure now why Bumble happened – was it really a game and a result of you not taking a break after your marriage? Or was it really your utter and complete lack of character? You were so sincere and poured so much of yourself into all those emails you sent me this summer. And I did read some of the exchanges you had with those Bumble women. They were benign, but you were playing games with women's emotions – women who really thought that you were interested in them – and that is wrong on **every** level.

I believed you and believed IN you, because when someone like me has spent their entire life trying to be the best version of themselves, they want to believe in the integrity of everyone else. But I don't think you had any intention of ever telling me you had begun seeing someone else. You knew I was on to you, because I had already told you three times recently that "You are making me feel like you are seeing someone else." You must have been amused by my "spidey" senses as you witnessed them again and again during our relationship. I know you believed in them – hell, you cancelled your 2020 Everest trip! You told me seventy percent of the reason you canceled it was because I told you that, psychically, I didn't see you summiting. Lucky you – my spidey senses saved you thousands of dollars.

Good riddance to you! Good riddance to the man who told me, "I have been trained to beat lie-detector tests." Do you know who says that? A LIAR. I'm sorry for you that my future thoughts about you will be unkind. But soon enough you won't even be a thought to me. That is sad, since you told me not long ago, "When every relationship I have been in was done, I never looked back. But if our relationship ended I would still want you in my life – I can't imagine not having you in my life!" Well, you won't have to imagine; now you get to experience it. You have lost your cheerleader, confidante, motivator, lover and friend. I am going to use a saying you loved: "So sad for you!" You may not feel it now, but in time I do believe your actions will be among your greatest regrets. After you texted me that you had "given your love to someone else," you had the nerve to send me a song called "Bridges" – about building bridges, not walls. Sorry, babe – I FUCKING TORCHED OUR BRIDGE!!

Goodbye, Wylie. I forgive you for all your faults and for what you did to me, but I will not **forget** what you did…

We are done in this lifetime.

Laurie~

Chapter 52

Don't Shed a Tear

~song by *Suzanne Karr*

https://open.spotify.com/track/1WrF8vUTKfxtPBPgGI5uN7?si=H39ggC14SkKoxixCUMmhkg

I carefully packed the last of Wylie's belongings in a plastic grocery-store bag. The tee-shirt with his lingering smell that I had so passionately worn to bed every night, just weeks earlier, now sat in a quart-size zip-lock bag, unwashed. There was a part of me that had wanted to bring it to the "Burning Man Party" – a name Sal had jokingly given to the ceremonial torching of the Wall of Adventure – photographs and memories I no longer cared to have in my possession.

 I had really debated whether or not to share my final thoughts with Wylie in person – to question *why?* Why had he promised he had so much respect for me that he would **never** end our relationship by seeing someone else behind my back? Why had he only weeks earlier – in response to my declaring I had no interest in being in ANY kind of relationship with him if he intended to see other people – hold my hand while looking in my eyes and tell me his energy wasn't open to other people; then assure me by saying, "I don't want you to worry about that." Finally, why only 11 days before the unannounced stop-by event did he sit across the restaurant table caressing my hand and proclaiming more than once: *"I promise you, I won't string you along"* – and later that same night send me the text message: *I love you. Don't forget.* I just couldn't reconcile all these "talk tracks" with his actions. The only words that connected the dots were: pathological liar.

 In the end, I decided he didn't deserve to see me again. He did not need any other ego strokes that could make him feel I had *any* motivation or intention to keep him in my life – which I didn't! He had declared in an email that he was leaving in a couple days to explore some options in Colorado. I assumed he was hunting for some type of career replacement, since his vocation had blown up with the rest of the world economy in the COVID-19 pandemic. I couldn't have cared less what he was or wasn't doing, so I decided not to open the door to any discussion. Instead, I taped a note to the door that read: "Thank you for dropping off my things. Please take yours."

I also slipped an envelope in the bag. Inside the envelope were two pieces of paper. The first was a printed copy of the poem that had "popped" into my mind during *Bumble-Gate*:

Choices

Bring your BEST to me because I won't accept less

I know what you are capable of and who you are

You can't hide from me in the made-up playground we have created here

I've known you through millennia, know how you tick

You made a contract with me and I want it to stick

It's all a choice now in this human realm,

Your human free will has taken the helm

It will steer you where you need to go for now,

but at some point you'll need to reconcile and pay the cost

I only hope in the process you have not lost,

the most precious thing you could have had on this Earth

LOVE in the way you planned before birth

The poem wasn't a promise of any future to come – more a reminder of the love we were destined to have which would no longer be. The contract I referred to was our Soul Contract, which was now complete. In my opinion his Free Will had taken him off the course we had planned together before coming here to this earthly plane. I believe as Souls, that love is our greatest lesson to learn. The strength of the love Wylie and I had together was indescribable with words, and he had *many* times expressed his fear of the tremendous strength of our love. Ultimately he let his fear overcome his desire to further experience it here, and to grow in love on a Soul level.

The second piece of paper was a handwritten note...my final correspondence. I wasn't sure whether he would be relieved that he wouldn't have to face me in person, or disappointed he wouldn't be able to share his ideas for the future. For a very long time I had played the role of confidante. He had someone new to take that role – but old habits can be hard to break.

Wylie —

There is no benefit — for either of us — to continue any more conversations. You showed your hand and told me who you truly are. I don't need to know anything more. This relationship — you — were not what I thought you were. The person I fell in love with <u>never</u> existed. We approach this life with a different set of rules that just don't match up. You have your boundaries, I have my ethics. I'm good. I have easily moved on. I have removed my energy from you and cut the cords. We are FREE. Good luck. I do hope you can find what you are looking for — but you have been looking in the wrong places — you need to go within and fix all that is wrong/missing for you there. My greatest hope for you is that someday you will be able to stand in your truth instead of in your lies — because what do you have if you don't have your word*?

(*hint - the answer is: <u>nothing</u>)

    Laurie

Chapter 53

The Captain of Her Heart

~song by *Double*

https://open.spotify.com/track/5EwItLwI9hRLyiTUAjMsQ6?si=jAdDMOvDRKm1WP3iWkU88w

Two beads of sweat poured out of each armpit as I sat waiting in my daughter's bedroom...while nervously watching out the front window for his vehicle that would be hauling the last of my hiking gear back to me, back to where it belonged. He was going to be greeted by a note on the door instead of by me. Would he feel relieved at not having to face me? I'm sure the anticipation of confronting the one you had betrayed with your words and your actions wasn't a pleasant thought. I semi-enjoyed the thought of him having to anticipate the encounter – half hoping it left him feeling slightly off balance.

He was in and out within minutes. He left the wheeled cooler I had requested in front of my door. It was filled with *most* of the gear I had asked to be returned. I cringed at the thought of still having to deal with him to get the remaining items back.

Sitting on top of the army-green sleeping bags rested a check in the amount of $8,203 – the remaining payment of his half of our jointly owned timeshare. I felt relief at not being stiffed by him. Almost no one in my life thought he would come through with the money. Not my kids, or my parents, my sister, nor my closest friends. Even the Angel-card reader I had visited two weeks earlier saw in the cards that he owed me money. She gently affirmed, "I don't think you'll be getting your money back." They all had almost convinced me that I would never see a dime, giving me even more ammunition to hold a grudge against him. Only Dawn had believed he would. I remembered several conversations I had had over the summer during *Bumble-Gate*, where I adamantly defended to others his honor and insisted that he would pay me back. I had no doubt in my mind he would do the right thing by honoring our financial agreement. But as I learned more and more about his true nature and character, I began to question my own gut feelings and was slowly being persuaded into thinking they might all be right. But in the end, I held the check in my hands.

Nevertheless, I flipped the check on its back and signed my name, then quickly jumped into my Jeep and headed to the bank the check had been written against. Spirit was smiling down upon me that day, in that his check's bank turned out to be the same bank I personally used – meaning I would be getting my money immediately and he wouldn't be able to have second thoughts about paying me. The check was deposited in my bank account before he would have even reached his house, 35 minutes away.

Good riddance!! Good riddance to the person I didn't really ever know. Relief flooded my body. It was really and truly over. Now I had some work to do. I turned back to the business of raising my vibration back up to the higher vibrations I had not been able to consistently maintain over the previous several months. He had literally been sucking the life force out of me. He had been trespassing on my land without the proper permits, and I had now thrown him off of it!

I needed to take the helm and become the captain of my heart and my Soul. It was time to get my power back. I turned to my Guides and Spirit Team, asking them to help me fully absorb the lessons I had learned. Perhaps my experience wasn't in vain – after all, no lesson is ever wasted. Maybe by sharing my story, others could learn from my lessons. It wasn't too late to change the ripple effect Wylie had put into motion, into something more positive. This would be my inspired gift to the World...

The End

(But just the beginning of the Spiritual Lessons)

Epilogue

What a journey! In the over two years I was with Wylie, I had never once had a thought of writing a book about our story. I don't think this book would have been written had he not sent the text stating, "I've given my love to someone else, please forgive me for not telling you sooner." I realized in that moment it had been a calculated betrayal, as he had purposely been telling me things to throw my intuition off.

The last correspondence – my handwritten letter to him – became Chapter 52 of this book on the day he came to pick up the last of his belongings. Two days later, in just one sitting, I wrote the entire outline for the book and selected all the songs for the chapter titles. The book then began to flow out of me like lava from an angry volcano. I spent almost every minute of my free time for seven weeks writing this book. There were times it would flow so quickly I could not type fast enough to capture the torrent of words. Luckily, I had saved every text message between Wylie and me, every email, and the long notes I made after almost every major conversation we had – all of which allowed me to often write verbatim what my mind would not have remembered over time.

Our relationship was so complex! He would express all sorts of feelings to me, but then would need space and pull away to retreat – and I might not hear from him for days. In order to keep my sanity and to reconcile what he was saying with what he was doing, I began to write all the notes to myself. And when our connection would feel disconnected, I could go back and read the words he had communicated about how he *really* felt about me and about us. It would bring me comfort and help me stay in my heart-space, instead of retreating into my head-space where I might tell myself stories that didn't serve me or our relationship. Having all this documentation made it feel almost as if this book, from the beginning, were destined to be written. In no other relationship had I ever written notes to myself after *any* conversation.

I cannot dismiss the huge Spirit presence around this book. I talked a lot in this story about Mark Abrahamian, my love on the Other Side. I believe he is my primary Spirit Guide. He had already been speaking to me through music for many years. The frequency at which the song titles from chapters of this book would play while I was writing it – and even for months afterward – was astounding. They played on the radio in my car, on my TV, over loudspeakers in stores, in the background of movies, and even once from my neighbor's backyard.

I would often spend only 15 minutes a day in my car, yet hear two songs in that brief time.

The way this book poured out of me also seemed very Spirit inspired. I described it to my friends and family as an "exorcism." I felt like I *had* to get it "OUT OF MY BODY!" Ultimately, I wrote 131,000 words in seven weeks. I spent at least the first five of those weeks in waves of anger and, as a breakup of this magnitude, it felt like a death to me. I think I skipped right past the sadness of the grieving stage because I had already spent so much time in that emotion over the last eight months of the relationship. I finally settled into acceptance over the last couple weeks of writing. I only wished Wylie well, but I was supremely thankful he was no longer in my life. Even so, it was hard hearing from two really good male friends that they had Wylie pegged from the beginning and had been very vocal about it to everyone but me. But I wouldn't have listened anyway – Wylie was my lesson to learn.

Lessons are the reason we are here on Earth, and I do believe our greatest lesson to learn is about LOVE. Every failure in love just prepares you for your next love. Eventually, you are ready to attract the one that makes you look back and thank your lucky stars for the lessons that helped you evolve into the person you are now, preparing you for the greatest love of your life.

Spiritual lessons are so important for our growth, and yet many people don't understand that once we learn a lesson, we are *allowed* to move on from it – we don't have to repeat it over and over again. Often, we won't understand the full scope, breadth and depth of our lessons until we have our Life Review on the Other Side after we die. I have written the last part of this book to hopefully shed some light and perspective on the Spiritual lessons related to this book. I wanted to share some of my insights, and I hope it helps you better understand your own lessons. I've been writing about Spiritual topics like these since 2013, and I would love for you to connect with me by typing any one of the following in the indicated search line:

On Facebook: @SoulHeartArtXO

On Instagram: @LaurieMajka

YouTube channel: @Laurie Majka (Be sure to hit the subscribe button.)

Podcast: Powerful Soul! with Laurie Majka (found on Spotify, Google and Apple Podcasts)

Website: https://www.LaurieMajka.com

Website: https://www.SoulHeartArt.com (where you can sign up to receive the Daily Soul Whispers via email)

I have learned so much and continue learning more every day! Each day on this Earth is a gift, and every one of us is an evolving work in progress. And when the lessons here are done, we will continue them in another realm. Perhaps we will take a break on the Other Side for a while, or maybe we will come back here to try again. No worries – the only thing I know for sure is that things are unfolding perfectly, and I am so glad you are here...xo Laurie

A Cheater...

~~Once~~ A Cheater...

Part 2 Lessons Learned

You Learn

~song by *Alanis Morissette*

https://open.spotify.com/track/1HsbGJnOXPWfocSS6FoR60?si=PpU9b55nQXqfqHs2H_btVA

~~Once~~ A Cheater...

Your Soul's Vibration

The power & beauty of your Soul is beyond human comprehension 🕊

Everything in the universe has a vibration. I'm not referring to your cells or the molecules within your body; I am talking about pure energy – specifically, your Soul's energy. You don't have a Soul – you ARE a Soul. You HAVE a body that you use in this earthly realm, which allows you to play the game and have experiences for the purpose of learning lessons while you are here. You yourself are eternal and cannot be harmed, since energy can neither be created nor destroyed. That might be a difficult concept to grasp, but on the Other Side, in the spiritual realm, you consist of nothing but love. You are, in fact, PURE LOVE. The vibration of the Universe *is* Love. Love is your birthright! How do I know? I have left my body and taken multiple trips to the Other Side and have experienced the vibration of my Soul and the feeling of that love.

It is not easily described with human words, but our Soul is ENORMOUS. From what I have experienced, we shrink our Soul down in size to fit into our body. I also now understand that only the smallest portion of our Soul enters into this body. The portion of your Soul that enters your body varies according to the experience you are trying to achieve here, and the job and/or lessons you are fulfilling. The vibration I experienced of my Soul would be like setting a jackhammer on the highest setting then multiplying that by a million percent – yet at the same time the vibration has the gentleness and smoothness of a hummingbird's wings.

I have also been with "The Light." You can call it God, Universal Consciousness, Source or any name you like. I choose to use "The Light" because any other name seems to diminish the intensity of what I experienced. I also love the name God, but I feel it is often tainted with human definitions that do not encompass the true magnificence, and instead conjure up more of a human vision – which it is not. The vibration of light that emanates throughout the Other Side is, once again, not fully describable with words, but is a feeling of pure, unconditional love and is the best feeling I have ever experienced. In that "space," you understand that your Soul can never be harmed. There is nothing evil on the Other Side, and nothing bad could ever happen there. The evil and bad things we perceive here are bound to this earthly incarnation and existence. You may be able to reach a similar feeling of euphoria on Earth through mediation, orgasm or kundalini energy, or on a medicine journey. But truly, I have not been able to even touch the enormity of that feeling while *in* my body here on this earthly plane.

We have a lower vibration while we are here in our human body. Spirits on the Other Side vibrate at a much higher frequency than we do on this Earth plane. In order for them to communicate with us, they have to lower their vibration. The higher your vibration, the easier it is for them to reach you and to get your attention with signs. If you would like to understand this in greater detail, you can read my book *Signs Surround You, Love Never Dies*. In that book, I tell the story of Mark Abrahamian, my passed-away loved one, and the story of the signs he sent me in the first two years after he died. It was my hope that by sharing that story, you would see how signs worked for me, and that it would help you recognize your own signs.

We all vibrate at different frequencies, and I have referenced many times in this current book my efforts to "raise my own vibration." The way to raise one's vibration is by working on the spiritual aspects of higher self and trying to get to and stay in elevated states of emotion. To name just a few of them:

Acceptance

Bliss

Empowerment

Gratitude

Happiness

Inspiration

Joy

Love

Truth

Wholeness

As you connect with these higher emotions, your vibration naturally increases. Every emotion carries with it a different vibration. For example hate, anger, fear and even sadness are all lower vibration emotions. Think about being in a room when an argument breaks out; you might be sensitive enough to feel a heaviness fill the room as the overall vibration lowers. Other times, you might feel lower vibrations emanating from a particular person and have an instant feeling of not liking them or trusting them. On a subconscious level you "read" energy every day, all day. Furthermore, you draw to you, or attract to you, the same frequencies of energy that you send out into the world. It would be uncomfortable for a very high-vibration Soul to hang out with a very low-level vibration Soul – uncomfortable for both sides. This is why, as you evolve, you will find you attract new Souls to you, and some Soul relationships will naturally fall away as they are no longer a match to you. This is in no way good or bad, better or best. Each Soul is playing a role, and a very highly evolved Soul may come here just to play a role to learn something or to assist someone in learning a lesson. The capability of judgement is a human quality. But how can you possibly judge something you cannot fully understand with our human mind?

We are all human, and it can be difficult in this world to avoid emotions that bring our vibration down to lower frequencies. Awareness is a good starting point; this includes awareness of what you surround yourself with, who you surround yourself with, and an awareness of the thoughts you have, as they are energy vibrations you send into the world. Many times over the course of my relationship with Wylie I could feel my vibration slip downward as I often had feelings of anger, annoyance, dissatisfaction, or sadness over events that were happening. I would try to do things to change my emotional state: I would hike, since exercise is a good way to move your energy and raise your endorphins. I would spend time in nature, talk to a friend, or spend time in the space of unconditional love with my dog Storm. Similarly, things like listening to upbeat music, watching videos about inspirational topics or watching funny movies – have all helped me raise my vibrations – as has eating chocolate, something I love that makes me feel good. There are lots of things you can do that make you feel better in your own skin, such as getting a haircut, wearing an outfit you like that makes you feel good about yourself, or even something as simple as painting your toenails. In my case, I would also start a project that made me feel productive, or create a new painting, beautify my yard, or fix something that was broken in my house. All of these things served to take my mind off of what was negatively affecting me and allowed me to refocus my energy on something that made me feel good.

Helping someone else is another thing that often takes your mind off your own problems; for example, helping a friend or family member do something they couldn't do on their own. On the other hand, watching the news is off limits, at least for me personally. It's too negative and it attempts to elicit a certain response, because there are too many topics coming at me and I can't control the emotional effects on me. I have noticed that among people who achieve higher vibrational levels, drama and negativity in general are avoided. I will occasionally read the news, but I never watch it. To interpret things for myself, I want to control which emotions influence me.

You, too, need to stand in your truth, whatever that is for you, in order to raise your vibration. When you present yourself as someone you are not, you lose a piece of who your Soul actually is – that is, who YOU actually are. You have accomplished a lot in your Soul's evolution by even coming to this earth plane. Be true to your authentic self!

Operating from your heart-space means staying in the elevated states of emotion and focusing on the *present moment*. When we operate from our head-space, we toggle between the present, the past and the future. Many times this transfers us into lower vibrational emotions because we can't change the past and we can't predict the future; we can really only be in **this** present moment. Of course, we can and should make plans for the future – we just don't want to be in our head-space all the time, because we would miss out on the beautiful things happening in the here and now. Listen to the whispers from your Soul and let them guide you where you need to go.

Wylie exhibited three stages of vibration, in my experience with him. I believe that when we first met our vibrations were very similar. I had just exited the relationship with my ex-boyfriend John, and I was in much lower vibrational emotions. Right after that exit was when Wylie and I first met, and I believe we would not have come together if we hadn't been in the same general place vibrationally. Still, he struggled for months with not wanting to be in *any* relationship. Then he transitioned into being in love with me, and we both raised our vibration as our love for each other grew. He also began his healing medicine journeys and was working on overcoming the emotion of fear. He then transitioned into feeling that at some point he would need to take a break from our relationship. And it was right after he went on the Bumble app that he began talking about the strength of my love being too intense. I don't think he understood the feelings he had for me, because they were *not* a result of my love being too strong. I believe they were more about his own fear.

I had significantly raised my vibration with the spiritual work I was doing and with my own medicine journeys – while Wylie had significantly lowered his vibration by not standing in his truth. He was blatantly lying and withholding information, and being generally deceptive in our relationship. All of these actions would have lowered his vibration, probably making my higher vibration feel uncomfortable to him – which he called too strong and overwhelming. Notice, he did not express this until during and after *Bumble-Gate*. Unfortunately, I didn't figure it all out until I had the proper hindsight and was able to fit all the missing puzzle pieces into place.

Understanding Soul Mates

The Soul Mates appear when each is ready for the lesson

Soul Mates: just the very word can conjure up images of a forever partner and a life of happily-ever-after. But in reality, we are all Soul connected – and I do mean that each and every one of us is woven into a complex web that crisscrosses through space and time, connecting us in unfathomable ways.

We are connected to some Souls more than others. I want you to picture a giant tree with an enormous trunk and huge branches the size of smaller tree trunks. Extending from each huge branch are large branches, and from each of those are medium-sized branches, and then smaller and smaller sets of branches – all filled with leaves. Take a closer look at a smaller branch with only about 15 leaves on it. One of those leaves is you, and all the other leaves on your branch are your VERY closest Soul Mates. Not all of them will have incarnated with you in this lifetime; several may have stayed behind on the Other Side to help guide you on your journey. When you encounter these VERY closest Soul Mates, you will have an immediate Soul Recognition. You may feel very drawn to them but not understand why. It is because on an energetic level your vibrations are very similar, and you may feel like you have known them forever – because you have! I believe you will only encounter a *very* small number of these closest Souls in one lifetime. Most of the Souls you associate with will be "from" other branches.

Look again at the leaf that is "you." Now look at the tiny branch next to the branch you are on, with its own set of leaves. The leaves on the branches closest to you are also *very* significant Soul Mates. They too can have an influential or even monumental role in your life, similar to the Souls on your branch. Soul Mates are not always lovers – oftentimes they are *not* lovers. They could be a parent or a child, a sibling, a best friend, a grandparent, a spouse, or even a mentor. If you think about it, you can probably name several Soul Mates right now in this category. The relationship could be one of the best of your life, or a complete disaster (I will address this further in the section titled "Soul Contracts"). There is no one of any significance in your life whom you have not known before. In other words, if you have a significant relationship with someone, you have known them in other roles, in other lifetimes. Each of these Souls has again joined you to be a part of your journey and you a part of theirs.

Look at your leaf again and look at the leaves that are on a branch two away from yours. These leaves are also Soul Mates, and they might be relatives, neighbors, co-workers, friends, classmates, teachers, or a lover. They can mean a great deal to you as well; you can be connected to them and have strong feelings, and also for the people they are connected to in their lives. When you meet these Soul Mates, you might not immediately connect with them, or as quickly as you would with your closer Soul Mates, but you will still have a comfortable feeling with them. It may be that you are just meeting one of them for the first time in this lifetime, but it might feel like you have known the person before – because in reality, you have. These relationships can accelerate quickly, since you already have a history with each of them.

Now look at your leaf again, and look at the branches that are three away from yours. The leaves on these branches are still Soul Mates. You are all on a common branch together, but these Soul Mates play less significant roles in your life. They might be acquaintances, someone you went on one date with, a classmate you went to school with for a couple years, your dentist, etc.

Look at your branch again, and start to look at branches further away from your branch but are still connected to your common branch. These are also Soul Mates, but they will have less significance than the ones on the closer branches. They might be people who work at your company, people who live in your community, or people you went to high school with. They do not play a significant role in your life, but you may have formed bonds and even friendships with these people. You may also have learned lessons in those relationships that have contributed to making you who you are as a person, such that they did influence you. But they weren't meant to be with you for your entire life; their purpose with you was to teach or learn a lesson.

Now look at the branches connected to a different large branch that is not your common branch. These won't be Soul Mates, but they are still Soul connections, and you are all part of a larger, primary branch. These Souls may all live in your city, for example, or you may all be affiliated with a political party, or maybe you are all in the same profession. You might not ever personally encounter these Souls in your life, but they do influence your Soul group in some way. Lastly, look at the very large-sized branches; the leaves on these could represent the Soul connections you have to everyone in your country; or all of the mothers or fathers in the world – you get the idea. Over time, each Soul weaves in and out of the tapestry of souls, creating a part of the picture and ultimately making up the whole.

Now look at the giant main trunk of the tree. The trunk connects every large, medium and small branch and every leaf on the entire tree, as we are ALL connected. That connection is Love, Universal Consciousness, God, Source (feel free to give it any name that resonates with you). In this way, each and every Soul is a part of the whole. We are all connected and dependent on each other to learn, grow, and evolve. The whole makes up the entire population on the planet, and we are all here to learn and grow in love. I do believe this is a lesson all Souls never finish learning while they are here on Earth. We cannot forget that we are all part of each other, since we are part of the whole.

One of the most important concepts about Soul Mates of all kinds (not just the romantic ones) is in how you meet them. When you are both ready for the lesson, or when the conditions you agreed upon in advance are in the perfect timing for you both, you *will* come together.

I often hear mediums express that a former lover now on the Other Side not only approves of your new love, but they may have had a hand in sending or connecting you with that person. Through the medium Thomas John, my love Mark gave me the message that he had had a hand in bringing Wylie and me together. You don't have to search for your Soul Mates – it would be impossible for you *not* to meet when the timing is right, as the Universe will conspire to make it happen.

I also want to acknowledge the significant role our parents play in our lives. *We pick our parents.* This is a fact you may not be familiar with, but is important. Often our parents, more than any other Souls, influence who we become. And we choose whoever will help us to become who we are meant to be in order to accomplish our Soul's life purpose – loving parents, cold parents, actively involved parents, distant parents, adoptive parents – every role plays a part. Parents shape you into who you will become, and without those experiences, you would not become you – and thus you would not have created the circumstances you needed to learn your lessons.

The above is just a small sampling of the ideas behind a very complex matrix that I don't think our human brains can fully comprehend while we are here on this Earth. There are so many aspects of this life that we can't understand, including why we are here at this very moment in time.

~~Once~~ A Cheater...

Twin Flames Explained (kind of)

Twin Flames accelerate the lessons, and hold your feet to the fire 🔥

Twin Flame. I had never heard the expression until my reading with CJ Martes, the Angel Connector. Although I had scheduled a reading with CJ to connect with my Angels, when I walked into her house for the appointment, she said, "Oh, I see you brought a man here with you; he is always with you." Ultimately, she did connect with my Angels, but she primarily connected with Mark, who had been on the Other Side for three years by that time.

It was in reference to Mark that CJ first spoke to me about Twin Flames: "Your connection comes with a profound amount of love. You really are like a yin and a yang – he was your Twin Flame, your perfect mate." She then used a physics term to describe how well our vibrations matched: "You both moved in *real frequency*." After that reading, I began my search to try to understand Twin Flames.

When I connected with CJ two years later, she immediately brought up Wylie, "knowing" (without me telling her) that I was in a relationship with someone new. She knew things about him – that he was an Aries, as well as the sex and ages of each of his children. Then she said, "He is your Twin Flame." I immediately became confused, as I understood Twin Flames to be the same Soul, split into two Souls – one half masculine, one half divine feminine. (This doesn't mean that one Soul has to be male and the other female.) I couldn't figure out how a third Soul fit into that picture, and I remembered CJ had told me two years earlier that Mark was my Twin Flame. I questioned her, asking if you could have more than one. She said no. I then reminded her of what she had told me about Mark in my last reading. She replied, "I will need to consult with the Angels." While she was "consulting," I was busy thinking – wondering if she just told everyone they had a Twin Flame. But I also remembered how I had come to find CJ, and the credibility that came with that. (You can read this story in the section "Psychic Mediums & Angel Connectors," under the subsection "CJ Martes – Angel Connector.")

The Angels explained to CJ that Mark had been my *true* Twin Flame, but after he died Wylie and I, as our Higher Selves, agreed to come together and *contract* as Twin Flames. We now had Twin Flame energy and a very profound connection. This made sense to me on a psychic (intuitive) level, but I was going to need to do further research to understand Twin Flames. The first thing I did was to contact five other people I knew who had had readings with CJ. I wanted to know if she had told any of them they were in Twin Flame relationships. It wasn't that I mistrusted CJ – my skeptical left brain just didn't want to leave any stones unturned. I needed to make sure it wasn't something she told everyone. After talking to each person, I was surprised to learn that *none* of them had been told they were in a Twin Flame relationship.

Prior to my quest for knowledge about Twin Flames, I had learned that there are many highly evolved Souls on the planet: Light Workers, Healers, Channelers, Ascended Masters, Empaths and Psychic Mediums, to name several. They have incarnated in this lifetime not so much for their own Soul growth but to help evolve our planet as a whole. The highly evolved Souls who are here now, having a human experience, are working to help others awaken to who they really are. As this happens, the human collective is gradually moving from a materialistic society to a more loving and cooperative one. It is an evolution that has been a long time in the making, perhaps for thousands of years. We humans have begun to see ourselves as Souls who are not separate from one another but intimately connected.

With regard to Twin Flames, I've learned that the connection is unique, and that in the past they rarely incarnated in the same lifetime together: One would remain on the Other Side as a guide for the other because the relationship had the tendency to be tumultuous when both incarnated together. In recent years, Twin Flames have been incarnating together in the same lifetime with greater frequency. They are meant to come together to help change the energy of Earth. This may have to do with the evolutionary stage of the Souls who are choosing to bring in Twin Flame energy, as all Souls would not be ready for this type of work. When Twin Flames combine their energy they are able to use that energy to help evolve the planet in a way they could not accomplish alone.

Twin Flame energy in a relationship can be very difficult, because in order to do the planned work each must hold the other to a higher standard, and this reflects both the weaknesses and the strengths in the other. Twin Flames are a mirror to one another. Their work seems to be a higher calling that holds a lot of importance, and there is a lot of Spiritual help and energy from the Other Side around the Twin Flames – which might also feel like pressure to the Souls involved. Twin Flames often enter into a romantic relationship, but not always – Twin Flames are about awakening! In my relationship with Mark, he was the spiritual teacher who awakened me. He challenged me to examine everything I had ever thought and believed, and he helped me see things in a different light. I often say, I grew more with Mark's influence in the less than two years we were together than I had in the entire 38 years before we met. With Wylie, I was the Spiritual teacher who awakened him. Then, together, we both grew and evolved until it was too painful for Wylie to evolve into the next higher state he needed to be in for us to complete our contract.

Finding one's Twin Flame is a unique experience that feels unlike any other relationship, because when you truly unite you feel you are one complete Soul. Both Souls understand and feel the significance of the connection, even if they had never been exposed to the idea before. Hearing the label might be a relief, in that there is a name that explains the uniqueness of the connection. This is a most intense relationship. Often one or both Souls will at some point want to run from it because this type of awakening can be very painful, yet they must transform to keep evolving with one another. One Soul may at some point choose not to stay. Free Will always has the final say, but even when it feels like it's over, it *never* is. A connection of this magnitude brings with it a bond that cannot be broken. Any "ending" between Twin Flames is just an illusion. The Souls may choose not to be together physically, but each will still feel the other, regardless of time or distance. Your Twin Flame gets under your skin and will not leave your thoughts – probably ever. This is by design, because there is a unique contract between the two of you. Even after death, Mark came back to me immediately in Spirit. We have continued our relationship and our Spiritual work together through my artwork and books. He sends me dreams, "downloads" from Spirit, and signs as confirmations. The work we do together I could not do alone; it can only be accomplished when we combine our energy to do it.

When I met with Holly Power, the oracle, she talked about "Twin Flame aspects." She explained that each of us has a Higher Self that, as we grow and evolve, may choose to incarnate (come into the body). Additionally, the whole of our Soul does not reside in our human body; only a part of it is there. After one of my experiences on the Other Side, I came back with the knowledge that in regard to my Soul, it was as if its essence – the part that is in my body now – is a portion of my Higher Self equal to my pinky fingernail in relation to my whole body. (It is different for each person, from what I understand.) Imagine the power of a higher, more-evolved version of your Soul dropping into the body – that would quickly accelerate your energy.

Another way Twin Flames come about relates to what Thomas said: *Mark went back for the love of Wylie.* As I understood it, this meant that after Mark died, he was instrumental in helping Wylie and me change our future contract to a Twin Flame connection in order to continue where Mark and I had left off as earthly Twin Flames. This would match what CJ said about the contract between Wylie and me changing after Mark died. But there are aspects of Twin Flame connections that cannot be explained or understood with our limited human knowledge.

I was shown in one of the Toad ceremonies when I was on the Other Sid, that other than my children, there was no other Soul on the planet with whom I had a more profound love and connection than Wylie. That is not to say I cannot in the future find an amazing love in another Soul Mate. Our Souls know no boundaries when it comes to love, but Soul Mate connections are more rooted in love, whereas Twin Flame connections are more rooted in awakening. But I don't have all the answers – understanding Twin Flames is a continuous work in progress.

Holly the Oracle also said she could see no reason I would ever, *ever*, want to leave my relationship with Wylie. At the time of the reading, Wylie and I had been together for eighteen months, and his Free Will choices contrary to our

A Cheater...

contract had not yet been made. I believe Wylie and I had the potential to fulfill our Soul Contract and to blend our energies together to create a business that would have brought a very positive ripple effect into the world. But in order for that to happen, *both* would have had to make the choice and follow through. Even in a Twin Flame relationship as intense as Mark and I experienced, we both made Free Will choices to turn away from our earthly connection, and we had not come back together before he died.

There are parts of me that wouldn't wish the intensity of a Twin Flame relationship on anyone! Give me a loving Soul Mate connection instead. But there are parts of me that are eternally grateful I got to experience the intensity of each of those Twin Flame relationships. The growth and learning that came *afterwards* may have been more important for my Soul's growth than the learning that happened while *in* the relationships. They were, after all, an "awakening by design," and once awakened it would have been impossible to return to my life as it had been. If I could go back right now and wave a magic wand to change anything about either of my Twin Flame relationships, I actually would not change one single thing – or I would not be exactly who I am at this moment. I have to believe everything is unfolding perfectly, even if I can't understand why and sometimes wish other choices had been made by my Twin Flames.

Are you experiencing a Twin Flame connection? Look for these signs:

- An overwhelming attraction to each other that feels magnetic (does not have to be a romantic attraction)
- A destined meeting in an unusual place or circumstance
- An immediate and intense connection that is unstoppable
- An urge to enter into a relationship with one another
- Synchronistic events surrounding your connection (I saw Wylie's name on license plates five times)
- Frequent sightings of 1111, 2222, 3333, etc.
- Many similarities to one another: same birthday, upbringing, etc.
- An ability to feel what the other feels
- An uncanny "knowing" about the other
- In a physical connection, the experience is intense
- Pain, pain and more pain
- Shared nonphysical experiences like dreams
- Requiring that your Twin hold themselves to a higher standard
- Helping each other become the best version of yourselves
- Multifaceted connection, e.g. best friend, lover, business partner, therapist, teacher, confidant
- You feel more "in your own skin" in the presence of this person
- Soul starts awakening to Spiritual growth
- Intensity of the connection produces an awakening in one or both
- Ultimately, love with non-attachment (maybe the most difficult to achieve)

Soul Contracts

I've known you through millennia, know how you tick.

We made a contract and I want it to stick 🫶

A Soul Contract is first of all a contract you make with yourself for your Soul's growth. It is made with yourself, but ultimately with God as you are an extension of that beautiful intelligent Divine loving light. It can also be called your Life Plan or your Life Purpose.

Designing a Soul Contract

Think of writing a Soul Contract as writing a play about your next life. You begin by deciding what it will be about. You may have only one lesson to learn. For example, you might want to experience in a human body what unconditional love feels like. Based on that, you pick your parents and your Soul enters into the body of a baby whose birth is infused with love. You are held and loved unconditionally by your new parents, and you leave the Earth within hours of your arrival, returning quickly back to the Other Side, as you have completed the contract for your Soul. Perhaps you only wanted to dip your toe in an earthly experience and then serve as a guide to your parents, with whom you also had a contract. One (or both) of your parents could be a member of your closest Soul team, or another Soul Mate. They may have had a lesson to learn from loving you and losing you. Maybe they wanted the opportunity to overcome this tragedy in their life so they could make different choices than were made in previous incarnations. Perhaps through your death, something will be discovered and mandated that saves future babies from dying. Your death gives them a special project and gift to send into the world. The simplicity or complexity of Soul Contracts can vary greatly from Soul to Soul. Either way whether simple or complex, everyone involved agrees to the contractual lessons to be learned.

Most Soul contracts are not that simple. Imagine the complexity of a Soul Contract for someone who lives to be 100 years of age; imagine all the Souls they encounter and all the potential lessons that could be gained during that lifetime. Not that the lessons would have to be numerous – you could still have only one primary lesson, such as wanting to remember while on Earth that you are a Soul. Or you may contract to have something horrific happen to you, and the lesson is learning compassion or empathy or forgiveness.

You will decide on every facet of the play of your life and your Life's Purpose. Where in this world will it take place; where specifically will you live throughout your lifetime? Maybe you will live in a small town you never leave, or maybe you will join the military and traverse the world. You leave nothing to chance, as each location offers opportunities for other Souls to help you on the journey, or for you to help them.

You choose the precise moment you will be born, and thus the astrological sign you will be born under, as that influences your personality. That is, you pick how the planets will align so as to give you the characteristics that will best help you accomplish your lessons. You also pick what your body will look like: will you be strong or weak, tall or thin, attractive or homely, introverted or extroverted? Will you sing, or have some other special talent? The YOU that is created will be so unique that there has never been or ever will be another person exactly like you. You pick your parents, as they can set the stage for who you will become later in life. Will you have obstacles to overcome in childhood, such as a disease? Or will you be the target of bullying – or be the bully? All of these attributes and conditions contribute to your ability to learn specific lessons.

You turn to your Soul Group – your cast members – and you all choose roles to play with one another. Your play interlocks with their plays, and you all take on supporting character roles. Some may be in your play from beginning to end, such as a sibling. Others will only take a minor role, but their influence – no matter how brief – has the capability to impact the rest of your life. Once you have worked out and gotten agreement for the most influential roles, you may have other Souls with whom you have Soul connections ask you to play a role in their play. Some may be Souls you have never worked with before; others you have been with through many lifetimes. You may be asked to play a villain or perhaps a short-term lover or friend. Each role has some particular significance and the perfect timing for you to encounter one another when each is ready for the lesson to be learned. This is why I often say that even though it might not seem like it at the time, things are unfolding perfectly!

Lastly, you have to plan your exit. How much Earth time will you need to complete your lessons? Maybe, like the example of the baby, you have childhood lessons to learn, and your death serves to help your brother – and you become his guide after you die. You may not be sure that you will grasp the entirety of a lesson the first time you encounter it, so you may plan out a few opportunities over time to learn that lesson. You may even plan a few death scenes or exits for your Soul, which depend on whether you have achieved your lessons. This gives new meaning to the phrase "It was just their time." I have often heard about loved ones left behind lamenting to a medium over the "what if's" surrounding their loved one's death: *What if* I had been there that night when he got in the car and could have stopped him? *What if* I had been there to administer a procedure to save her? *What if* I had insisted he see a doctor about his condition? And the medium would say there was nothing you could have done – if they had not died at that moment, they would have died soon after. Those Souls had an exit point that had been reached and nothing could stop it from being *their time*.

We have not even added Free Will into the mix. We always have Free Will, which is what makes the play interesting. Much like a dress rehearsal, you may have a plan directing how things are going to unfold. But in the middle of the actual play someone exercises free will and pulls the fire alarm and yells "Fire!" and that adds unexpected variables. (I will address free will more fully in the next chapter.)

Your Spirit Guides and Team

Your Contract may be designed by you for you, and you have the final say, but just like you being the playwright, someone has to direct the play. You will solicit help of various kinds from others, and you will consult with the Souls who will serve as your Guides during your incarnation. You may have a primary Spirit Guide who has never been in a lifetime with you but has guided you through millennia. You also have Angels who will take roles to protect you and whisper guidance, helping you to keep on task. You also have Guides who help you through just one specific period or activity in your life. If, for example, you decide you will play an instrument professionally, you might be guided by a Soul who lived a life as a professional musician and played that instrument. The number of Guides you have is unknown to you. But make no mistake – you have lots of help during your life!

Reviewing your Contract

No one is just going to let you put on a play without adequate assistance. You need a producer who will help refine everything and help you make it perfect so it can become a real-life production. Once you have tweaked your Soul Contract, you must present it to a group of elders for their input. These are highly evolved Souls who have had countless experiences on Earth and no longer incarnate here; they may tell you your plan is too aggressive and ask you to reconsider pieces of it. I do believe that other than cases involving mental illness, there are Souls who commit suicide because they took on a Soul Contract that was too difficult; or they may have made so many Free Will choices in conflict with their Soul Contract that their life feels "off the rails" or out of control, causing them to want to exit early. You may disagree with the elders' advice and believe so fully in your ability to overcome obstacles that you decide to execute your Soul's plan AS IS. Other times, you may reconsider and make changes.

When all the agreements on roles have been considered and reviewed and all the contracts "signed," you are ready to test your Soul.

Synchronicity is one sure sign you are on your highest Soul path. When things are happening in the way you envisioned and planned in advance, and you are following your guidance, your life will be moving along smoothly. The right people will show up at the right time, and things will fall into place seamlessly. Anxiety and disarray, where nothing seems to be going right in your life, may be an indication you are off course. Try to reassess; and pay attention to the whispers of your Soul, as they will continue to guide you. Don't be afraid to ask for help! You have a lot of it available, but you do have to ask, as there are rules around Free Will requiring you to ask for help when you need it. You can get help by praying to God, your Angels, your Guides, or passed-away loved ones, who will offer comfort and guidance where they can.

Ending a Soul Contract

Souls come into your life for a moment, a season, or a lifetime. You may encounter a Soul you contracted with to have a car accident where you might suffer only minor injuries, but it causes you to awaken to the precious gift that *is* your life, and you decide to be more present and less reckless. The Soul Contract between the two of you is now complete; they helped you learn the lesson, and you are finished with them for this lifetime.

As another example, you might get married to one of your Soul Mates and have two children, raise them through high school, and ultimately divorce when the kids go off to college. Your contract may simply have been to have and raise your children together, and now that it is complete you both will move on to find new love and new lessons. You may or may not remain in each other's lives, but your contract together is finished. Either way, you will still encounter each other because you both have open contracts with your children that last the rest of your lifetimes.

Contracts may also end early because one of the Souls "decides," maybe subconsciously, through Free Will not to honor the contract any longer. For example, your Twin Flame has a contract with you to build an amazing business together, but they make choices that prematurely end the contract. Or, you might have a contract with your sibling to support each other, but one of you gets into drugs and you part ways, ending the contract. It is possible to revive a contract, but you may have to go back to the Other Side in a dream state to make changes through your Higher Self. Then again, a large part of your Soul may still be on the Other Side, orchestrating changes as you move through your life. There are so many unknowns about the intricacies of a Contract and of our Soul.

Death and Life Review

So you wrote your Soul Contract and executed it to the best of your ability, and now your life is finished. You will exit your body and your Soul will return home – back to the Other Side. You will "choose" what your heaven will be like. If you expected to see St. Peter at the pearly gates, holding a list with your name on it, that is what you will experience. If you expected to be reunited with your loved ones on the Other Side, that is what will happen. If you had a particularly traumatic life, you may be whisked into a hospital type of setting to acclimate and heal; in that setting there are advanced Souls available who specialize in helping Souls heal. If you believed you would die and become nothing, then you will experience a dark nothingness. But in time, you will realize that all of these endings were based on perceptions from the life you just exited; you will remember that you are the eternal, powerful Soul you have always been, and you will see things as they truly are. You will retain your personality, and you will show your Soul self to others in the way they remember you. You may show your older self to your grandchildren; a version of yourself in your 30's to your life partner; and your seven-year-old self to a childhood friend. We can project whatever we want to show.

You will continue to watch, know about, and/or guide all the Souls you cared about, who will live out their lifetime on Earth. You will still care about them, deeply love them, and know what happens in their life. If you will miss attending an upcoming wedding in person, you will attend it in Spirit. You don't become all-knowing when you leave the Earth, but you do gain a perspective you didn't have while you were here – you will see things for how they *truly* are, not how you perceived them on Earth. You can send your loved ones signs so they are able to feel your presence in their lives. But when you leave them, you will not miss them the way they miss you. Souls on the Other Side feel like they saw you just yesterday and that they will see you tomorrow even though a loved one may live 60 more years after your death. Time is very different on the Other Side, because in this earthly realm, time is an illusion. Love, first and foremost, knows no limits of time.

You may leave Earth and experience your Life Review immediately. I have even heard of people having a Life Review during a Near Death Experience (NDE), then returning to Earth and making significant changes based on their new knowledge. You may experience your Life Review alone, with a Spirit Guide, with a wise, ancient Soul, or even with God directly. You are shown every single moment from your life, and you see every one of them from both your perspective and the perspective of others. You experience your own emotions and *their* emotions. You can also see the ripple effect each and every act had on you, on others, and on the world. I know of one person who was shown an act of throwing their garbage out of an open car window and the ripple effect that act had on the Earth itself. That was just one simple act by one person, but with many people doing the same, the effect was to fill the ocean with garbage and this affected all earthly inhabitants. To me, *this* is Karma. It is not actually a punishment – it is giving the person an awareness of cause and effect as a result of one's actions. I'm reminded of a popular bumper sticker that says *Do No Harm*, and I think this is a goal of our Soul.

We review our Life Plan and we evaluate how well we embraced our lessons – the lessons we *chose* to learn. We look closely at the ways we loved ourselves and loved others, how kind we were and how often we helped others. We see everything we did while others were looking, and what we did when they weren't. The Souls who review this with us don't judge us, as ultimately *WE* are the judge of ourselves. There will be Souls who are horrified when they see what their actions caused, and others who will be surprised to see how the actions they sent into the world had a positive effect. Even the smallest act of kindness or unkindness can have huge repercussions.

We decide when *and if* we will go back to Earth again, and we think about lessons we might want to try to master in another lifetime, where we make different choices. Or we may have mastered everything we had set out to learn and decide to have our next lesson elsewhere, in another realm. Maybe we will take a long break and return to Earth in the next century, or maybe we will go back sooner to become the Soul of our grandchild.

There are an infinite number of classrooms and we have eternity to learn, grow and evolve. It's all a choice – our choice. Not all Souls chose to live a life on Earth. I read the account of a woman who had an NDE during which she found herself in a large auditorium setting where many Souls had gathered to hear about her journey. She said she had been revered by those Souls, as none of them had ever chosen to go to Earth to learn their lessons. Coming to this Earth is a difficult decision for most Souls, because we feel separated from the whole while we are on Earth; we feel separated from God and from feeling the all-encompassing LOVE that we are. Many Souls will make choices to learn in less difficult settings than Earth. Perhaps the Souls who incarnate on Earth are the daredevils of the Spirit World.

I don't think I can adequately cover the complexity of all that happens in carrying out a Soul Contract, as I don't think our human mind can comprehend that level complexity. I'm using my years of study combined with knowledge gained from my personal trips to the Other Side, to explain with my limited human mind the way I understand things to be.

Free Will
Your Free Will has taken the helm… (it is ALL a choice) 🙂

Free Will is a complex Spiritual topic. For me, when I hear the words "Free Will" it evokes a knee-jerk reaction of feeling "*Why would you do that?!*" In the previous section, we discussed Soul Contracts – the agreements Souls enter into before they come together in a life on Earth. Without the gift of Free Will, our whole life would just be a scripted play. With the addition of Free Will, our lives become more of an improv than a play.

Meant to Be

Is everything *meant to be*? The answer is yes – and no. I believe that for the most part, the events planned out in our Contracts are divinely orchestrated and destined to happen – otherwise, you might lose out on your purpose for being here in the first place. So yes, I do believe there are events in your life that are absolutely meant to be. If, for example, you are meant to have children with one of your Soul Mates, the meeting of that Soul Mate would itself be predestined – and it would feel very much that way to you. I believe that meeting my ex-husband, Mark, and Wylie – each one of them – was very much destined, and each meeting had that feeling.

But I also think there are chapters of one's life that, although they were predestined since before we were born, can still change drastically as our life progresses. Such changes can happen when our life is derailed or, to the contrary, accelerated due to Free Will choices made by ourselves or people we are connected to. Thomas spoke specifically about this in reference to choices I had made in response to life events, which accelerated my Spiritual growth. I believe that whenever my life changed, I would likely have gone to my group of elders for counsel, and increased or decreased my workload or changed my trajectory. I don't think it is hard for our Higher Self to have interactions with the Other Side in our dream state. We spend a great portion of our life sleeping and dreaming, and in that state it would be very simple for our Soul, throughout our lifetime, to cross the veil in order to conduct business on the Other Side.

~~Once~~ A Cheater...

No Accidents

Do I believe there are no accidents? Yes, mostly. Yet when mediums connect with Souls on the Other Side, those Souls will often apologize to people still on Earth for their actions that changed someone's course in life. But I do believe the course of someone's life can only change if there is still a way the Souls involved would have the opportunity to learn the intended lessons. I believe either God, the Angels, or our Guides will intervene in our lives if an action against us would spoil the entirety of the Contract plan. Otherwise, what would be the point of coming to Earth to accomplish the plan and learn lessons? So I don't believe in accidents – and I do believe in a higher purpose behind things that happen, even if we can't understand it at the time.

No Lesson is Ever Lost

No lesson is ever lost, because every situation offers our Soul an opportunity to learn, grow, evolve or help another grow. There are lessons our Soul never tires of learning – like love, since there are so many facets to love. Even when someone exercises Free Will and ends a Contract with us, we have an opportunity to further our own growth and development by the way we respond. For example, when you experience the death of a loved one, you can choose to stop living your life, curl up in a ball, and retreat from the world. But you also have the choice to turn that death into something positive, such as a scholarship fund in memory of your passed-away loved one, thereby giving your life a new purpose and helping preserve the memory of the one you loved.

My Lesson in Free Will

I don't believe my Contract with Wylie was completed, in that I was told by various psychic mediums that we had special work to do together – and I myself could intuitively feel that. Neither can I disregard the "hold the line" signs I received more than 30 times from Mark, and they have continued while writing this book.

I was also asked by Spirit to be patient where Wylie was concerned – to "hold the line" for him. But being patient with someone does not mean letting them treat you in a way that doesn't honor your relationship. Wylie made significant Free Will choices when he downloaded the Bumble app and began having conversations with other women – especially when he crossed the line from it being an online game, to him actually meeting someone in person. These were *all* choices he knew had the potential to damage our relationship. He did it anyway – he exercised his Free Will. I too exercised my Free Will choice and pulled out of the relationship. Was Wylie's choice a symptom of him needing to take a break? Perhaps it was, and maybe it was his way of sabotaging our relationship so that I would be the one to pull out, since a part of him did not feel worthy of my love. Wylie was fully aware that he was sabotaging our relationship, as his past experiences had taught him over time what his actions had the potential to do.

I could make a lot of excuses for Wylie; his childhood experiences of love had not prepared him to accept mine. I think my leaving our relationship after Bumble-Gate was the turning point for us. After I left, Wylie expressed how surprised he was with my action – he had believed our love could withstand any blow. Based on what I know about his experiences of conditional love during his childhood, I think a part of him no longer believed in or trusted my love after I left. Of course, you can reason how that doesn't make sense, as I had left in direct response to *his* actions. But that kind of reasoning is no match for childhood damage. I think when I pulled away, my action put an irreparable crack in the foundation of our relationship. And the final blow was when I ended things on the phone with him after he returned from his Island Peak hike. My leaving again, in response to the final straw of him not contacting me for five days, robbed him of the assurance he needed that he could trust in my love. Just like he had experienced with his mom, all along I had sent him the strongest feelings of love he had ever known, and then unexpectedly took it away from him. I really believe he gave up on us after that action, and eventually fell into his old habits of infidelity. Of course, he probably justified it by telling himself we were not "fully" back together, yet at the same time he *was* trying to hold on to our relationship. But it was by manipulating me with his words and his lies. Ultimately, through his Free Will actions, he lowered his own vibration and we were no longer resonated with each other.

Another part of the situation for Wylie was that he was also feeling overwhelmed by his recent experience climbing the mountain, and said he was feeling depressed. But to me, it comes down to values and standards we hold ourselves to, and whether or not we can and will do the work it takes to be in a *real* relationship, one that is committed. The ultimate answer is he was not willing to do the work, and as much as I loved him, I could not compromise my values and accept less for myself than I deserved. These situations are very complex, and many factors played into Wylie's and my final Free Will decisions.

People Tell You Who They Are Up Front

You can ask me to leave now; I wouldn't blame you 😊

When I was 15 years old I began dating PJ, a boy one grade ahead of me. He had dated a friend of mine who introduced us. He told me multiple times, "You're too good for me." My 15-year-old self would laugh and tell him that wasn't true. Within a month, he proved me wrong. We were supposed to go out one Saturday night, but he cancelled. He said his dad had grounded him because of his grades – which was believable (lol – he wasn't the best student). On Monday, at school, I heard from several people that he was at a party that same Saturday night, kissing a girl a grade younger than me. I promptly broke up with him.

His ex-girlfriend, my friend, heard about his shenanigans from me, and she read him the riot act. He then got really angry at me. (I think he still really liked my friend. Time would tell – they would much later date again.) The next weekend my house got egged, and he was the only one I suspected would have done such a thing. At 11 o'clock that night, I had to work quickly with my family to hose off the house before the egg dried and ruined the paint. My dad advised me not to tell anyone it happened. He explained that boys like PJ would want the story to get back to them. If it didn't, they would start telling everyone about it themselves, and it would get back to them that way. My dad is a pretty smart guy, and he was right – by the end of the week, I heard the rumor. Several people asked me if PJ was the one who had egged my house. The moral of the story is, PJ knew who he was and told me up front, but I had not listened.

In over 30 years, I had not thought about this boy. As I was writing the above story, I became curious about him and decided to look him up on Facebook; I found him. He had only two pictures of himself posted – one of him in his 20s, and a more recent photo. In the recent photo I noticed in the background words written on a wall behind him that he was standing in front of. The largest and the only fully legible word said "Jerks" – my hand to God, I cannot make this stuff up. It was as if Spirit was sending me a confirmation because some things never change.

People telling you up front who they are is not necessarily a bad thing. I remember working with a woman at my first job out of college, who was talking in a matter-of-fact way about all the friends she had and her busy social schedule.

The year I knew her she was a bridesmaid in six weddings! She was and still is an amazing friend to many.

Wylie told me on our second date who he was – he was a man who had cheated in almost every relationship he had been in. He also expressed that this was not who he *wanted* to be, going forward, and I believed what I wanted to believe. I often see the potential in someone, and I want to believe the best in people. But the truth of the matter was that Wylie, in his entire adult life, even in his marriage, had been free to do *whatever* he wanted. He cheated on his wife less than two years into the marriage, and later turned their relationship into an open marriage so he could continue doing whatever he wanted. He cheated on "28" with me ("28" was the name I privately gave to her, as she was only 28 years old – more than 20 years younger than Wylie). I had never really thought of their dating as cheating on his wife, since he had begun the relationship during his open marriage, and "28" knew that was the arrangement. But she didn't know about me, so in a way, he also cheated on me with "28," as he had given me the impression I was the only one he was seeing.

I was the first person Wylie had ever been with who held him to any kind of standard and asked him to answer to the relationship. He had been in a couple of long-term relationships during his open marriage, but those women could not hold him to any standard as they were at the mercy of his situation. I'm sure each one ended in heartbreak, with the women thinking he would choose her over his wife. I wanted so badly to believe in the strength and love of Wylie and that our unique connection would be enough for him to want to be faithful to me. I believed we could move forward together as a couple in a real relationship – just the two of us. But it was not sustainable for him. He was – as he told me up front in so many words – a serial cheater – and he failed miserably in changing that behavior. Bumble-Gate violated our relationship in that he put himself in a situation in which he would be open to someone else.

I am not saying people cannot change – because they can! People grow and evolve, and when circumstances are different they can and do make new choices, breaking a cycle that didn't serve them. But in my case, I entered into the relationship with Wylie with eyes wide open – I knew there was a chance he would fall off the monogamy wagon. What I failed to pay attention to were the lines he continually repeated about not cheating on me. If someone has to tell you over and over again what they *plan* to do, they are probably trying to convince themselves and not you. Another mistake I made was I trusted Wylie would tell me the truth. He had been so raw and honest about his past that it gave me the sense he would continue to be completely honest in our relationship. I don't think he ever volunteered the truth again after that first conversation; he would only be truthful if asked a *very exact question* with no wiggle room to manipulate the answer. Maybe in his mind he wasn't lying if he merely withheld information; or could get away with answering exactly what I asked, without having to disclose additional information that could expose his manipulations and intentions.

My situation may have gone a little deeper than a case of not believing someone who tells you who they are up front. Towards the end of the relationship, Wylie was blatantly lying. I'm not a doubting, skeptical person designed to be a human lie-detector. And he knew me well enough and was smart enough to know exactly what he could tell me to be convincing. Sometimes there is nothing you can do when someone deliberately sets out to deceive you the way Wylie did in our last few months together; especially on our last date, 11 days before our break up, when he said, "I promise I won't string you along" – when that was precisely what he was doing. He was already most definitely seeing someone 11 days before the "This doesn't work for me!" confrontation. Perhaps he had even set out to deceive me and was lying when he declared two months earlier, "My energy isn't open to anyone – I don't want you to worry about that." There are things I will never know...

I recommend standing in your truth. Don't go along with the crowd if you don't agree. Don't make up stories or cover things over because of your perception of what your truth will do to someone else. That is their journey, not yours. I believe if Wylie had been able to stand in his truth with his kids, his life during the transition out of his marriage would have gone smoother; his withholds and cover-ups hurt them as much as they hurt him. If you can't be your true self with your closest Soul Mates, then who can you be true to? Overall, Wylie didn't give many people in his life the credit they deserved. Perhaps to him it was self-preservation as he was afraid of losing their love. But love starts with self-love, and if you don't have love for yourself, it's difficult to receive it from another.

~~Once~~ A Cheater...

Learning to Trust Your Intuition

You know (you've always known) the trick is leaning to trust what you know 💋

We are born with intuition. But what is intuition? It is the inner knowledge and immediate perception we have of truth, facts or insights. We use intuition more than anything else to navigate the world around us. You might call it an inner knowingness, something that you understand to be true without using your logical brain. We can be deceived by words or actions, but intuition cannot deceive us since it is an inner knowledge that can't be distorted by worldly factors. As we get older, we begin to discount or ignore our intuition because our logical brain weighs in more often and clouds our judgement. We second-guess the accuracy of our intuition. I have more examples than I can count of times I've discounted my intuition and let my logical brain take over, only to later discover my intuition had been precisely correct.

I can vividly remember several conversations I had with friends three months into my relationship with Wylie. I had become very confused, as I felt him pulling back from me. He was often inconsistent with his communication and would not make an effort to see me as frequently as he had in earlier months. I would make excuses to myself about him needing to juggle the obligations he still had to his family, but my intuition told me it was something else. I talked to my friends many times about leaving the relationship, or pulling back from it. I felt that might give Wylie some space to deal with whatever he was going through, and also let him better assess the relationship he was building with me. I was encouraged by my friends to "wait it out," because to them it merely seemed to be a temporary condition related to his divorce not being final. Later, I learned that he was having issues at that time in his relationship with "28," the young woman he was dating when we met. The last straw was that he told her he was dating me, and that revelation seemed to end their relationship. In the end, she "ghosted" and he had been very bothered about it. Looking back at text messages during that time frame, I was reminded that he had expressed feelings of melancholy. This was definitely a time I disregarded what my intuition was urging me to do. I probably should have listened and pulled my energy back.

Over the course of the relationship, there were countless examples of me discounting my intuition, especially towards the end. Even when you are aware that your intuition is consistently dependable, when someone deliberately sets out to deceive you, it is difficult to combat. One way we can get better at listening to our intuition is with practice. As well, sometimes we need to get better at recognizing the red flags that back up our intuition. I'm going to share some red flags in the subsection below.

The Red Flag of Being Hidden

There can be legitimate reasons to keep a relationship hidden. For example, when my kids were younger I would not expose them to someone I was dating until I had been with that person for a relatively long time. Wylie's and my relationship was unique, and to a certain extent I could understand it being hidden. He was just beginning to tell the people in his life about his divorce, and he didn't want them to think I was the cause of it, because I was not. I wanted to be respectful of Wylie's situation and his divorce, but being hidden in a relationship is not a healthy thing and should have a time limit. Without a lawyer, the divorce took a very long time, and after it was finalized, he continued to keep me hidden from friends and acquaintances. This was super unhealthy for me, and I should not have allowed it to go on for as long as it did.

Wylie was an excellent communicator and would have very detailed responses that made logical sense, but they were intended to keep me from discussing the issues. He may have even kept me hidden in order to keep his options with other women open. After all, if no one knew about me, he was free to engage in deceitful behavior undetected. I found it telling that, after we got back together, he had not told his roommate we were seeing each other again. I believe he was hiding that from her because it would make him look bad to bring the new woman around while he was still seeing me. If I had listened to my intuition when he wanted to meet me out at a restaurant instead of his house, I would have realized this was not normal behavior. Pay attention when someone will only see you on their terms – when and where, etc. – as there may be something they are trying to hide.

The Red Flag of Excuses, Excuses, Excuses

Hindsight being 20/20, I decided to examine the excuses Wylie had been using to throw me off his scent so he could continue the relationship with me. He knew I was on the verge of leaving, and he wanted to keep seeing me, so he created excuses that were designed to keep me from doing so.

Wylie is an empath. An empath is someone who can feel the emotions of other people. When such a person is not aware that they are an empath, they will often unknowingly take on others' emotions as their own. In the beginning of our relationship, Wylie talked about having bouts of what he called melancholy; and toward the end, he told me he had been suffering from depression. I have seen firsthand what depression looks like – my sister has suffered from moderate to severe depression for her entire life. But I just didn't see it with Wylie. I spent almost three years in a relationship with this man, and for the most part, his temperament was even keeled. On top of it all, it seemed very odd that his self-diagnosis came on suddenly, toward the end of our time together – just when I had begun voicing my concern about the lack of time we were spending together. Wylie is a very smart man, and I think he used depression as an excuse that would make logical sense to me so I would let him off the hook. As a result, he wouldn't have to be responsible for his behavior. I had the feeling that someone else in his life was taking all his time and attention.

He knew he was acting uncharacteristically, and that a person's personality doesn't change drastically overnight unless there is something wrong. If Wylie had really felt something was psychologically wrong with him, he would have sought help from his psychologist as he had done in the past. On my part, I was ignoring what my intuition was telling me – nothing about this depression made sense. He used it to buy time and as an excuse for not seeing me, claiming that he didn't feel like himself and needed to "sort things out." I thought it was because he was trying to avoid sleeping with me, as he knew how strongly I felt about only having sex in a monogamous relationship. Maybe he was trying hard to honor that requirement; he had begun a relationship with someone new and may have wanted to buy time to see if he was more interested in her before letting our relationship go. Ultimately, when someone wants to be with you, they will make excuses to see you – not why they *can't* see you. I made as many excuses to explain why it was happening as he had made in doing it. In a healthy relationship, you don't need to constantly make excuses for someone. This should have been a bigger red flag for me than it was.

Red Flags with Social Media

We live in a social-media society, and this aspect of life is not going away. Pay attention to how someone interacts with you with regard to social media. I should have known when Wylie hid all posts of us pictured together that there were bigger issues. I also realized in hindsight that Wylie *not* hiding Jane probably meant there was nothing between them. I'm still not totally ruling out the possibility of some sick, twisted relationship between them…kidding! But ultimately, I don't know if there was or was not something between them. If I listen to my intuition, it says Jane had feelings for Wylie. My intuition also tells me he was using her for what she could do for him financially, and I don't believe he would chance messing that up by getting involved with her romantically. If he had an age issue with me being 50, then he surely had an age issue with her being 57 (even though neither of us looked our age).

Red Flags of Unreasonable Boundaries

Boundaries are necessary in every relationship and can be defined on an individual basis. Wylie's boundaries with me felt unusual, and he announced his expectations in such a way that it just threw me off, when it should have sent up red flags. Wylie said he had had issues with boundaries in his past relationships. I should have questioned what those boundaries had been and why he felt that way, in which case I may have been tipped off much earlier. He also said this was something his therapist wanted him to specifically work on. He had so sternly warned me to never stop by unannounced that, after the first time, I didn't do it again until the last day of our relationship. Other than that, I had always been very careful to call or text in advance to ask for permission. This was reasonable early in our relationship, but shouldn't have been an issue after almost three years. Pay attention when someone insists on being alerted in advance every time they see you. If you are not allowed any element of surprise or spontaneity, it may be because they have something to hide. In a loving, committed relationship, there should be nothing wrong with you dropping off cookies unannounced, or stopping by because you were in the neighborhood. If Wylie had stopped by my house at any time to surprise me, I would have been so happy to see him. I would have welcomed him with open arms – and lips!

Friends

I want to address the topic regarding the many friends and family members I confided in during my relationship with Wylie. Several of my friends got to know him *very* well, including Stacy and Sal along with Dawn and Dale. Wylie had so many beautiful, redeeming qualities, and he was genuinely liked by them. Stacy, especially, saw the difficult struggle he had had in our relationship because he felt he had not properly ended his marriage. Much of the advice I got from her and others was based on time they had spent with him and with us as a couple. There was a reason many of my friends held out hope for us and our relationship...

Forgiveness

~Forgiveness is about YOU, not about them 🕊

Forgiveness is so often misunderstood. Forgiveness is not about the other person. Forgiveness is about releasing all the lower level emotions surrounding an event, so YOU can move back into your heart space. Forgiveness is an acknowledgement that even though you don't know why things happened, you can't let the actions another Soul made against you, or against someone you love, take away your ability to **live your life in love**. Forgiveness is about LOVE. It is about loving yourself enough to admit that you don't have all the answers. Forgiveness is about admitting you don't know why or how something happened. Forgiveness is not about forgetting; it's about letting go!

Many years ago, I remember watching a TV program that profiled a murderer. The story took the viewer back to the beginning of the murder's life, and retraced the many terrible events that had happened to him. The reporter gained sympathy in seeing events that shaped the murder's life. The reporter acknowledged the rotten hand the murder had been dealt, and could now, in some small way, understand how the murder had reacted to events based on his past experiences that brought him to that lowly fate. The reality is that if we walked in a person's shoes for the entirety of their journey – experiencing from their perspective every event that made them who they are – we would better understand why people make the choices they do. Perhaps they had terrible role models and examples to follow. Perhaps the lack of love they experienced as a child, numbed them as an adult. Maybe their family had a history of mental illness or they made horrible Free Will choices. If you could see every moment from their life, you would gain a perspective that induced understanding. I'm not making excuses for murder, because if you had walked that life instead, you might reason, that *you* would have made different choices. Perhaps you would, perhaps not. This level of understanding would make it easier for you to forgive. Most times we are not privy to that level of knowledge, and we are only left with a disbelief in the choice another person has made. The more you know or understand, the easier it is to forgive.

I am a big proponent of non-judgement, as much as I can be. Mostly I am aware that, from a Soul perspective, there are lessons we are here to learn – on both sides of a relationship. What were my lessons with Wylie? I suspect because we are Twin Flames that we had a bigger job to do together; so in my opinion he made Free Will choices that ended our contract. But, what if as my Twin Flame, he agreed to a contract to play a role with me where he would violate my trust and end our relationship in a despicable way – in order to give my Soul a choice to react to his actions. What if THIS book is the product of our Soul Contract, and is the "bigger thing" we were meant to send into the world? What I've written here about Spirit and spiritual lessons will help many people, and have a new ripple effect on the World. What if you enter into a new relationship, and because of reading this story and the lessons I've learned, it helps you see red flags it your relationship. And ultimately that helps your Soul make different choice, and through those choices you raise the vibration of your Soul. The ripple effect from these lessons is unknown and unknowable.

After reading this book you may wonder if I believe that Wylie is a good or a bad person. I think he is mostly good, despite what he did to me at the end of our relationship. He is one of the most interesting people I have ever encountered, but he clearly has relationship issues. I can't underestimate the effect his extremely dysfunctional childhood had on his adult relationships. According to Wylie, his mom had an undiagnosed personality disorder. She was married six times, which caused instability in his childhood. She was an exotic animal owner (it takes a very unusual person to do this) and with the recent *Tiger King* show, need I say more? Her cougar graced the cover of John Cougar's first album. Wylie discovered, in his 30s, that his Godfather was his *real* father and that he was conceived when both his father and mom were in other marriages. Wylie never witnessed an example of what a health, monogamous, relationship looked like. Maybe by reading this book now, and seeing things from my perspective – it will feel a bit like a life review to him. Perhaps, with this new perspective, he can make better future choices and change his own ripple effect. And *that* could be the life lesson he was meant to learn from me. If Wylie was not able to accept love from me on the scale, intensity, and honesty I was offering it, maybe he can now see it from a new perspective. If nothing else, I hope he could understand that he *is* deserving of loving himself.

As for his mother, according to Wylie, you were either on her good list or what he called her "shit list," never knowing what one you might do to land yourself on the other list. That means the love coming from his mother was *very* conditional, and he could not count on it. I think the demise of our relationship began when *I* pulled out of the relationship first over Bumble-Gate. Not because of his violation or because he had any real interest in another woman, but because *I left the relationship*. Even though I made decisions based on *his* actions, I think Wylie felt he could no longer believe in my love (as I typed that the music playing in the background said, *"I pray you learn to trust, have faith in both of us,"* and I think that Spirit is weighing in on what happened). Then, when I pulled away a second time after he came back from Island Peak because he didn't communicate with me for five days, he decided he could not count on my love. My love *was* somewhat conditional because, but my pulling away was based on his actions, not on my feelings for him. I am not saying I am right, or that he was right. I just knew I could no longer except from him less than I deserved, and he felt he could no longer count on my love. It didn't matter that the actions were facilitated by *his* choices and actions because...

Perception = Reality! What's true for you is true for you.

Just remember, perception does not make something true. So FORGIVE where you can; it will lighten your burden and allow you to open your heart to love again. Failure to forgive is just a block you are holding on to. Forgive so you can accept or let LOVE in – that is your birthright!

~~Once~~ A Cheater...

Your Super Power

What you tell yourself becomes your reality, good or bad 🦋

Everyone is born with a Super Power, but most people either do not realize they have it, or understand how to harness it to help improve their life. Your Super Power is your ability to control your thoughts, because what you tell yourself becomes your reality – good or bad. The reason this is your Super Power is because you have POWER over what you tell yourself and over what you believe about what you tell yourself. If you tell yourself you can do something then you will direct your energy towards accomplishing that task and conversely if your tell yourself you can't do something you will manifest that instead. Thoughts are very powerful; do not underestimate the impact they have on your life.

I have created several videos to address your thoughts as your Super Power, and I want to share this particular one with you here:

https://www.youtube.com/watch?v=4Ic_kBcGym8&t=139s

After Wylie revealed the relationship he had with "28" while we were beginning our relationship together, it activated my thoughts in a way that did not serve me. In order to work through them I needed to protect myself from what I was telling myself about their relationship and about another woman in general. I was very bothered that although he had ended the relationship many months ago, he was still upset that she would not communicate with him after their relationship was over. I didn't see any reason he needed to be in contact with her, and his reaction took something away from me somehow – making me feel like I, and our relationship, was not enough for him. To combat those thoughts I needed to block them and replace them with something else. I created the following note in my phone, and when I would feel my thoughts slip I would read this list to remind myself of the value I brought to *any* relationship...

"28's" Got Nothing On Me

Age = experience = confidence

Because I've had children:
*I can put someone else's needs before my own.

*When you love a child you know the real depth of love, an experience that someone who is young, and without children, might not fully understand.
*In a relationship, I know that my partner's children will always come first for them, and I wouldn't want or expect anything less. ("28" couldn't grasp this)
*I know how to relate to what you are going thru with your kids, so I can better relate to you, and we can be a sounding board for each other.
*I'll never make you choose between your kids and me. ("28" tried to leverage that)
*I understand how much time, effort and money go into having kids.
*I'll never resent you for not having kids with me.

*I have a spiritual depth that most people don't begin to experience until after the age of 35. (there have been studies about this)
*There will be a depth with me because of my extensive experiences.
*I've been through many phases that began by: focusing on me, then on my house, then on my kids, and then back to me. This makes me grateful for all I have. "28" can only relate to phase one, herself.
*I've had deep, long lasting friendships that extended beyond 28 years.

*Long lasting relationships taught me skills like compromise, communication, loyalty, and time investment that make me appreciate and value them.
*I created Soul Heart Art which allows me to create something meaningful to send into the world – to do something big to help make the world a better place.
*I've been able to build a 30 year career, teaching me how to: collaborate, get along with people, be tolerant, and negotiate.
*I have an understanding of who I am that didn't happen until my 40's.
*I've been working on a spiritual understanding for the last ten years that help me be less judgmental and to better navigate the world.
*My extensive life experiences make me better able to relate to yours.
*We (Wylie and I) are the same age – we have the same references to events, songs, how we grew up, and childhood experiences, this level sets us. When we make reference we both understand them and where we are coming from.
*Because we grew up in the same generation, we have the same expectation of how life should be – we see it from the same reference point. The younger generations have become more self-centered and expect life to be centered around them. They expect to be taken care of in a certain way which seems to be more materialistic.
*I know what I don't like and don't want – you only discover that when you've had enough life experiences. I didn't know that until probably 35 or 40 years of age.
*I have a heightened perspective about what life is and how precious it is because by this age I've also experienced many profound losses.
*I've been through a divorce, so I can relate to yours.
*I will have no issues or problems when you want to have a "family" experience around the holidays etc., because I'll need those too with mine.
*When your kids get ready to get married and have kids, I'll be ready for those stages of life because I'll be right there with you too.
*I have a better appreciation of money. I've earned it and am independent. I don't need someone to fund me.

*I'm stable. I own a house and have an established life. I'm steady, consistent and safe.
*I've experienced deep loss, it changes how I see life. It has made me a better, more empathetic person.
*Our relationship is between two equals.
*I'm mentally tough. Some of that is just who I am, some of it is from my lifetime of experiences.
*I have a confidence that can only be earned through experiences over time.
*I have a maturity and that only comes with time. I'll approach our relationship with that same maturity. I'm not interested in proving myself or being right; I'm only interested in making things work.
*I have way more sexual experience, which lets me be more uninhibited and lets you be the same.
*She may have no gray hairs, fewer wrinkles, and perhaps a tighter body…and she may even be prettier by popular standards, but truly she has nothing on me!

Real Love

*When someone **really** loves you, you will never question that love,*

they will prove it in every way, with their actions 🫶

If I could erase one line from a movie, it would be the line from *Jerry McGuire:* "You complete me." Because, in fact, there is NO Soul on the planet destined to complete you, because YOU COMPLETE Y-O-U!

Real love is not about completion – it is about acceptance. It is about seeing someone for who they are, and loving them anyway. We are all riddled with faults, but that's because we are seeing ourselves with our human eyes. In our Soul state, we love and accept ourselves exactly as we are. It doesn't mean we don't have areas of growth yet to experience, it means simply that – we are love. Love starts and ends with loving ourselves.

Most of the love we experience on this planet comes with conditions, and that's ok. Unconditional love is a high aspiration. We may have been on the receiving end of unconditional love from our pets; they are the best example of this type of love. It should be what we aspire to give.

Romantic relationships are about experiencing love with another Soul. Ultimately it does not matter what the Soul relationship is: a Soul Mate, a Soul Connection, or a Twin Flame. But there is one specific aspect of love you should pay attention to: when someone loves you, you won't have to question the love, you will feel it from them in every interactions with you. You will not wonder, you will *know*, without a doubt, when someone loves you. You will also not need to hear affirmations, because the actions and the energy will align with the feelings. The person who loves you will make time for you. They will make excuses to see you, not excuses to NOT to see you. They will make you a top priority. They will make plans to see you, because they can't wait to see you again. They won't look for excuses or reasons why seeing you won't work. They will make you a priority on their calendar and they won't cancel plans after they've made them. They won't want to keep you off balance, or keep you wondering about their feelings because they will not take the chance to lose you because you didn't know how they felt.

I want to liken this example to a story of buying a one of a kind big ticket item, like a house. You might need to see that house a few times before you ultimately decide it's the one you want to live in and spend time in. Once you have made the decision that you want to buy it, your attitude changes. You are no longer looking for deal breakers that will keep you from going through with your purchase, instead you become worried that someone else might buy the house before you can. You realized THIS is the house for you, and now you'll do everything to assure you will close on this/the house. You'll now overlook some flaws that might have chased you away before you made your final decision. You will instead find a solution to make them work. Then you'll begin doing things to help assure that you can close the deal. In other words, you will do the work to assure you get what you want. I might be slightly simplifying love with my house purchase example, but that's it in a nutshell. When you know it's love, when you understand how rare, special and precious the gift of love is, you will grasp it with both hands and not let go. You won't keep looking for it everywhere else you go, you'll know what you have and proudly display the SOLD sign in your yard. And if love doesn't feel like that – run, it wasn't the one for you. You have probably heard countless couples declare: *You'll just know*. Because it's true.

Not everyone is ready for love, and you can't force anyone to love you. Love is not about manipulation. Love is about kindness and generosity and freedom. Love is not a trap or based on revenge or ownership. Love is built on a strong foundation of trust and communication and understanding.

No two love stories are the same. People give and show love in many ways. But when someone loves you, you won't lose any sleep wondering if they love you, the only sleep you may lose is worrying that the love could be taken away too soon, in tragedy. But I will gladly endure the heart break of a love that is lost, rather than a lifetime without feeling the intensity of love. Love is always worth the effort; you are worth the effort.

Pick Them, Don't Pick Them

Only you know what is right for you🖂

The decision to stay in a relationship or to leave it is so personal that the ONLY one who can make it is you. Baring physical or mental abuse – which should ALWAYS be a reason to leave – the choice to stay is yours and only yours. People will want to give you their opinions but unless someone has walked in your shoes throughout your entire journey, they only have a perception to base their opinion on. The only way you can assess what feels right is to consult your heart, look for signs and listen to your Soul Whispers. You will know if there is something that keeps drawing you back to finish a lesson, and you will know when you have had enough and it is time to walk away. These are *your* spiritual lessons to learn and the people in your life may want to protect you and help you avoid pain or pitfalls because they love you, but sometimes you need to finish a lesson in your own perfect timing. People who love you for the right reasons – for who you are, not for what you do – will respect and honor your decision even if they don't agree with it. And if they don't maybe you need to reevaluate your support team.

People are broken and will sometimes do things to hurt you. It does not mean they are all bad. Many times the way someone treats you says more about them than it does about you. There are times you will give someone the benefit of the doubt then let them have a second chance, or a third or a fourth – even if people in your life don't feel they deserve it – as you may need to feel like you have given a relationship every opportunity for it to work before you can move on and leave it behind. Only you live with the choices you make.

It is ok to let someone go. Sometimes things just don't work out no matter how much potential you can see in them. It does not mean you failed! On a Soul level no lesson is ever wasted and usually with hind sight you will understand later why things played out the way they did. And there may be times you make decisions and you are left with regrets because sometimes we just make decisions that don't serve us. Don't be too hard on yourself, you will have a chance to learn the lesson again.

It is ok to pick them. Sometimes we share the worst of our relationship with the people in our lives blinding them to understand why you would choose to stay with someone. Only you live with your choices and sometimes you will feel compelled to try again. I was married for 18 years when I began to divorce my husband. We were separated for two years and ultimately decided to reconcile. It was a decision many friends in my life did not understand, but I had to try one more time. We stayed together for six more years and ultimately divorced, but I still believe it was the right decision for me. Many of my friends took an "I told you so" attitude, knowing it would not work out, and maybe I knew that too but I believe my husband and I had a Soul Contract to raise our kids through high school and that was what we did. When it was time for me to leave the marriage, everything aligned and fell into place and just felt right, that was because we completed our contract.

Love is not logical, listen to your brain but follow your heart. This is your life. You picked the exact lessons your Soul wanted to learn while it was here. This is your journey and yours alone. Others will judge and others will judge, so what. You need to learn how to stand in your truth, how to gather your inner strength and courage. You cannot let fear rule your life and paralyze you from making decisions. Sometimes you will make great decisions and sometimes you won't. If you choose not to decide you still have made a choice. Just remember you are not on this journey alone. You have lots and lots of help. Just ask God your Angels, passed away loved ones and your Spirit Team to help you and guide you. Connect to your Higher Self and ask for guidance and then make sure you listen for the answers. But above all remember the power of your Soul, the strength of the Love you are and that everything is unfolding perfectly. I believe in you and and I need you to believe in you! You've GOT THIS!!

Psychedelic Healing Spiritual Journeys

There is nothing more powerful than experiencing the LOVE of the Universe and meeting your Soul face to face 🌀

I hope you can see that these medicine journeys are not something that I take lightly. They are very sacred, done with a great deal of intention, and, for me – for the purpose of Soul Growth. I experienced my Soul, the Other Side, ascended masters, Source and the Universe. The biggest lesson I learned there is that the language of the Universe is LOVE. The stories in this book about medicine journeys are not to be considered encouragement for you to try them. I am merely sharing my experiences and the growth I experienced from them. Please educate yourself and consult someone who is a Shaman with a lot of personal experience, before you have your own experience.

I recommend three books that were the starting point of my education.

1. "DMT the Spirit Molecule" by Rick Strassman, M.D. This book focuses mostly on DMT. I had the pleasure of meeting Dr. Strassman and seeing him speak on this subject.
2. "The Divine Spark, Psychedelics, Consciousness, and the Birth of Civilization" by Graham Handcock. This book focuses on psychedelics and the personal stories from many people. I had the pleasure of meeting and of seeing Graham speak on this subject.
3. "How to Change Your Mind, What the New Science of Psychedelics Teaches Us About Consciousness, Dying, Addiction, Depression, and Transcendence." by Michael Pollan

I also watched many YouTube videos and listened to several podcast discussion. I first learned of Graham Handcock on Joe Rogan's Podcast, "The Joe Rogan Experience." I became a part of the medicine community. In that safe place I was able to integrate my journeys into my everyday life, and I learned a lot by listening to other people's experiences.

~~Once~~ A Cheater...

Psychic Mediums & Angel Connectors

The future is like a bowl of spaghetti 🍝

You are probably wondering about all of the readings and how they were all so consistent with saying they saw Wylie and my relationship going the distance and how Wylie "was not about other women", but then he cheated in the end and we did not go the distance. I addressed "Free Will" in *Chapter 5*, and I do believe at the time of the readings they were accurately connecting with where we were going *at that point in time*. Wylie was doing his best to follow the Contract he planned in advance with me. For the first six months he struggled with feeling like he hadn't planned to be in ANY relationship. I caught him completely off guard and I came in like a freight train he said, "I couldn't have stopped falling in love with you if I had tried." I believe at the point in time of each reading Wylie was trying to hold the intention to stay true to me. I think he battled with himself during our entire relationship. Ultimately, our demise was not about anyone else, it was about Wylie sabotaging himself over and over again. Those are his lesson to learn.

The list below includes an incredible group of Spiritual practitioners. They all have their specialties and I highly recommend each and every person. We all vibrate at an energy frequency and you may get a feeling about someone and feel drawn to them. That is how I like to choose who I connect with...

CJ Martes Angel Connector

I found CJ through a series of spiritual synchronicities that began with a call from my sister Stephanie. She called me excitedly telling me about a reading she had had with a woman named CJ, who not only connected with angels but was in fact *herself* an Angel Incarnate. Of course my logical mind had a difficult time wrapping its head around the fact that someone would come to this Earth as an angel. Nonetheless I was intrigued and called CJ to schedule an in person reading as I would be driving my car back from Chicago to Arizona in a couple of weeks. It so happened she was available the day I needed to meet with her. I noticed the music that had been playing on Pandora through my TV had suddenly stopped playing indicating "weak internet signal" but the screen was frozen on the song *"Count On Me"* by *Jefferson Starship* –Mark played this song at every concert. It seemed Mark was sending his approval of my upcoming reading. That same week I had a conversation with Mark's mom. She shared how she had become unsatisfied with her Medical Intuitive (someone who helps you discover energetically what health frequencies are out of balance in your body) She turned to the internet to find a new Medical Intuitive. It took her two days to sift through all of the choices until she found one to be excited about. She scheduled an appointment with CJ. Turns out we both had a reading scheduled with CJ! Me for an Angel Connection and her for a Medical Intuitive reading – our readings were on the same day one hour apart. The statistical chances of both of us being directed to the same person for different reasons on the same day would be astronomical. We both believed we were guided to CJ by Spirit, specifically by Mark. Of course Mark would have us both meet with a true Angel Incarnate and this spoke to her credibility. **CJMartes.com**

Dougall Fraser-Psychic Medium/Aura reading

Dougall was right in talking about Wylie's inconsistent behavior. But he also had a reading with me very late in our relationship, when we were in the deepest part of our break from one another. My reading with Dougall was more about reading my energy & my aura than it was about my relationship, where it had been a focal point in other readings. I absolutely *loved* my Aura reading with him and would recommend having a reading and or reading his book. **DougallFraser.com**

Holly Powers Matthews-Oracle reading

I really enjoyed my reading with Holly, she was the most different type of reading I have ever had, as she focused a lot of time on my past lives, and not necessarily lives you have lived on Earth, but lives lived in other realms. She did connect to the energy of my relationship with Wylie – with absolutely no prompting from me; and was able to answer questions. I learned about many new concepts during my reading with Holly. Although I do recommend her, at the time of this printing she is not conducting readings. **AZSpiritualMedium.com**

Moriah Rhame-Psychic Medium reading

Moriah once explained to me during a reading. *"The future is difficult to pin down. The future is like a bowl of spaghetti. Everyone is on their own strand – the Soul path they planned for learning – but people have Free Will and that can change the path and the outcome. Also time is weird over there* (on the Other Side). *To them they feel like they saw you yesterday and they will see you again tomorrow. So when they talk about time and timing, that might not be clear."*

~~Once~~ A Cheater...

I had my first ever medium reading with Moriah in 2006. I have had more readings with Moriah than with any other medium. She is beyond amazing as a medium and an even more awesome person! I can't recommend her enough!! I have had reading with her in person and by phone. Her speech cadence changes when she is interpreting messages from Spirit. I don't think there is anyone else who has brought through Mark's personality more accurately than Moriah. She has a no nonsense approach and will tell you exactly what she hears. She will bring through such detailed nuances of a person that you will have absolutely no doubt she is connecting to them. **MoriahTheMedium.com**

Stephanie Cochran-Psychic Medium.

She is my sister and she is amazing! She is my friend, my confident and a beautiful person inside and out! Many of my friends have had readings and have been astounded with the information and insights she delivers. I highly recommend her! **IntuitiveReadingsByStephanie.com**

Thomas John-Psychic Medium reading

Thomas will Wow you. He names names and leaves you with no doubt he is connecting to the Other Side. The level of detail is superior, he shares many things that no one could have known. He talked about my Spirit team, life lesson and what he sees in my future. I think he is worth every penny, but he is by far the most expensive with the longest wait. Get on his email list, as they do run specials and have lots of ways you can connect with him. Highly recommend!! He has two shows *The Seatbelt Psychic* and *The Thomas John Experience.* **MediumThomas.com**

Signs I Received While Writing This Book

Signs Surround Me, Signs Surround You 🎵

You know from reading this book, that Spirit often speaks to me through music and send **lots** of music signs. I wrote the first part of this book over a seven week period, and I would hear a song from one of the chapter names almost every time I got in the car. There were *very* few days that I did not hear at least one song; it wouldn't matter if I was in my car for 30 seconds or 30 minutes. I am also very intrigued by the timing of receiving these songs as there are thousands of potential songs that one could hear on various radio stations. Spirit found lots of opportunities to send me signs. Here are the stories of a few of my favorites...

Five Minute Window for Spirit to Send Me a Sign

I had been working on my book all Sunday and I needed a break. I decided to run to a nursery that is located one mile from my house to look for a new planter for my yard. I discovered it was later in the day than I realized, and I would only have 20 minutes before they closed. I hurriedly got in my Jeep and had been driving for less than two minutes when I heard the beginning notes of *"Hold the Line"* start playing. I had been in deep thought about the chapter I was writing in my book and had not been playing attention to the music. The screen said *"Steely Dan" "Deacon Blues"* as playing on XM Yacht Rock Radio, but it was not. I pulled into the nursery parking lot and had to wait for the song to finish playing in the parking lot because my car ride there was so short. This was the 11th time *"Hold the Line"* had played and the first time it had played since my break up with Wylie. I pondered the meaning of the lyrics about Love and its timing and wondered it the song message was telling me to hold the line for love, or if it was just Mark telling me hello.

Story of Hey Nineteen

Dawn gave me a *Steely Dan* book that told the backstory of every one of their songs for my birthday. I read it that afternoon and stopped right after reading the story about their song *"Hey Nineteen"*

~~Once~~ A Cheater... 346

The next morning I moved the Jeep out of the garage then went back in the house to get Storm to load her in the car. I noticed the song *"Hey Nineteen"* was playing on the radio, and remembered how just yesterday that was the last song I had read about in my new book. But the screen said a *Carol King* song was playing. Wow that had only happened with *"Hold the Line"* but just seconds later the screen updated to the correct information and said *"Hey Nineteen"* was playing. I laughed, realizing it was probably just a lag in the XM satellite radio connection having just moved my Jeep out of the garage, there was just a delay in catching updating the screen info.

When the song ended *"50 Way to Leave Your Lover"* by *Paul Simon* began playing, but the screen did not change; it still said *"Hey Nineteen"*. Hmmm curious. I wanted to challenge what was happening so I changed to another XM station. A new song was playing but the screen stayed the same still displaying *"Hey Nineteen"* I tried a few other stations with the same results, including switching off of XM radio onto the FM stations. It didn't matter, the screen showed *"Hey Nineteen"* on the entire drive to my hike. When I returned from the hike and restarted the Jeep the screen was now back to normal showing the song that was playing along with the correct song name. As I drove home I questioned whether I had really even stopped reading my book at the *"Hey Nineteen"* song story or if my mind was just making it up. So later that day I got my *Steely Dan* book out and re-read the *"Hey Nineteen"* story and just keep reading. Everything after that story was new and I thought it had been a neat sign and confirmation. But that wasn't the end of the story.

Two weeks later I met Stacy to hike, she had been gone all that time, and I told her the *"Hey Nineteen"* story. I also had lunch with Dawn that same day and told her the *"Hey Nineteen"* story. They both agreed it was more than a coincidence and had been a cool sign.

I was running 30 minutes behind to hike the next morning, and was really upset with myself because it was going to be a hot day and I had intended to hike earlier to avoid the heat by getting an earlier start. I started the Jeep and *"Hey Nineteen"* was playing on the XM Yacht Rock radio. I laughed at the timing of me running so behind but being "just in time" to hear this song – as I had just the day before told both Stacy and Dawn the story. As I pulled up to a stoplight I snapped a quick picture of the screen just as the song was ending. All of the sudden the radio began playing *"Hold the Line"* and the screen still showed *"Hey Nineteen"* I think my eyes just about popped out of my head in surprise. You know from reading my book how the *"Hold the Line"* signs had been working for me. Never before had any of the songs named that were indicated on the screen ever actually played before being taken over by the *"Hold the Line"* song, so this was a new aspect. *"Hold the Line"* continued playing from the first note to the last note then when it finished the screen updated to an XM commercial then to the song *"Diamond Girl"* by *Seals and Crofts*; which was now actually playing. I was so stunned by all of the synchronicities that I used the replay feature on my car screen to rewind back to *"Hey Nineteen"* and I made a video to show what

~~Once~~ A Cheater...   347

had happened. You can watch the video here: https://www.youtube.com/watch?v=rC8cbYkT8Nc&t=1s

Spirit definitely does have a specific way of working with me, but this had been not only been a *"Hold the Line"* take over, but had been combined with another sign to make it an even bigger event. I went directly to my parent's house and we did a video call with my sister Stephanie so I could tell them all about this very big sign! I love being able to share this with my special family. It was the 12th time *"Hold the Line"* had happened to me in one year! After leaving my parents' house I need to run one quick errand to the store. I was in my car for only a few minutes when the song *"Rock the Boat"* by *Hues Corporation* began playing, the title of Chapter 23. I arrived at the store just as the song ended and ran in to get two things. As soon as I entered the store I heard the song *"What You Won't Do for Love"* by *Bobby Caldwell* Chapter 33 was playing over the loud speakers, and I exited the store just as the song ended. I had only a four minute drive home and *"She's Gone"* Chapter 39 by *Hall and Oates* serenaded me on the drive home!

Four Songs In One Day In a Series of Errands

I had spent so much time writing my book during every spare minute that my food supplies were running very low. I ran a series of errands to Walmart, and two grocery stores. I was in my car a total of 30 minutes at the most as all of the stores are within a five mile radius of my house. During that time four song Chapters played: *"Magic Power"* by *Triumph* Chapter 4 and *"Spirits in the Material World"* by *The Police* Chapter 24 played consecutively followed by *"Can We Still Be Friends"* Chapter 41 and *"Love Walks In"* by *Van Halen* Chapter 9 on the ride home. All four songs played on XM radio stations.

A Little Help From the Neighbors

My neighbors located behind my house love to play loud music outside. They had been playing country music all day but suddenly switched it up and the first song that played was *"Magic Power"* by *Triumph* the title of Chapter 4 that I had not yet written. I had been outside in my backyard all day working on my computer writing Chapter 30 *"Hold the Line"* which I had copied from my previous book Signs Surround You; as that chapter is the transition chapter there telling about my new book. I had intended to finish up reworking *"Hold the Line"* then be finished for the day. Except the way *"Hold the Line"* had been written in my other book didn't work for this book, and ultimately had to be divided into three Chapters, the majority of which ended up being in Chapter 4 *"Magic Power"* which I then finished writing at the end of the day. If you had asked me earlier in the day, there is NO way I could have predicted I would be working on Chapter 4 in my book. What a crazy confirmation for Spirit to send me *that* song through my neighbor's music on the very day the chapter was written.

Walmart Run

I had finished my workday and sat down to work on one chapter in the book. When I finished I needed to make a quick run to the store and there is a Walmart less than five minutes' drive from my house. I started the Jeep and *"Games People Play"* by *Alan Parsons Project* Chapter 1 was just ending. I went into the store and when I started my Jeep to drive home *"She's Gone"* by *Hall and Oates* Chapter 39 began playing before I left the parking lot. Car time total less than ten minutes, yet two songs chapters played during my short car time.

The Week I Finished the Book

The song "She's Gone" is the title of Chapter 39. It was such an important song to me because Wylie had not only added it to our *L.A. Woman* playlist, but it had played in my car just after leaving his house and seeing him for the very last time. We didn't see each other again after that incident. The Song "She's Gone" played **five times** during that week, and I was only in my car five days that week, as I had been on furlough for work and had stayed home three days in a row – not even leaving to hike – just to write my book. There are 59 songs referenced in my book, that is a lot, but to hear the same song five times in one week absolutely had significance for me!

One Year Anniversary of "Hold the Line" Signs

I woke up early to hike. I talked to Mark asking him to send me a special sign today, which I almost never make a specific request. I asked to hear a song from my book, but not just any song – I asked to hear one of the two songs from the chapters I had written the day before, or the song title from the last eight chapters I had left to write. I was asking to hear one of ten songs. I got in my car and drove the 12 minutes to my hike. When I finished I got in the car to drive home and as soon as the Jeep started the song *"Gold Dust Woman"* by *Fleetwood Mac* began playing. I was one of the eight chapters I had left to write! As if that were not amazing enough, a minute later I heard the last part of the song *"Hold the Line"* by *Toto* which was the sign woven throughout the book that I have received 13 times. It was playing but the screen said *"Brandy You're a Fine Girl"* by *Looking Glass* was playing – but it was not. The radio had been taken over by Spirit. When the song ended the screen updated to *"Diamond Girl"* by *Seals and Crofts*. This exact combo had been taken over by *"Hold the Line"* at my cabin last summer and was played that day in my rental car. Then I realized today was June 3rd, it was exactly one year to the day *"Hold the Line"* was first played over another song when I was with Wylie.

What an incredible combination of songs to receive at one time! The next day I finished writing Part One of the book, and there was no way I could have planned it – but *"Gold Dust Woman"* Chapter 27 by sheer coincidence was the last chapter I wrote. I finished the last word of that chapter at exactly 12:01 a.m. seven weeks after I had begun writing the book.

Two days later while driving home from my hike both *"Brandy You're a Fine Girl"* played normally followed immediately by *"Diamond Girl"* which also played normally. I thought it was funny to hear them again in that same order, only this time in the way Yacht Rock intended them to play.

Sending my Book Out for Review

I finished part one of my book and spent the next three days reading the book from beginning to end for the first time. I had it ready to send to my kids, my parents, my sister and my closet friends most of whom were in the book, to read and give me feedback. It was Storm's birthday and I wanted to take her on a sunset hike as it was cooling off at the end of the day. The trailhead was only a five minute drive from my house. I had texted everyone letting them know the copy of my book was now sitting in their email to read and several people began texting me back at once. I parked my car and quickly answered a text from Rachel as the song *"The Long Run"* by the *Eagles* began playing. Chapter 3's title. I went on a 40 minute hike then got in the car to begin my five minute drive home. Within one minute the song *"Magic Power"* by *Triumph* began playing Chapter 4 of the book. Immediately following that song was *.38 Special "Hold on Loosely"* which is referenced in Chapter 35. There are a total of 59 songs in my book. What are the chances three would be played in the short ten minute drive, especially on the heels of sending my book to the most important people in my life.

What a Fool Believes

I had spent several hours one Saturday working on Part 2 Spiritual Lessons of the book, and I was feeling mentally exhausted and just felt like I needed to get out of the house. I had already received two songs from the book that morning on the way to my hike *"How Long (Has This Been Going On)"* from Chapter 48 played and as I pulled into the garage after my hike *"She's Gone"* by *Hall and Oates* from Chapter 39 played.

I ran three errands and the last one took a really long time as I got delayed several times by the cashier at the grocery store. When I returned to my car *"What a Fool Believes"* by the *Doobie Brothers* was playing on Yacht Rock XM radio. I don't often hear this song, and joked with Mark in my head telling him I wished he had played *"Hold the Line"* by *Toto* (our special sign from Chapter 30) over this particular song. Other than that day back in December when I had specifically asked Mark to send me *"Hold the Line"* I had not asked for this song from him on demand. The song ended and the screen updated to

~~Once~~ A Cheater...

play an XM Yacht Rock 15 second commercial, except a commercial did not play. The screen froze and I heard the entire 3:55 *"Hold the Line"* song. I was very surprised at Mark's quick response to me. And while he did not freeze *"What a Fool Believes"* the song *"Hold the Line"* began playing within about 30 seconds of the request I made to him in my head. I actually pulled the Jeep over and made a live video showing the screen updating to play a song by *Firefall*. Four song chapter titles in one day plus hearing *"Hold the Line"* "on demand" felt like Spirit was giving me extra encouragement while I was writing about topics referring to them.

Feedback From My Book

I went to bed very late and slept in as a result, but I should not have because by 8 a.m. when I was ready to leave for my trail run it was already over 80 degrees. Of course Spirit had me just where they wanted me and played *"Magic"* by *Olivia Newton John* the title of Chapter 29 on the drive home. I had texted Thomas John yesterday congratulating him on his new TV show and today I was looking at a picture of Thomas I took while he was at my house spending the day with me as described in Chapter 4. I had not realized it before, but as Thomas was sitting on the couch smiling, the *Jefferson Starship* song *"Count On Me"* was playing on my TV screen at that moment, which would be a sign Mark was checking in. I had not noticed this before! A couple of hours later I had a video call with Ryan's fiancé Brittni who had just finished reading the book and wanted to share her feedback. We had a lovely conversation. I got in my car immediately after the call to meet Dawn for lunch and as I started the engine "So Into You" by Atlanta Rhythm Section as playing the title of Chapter 20. And while eating lunch with Dawn *"Gold Dust Woman"* by *Fleetwood Mac* the title of chapter 27 began playing over the restaurant speakers. Three song in one day is a lot.

Stacy sent this to me the day after Wylie's hateful text message. I thought it was fitting to end the spiritual Part 2 with this song: "Rescue" by *Lauren Daigle*

https://open.spotify.com/track/7r9kOxiNDnkAg5QKqtyjVk?si=evdp3z2eRQitBfjpN5tjtw

The End...

❧ **New beginnings are often disguised as painful endings** ❧

Acknowledgements

A book like this is never written alone. Thank you for the support of my friends and family and for everyone who helped me on this journey!

Wylie, I hope you find what you are looking for and that you can find your inner peace and happiness.

Marilyn, Thank you for your insights in helping me editing this book. Thank you for helping me find the perfect words placed in the perfect order. It was sometimes tortuous reliving this part of my journey over and over again; I appreciate your allowing me to vent and for always being on my side. God help us if we ever have to edit another book, lol! I love you. Mark is so proud of us!!

Shannon, Thank you for having the courage to share with me what many people would not. You are a true friend in every sense of the word. I love you my beautiful friend!!

Dad and Mom, Thank you for your endless love and support. The more I hear other people's childhood stories, the more grateful I am. I'm sorry you had to watch this unfold; I know it caused you a lot of pain too. My life is so much better now that you live five minutes from me. I couldn't have picked better parents! I love you both! Dad – thank you for your amazing proofing abilities!

Ryan and Rachel, I hope my experience serves as a valuable lesson to you both. Ryan I am especially grateful for the extra year I got with you. You are such beautiful Souls and I thank you for picking me to be your Mom. I love you both!!

Steph, I'm so glad we have each other to lean on through this journey called life. Thank you for being there when I needed you – like every phone call. I love you. Sisters are forever!

Stacy, You saw it all first hand. You always take the high road and want to see the best in others. I'm sorry he used you in several ways. Thank you for all the hikes where you listened endless to me. Thank you for your counsel and prayers, but mostly thank you for your beautiful friendship. You were a shoulder to cry on many times and I am forever grateful. I love you!!

Dawn, we are true soul sisters! Thank you for supporting me through every journey. I especially thank you for being there during Bumble-Gate and for trying to help me put the pieces together. I love you!!

LeeAnn, you wanted to see the best in Wylie and to give him the benefit of the doubt. Don't ever stop seeing the good in others. Thank you for every phone call and especially for being there in the middle of the night. I love you!!

Melinda, your timing is impeccable! Thank you for being there when I needed a friend. You saw Wylie in action first hand, thank you for encouraging me not to accept less for myself. Love you my beautiful friend!!

Angela, we have grown up with each other. Thank you for being there when I really needed you. Friends forever! I love you!!

Gina, thank you for always being there to listen. You are my little sister and a forever friend! I love you!!

Phyllis, thank you for your undying support and love. Our guitar guys on the Other Side are proud of us! Love you!!

Nikki, thank you for your assistance in my Soul Growth! I love you!!

Jane, You can have him! LOL Good luck with that!

About the Author

Laurie Majka is an *Inspirational Artist* – which means she receives the ideas for her artwork and writing in powerful "downloads" or fully formed ideas she "sees" in her mind. She believes these concepts are inspired from her Higher Self, Universal Consciousness, God and her Spirit Team. Laurie began receiving communications from the Other Side in 2012 when her Soul Mate Mark passed away, confirming her belief that love never dies. Now, with this book, she hopes through her story you will understand her signs in a way that lets you recognize signs from *your* loved ones. Laurie also believes her life's purpose is to send positive energy into the world. She created *Soul Heart Art* as a way to help do that by encouraging people to harness the power of their Soul. Her Daily Soul Whispers have inspired millions of people worldwide. Laurie grew up in Lawrence, Kansas and has a degree in Business Administration with a minor in Communication Studies from the University of Kansas. She built her career working for several Fortune 50 companies including Pfizer, IBM and Hewlett Packard. She has been a part of strategic teams selling multi-million dollar deals. Laurie lives in Arizona with her dog Storm. They enjoy hiking mountains and spending time connecting with nature. Laurie has two grown children, Ryan, a pilot for the United States Air Force and Rachel who is working towards becoming a Mental Health Counselor. You can connect to Laurie's YouTube channel: Laurie Majka, on her web site www.LaurieMajka.com and with her podcast Powerful Soul! She would love you to share stories of signs you have received from *your* loved ones...

More Books By Laurie Majka

More Books By Laurie Majka

www.ingramcontent.com/pod-product-compliance
Lightning Source LLC
Chambersburg PA
CBHW071259110426
42743CB00042B/1112